CITIES FROM SCRATCH

CITIES FROM SCRATCH

POVERTY AND INFORMALITY
IN URBAN LATIN AMERICA

BRODWYN FISCHER, BRYAN McCANN,
AND JAVIER AUYERO, EDITORS

Duke University Press · Durham and London · 2014

Library of Congress Cataloging-in-Publication Data
Cities from scratch : poverty and informality in urban Latin America /
Brodwyn Fischer, Bryan McCann, and Javier Auyero, editors.
pages cm
Includes bibliographical references and index.
ISBN 978-0-8223-5518-2 (cloth : alk. paper)
ISBN 978-0-8223-5533-5 (pbk. : alk. paper)
1. Slums—Latin America. 2. Urban poor—Latin America.
3. Marginality, Social—Latin America. I. Fischer, Brodwyn M.
II. McCann, Bryan, 1968– III. Auyero, Javier.
HV4050.5.A5C58 2014
307.3′364098—dc23   2013025655

IN MEMORIAM

Emilio Duhau, one of Mexico's leading urban sociologists, passed away on August 13, 2013. His contribution to this volume is but a small example of the rigor, originality, and optimism that characterized his extensive work on informality, poverty, and urban space. His voice will be sorely missed.

CONTENTS

INTRODUCTION

Brodwyn Fischer

Most Americans south of the Rio Grande live in cities that have never resembled a North Atlantic urban ideal. One in four Latin Americans lives
in an underserviced, poor, legally precarious neighborhood, part of what
has come to be known as the informal city.[1] Many of Latin America's other
urban residents know that their cities would not function without such
places. Poor, informal neighborhoods are often dismissed as slums, as unfortunate and accidental scars on the urban landscape. But they are in fact
thoroughly entwined with formal urbanity, and with more privileged iterations of informality. The formal city profits economically and politically
from the slum's illegality, and much "urban" culture originates in poor, illegal neighborhoods. The informal city provides a refuge from utopian urban
regulations that would otherwise exclude many poor Latin Americans from
city life. Neither city could exist without the other; the relationship between
them defines the Latin American urban form, and does much to shape Latin
American law, politics, and society.

The informal city is not exclusive to Latin America, or to the world's poorest countries. Informality itself extends far beyond the reaches of poverty.[2]
Slums have been written about often, even incessantly, an instantly recog-
nizable emblem of almost every perceived social ill. Much of this writing is
vivid, lustrously repelling, enthralling enough to be termed slum pornogra-
phy and sweeping enough to articulate theories of universal injustice. Why,
then, have we chosen to write another, less sensational book, focusing on
Latin American manifestations of a supposedly global problem?

The answer lies in two paradoxes. The first is that, while poor informal
cities are often described, discussed, debated, or deplored, the places themselves are not always the point of the conversation. Slums and shantytowns
are magnetic because they disquiet outsiders and contrast so sharply with

a normative vision of the modern cityscape. The settlements' photogenic misery allows them to serve as potent symbols in polemical global debates about poverty, capitalism, race, and state failure. The instant identification of these settlements with the "subaltern" makes them the natural locale for radical critiques of the powers that be. But the very proximity to hot-button issues that makes the informal city so attractive can also distort and obscure it. The symbolic value of informal cities usually lies in their dysfunctionality and capacity for resistance. But poor informal cities largely survive because their inhabitants are so adept at making these places function, in ways that usually link their fates to established networks of power and profit. Portraits of the informal cities that focus only on their pathologies, or their transformative potential, can easily miss their constitutive role in extant urban cultural and power relations, the settlements' functional vitality in the here and now.

The second paradox is embedded in the informal cities' dual role as global phenomena and intensely local social formations. At first glance, the world's informal cities can seem disconcertingly similar, a "planet of slums" that share striking physical characteristics and are universally characterized by poverty and subcitizenship.[3] Most settlements originate in roughly similar patterns of invasion, negotiation, or petty profiteering, and some form of populist political practice usually both sustains and marginalizes them. Residents usually create intense networks of exchange, commerce, and small-time credit, and varying degrees of violence and exploitation can coexist with expressions of community solidarity.

It is easy enough to link those features to global economic, cultural, political, and environmental transformations and to end up discussing the "slum" as if it were an epiphenomenon of global history, the inevitable symptom of our interconnected pathologies. And yet the thing that informal cities around the world hold most in common—what brings them into existence and allows them to survive—is their entrenchment in intensely local dynamics. The settlements' similarities are pragmatic, not determinant, and each depends on unique constellations of needs and intricate local relationships. The local rootedness of informal cities renders most generalizations about them fanciful, easily belied by one or a thousand divergent experiences. At most, one might say that the global informal city is also the rawest form of local self-expression, the space where literal and figurative façades thin away, revealing more transparently the relationships of power and culture that define each locality.

The chapters that follow engage vital global issues, and none binds the informal city exclusively to its local context. All are informed by the rich extant literature on global urban poverty, to which many of these authors have contributed. But these particular chapters share a commitment to building both sociopolitical theory and generalizations about the informal city from the local context outward. The resulting volume is both a fractured portrait of Latin America's informal cities and a multifaceted argument about the nature and consequences of urban informality itself.

Why concentrate only on Latin America? These chapters portray informal cities that come into being and survive in a particular historical context, where global economic and political trends have played themselves out in specific and patterned ways. U.S. influence has been more pervasive and direct here than elsewhere. The interplay of populism and authoritarianism has chronologically overlapped with intensive rural-to-urban migration, and debates about democratization have granted an unusually central place to questions of law and urban citizenship. Race, caste, and religion have been politicized loosely in most of contemporary Latin America, and understandings of urban social inequality have grown from regionally particular schools of urbanism and social science. Perhaps as important, this is a region where global twenty-first-century fears about gang violence and state failure have often coincided with palpable political and economic progress: dystopic terrors coexist with deep optimism and (in most places) unprecedented political openness. These chapters do not posit the existence of a specifically Latin American form of urban informality, but they collectively suggest that regional dynamics are at least as important as global ones in helping to shape the informal city.

Within those regional boundaries, the contributions range over broad geographical, methodological, and theoretical territories. Urban informality is by its nature an interdisciplinary theme, and we make no claim to comprehensive coverage. Economists will find relatively little quantitative work, geographers may wish for more frequent references to the spatial turn, and cultural scholars may desire a more studied focus on the literature, theater, cinema, and music of informality. Many of our chapters acknowledge these fields' contributions, but the selections mostly move through history, anthropology, and sociology, united by a common concern with local and historical embeddedness.

We begin with Brodwyn Fischer's chapter on the intellectual history of Brazilian and Latin American shantytowns from the late nineteenth century to the 1970s. Juxtaposing a critical reading of shantytown literature with insights from recent historical research, Fischer examines what has been gained and lost from the persistent presentism of shantytown studies, arguing for approaches that tether the informal city less firmly to contemporary crises. Fischer's chapter also provides an intellectual and historical context for the rest of the volume's selections. Edward Murphy's chapter takes up the historical thread in Chile of the 1960s, where he demonstrates how shantytown residents tied their demands for housing to national moral discourses about the importance of home and family. In the hands of Murphy's *pobladores* (low-income urban residents), demands for housing rights were radical in form, and in claiming belonging for neighborhoods usually dismissed as nests of social marginality. But these struggles expanded rather than overturned prevalent languages of morality and decency; the pobladores' fight for urban rights was part and parcel of a broader struggle to defend home and family against the corrupting effects of homelessness and poverty.

The next two chapters take on a more recent historical period at Latin America's two geographical and sociopolitical extremes by examining the evolution of informal settlements in Nicaragua and Brazil from the 1970s to the present. Bryan McCann's chapter on the interlaced histories of two adjoined Rio de Janeiro neighborhoods, one formal and another informal, illuminates the shifting practices, politics, and cultural alliances that at once tie these locales together and maintain the boundaries between them over time. McCann also draws attention to the larger ebbs and flows that shaped the informal city's local dynamics during this period: the inclusion of rights to the city in campaigns for democratization and broader citizenship, the corrosive impact of the drug trade, and the shifting strategies and aims of church groups, NGOs, and politicians. Dennis Rodgers's chapter on Managua's La Sobrevivencia settlement, drawing on decades of ethnographic fieldwork, explores the shifting interaction between neighborhood dynamics, political currents, and transnational transformations. In Rodgers's narrative, La Sobrevivencia's fate is inexorably tied to national and world events: the rise and fall of Sandinismo, the economic devastation of the 1980s and 1990s, and the growth of neoliberalism, drugs, and gangs. But the community's destiny is also negotiated from the inside out, on the basis of shifting patterns of community solidarity, conflict, and territorialization.

Emilio Duhau's chapter on Mexico City strikes a more optimistic note on the evolution of informality in Mexico City during roughly the same period. Duhau is less concerned with the internal politics of Mexico City's informal neighborhoods than he is with their impact on larger, spatial patterns of urban inequality. Drawing on decades of demographic and sociological research, Duhau demonstrates the fundamentally progressive workings of Mexico City's informal city—the ways in which it has promoted certain forms of social mobility and urban integration while actually lessening socioeconomic segregation over time. Ironically, Duhau argues that a current shift toward a more formalized production of low-income housing runs the risk of increasing segregation and marginalization. In this way, Duhau highlights the functionality of the informal city over time and calls into question the empirical basis of the current drive toward state-led formalization.

The collection's last four contributions focus on single places in the very recent past. Bryan McCann's annotation of photos taken by Rio de Janeiro's Ratão Diniz evokes the interconnectedness of formal and informal life, the daily routines and cultural and economic dynamism that animate poor neighborhoods, and the palpable physical improvements that are now as much a part of the informal city as the pockmarked scars of urban violence. Sujatha Fernandes's chapter on Caracas's Alameda theater explores the rehabilitation of a once-iconic neighborhood cultural institution. Like Dennis Rodgers, Fernandes is concerned with radical political change and with the interplay of local, national, and transnational forces in a poor neighborhood's most intimate spaces. In the theater's history, she finds memories of left-wing cultural radicalism, rehabilitated by a community alert to Chávez-era opportunities and then co-opted by political hacks. But in Fernandes's rendering, Chávez-era events are mediated and shaped by shifting patterns of local identity and cultural solidarity—their immediate impact as much homegrown as imported.

Mariana Cavalcanti's chapter, like Bryan McCann's, focuses on the borderlands between the formal and the informal. In Cavalcanti's case, those borderlands become crucibles for the very concepts of the favela and the formal city. Through intensive ethnographic exploration of real-estate practices and movement from the favela to the formal city (and back again), Cavalcanti portrays a liminal space in which the formal-informal divide is at once inconstant and vital, shaping inhabitants' spatial and social practices even as the poles that this frontier mediates are constantly redefined.

The collection ends with Javier Auyero's chapter on the Buenos Aires neighborhood of Flammable, a space where a ruinous combination of industrial misconduct, governmental half measures, and local paralysis has left residents in a netherworld of physical suffering and constant expectation. This chapter, a follow-up to Auyero's coauthored book on the same topic, opens up polemical questions about the long-term impact of poverty and environmental poisoning on a community's capacity for effective self-determination.[4] More broadly, the text highlights the political nature of the informal city, the degree to which the absence of effective rights renders inhabitants political dependents rather than rights-bearing citizens. While poor informal residents have often been able to capitalize on this process to prevent more draconian urban exclusion and gradually claim urban rights, Auyero's chapter paints a dark picture of the waiting—the constant, dependent expectation—that can envelope and paralyze the most vulnerable informal residents.

Collectively, these chapters have much to say about themes that have dominated debates about shantytowns and other poor neighborhoods for decades: social marginality, demagoguery, collective social movements, and cultural dynamism. But the contributions' comments on these old themes are also shaped by new paradigms and developments. These chapters note from the inside out the ways in which Latin America's informal cities have been transformed by democratization, the rise of Latin America's "new Left," the recent centrality of rights-based approaches to urban poverty, the acceleration of international migrations, urban environmental degradation, and the expansion of the drug trade. They also engage (often critically) new paradigms about subaltern politics, neoliberalism, and race.

The hope and aim, however, is that the chapters discuss these issues only in as much as they emerge from and are crucial to local dynamics. The volume's central questions are about the nature of Latin America's poor informal cities themselves: their relationships to the larger urban form, their political roles, their transformations over time, and their nature as sites for the reproduction or transcendence of poverty and subcitizenship.

This local perspective, far from limiting this volume's broader significance, allows for its most significant contributions. The urban neighborhoods that emerge from these studies are diverse, historically rooted, and inseparable from the formal city. Their informality is often functional in and of itself, and not simply a side-product of poverty and need; the use value of illegality—for purposes both hopeful and exploitative—emerges everywhere, calling into question popular policies that aim to solve the slum problem through simple legalization. Progress is a delicate and often cyclical process in these neighborhoods, as it is in the broader urban ecology. Above all, the informal cities that emerge from these pages are building blocks of Latin American urbanity, not the unfortunate side effects of modernist city building. Urbanization, from this perspective, involves far more than physical upgrading and the elimination of illegal settlements. It demands that cities recognize the needs and interests that poor informal cities serve, the multiple ways in which they are embedded in urban life, and that they expand the limits of the formal city to incorporate what informality does best. Urbanization demands, in short, that we recognize that Latin American cities are defined rather than deformed by the dynamic intersection of formal and informal urbanity.

NOTES

1. UN Habitat, *State of the World's Cities 2010/11: Bridging the Urban Divide* (Washington, DC: United Nations, 2011), 32.

2. Ananya Roy's article "Slumdog Cities: Rethinking Subaltern Urbanism," *International Journal of Urban and Regional Research* 35, no. 2 (2011), highlights the perils of conceptualizing urban informality as the exclusive domain of the poor, preferring to use the concept to focus attention on the processes by which poor informalities are criminalized while others are valorized. This collection, however, is less interested in informality as a concept than in the spaces where poverty and informality intersect and will generally use the term *informal city* to denote only those places.

3. The phrase *planet of slums* is from Mike Davis's book *Planet of Slums* (London: Verso, 2006).

4. See Javier Auyero and Débora Swistun, *Flammable: Environmental Suffering in an Argentine Shantytown* (New York: Oxford University Press, 2009).

ONE

A Century in the Present Tense

CRISIS, POLITICS, AND THE INTELLECTUAL
HISTORY OF BRAZIL'S INFORMAL CITIES

Brodwyn Fischer

In 2006 an impressive array of luminaries graced the cover of Mike Davis's *Planet of Slums*, extolling it as "magisterial," "profound," and "brilliant," the latest word on the future of the global city. Davis's book began with a neo-Malthusian analysis of "the urban climacteric," in which he dramatized the impending "watershed" moment when the world would become more urban than rural. He provided a fearful description of what such accelerated urbanization implied: "Instead of cities of light soaring toward heaven, much of the twenty-first-century urban world squats in squalor, surrounded by pollution, excrement, and decay."[1]

Davis sketched a meta-analysis of global slum development in which only the poor escaped blame. Colonial oppressors, populist national governments, urban planners, military dictatorships, international aid agencies, NGOs, and neoliberal policymakers had collectively failed to create a cityscape capable of accommodating an undifferentiated global army of underemployed, unempowered, and sub-urbanized human beings. The result was "peri-urban poverty," "the radical new face of inequality," "a grim human world largely cut off from the subsistence solidarities of the countryside as well as disconnected from the cultural and political life of the traditional city."[2] Here, in an atmosphere of chronic unemployment and environmental catastrophe, little was beyond the pale: Davis invoked drug trafficking, armed violence, organ sale and theft, terrorism, and even witchcraft as signs of "an existential ground zero beyond which there are only death camps, famine, and Kurtzian horror."[3]

When it came to Latin America, however, the power of Davis's scathing critique derived from moral resonance rather than intimate knowledge. Davis's doomsday prose draped rickety empirical scaffolding; an accumulation of inaccuracies that together created an ill-defined caricature of the actual features and dynamics of Latin America's poorest neighborhoods. His errors — mischaracterized neighborhoods, misused Spanish words, mistaken historical facts, misplaced cities — were individually petty.[4] But they would have been immediately obvious to any local inhabitant, and suggest collectively that local perspectives had little role in shaping Davis's confident exposé. Davis's sense of the informal cities' history extended back only a generation or two, and his analysis of the social, economic, and political networks that sustained these intensely local places was thin. Despite an attempt at typology, Davis's focus was simply too broad for the world's urban poor to emerge as anything but an undifferentiated suffering mass. This was clearly — and ironically — an argument built from the top down, aimed at marshaling evidence of urban disaster to indict the global order's unjust march.

Given the ubiquity of urban injustice, it is tough to fault Davis too much for his unsound detail. He meant to jolt a general public into awareness of the worst things that are happening in the world's dystopic "edge cities," and in this he succeeded in spades. What is significant about Davis's approach, however, is that it is the rule, not the exception. The sacrifice of local, grassroots analysis for urgent, sweeping political argument began at the very nineteenth-century moment when shantytowns emerged as distinct urban phenomena; since then, the urgency of now has reigned supreme. Poor, informal cities have emerged as symptoms of present-day ills, or as bellwethers of terrible or (rarely) utopian futures. Critics have associated such neighborhoods with a litany of dangers: to public health, to racial purity, to public safety, to political stability, to family values, to economic development, to urbanism itself. Informal residents and their advocates have roundly debunked such critiques, in the process helping to defend their place in Latin America's urban landscape. But shantytown defenders have rarely escaped their critics' conceptual constraints and have often strategically avoided close examination of the neighborhoods' less idyllic features.[5] Arguments over poor communities' elimination have thus become entwined with the language, social categories, and moral polemics of successive generations. Informal cities have frequently occupied center stage in Latin America's sociopolitical arena, but they have largely done so in the service of larger debates about the nature and tolerability of social inequality.

What does it mean when an enduring feature of urban life is persistently defined as a symptom of contemporary crisis? How has this emphasis on immediate conjunctures influenced how Latin America's informal cities are understood and misunderstood, and what can be learned from so many decades of sedimentary debate? This essay considers the problem of presentism in Brazilian and Latin American "slum studies," from the late nineteenth century to the 1970s, focusing particularly on the Brazilian cities of Rio de Janeiro and Recife. Within this vast literature, I examine three especially important waves of writings: a first in the late nineteenth and early twentieth centuries, a second between the 1920s and the early 1940s, and a final "boom" that extended from the 1940s through the early 1970s.

During all of these periods, informal cities remained central to the hemispheric polemics of race, poverty, development, citizenship, revolution, and cultural modernity. Each generation attached shantytowns to its own urgent paradigms, and traces of older templates stubbornly persisted, forming rich and complex intellectual sediment. Yet, until very recently, fundamental questions about the shantytown's origins, functionality, and networks of social and political sustenance remained in an intellectual shadow land, explored mainly when they touched upon seemingly more vital contemporary issues and avoided when they pointed toward politically inconvenient territory. As a result, our historical understanding of this particular form of urban poverty — informal, often precarious, bereft of most "public" services, yet defining and facilitating urban life for the region's poorest people — remains weak. For most places, at most times, we still do not know how poor informal cities came into being, what range of ties bound them to their urban contexts, what allowed them to persist over successive generations, or what their presence has done to transform Latin American or Brazilian urbanity. In tracing what was learned and lost through nearly a century of study in the present tense, I hope to highlight the potential of alternate intellectual paths and also to identify the polemical magnets that threaten to distort contemporary understandings of the settlements that Mike Davis so correctly identified as bellwethers of Latin America's urban future.

WHICH CAME FIRST, THE INFORMAL OR THE CITY?

Latin America's poor, informal cities existed long before they were named. While modern-day definitions of Latin America's underprivileged and peripheral neighborhoods vary, they tend to converge on a few basic features: illegal or semilegal land-tenure arrangements, substandard construction, lack of formal urban planning, a mostly poor and nonwhite population, and little or no access to public goods and services. By these criteria, all kinds of colonial and nineteenth-century urban settlements could have been called "informal slums," had they been unusual enough to merit a label. Spanish America has often been distinguished from Brazil because of its relatively orderly city planning, but even there urban regulation was quite circumscribed: borders blurred between urban centers and rural settlements, and it was often taken for granted that the poor (and especially the indigenous poor) would live in "informal" neighborhoods distant from the city squares. Richard Morse dated such phenomena in Mexico to the sixteenth century, citing George Kubler's description of "indian districts comprised of casual, dense agglomerations of huts."[6] Asael Hansen described analogous social geographies for colonial Mérida,[7] and Morse also cited an eighteenth-century shantytown populated by two thousand *castas* (persons of mixed race) near Callao's central square, dispersed with a resettlement policy eerily similar to those pursued throughout Latin America in the twentieth century.[8] Such references confirm what common sense suggests: in Latin America's colonial cities, as in modern ones, "urbanized" regions coexisted with rustic and improvised dwellings, which were often accepted as the inevitable result of poverty or necessity and merited mention only when they became dense or central enough to disrupt the urban core.

Well into the nineteenth century, when Latin American social thinkers had already begun to problematize urban poverty and to equate urbanism and progress, poor people's improvised huts were only very rarely distinguished from the general landscape of urban indigence. Even a keen polemicist such as the Colombian liberal Miguel Samper — who in 1867 tied a blistering description of Bogotá's urban dysfunction and promiscuous poverty to a wide-ranging condemnation of colonialism, political chaos, and Colombian national backwardness — saw no reason to single out informal dwellings as a particular ill.[9] Neither did Juan Capelo, who explored the links between urban form and social evolution in his pioneering *Sociologia de Lima* (1895).[10] Although early censuses often suggest the ubiquity of improvised housing and scarce urban services, the many guides that chronicled Latin America in the late nineteenth and early twentieth centuries scarcely mention them. William Eleroy Curtis's *The Capitals of Spanish America* (1888) contained evocative sketches of shacks and improvised neighborhoods in Caracas, Guayaquil, and Rio, but such places appeared nowhere in Curtis's text. Curtis did describe a good part of Lima's housing stock as "mere shacks of bamboo reeds, lashed together by thongs of raw-hide, and plastered within and without with thick layers of mud."[11] In Valpa-raíso, he wrote, "there are whole blocks . . . in which nothing but corrugated-iron houses can be seen, both roof and walls being of the same material."[12] And yet these places merited no specific terminology; they were simply an expected feature of the "primitive" Latin American cityscape.

Interestingly, some of the most explicit early references to informal dwellings come from belle epoque Buenos Aires—already the most European and formalized of Latin American capitals. James Scobie uncovered numerous late nineteenth-century photographs of shanties and huts in the ecologically precarious outskirts that would become Buenos Aires's "black belt"; these were also cited in an 1896 article about the area published in the *Revista Municipal*.[13] The French prime minister Georges Clemenceau's *South America To-day* (1911) disgustedly compared Buenos Aires's impro-vised slums to similarly degraded areas of Paris. It is perhaps their very scar-city that made the slums notable; Clemenceau's enraptured portrait of Rio de Janeiro made no mention of the favelas that already occupied most of the city's downtown hills, perhaps because he found them a more "natural" component of Brazil's rustic urban scene.[14]

THE INVENTION OF A PROBLEM

In light of so many centuries of urban informality, an obvious question emerges. Why, sometime between the late nineteenth and early twenti-eth centuries, did Latin America's informal dwellings begin to be named, photographed, and conceived of as a discrete problem? The specific histo-ries are unclear for most places, and one suspects they are as varied as the terms that emerged to describe the settlements: *colonias populares* or *prole-tárias* in Mexico, *tugurios* in Colombia, *barriadas* in Peru, *callampas* in Chile, *ranchos* in Venezuela, and *favelas* in Brazil.[15] There is every indication that some of the explanation boils down to the concurrence of ascendant urban-ism and quick informal expansion. But writings from the early twentieth century about Brazil's favelas and *mocambos* (shacks) suggest that the terms were invented not so much to describe the places where poor people lived as to spell out the relationship between such places and their surrounding cities. While shacks and small informal communities had existed for cen-turies, their emergence as a category of urban pathology largely depended on Brazil's integration into international debates about poverty, sanitation, racial degeneracy, and urbanism.

In order to understand the slums' invention it is necessary to reconstruct what we can of their literal expansion in the nineteenth and early twentieth centuries.[16] This was typically a practical matter, and it satisfied multiple and conflicting interests. In Recife and Rio de Janeiro, both isolated *barracos* (huts) and small groupings thereof were common throughout the nineteenth century, associated mainly with slaves, *libertos* (freed persons), and the free poor.[17] Gilberto Freyre wrote of "the villages of shacks, huts, or shanties that grew up in the cities under the Empire," surmising that such settlements "represented the desire on the part of free Negroes or runaway slaves to revive African styles of living or association."[18] In subsequent writings, Freyre emphasized African etymology of the word *mocambo* (the northeastern term for a rustic shack) and emphasized the link between mocambos and freedom among liberated slaves.[19] In Rio, some informal settlements seem also to have emerged from the process of freedom, either as small "abolitionist quilombos" (maroons) housing runaway slaves or as backyard shacks "given" or rented to ex-slaves or other dependents.[20]

More prosaically, Recife's mocambos multiplied during economic downturns or urban population crises such as the great drought of 1877–79. Rio's shacks proliferated in periods of urban reform and sanitary crackdown, when the razing of inner-city tenements left thousands homeless, or when military mobilizations involved larger numbers of soldiers than the barracks could handle.[21] There was, everywhere, ample evidence of profiteering: a poor worker could squat on a small piece of land and rent out part of it, a widow would allow a family to build a hut in exchange for petty services or a small fee, tenement managers often encouraged "beehives" of improvised dwellings to expand well beyond their property lines, exalted members of high society extracted rent from lands tied up in judicial conflict.[22]

Political expediency could also spur informal settlement. By the mid-1880s, Rio's municipal council had resolved to allow some shacks on the centrally located Morro de Santo Antônio, and one illiterate supplicant appealed to the minister of the Brazilian empire for permission to construct a "barraca" from scrap wood on the hill "as others have been allowed to do."[23] Ten years later, officials gave homeless soldiers leave to build shacks on Santo Antônio in the wake of the Revolta da Armada (Navy Revolt); around the same time, when public-health officials destroyed a massive tenement at the foot of Rio's Providência Hill, they allowed the slum's owners to rent adjacent hillside land to evicted tenants, who apparently built their homes with scrap from the destruction.[24] Five years later, soldiers returning from Brazil's famous Canudos conflict swelled Providência's shacktown, dubbing it the *morro da favella* (favela hill) after a northeastern desert plant.[25] When Rio implemented a sweeping building code in 1903, a clause allowing hillside shacks provided a residential escape valve. The morros were a cheap alternative, too, for poor residents swept from their homes by Rio's massive twentieth-century urban reforms. Rio's shantytowns thus served as places of refuge, as emergency shelter, or as sources of private profit. But they were also a steam valve, a way for politicians to ease social tension and reap political capital by protecting poor populations from laws and policies that fit crudely with the city's material, social, and cultural realities. In Recife, considerably less evidence exists for this period, but similar political expediencies were noted in the 1930s, and repeated statutes banning the mocambos were routinely ignored, suggesting an analogous phenomenon.[26]

All of this added up to significant informal urban settlement by the early twentieth century. Nearly 44 percent of the homes counted in Recife's 1913 census were classified as "mocambos" and another 22 percent as "mud houses."[27] The 1923 census counted 19,947 "residências in mucambos" as opposed to 19,079 formal "residências."[28] In Rio, there is little exact information before the 1930s, but the Santo Antônio hill alone contained more than four hundred shacks in 1901.[29] By 1913, health officials counted some 2,564 shacks in just Rio's central districts.[30] The building census of 1920 noted numerous houses on morros, and the census's main author lamented the presence of numerous *barracões* (shacks), *tocas* (miserable huts), and homes with *sapé* grass roofs.[31] By the mid-1920s, one real-estate developer and city booster estimated that the morros housed about 100,000 people, more than 8 percent of the city's population.[32] According to the building census of 1933, 26 percent of Rio's structures were made of materials other than brick.[33] Although other Brazilian cities lack exact statistics, it is likely that a similar pattern prevailed, especially in the Northeast. Even in São Paulo — a city, like Buenos Aires, where shantytowns are usually traced only to the mid-twentieth century — Preston James noted in 1933 the presence of "congested slums analogous to the favellas [*sic*] of Rio de Janeiro" occupying "the narrow bottoms of the valleys heading back into the main ridge."[34] By the early twentieth century, Brazil's informal cities were already part of the urban fabric, not only as temporary refuges for the homeless but as sources of profit and social mobility, as political poker chips, and as the loci of increasingly dense social and cultural networks.

The informal city's deep presence did not automatically signify the emergence of "favela" or "mocambo" as a socio-spatial category. That process was different, and in many ways separate. Throughout the late nineteenth century—even as small groups of shacks swelled into informal communities in both Rio and Recife, and even as wealthier city residents quietly tolerated or even propelled that process—public pronouncements about the settlements as a distinct form of urban poverty remained sparse. In the early twentieth century, however, increasing concerns with urbanism and public health, augmented by more liminal fears about Brazil's insertion in the "civilized" world, spurred a growing interest in urban informality.

In Rio, as shacktowns swelled, a trickle of printed material began to fix the phenomenon in outsiders' imaginations. It was largely in print that Rio's shantytowns became "favelas"; small groups of hillside barracos that might have escaped remark twenty years before were now recognized as a distinctive type, one that stood in increasing contrast to the electrified, sanitized, well-communicated city that was taking shape in the valleys below. Early favela writings are an eclectic bunch, and many of them exhibit a healthy appreciation of both the practical impulses driving the favelas' expansion and the hardworking nature of many poor residents.[35] But their authors were also deeply preoccupied with defining the favelas' separateness, and their portrayals were profoundly shaped by their era's concern with European standards of civilization, culture, hygiene, and race.[36]

Thus the earliest portraits of the "favela" shared several distinctive features. The favela was portrayed as a place without a history, by its very nature spontaneous, reactive, and transient. Both its physical and abstract connections to the formal city were thought to be precarious, and there was no hint that outsiders had any interest in its continued existence. The favela was also a deeply antimodern place: a reminder of rural backwardness, a refuge of unproductive economic activity. Many of its residents evoked the slave past, both in their physical presence and in their sociocultural practices. It was considered a place of filth and disease, a nineteenth-century atavism in an age when Brazilian cities were finally ceasing to be sick places. While Rio's favelas might have provided the occasional adventure for flaneurs and bohemians, they were fundamentally separate from the urban sphere—relics, curiosities, or blights, but never part of the urbane world that observers so self-consciously pertained to.

No one captured these crosscurrents so effectively as Rio's acclaimed chronicler, Paulo Barreto (João do Rio). In a breathless 1908 essay, Barreto described a nocturnal visit to the already "celebrated hill" of Santo Antônio.[37] The adventure begins past midnight, in a plaza adjoining Rio's most famous belle epoque boulevard. After spying a motley group of *malandros* (rogues, shysters) — one man in an unnumbered soldier's outfit, three or four "*mulatos* clutching guitars" (143) — Barreto's narrator resolves to follow them to a hillside samba jam session. The crew leaves the plaza, passing the lyric theater, then ascends a broad and utterly ordinary street, past reassuring urban fixtures: a hospital, an astronomical observatory, family homes. But suddenly, at the top of the hill, his guides descend into "a sort of corridor, covered by weeds and vegetation" (145). On the other slope he apprehends "another world"; the path becomes narrow and rough, the lights disappear, the dwellings are shacks made of scrap wood. They are "in the fields, the backlands, far from the city" (146).[38] In this "city inside the great city" (147) — which he compares both to Euclides da Cunha's first view of Canudos and to a giant chicken coop (147) — they buy cane liquor from Baiano, the black owner of a *botequim* (bar) who greets them "with the air of someone who has been a servant in a wealthy household" (147). Barreto's narrator sees in Santo Antônio a "mimicry of an organized society" (148), where everything is a twisted and primitive version of the city below: there are alternate authorities, beaten paths that imitate streets, "bars" and "restaurants" housed in tumbledown shacks. There are prostitutes and malandros, but also families of *operários parados* (laid-off workers) who eke out a living from petty services or street vending. The inhabitants live in drunken and crowded squalor, forming a community where "each man is an animal of impulsive instincts" (148), but where "they don't want anything more" (149) and live in a "permanent festive state," which Barreto's narrator enjoys until three in the morning. When he is finally escorted back to the "civilized" hill, the narrator's final words encapsulate the dominant images of early *favelologia*:

> When I arrived again at the top of the hill, gazing once more at the city sleeping in lamplight, I imagined I had arrived from a long journey to another earthly point; from a rush through a hamlet of sordid happiness, a passage through the unconscious horror of seductive misery. I

envisioned the huts and faces of that vigorous people, making merry in indigence rather than working, managing to construct a camp of indolence in the midst of a great city, free of all laws. I suddenly remembered that smallpox had hit ferociously there, and that I might have been touched by infection. So I hurried on. The palpitating stars began to pale in dawn's pearl, and the roosters began to sing melodiously behind the high grasses of the neighboring yards. (152)

The favela here is the antithesis of the urban aspirations of Rio's republican elite; an anticity without work, without discipline, without law, without sanitation, a distorted mirage that existed for an observer such as Barreto only in the deep of a *carioca* (Rio) night.

Recife's mocambos attracted less bohemian attention. But observers—particularly politicians, engineers, and public-health officials—viewed the settlements with prejudices and preoccupations similarly tethered to their city's point in history. Recife was the principal port and political capital of a northeastern state where a small spurt of belle epoque industrial growth made little dent in a generalized economic decadence. Unlike southern Brazil, Recife had few foreign immigrants, and the city's poorest population was composed overwhelmingly of migrants from the region's drought-afflicted *sertão* (backlands) and miserably exploitative sugar zone.[39] Although there were scattered attempts and urban remodeling, no campaign reached the scale or intensity of the reforms undertaken in Rio by prefect Francisco Pereira Passos.[40] All of this added up to an *urbe* that was far smaller, poorer and sicker than Rio—where mocambos were the norm rather than the exception, and where urbane pretensions stood on far shakier foundations.

Early twentieth-century writings about the mocambos reflected these realities. The first public depictions of Recife's shacktowns viewed them mostly through the lens of the city's abysmal public-health conditions.[41] In 1907 the prominent hygienist Otávio Freitas noted that both mocambos and tenements contributed greatly to high mortality levels, and that "their living conditions are a serious threat for that part of the population more favored by fortune."[42] Such sentiments seem to have shaped the city's sanitation plan of 1909, which formally banned most mocambos, and they were heavily present in the writings of subsequent health and welfare officials. In 1908 the noted lawyer, jurist, politician, and journalist Artur Orlando laid out the moral and physical dangers the settlements were thought to represent: "In the Recife neighborhood of Afogados, at the city's very heart, so-called mucambos are not lacking. . . . [There are] shacks without air, without light, built upon miasmatic swamps, with scraps salvaged from packing crates and kerosene cans, with no internal divisions, lacking sewage and water to wash with or drink, with all of the tenants—men and women, parents and children, young and old—filthily piled up in a state of repugnant promiscuity."[43]

Writings on the mocambos also incorporated Recifenses' fears about their city's racial identity and international reputation. The authors of a 1913 census worried about the "disagreeable aspect" the mocambos lent to great parts of the city; health and welfare head Amaury de Medeiros lamented that the mocambos were akin to "Negro settlements in Senegal," and fretted that they caused "an inevitable air of pity and disgust" among "civilized men and women from the world over."[44] Paulista poet Rui Ribeiro Couto noted in 1928 that Recife's inhabitants were humiliated by the mocambos because "tourists take pictures of their straw cabins."[45] Rio's boosters voiced similar concerns—"leprosy" was a favored metaphor for the favelas—but Recifense writings revealed a much deeper repugnance for dwellings that not only stained the city but characterized it.[46] In an emblematic article written toward the end of the 1930s, Pernambucan governor Agamenon Magalhães noted a friend's horror in seeing a mocambo depicted on the dinner menu of an elegant flight from Recife to Paris, with a caption defining it as the typical "lodging of Pernambucan natives": "The city's avenues, the bridges, the river, the landscape of the suburbs with their leafy swamps and century-old jaqueira trees, all of this disappears for the tourist in the face of the spectacle of the mocambos."[47]

These writings reveal little about the mocambos themselves: how they came to be, the nature of their daily life and microeconomies, why they continued to dominate the cheap housing stock, whom they benefited, and how they related to Recife's political power structures. Instead, the writings speak to the mocambos' significance in some Recifenses' quest to promote a salubrious and civilized urbe in place of a degraded and Africanized city. Rio's favela became fixed in outsiders' imaginations as an atavistic and curious evocation of exoticism, rurality, and disease; Recife's mocambos represented the city's all-too-continuous distance from an urban ideal.

None of the earliest iconic images of Brazil's shacktowns has ever faded: new associations with filth, disease, atavism, rurality, Africanness, and bohemia have emerged with every generation. But between the 1920s and the 1940s, a series of new political questions and social categories animated Brazil's political and intellectual landscape, inevitably redefining the informal city. Partisans in the era's intense debates about race, popular citizenship, and urban design found in the mocambos and favelas both objects of discussion and sites of political and cultural organization. Were informal cities a healthy expression of *mestiçagem* (racial mixture) or warrens of racial degeneracy? Were their residents biologically tainted or simply the transient victims of malnutrition, disease, and inadequate education? Were workers housed in favelas and mocambos victims in need of state solidarity or threats to Brazil's political stability? Could people morally deformed by the favelas' "promiscuous" conditions be reformed by "proper" housing? How could the shantytown's political potential be marshaled or repressed? In Brazil, as elsewhere in Latin America, these questions became central to national and local politics. The foreign gaze weakened, and shantytowns tended to be considered more fully within their local socioeconomic and political contexts.[48] But even as writings about the favelas and mocambos proliferated, their depth and range continued to be constrained by the settlements' contentious place in the era's central political and economic debates.

Archival evidence suggests that mocambos and favelas retained some core features between the 1920s and the 1940s. They still housed poor and migrant populations who might otherwise have been driven out of the city, they were still characterized by precarious construction and by the absence of urban services, they still provided political power and profit to actors up and down the social scale, and they still appeared mainly illegally and on marginal lands unsuitable to formal development. But favelas and mocambos expanded quickly, and that very expansion radically altered their place in the cityscape, physical and imaginary. Outsiders could no longer ignore informal cities, or realistically imagine that they would disappear with economic growth or rising urban prosperity. Indeed, cities' rising fortunes—along with a generalized rural crisis—likely drove the shantytowns' expansion. By 1933, 51,625 of Rio's buildings (about a quarter of the city's total) were wooden shacks or other precarious structures. In 1940 the Yellow Fever Service estimated that there were some 63,000 wooden shacks in Rio, and the 1940 census counted about 60,000 wooden or precarious structures in the city (21 percent of the 285,000 total).[49] In Recife, more than 45,000 of 70,000 total dwellings were mocambos in 1939, and nearly 50 percent of the city's 342,000 inhabitants lived in them.[50] In both cities, shantytown residents were often migrants from rural areas or small interior towns — some rendered destitute by drought, others left landless and unemployed by changing forms of agricultural production, and still others drawn to an urban way of life that was improving at a much quicker pace than in the countryside. Josué de Castro, among the first social scientists to spend significant time in the favelas or mocambos, described the movement to Recife as a great "draining" of excess population from the exploitative sugar mill complexes and drought-ridden backlands.[51] Mário Lacerda de Melo, writing in 1940, injected a culturalist reading, noting the city's attraction for all levels of rural society: "Rural life is increasingly disdained. To live in the rural interior is more or less to be a bumpkin, a hick, to be unfamiliar with civilization and progress, to gape openmouthed at city things, to 'comprar bonde' [fall for a ruse], as they say in the south. Everyone wants to live in the capital. And no one takes pride any more in the title of *senhor de engenho* [sugar baron], once worn with such dignity."[52]

The growth and diversification of Brazil's shantytowns entailed paradoxical changes in their relationship with the urban environment. The settlements' expansion — together with heightened expectations about urban life and rising values for once marginal lands — initially intensified calls for eradication. After widespread discussion in the 1920s and early 1930s, both Rio and Recife attempted full-blown clearance campaigns during the Estado Novo (New State; 1937–45). Both cities also intensified efforts to remove individual shacks for public-health violations and to evict tenants so that shantytown lands could be sold to higher bidders. Such campaigns proved more effective in reorienting the geography of informal settlement than in eliminating it. Rio's shacks began to concentrate in larger and more clearly demarcated favelas and expanded especially quickly in the less-regulated suburban and rural areas.[53] In Recife, some central swampland mocambos disappeared, others became more concentrated, and still more sprung up in the hills to the northwest of the city center.

Larger numbers, increased geographical concentration, accelerating land values, and rising threats of removal forced significant political and economic shifts. Political expediency had long undergirded shantytowns' growth. But crosscurrents from the 1920s through the 1940s created new urban dynamics, which would endure for much of the twentieth century.[54]

If public outcry forced politicians to make a show of slum clearance, the sub-terranean requirements of emergent mass politics required something else entirely. Communists brought pressure from the Left, using eviction threats to effectively organize numerous communities and riding to considerable electoral success in the municipal elections of 1935 and 1947.[55] Mainstream politicians sought to decompress such pressures, and also found in urban shantytowns the cheapest possible source of political support; in exchange for a water spigot, or a little protection from an avaricious landlord, or a willingness to block enforcement of a whole range of laws banning settle-ment, a politician could gain votes from thousands, none of whom could legitimately demand expensive urban services. At a local level, those able to organize a community and deliver its gratitude in votes became newly criti-cal cogs in the urban political machine, often using the experience to launch political careers. This dynamic accelerated after 1945, as in-migration and a widening voter base revolutionized the practice of urban politics.

In economic terms, mocambos and favelas also became steadily more entrenched. Even as prominent citizens decried illegal slums as affronts to civilization, some built enduring networks of profit on the settlements' backs. The informal city opened up surprisingly lucrative opportunities for everyone from destitute squatters with a little spare space to real-estate speculators with titling problems to decadent nobility seeking additional income. Each incremental expansion—every mocambo that added on a space for a renter, every bit of ground leased for shack construction, every illegally held area subdivided and "sold" off the books—extended the net-work of individuals with a significant interest in informal cities' persistence. As in politics, the shantytowns assumed economic importance not despite their illegality but because of it. With the partial exception of São Paulo, most Brazilian cities simply did not possess the economic infrastructure to guarantee legal, idealized urban conditions or rapid social ascension to legions of poor workers. Politicians, speculators, and the residents all came to depend on the opportunities for profit, power, or mere urban subsistence offered by this parallel, sub-urban city. Over time, so many interest groups gained a stake in the existence of tolerated illegality that urban society be-came inconceivable without it.[56]

Historical research suggests that such political and economic rooting was at the core of the favela phenomenon. But public discussion at the time veered toward issues with more obvious public resonance. Politicians and journalists decried the favelas' exploiters, but none systematically traced the economic and political foundations of favela persistence or seriously analyzed favelas' role in a new urban environment. Instead, most observers simply fit the phenomenon into politically convenient or sociologically current meta-analyses of the Brazilian conjuncture, exploring the informal city only in the context of well-worn ideological debates.

The discussion about the favelas' racial characteristics was a case in point. Favelas and mocambos had long been associated both with Africa and African descent: residents were disproportionately Afro-descendant, the mocambos' mythical and actual roots were entangled with slavery, and observers read their own prejudices into the settlements' "primitive" physical form. Black or mixed-race characters inhabited outsiders' titillating accounts of samba sessions or Afro-Brazilian religious rituals in Rio, mostly in the form of a few stock types—the *cachaça* (cane alcohol)-swilling, guitar-toting malandro, the entranced *macumbeiro* (practitioner of Afro-Brazilian religion), the *mulata baiana* (Bahian mulatta), and the *valente* (thug), razor or club in hand.[57] Even so acute an observer as the young Josué de Castro evoked Africa in an early description of the mocambos: "'Afogados,' 'Pina,' 'Santo Amaro,' zones of swamps, of workers, of unemployed, of misfits, of those who came from the backlands in hunger and couldn't make it in the city, of the rebellious and the resigned—of the vanquished. Zones of 'mocambos.' An aquatic city, with houses of beaten clay and sticks (*sopapo*), roofs of wild grass, straw, and corrugated tin. Black cambuca fruit floating in the water. Mocambos—residual slave quarters splintered around the Big Houses of the American Venice. Primitive poetry of blacks and mestizos practicing voodoo and singing samba. African physiognomy."[58]

Even as such depictions persisted, however, new intellectual and political currents inspired both a cultural valorization of African roots and a gradual de-racialization of favela and mocambo policy debates. In Recife, an ascendant discourse of *mestiço* (mestizo) regional identity glorified the mocambo as an architectural emblem of cultural cross-pollination, celebrating its African and indigenous roots and praising its adaptation to the tropical climate.[59] In Rio, samba musicians skillfully appealed to these electric intellectual trends, catering to white Brazilians' sense of the exotic and to their imaginings of racial cordiality, while simultaneously affirming Afro-Brazilian cultural identity and the favelas' deep connection to it.[60]

At the same time that outsiders began to celebrate informal cities' cultural links with African or mestiço culture, politicians and policymakers began to silence the overt racial content of debates regarding shantytown policy.

Urban sociologists and anthropologists, echoing international trends, began to emphasize ecologies of migration and class formation over racial determinism. While some public-health officials, urban planners, and city boosters still tarred the informal city with racist invective, others began to adopt more transient categorizations. Shantytowns were not the "natural" habitat of a backward race. Instead, they resulted from mutable social conditions: poverty, lack of public sanitation, ignorance, rural mentalities, poor planning, or official neglect. Politicians—anxious to build urban bases in an age of incipient populism and eager to snuff out the appeal of color-blind communist rhetoric—followed suit, depicting favelas and mocambos in increasingly deracialized terms. By the late 1930s, when Agamenon Magalhães led a pioneering campaign to eradicate Recife's mocambos, racial discourses were significantly muffled: the city's much-vaunted mocambo census did not even publish racial data.[61] The process of official deracialization was by no means linear and certainly did not indicate the elimination of racism itself, but overt racial references gradually became the exception rather than the rule. By the mid-1950s, it was possible for Brazil's national congress to debate a national favela law over the course of an entire year without a single acknowledgment that shantytowns' populations were majority Afro-descendant.

This trend was stronger in some places than others; São Paulo, in particular, was always an outlier when it came to Brazilian racial silences. But the muffling of racial discourse exemplified the ways in which the terms of debate about informal cities could turn on currents generated far from the settlements themselves. People living in mocambos and favelas did not become any less black in this period. Racist attitudes endured. Judging from available correlations between race, socioeconomic indicators, health, and city services, Afro-descendants faced no fewer disadvantages in the urban milieu.[62] But while observers mostly ceased to explain the mocambos' informality and poverty with reference to racial torpidity, they also mostly ignored racism; new analyses placed more emphasis on nutritional deficits, poor education, low salaries, and faulty public policy. The shift arguably allowed shantytown residents to build cross-racial solidarity and to win greater sympathy for favelas and mocambos among white and mixed-race Brazilians, thus contributing to the settlements' long-term survival. But the new lenses were no less tinted than the old; the new focus on mutable causes of informal poverty obscured for many decades the racial dimensions of urban marginalization.

Discussions of work and poverty also greatly influenced debate about shantytowns during this period. In concert with president and dictator Getúlio Vargas's corporatist celebration of the urban working class, politicians and policymakers actively contested stereotypes of vagrancy and *malandragem* in Brazil's shantytowns, and strove to incorporate mocambo and favela residents into the fold of a respectable, loyal, family-based working class.[63] In Recife this effort accelerated in the wake of extensive radical activism in mocambo communities.[64] Agamenon Magalhães structured his mocambo-eradication campaign around the idea that residents were a redeemable population, ennobled by work and exploited by a class of vicious speculators and profiteers. In a 1939 article, Magalhães celebrated the Recife census's findings that the vast majority of mocambo residents were honest workers: "What kind of population is this? One of illiterates? Unemployed people? No. Two-thirds . . . know how to read and write. They are literate. Almost the whole population of the mocambos works. They have occupations. The percentage of unemployed is minimal, only 3.3 percent. The heads of family are artisans, or work in factories, in commerce, in transportation. The women wash, iron, when they are not occupied in other domestic jobs. The children of the mocambos go to school, 62.78 percent of them."[65]

Magalhães concluded by placing responsibility for bettering mocambo conditions squarely on the backs of employers and the national state. The head of Rio's eradication campaign portrayed at least some favelas as home to virtuous, working families.[66] A propaganda piece from 1941 emphasized similar qualities.[67] Such views hardly became hegemonic; the finding that most *favelados* (favela residents) were workers would still be celebrated as pathbreaking in the 1970s, when Janice Perlman published her well-known *Myth of Marginality*.[68] But writings that emphasized shacktown dwellers' work and family values, like those that deemphasized race, posited that shantytown conditions resulted from mutable factors and that society had a significant responsibility for remedying them. Mocambos and favelas didn't grow from sloth or vice but were rather the result of "lack of comprehension of social problems," low salaries, or the profiteering of exploiters.[69] The portrayal of shantytown residents as working people was especially important in light of the Vargas-era linkage of work and citizenship, which legitimated the civic demands of workers in multiple realms.[70]

Yet glorification of favelados often obscured politically inconvenient socioeconomic realities. Many Vargas-era officials sidestepped deep issues for which they could offer no solution: the structural and political conditions that favored informality, underemployment, and illegally low wages;

the fact that gaining the status of a formally recognized worker entailed far more than the fact of working; and the very real networks of money and political influence that had grown up around the favelas. By the time Vargas was ejected from office in the mid-1940s, much time and effort had been spent stating what ought to have been obvious: most people who lived in shantytowns worked for a living and did their best to support their families and achieve some measure of social mobility. But it was not clear whether decency, loyalty, and work were enough to eliminate shantytowns and the sub-urban form of citizenship they implied.

Regardless of the Vargas-era's failings, it was a period in which the terms of debate about favelas and mocambos changed irrevocably. Deterministic views of social inequality now competed with affirmations that Brazil's perceived economic and social backwardness was primarily rooted in misguided economic policies, poor governance, and negligence of the social fabric. Collective responsibility for urban social problems was broadly acknowledged, policymakers favored new and mutable categorizations of social inequality, and the favela debate became more closely attuned to the settlements' empirical realities. But Vargas-era images of the informal city were unrealistic in their view that Brazil's shantytowns would be easy to erase. Even as demographers gathered the first generation of solid data about the social conditions they had targeted for change — scarce formal housing stock, illiteracy, low wages, lack of access to nutritious food, medical services, and sanitation — it was clear that the national government had nowhere near the resources necessary to alter them. And there was relative silence about issues less compatible with the political discourse of the day, particularly regarding the quiet, steady intertwining of informality, economic gain, and political power. Racial and other types of social discrimination, widespread exclusion from citizenship, scarce public resources, and the benefits that informality brought to actors up and down the social scale were brushed aside, and the notion that historical thinking had any role in understanding the informal-city phenomenon never even entered the conversation. It is thus unsurprising that Vargas-era policies barely slowed shantytowns' proliferation.

SLUMS IN THE AGE OF DEVELOPMENT

Between the 1940s and the 1970s, favelas and mocambos occupied an enormously important place in Brazilian public life. Informal cities grew precipitously, their populations swollen by high rates of migration from the

Brazilian interior. Rickety wooden shacks clinging to the hillsides above modernist apartment towers became iconic symbols of Brazilian inequality and underdevelopment. The settlements' political importance increased in an age of democratic elections and sporadic left-wing mobilization, and heterodox local leaders leveraged these new politics to impede evictions and reinforce residents' claims to urban territory. Shantytowns took center stage in thousands of newspaper articles, photo essays, paintings, sermons, political manifestos, novels, movies, songs, policy papers, statistical surveys, books, and academic theses, foreign and domestic. Favelas and mocambos periodically dominated debate in municipal councils, national legislatures, and political campaigns across the country. Shantytowns also became pawns in international diplomacy as the United States led initiatives to destroy potential sites of communist infection throughout Latin America.[71] The monumental construction of Brasília was based at least in part on the quixotic hope that the new capital would avoid the perceived scourge of informality; at least some small part of the post-1964 military government's initial appeal derived from its promise to control the social and political dangers spawned by the favelas.[72]

These developments spurred extensive research and reporting. For the first time, polemicists had abundant data with which to describe and analyze certain dimensions of favela life: employment patterns, formal family structures, residents' states of birth, income levels, literacy rates, housing conditions, religiosity, and participation in formal politics and associational groups.[73] For the first time too, some writers broached the subject of the profit networks that undergirded informal life, and many connected the favela phenomenon to deep and intractable dysfunctions in Brazil's national economy.[74] Occasionally, observers even began to study the shantytowns on their own terms, leaving behind an array of stock types and established categories of social difference and focusing on more organic phenomena: networks of daily interaction in the *birosca* (corner store), in the botequim, at the water spigot, or in the laundry line; structures that regulated property and behavior in the absence of formal law; webs of political connection; or informal networks of kin and friendship.[75] History remained sketchy in midcentury portrayals, many of which incorrectly argued that informal settlement had begun in the 1930s, and most of which defined the informal city by its precarious, ephemeral, urgent place in the present tense.[76] Scarce too were unmediated firsthand accounts of favela life, and those that did emerge were often highly problematic.[77] But the sheer volume and diversity of favela and mocambo portrayals, and the quality of mind of many favela observers, made it possible for outsiders to understand the settlements more deeply than ever before.

Partially as a result of such studies, and partly out of sheer pragmatism, many policymakers acknowledged that informal cities were an intractable part of the Brazilian urban landscape and focused their energies on improvement rather than elimination. This was an international trend. By the early 1960s, it was already obvious to many observers that shantytowns would linger for as long as urban incomes remained insufficient to pay for formal housing, and most policy recommendations leaned toward a pragmatic self-made housing model rather than large-scale removal campaigns.[78] The question of favela elimination was highly contentious in Brazil. Spurred by Alliance for Progress funding, virulent antipopulism and anticommunism, and outright kowtowing to real-estate speculation, Rio's governors conducted several spectacular mass evictions in the 1960s.[79] But such removals did little to dampen the growth of informal cities; the broader trend was toward disquieted entrenchment.

The predictable irony was that neither deeper knowledge nor a ground-level shift in favela policy was enough to prevent the central political and intellectual polemics of the time from defining the shantytown debate, particularly in the international and popular arenas. Iconic notions about favelas and mocambos stubbornly resisted empirical debunking, and new and seemingly urgent sets of questions bounded a now-internationalized debate. Were favelas and mocambos rural places, inhabited by people unprepared for modern industrial life, destined to degrade both development and urbanity? Did informal poverty distort the poor, making them immune to well-intentioned improvements in material conditions? Were shantytown residents a potential source of cataclysmic or utopian political radicalism? These three sets of questions made political tinder of the informal cities' fates, linking shantytowns to epoch-defining hopes and fears about revolution, underdevelopment, and the social potential of the so-called third world. The very survival of many communities—and that of the networks of profit and power that sustained them—could hinge on their leaders' capacity to contest the myths of marginality that reduced informal cities to nests of degradation, anomie, and radicalism. These high political stakes significantly hindered open public debate. Politicians, bureaucrats, and community leaders necessarily aligned their rhetoric with political imperatives. And even some researchers took great pains not to undermine their positions in the era's great debates, avoiding touchy question about the favelas' complex origins and internal workings and tending toward optimistic assessments of the settlements' impact on socioeconomic inequality and political culture.

COMMUNISM IN THE HILLS

The ideological battle over Latin American communism brought an international urgency to midcentury slum studies. At the dawn of the cold war, many U.S. observers already sensed revolution in Latin America's "festering" shantytowns. U.S. reporters anxiously followed the rising fortunes of Latin America's Communist Parties, sure that widespread poverty and inequality would eventually translate into political instability. In 1949 the *New York Times* reporter Milton Bracker spelled out the dangers: "Nature has perversely hung a millstone of hunger and want around the necks of South Americans living amid a spurious plenty. Thus, we find squalid housing, infected water, chronic intestinal parasitism, ignorance, hatred, fear, and often a blind and unreasoning nationalism. The demagogue always sounds louder to men who are poor and hungry."[80] Throughout the 1950s and early 1960s, U.S. Roman Catholics added fuel to the fire, transmitting urgent calls for social reforms to head off moral and political catastrophe.[81] As the Cuban Revolution veered left, fears about the region intensified: a *Life* magazine series from 1961 titled "The Crisis in Our Hemisphere" opened by warning that "the messianic eyes of Fidel Castro, hypnotic and hungry for power, summon up a new and nightmarish danger for the US."[82] By the early 1960s, reporters swarmed the continent in search of the next cataclysm. Their fears focused on the burgeoning shantytowns: one described Lima's "unimaginably evil slums" as "foul dumps, ravaged by herds of rooting pigs, heaped with garbage smoking through spontaneous combustion: A Dantesque inferno."[83] In the throes of such hyperbole, it is little wonder that Sargent Shriver, after a visit to "the hillside slums of Caracas," quipped: "If I were a communist agitator and couldn't organize a revolution in those slums in six months, I'd quit."[84]

United States academics often piled on the bandwagon, reasoning that shantytowns concentrated a frustrated population of rural migrants whose hopes for social mobility had been dashed by scarce jobs and urban resources; in their anomic despair, they were low-hanging fruit for communist propagandists.[85] Samuel Huntington noted in 1968 that "the most promising source of urban revolt is clearly the slums and shantytowns produced by the influx of the rural poor.... At some point, the slums of Rio and Lima ... are likely to be swept by social violence."[86] Even the dynamic Argentine economist Raúl Prebisch advocated a version of this theory, arguing that Latin America's economic distortions had led to the "surge" of "poverty, frustration, and resentment" from the country to urban areas, a process that he saw as "proof of explosive social polarization of development."[87]

In Brazil, as in Chile and Peru, fears and hopes about the radical potential of the shantytowns had deeper roots, and were often well founded.[88] In the late 1920s, communist lawyers were already helping mocambo residents to organize and resist eviction efforts; similar efforts would continue into the 1960s.[89] By the 1930s, the Communists won enough votes to form the second largest bloc in Recife's municipal council, due in part to their support among the mocambos, and an entire novel was written to promote class consciousness in the slums.[90] In this and subsequent decades, Recife's communists poured enormous energy into documenting the physical suffering of mocambo residents and organizing local associations to defend residents against eviction and demand physical improvements.[91] In Rio, from the 1930s forward, communist lawyers also came to the aid of favela residents, sometimes winning occupation rights and frequently staving off eviction threats. In the 1940s, Brazil's Communist Party explicitly favored neighborhood-level organization and integration into "popular" cultural traditions; such organizations were at the base of Communist success in the municipal elections of 1947.[92] Communist city council members and federal deputies defended large settlements from eviction during the party's brief legality, and neighborhood associations and favela advocacy were critical to the Party's clandestine life from 1948 forward. The communist press followed stories about favela activism as assiduously as strike movements or Yankee imperialism. Ironically, though favela activism is rarely mentioned in histories of Brazil's Communist Party — and was, in fact, viewed by Communist leaders as a strategic ploy to infuse the urban masses with proletarian consciousness — communists were critical in assuring informal cities' survival.

Brazilian politicians actively combated communist activism in the hills. Agamenon Magalhães's campaign against mocambos in the 1930s explicitly aimed to eliminate "cells of discontent" that opened opportunities for "enemies of order."[93] In the late 1940s, Rio's fiery anticommunist journalist Carlos Lacerda led an ambitious press campaign to eliminate Rio's favelas; like Magalhães, Lacerda was careful to affirm the favela residents' humanity and moral character and to reject draconian destruction of the settlements, precisely because he believed that humanitarian "recuperation" would deprive communists of a natural organizational catalysts: "o desengano, que é seu aliado, o desespero, que é seu cu(o)mpincha" (disillusionment, which is their ally, and hopelessness, which is their crony).[94] Throughout the 1940s and 1950s, as battles raged about favela evictions throughout Rio, municipal politicians frequently attributed favela protest to communist agitation.[95] From a different perspective, Catholic social activists and moderate community-development advocates urged attention to the favelados' legitimate social demands, lest the city become "an arena of class struggle."[96] In the early 1960s, when Lacerda, then governor, led an unprecedented favela eradication campaign, he and his appointees leveled similar rhetoric both to justify the violent removals and to attract Alliance for Progress funds for low-income housing blocks.[97] Throughout this period, the political police closely tracked favela and mocambo organizations and imprisoned and harassed communist activists; the post-1964 military government stripped many neighborhood leaders of their political rights and imprisoned or tortured them.

The great irony, for both sides, is that communist favela activism never implied a mass "tomada de conciencia" (awakening of consciousness) along communist lines. In both Rio and Recife, residents were always careful to hedge their bets when it came to community defense. Many embraced communist legal and organizational assistance and may have harbored genuine ideological sympathy. But informal cities were too precarious, and chances of revolution too slim, for communities to stake everything on the communist cause. Residents collaborated with communists, but they also forged links with Catholics, social workers, populists, and local bosses. Residents' public statements were scrupulously ideologically neutral, attentive to the very real dangers of communist identification. Rio's Morro do Turano was one of the two communities where communists were known to influence resistance movements in the late 1940s; as a result, recounted one father of five from Minas Gerais, the local landowner and his henchmen committed "violências" against all residents in the name of anticommunism.[98] Rio's pioneering Union of Favela Workers was also punished for its leftist sympathies; its meetings were infiltrated, its leader arrested multiple times, and its legitimacy questioned by factions within informal communities. Little wonder that favela organizations in both Recife and Rio studiously avoided revolutionary language.[99]

All of this was surely strategic, and the result of violent repression—who wouldn't deny communist sympathies in the oppressive context of Latin America's cold war? But by the end of the 1960s, shantytown scholars from across the Western Hemisphere argued that strategic thinking was a symptom of deeper conservatism or pragmatism. Beginning in 1960, when Charles Stokes first posited that settlements of recent migrants ought to be called "slums of hope," Latin Americanists began to probe assumptions about the supposed anomie and radical tendencies of Latin America's informal cities. John C. Turner and William Mangin were especially effective advocates of the notion that Latin America's shantytowns were in fact a kind of safety valve for massive social unrest, and that residents' values were essentially entrepreneurial and individualistic, in no way compatible with political radicalism. Mangin wrote in 1967:

> The dominant ideology of most of the active barriada people appeared to be very similar to the beliefs of the operator of a small business in 19th century England or the United States. These can be summed up in the familiar and accepted maxims: Work hard, save your money, trust only family members (and them not too much), outwit the state, vote conservatively if possible, but always in your own economic self-interest; educate your children for their future and as old age insurance for yourself. Aspirations are toward improvement of the local situation with the hope that children will enter the professional class. All of the above statements pertain perfectly to favelas.[100]

Eric Hobsbawm wrote in 1967 that rural migrants were doubly dissuaded from the radical action that might otherwise be expected of them, first by their complete lack of exposure to nonpatriarchal forms of political power, and second by the fact that urban conditions were so much better than those they'd left behind in the countryside: migration was, in this sense, in itself a revolutionary act.[101] By the early 1970s, sociologists and political scientists such as Alejandro Portes (Chile) and Wayne Cornelius (Mexico) had come to essentially the same conclusions. In Brazil, most academics studiously avoided reference to communist activism, and even right-wing politicians came to portray communists as only marginal agitators within an essentially "decent" favela population. The communist specter would continue to haunt shantytown politics—justifying brutal oppression from Chile to Peru to Guatemala—but by the 1970s few truly expected revolution to descend from the shanties.[102]

A relatively levelheaded view of shantytown radicalism thus eventually settled into place. But in the thirty years in which communism shaped debates about Latin America's informal cities, what had been learned about shantytown politics? Beyond a general awareness of the importance of cheap populism and demagoguery, did anyone understand how the shantytown's political networks functioned, who benefited, who lost out, and how the web of support for favela permanence managed to resist calls for eradication? Was it clear what role the Communist Party and the Catholic Church had played in defending the settlements, even if neither had achieved the allegiances they desired? Perhaps most important, had any analyst found a way of understanding what ground-level shantytown politics meant for the political culture of cities in the midst of such enormous demographic transition? The answer, in all cases, was mostly no: the communist question had siphoned so much intellectual energy that these more open-ended and enduring issues can only be pieced together from the margins.

BRAZIL AND THE CULTURE OF POVERTY

The notion that urban destitution begat a specific, generationally transmissible "culture of poverty" was the second ideological vector that came to define midcentury slum studies. The idea that the poor held some blame for their state had deep roots, appearing everywhere from Christian teachings about the deserving and undeserving poor to nineteenth-century European writings about the supposed laziness, promiscuity, and moral degeneracy of an urban pauper class. Robert Park, an early intellectual dean of the Chicago School of urban sociology, wrote in 1915 of "moral regions" in which the "poor, the vicious, and the delinquent, crushed together in an unhealthful and contagious intimacy, breed in and in, soul and body," thus reinforcing their shared cultural deformation.[103] Park's ideas were updated and racialized in St. Clair Drake's highly influential account of black Chicago, which painted a sympathetic but powerful portrait of cultural withering grounded in Great Migration–era segregation. Brazilian observers as diverse as the novelist Aluísio Azevedo and the engineer Everardo Backheuser had chronicled the moral (and racial) degeneracy that supposedly threatened Brazil's honest poor.[104]

Early twentieth-century reformism modernized these ideas without supplanting them. In both U.S. ghettoes and in Latin American shantytowns, the causes of poverty came to be portrayed as structural: unequal property distribution, insufficiently developed economies, lack of opportunities for education and the development of marketable skills, and racial segregation. But poor people's reactions to such structural conditions were said to lead to a kind of transgenerational cultural breakdown: broken families, self-defeating solidarity with family or neighbors, defensive rejection of values needed to escape poverty (hard work, planning ahead, saving, rational use of available resources), superstition, and overvaluation of ephemeral pleasures (parties, sex, drugs, alcohol). Formal blame for the economic fact of poverty had shifted—poverty did not in itself spring from moral or racial degeneracy—but poor people were still seen as obstacles to their own progress.

For Latin America, the central academic articulation of these ideas came from Oscar Lewis, an American whose pioneering studies of Mexican rural-to-urban migrants and their families transformed the practice of urban anthropology in the late 1950s and early 1960s.[105] Lewis had initially argued against the inevitability of social marginality among poor migrants, highlighting the possibility of "urbanization without breakdown" and giving far more weight to the structural determinants of poverty than his many later critics gave him credit for.[106] By the early 1960s, though, Lewis's in-depth, biographical studies of small-town migrants to Mexico City and Puerto Rican migrants to New York had led him to the notion that there was a transnational "culture of poverty"—sometimes born of displacement, but not a direct continuation of rural ways of life in an urban context—that ensnared inhabitants of ghettoes and shantytowns around the world. Members of such cultures were "marginal people even when they live in the heart of a great city."[107] They made little use of urban or governmental institutions; they restricted solidarity to members of their immediate families; they were uneducated; they struggled constantly for economic subsistence; they were given to "gregariousness," alcoholism, violence, and precocious and casual sex; they displayed "a strong present-time orientation" (which translated into an inability to delay gratification and plan for the future); and they had a strong sense of resignation and fatalism. Once ingrained, these habits of body and mind tended to transcend generations, a *culture* in the deepest sense of the word. Lewis argued abstractly that such adaptations could be functional, but his exhaustive biographical accounts left little doubt that the main product was urban pathology.[108]

Lewis employed highly innovative research methods and narrative forms, and he was careful to emphasize that the culture of poverty could be a coherent reaction to extreme destitution. But his writings had much in common with earlier pathologizations, and his arguments' unintentional effect was to give serious academic sheen to even the most exaggerated distortions of poor people's existence.[109] Numerous researchers contested Lewis; after exhaustive discussion in the 1960s, Latin Americanist scholars and thoughtful journalists resoundingly dismissed the "culture of poverty" as myth.[110] But many writers, especially early on, applied Lewis's notions bluntly and universally; others accepted his ideas in part if not in whole, or even claimed that the notion of "culture" gave too much coherence to the disorganized squalor that they saw in the worst of slums.[111] In books written for a popular audience, the culture of poverty soon merged with generalized prejudice in descriptions of Latin America's shantytowns as "malignant sores," "stinkweed," "scabrous crusts" or the "septic fringe" of the region's cities.[112] Just as U.S. ghettoes were seething nests of immorality, vice, and corruption, Latin American shantytowns were inhabited by people whose cultural proclivities blocked their own socioeconomic advancement.

In Brazil, as in much of the rest of Latin America, culture of poverty theories surfaced most overtly in the writings of foreigners, and especially foreign journalists. One especially arresting example was Gordon Parks's 1961 *Life* photo essay on twelve-year-old Flávio da Silva and his family, residents of Rio's Catacumba favela, which clung until the late 1960s to an impossibly steep hillside between Lagôa and Copacabana.[113] Parks was among the most acclaimed American photojournalists of the twentieth century, known especially for his elegant, seething portraits of black urban poverty and racism.[114] The essay on Flávio and his family, "Shocking Poverty Spawns Reds," was part of a five-part series, intended to document sources of radical discontent across Latin America. Parks's account, however, ignored politics, focusing only on the "dark world" he had found within the favela. Parks had chosen to profile a white family, refugees from the drought-ridden Northeast: an injured and unemployed father, a mother pregnant with their ninth child, surviving by washing clothes with water from a feeble public spigot.[115] Flávio was the oldest child, and the most sympathetically portrayed. Parks's photos emphasized the overwhelming squalor and tragedy of the family's daily life: the pregnant mother, two girls clinging to her, climbing the favela's steep, muddy paths with an enormous tin can of water balanced on her head; a naked boy, howling after being bitten by a vicious stray; a bare-bottomed toddler clambering alone among the precarious wooden stilts that bind a home to the rocky hillside; Flávio stuffing handfuls of food into the mouth of his filthy baby brother; an Afro-Brazilian neighbor, dead and laid out for her last rites on a candle-lit bed resembling a cross. On the opposite page was the most haunting image of the series: Flávio, who suffered from severe asthma, lying prostrate among dirty blankets with the caption: "I am not afraid of death . . . but what will they do after?" The only uplifting pictures were of Flávio and his brother playing for the first time in their lives on the world-famous Copacabana beach, and of Parks himself carrying the family's baby up the hill "to be cleaned up," the baby's whiteness especially stark against Parks's dark skin and black shirt.

The text, composed mainly of excerpts from Parks's field journal, gave an overwhelming impression of miserable poverty, filth, family breakdown, pathology, and anomie. The parents are "beaten people," "their mother doesn't have the time to give the love they need—and the father seems incapable." One of the children, Isabel, "a small flower of bitterness," pierces her foot with a nail. Parks pulls the nail free, and while the mother sops up the blood and applies rubbing alcohol, the father doesn't "even bother to look at her foot—although he was less than three feet away." The children, semiabandoned, show all the signs of budding social breakdown; they argue foully and strike out physically at the slightest provocation, biting, kicking, and scratching. They accost Parks with demands for money, and are incapable of sharing any small good fortune, seeming to revel in each other's envy and misery. Only Flávio seems almost miraculously capable of care, nurture, and hard work, but "in the tormented, closed world of the shack, assailed by the needs and complaints of his sisters and brothers who are always a little hungry, he fights a losing battle against savagery and disorder."

Flávio's story struck an extraordinary chord in the United States. *Life* magazine collected $30,000 in reader donations, and Parks returned to Brazil to bring the boy for free treatment at a hospital in Denver and to resettle his family in a small brick house. Parks's article was also unusual in his choice of a white family, itself a wordless critique of the racialized culture of poverty theories then current in the United States. But Parks's account nonetheless lent strength to the basic notion that favelas were nests of self-perpetuating misery. In an era when the U.S. government and other international organizations were beginning to make influential investments in Brazilian housing programs, such images had enormous practical consequences. If favelas were nests of vice and social disintegration, they had to be eliminated, a conclusion that directly contradicted the more realistic plans for on-site urbanization that had gradually and tenuously taken the lead in Brazilian policy circles in the tumultuous 1950s and 1960s.

In Brazil, *Life*'s presentation of Flávio's story sparked a small tempest of nationalist outrage. *O Cruzeiro*—*Life*'s Brazilian counterpart—published an extraordinary mirror image of the story, focusing on a white Puerto Rican family living in a New York City tenement, complete with staged photos of cockroaches crawling on a young child.[116] But anger at foreigners' airing of Brazil's developmental dirty laundry was only one facet of the country's complex relationship with ideas about the culture of poverty. Many Brazilians harbored prejudice against the poor, but the realities of populist-era politics; the persistent arguments of hundreds of activists, academics, and social workers; and the sheer demographic weight of the "poor" population pointed toward a less exoticized and homogenous vision. Neither perspective triumphed, but the debate indelibly shaped favelas' place in Brazil's cities and national imaginaries.

It is not difficult to find arguments about the social pathology of the poor in midcentury favela and mocambo literature. Occasionally, as in the 1949 census, such theories would be overtly racialized; the author of the census's introduction blamed Afro-Brazilian poverty on ex-slaves who "could not or would not take advantage of their liberty," and instead allowed the rebirth of their "atavistic sloth," hanging on at a bare subsistence level and spending every spare penny on drink and carnival.[117] More often, indictments of poor peoples' "culture" avoided explicit racialization, focusing instead on a familiar hornets' nest of interrelated social practices: female-headed families, unemployment, overcrowdedness, violence, early exposure to sex, and lack of ambition or connection with the outside world. In the 1930s, the labor minister Waldemir Falcão said that Recife's mocambo was "a house of mud that gradually transforms its residents into mud."[118] Pernambuco governor Agamenon Magalhães called the mocambo "a factor in the psychology of social depression," wherein residents lost all "elán for a happier life that forms the moral force of our collectivities, the precondition for progress, perfection, and civilization."[119] Engineer and housing specialist Armando Godoy Filho argued that "the promiscuous environment of favelas" was unlikely to produce "individuals that will come to be really useful to their country or to humanity."[120] Longtime social-service official Victor Tavares de Moura expressed progressively darker views regarding Rio's favelas. By the 1950s, he was quite explicit in naming them as "areas of social disintegration," largely in view of the residents' individualism, promiscuity, and lack of trust.[121] A generally sympathetic 1965 study of Recife's mocambos argued that "a long stay in these conditions atrophies . . . the residents . . . and facilitates the creation of negative habits that hamper family attempts to move forward and snuffs out the individual's internal desire for improvement."[122] Periodic antifavela campaigns in Rio were pushed forward in the name of eliminating social marginality, and the press frequently portrayed favelas and mocambos as sources of disease, crime, and social disorganization. It was not unheard of for favela residents to describe their neighborhoods in similar terms. President Vargas and Guanabara (Rio) governor Carlos Lacerda, both received numerous letters from favela residents willing to use culture-of-poverty concepts in the service of pleas for "proper" housing.[123] Carolina Maria de Jesús's tortured account of favela life in São Paulo, while probably significantly shaped by the journalist who "discovered" it, portrays slums as the very nightmare that culture-of-poverty theorists imagined.[124]

From very early on, these perspectives were contested from high and low, for myriad and sometimes contradictory reasons. As noted earlier, politicians across the political spectrum had begun by the 1930s to see the political advantages in portraying shantytown dwellers as mostly hardworking, family-oriented, and decent, victims of circumstance rather than their own cultural failings. This tendency intensified between the 1940s and the 1960s, as shantytown politics moved to the very center of local and national political debates and politicians scrambled to gain a greater share of the urban electorate. Shantytown residents, recognizing that the negation of the culture-of-poverty thesis was critical to their communities' survival, made their case loudly, with or without the assistance of Communist Party organizers, Catholic activists, or local bosses. In dozens of letters to Vargas and Rio's various mayors, poor residents consistently portrayed themselves as hardworking, morally upstanding victims of circumstance, asking for and receiving everything from building materials for new shacks to protection from public or private evictions. Samba composers in Rio confronted antifavela prejudice by asserting the settlements' solidarity, integrity, and cultural prowess, and some went further still with overtly political calls to avert favela removal.[125] In both Recife and Rio, settlements threatened with eviction sent delegations to local governmental institutions and newspapers, which were often more than ready to publish their words. In 1949, the pro-Vargas *O Radical* newspaper quoted a resident of Rio's enormous Jacarezinho favela asserting the residents' values while arguing for the community's need and right to exist: "We are hardworking men, we have families, and we just want the right to a roof to live under."[126] In Recife, the communist *Folha do Povo* newspaper gave consistent voice throughout its 1947–

1962 run to "housewives," "workers," "widows," and "heads of family" who insisted that mocambos were simply a rational and energetic reaction to poverty and inflation. From quite a different angle, the self-declared *encarregado* (property manager) of Rio's Santa Marta favela argued at length in *O Globo* that "his" favela, oriented by a local Catholic group, fit none of the negative stereotypes; the residents were organized and hardworking, the local store didn't even sell alcohol, and the neighborhood association kept strict order.[127] In the 1950s, residents of numerous communities in both cities went further still, rallying thousands to fight mass evictions with a language that emphasized the importance of favela homes for families and workers.[128] Discursive strategy only partially explains these communities' survival; the networks of political and financial gain that permeated Brazil's informal cities were probably more critical. But residents' persistent emphasis on their own moral and familial integrity was a critical element of their defensive strategy.

Social workers and academics reinforced the residents' own arguments. From the mocambo census of 1939 forward, statistics stubbornly contradicted the culture of poverty's demographic presumptions. Favela and mocambo residents were mostly employed, they lived chiefly in two-parent homes, and the children mostly went to school. Social workers and members of Catholic social-action groups stressed these facts, placing strong emphasis on the residents' basic humanity and frequently citing their capacity for transformation and self-help. The scholar José Alípio Goulart succinctly summed up the growing academic consensus in Brazil in 1957: "To say that the favelas are dens of shysters and bums is to commit a grave injustice against the majority of their inhabitants. The truth is that these people are victims and not creators of the miserable situation in which they live."[129] By the 1970s, scholars such as Anthony and Elizabeth Leeds, Antônio Machado, Carlos Nelson Ferreira dos Santos, and Lícia do Prado Valladares had written extensively about the social and political networks that tied shantytown residents to one another and to the city at large, and Boaventura de Souza Santos wrote an internationally influential account of a homegrown favela legal system, which emphasized poor peoples' capacity to create alternate, informal systems of justice.[130] In that context, Janice Perlman's *Myth of Marginality* (1976) only reaffirmed a line of argument that had long since been widely accepted among academics and long-term social and religious activists.[131]

None of this eliminated widespread prejudice against the Brazilian poor.

But it did place condemnatory culture-of-poverty theorists on the defensive. While many reporters and policymakers still agreed that "social marginality" was a fact of favela life, they took pains to attribute it to specific rather than general causes: it sprung from the corroding influence of a minority of "criminal elements"; it was the transitory consequence of rural-to-urban migration; it existed in some favelas, but not in others; it resulted from inadequate education and moral training, the product of societal negligence rather than cultural failure. Lack of a proper "home" was indeed a seed of social disintegration, but it was a correctable state, not a transgenerational inheritance. Conservative policy recommendations increasingly focused on recuperating favelas as well as destroying them — sometimes with a show of input from the residents themselves — and both recuperation and removal projects took pains to distinguish "workers "from "criminals" and "paupers." Such articulations were often condescending, and did not preclude draconian policy recommendations. Carlos Lacerda and Sandra Cavalcanti, who spearheaded a number of massive favela-removal campaigns in the 1960s and 1970s, both heaped cloying praise on "good" favela residents, insisting that these policies were meant to rescue them from favelas' noxious environment.[132] But by the 1970s, the idea that all shantytown residents were uniformly deformed by a culture of poverty was more political subconscious than explicit doctrine.

Favela and mocambo residents benefited considerably from this discursive shift. Outsiders had a harder time blaming the residents for their own troubles, and even the military government failed to make the case for wholesale eradication. But the question of what was lost remains. Amid thirty years of debate about the moral and intellectual capacity of the poor — debates carried out with the highest-possible political stakes — it had become very difficult to conduct any honest public discussion of certain kinds of problems: the ways in which poverty and public violence shaped shantytown cultures; the ways in which informal systems of regulation could become small fiefdoms; the ways in which the struggle to get by in extremely degraded conditions could fray psyches, families, and communities. Discussion of any of these issues was so easily distorted, and so politically consequential, that a generation of observers mostly chose to ignore them. Once again, the choice to view shantytowns as a fulcrum of contemporary crisis led to an enduring intellectual vacuum.

Though culture-of-poverty theories generated enormous intellectual and political heat, the sibling notion of "rural marginality" may have had deeper resonance in Latin America. The basic idea — that "rural" and "urban" were important social categories, and that the midcentury migrants who flooded into cities in the northeastern United States and across the global South were fundamentally unsuited to modern urban life — had varied and cosmopolitan roots. At the height of European industrialization, musings about internal migrants had helped shape a generation of sociology and literature, from Émile Durkheim to Friedrich Engels to Émile Zola. In the United States, anthropologists — most notably Robert Redfield and then Oscar Lewis — wrestled with the notions of "folk" and "urban," debating whether rural values and ways of life were fundamentally antithetical to modernity.[133] In the wake of the Great Migration, urban sociologists began to reevaluate nineteenth- and early twentieth-century ideas about cityward movement and urban ecology, frequently concluding that the newest generation of poor rural migrants were crippled by their degraded rural origins, disoriented, and racially stigmatized in their urban destinations, and thus unlikely to follow in the footsteps of previous, socially ascendant migrant groups.[134]

Latin Americans had their own complex historical relationship with the rural-urban divide: antirural prejudices had rested successively on fears of Indian, slave, or peasant rebellion; shame about African and Indian cultures and lifeways; or horror at rural disease, ignorance, and hunger. But at midcentury, with the rise of "development" and "modernization" as generalized regional aspirations, antirural prejudice gained a new form. Both concepts placed great emphasis on the backwardness of agricultural and primary-export economies, and they promoted the notion that emancipatory growth would be driven mostly by a few, predominantly urban, economic sectors.[135] Yet at midcentury, while some Latin American cities had begun to imagine themselves as part of a modern, industrial economy, the Latin American countryside was still dominated by large, underproductive landholdings; stagnant technology; brutal labor conditions; and miserably deficient levels of health, nutrition, and education. This imbalance generated levels of rural-to-urban migration far beyond the cities' absorption capacities, and rural workers were viewed as lacking the mental capacity and skills to fully participate in the development process. For all of the advances in steel milling and auto manufacturing, most Latin American workers were rural people, sickly, dependent, uneducated, and unskilled in urban occupations, with incomes so low that they couldn't begin to take part in a mass consumer society. By the late 1950s, most experts regarded shantytowns and their migrants as the urban manifestations of enduring rural backwardness, a rankling reminder that development remained more promise than reality.[136]

Some analysts went farther, arguing that mass migration from rural to urban areas was in itself an obstacle to development. It left rural areas short of labor, hampering commodity exports, creating food shortages, pushing up urban prices, and forcing wage hikes and labor unrest.[137] Migration sucked resources into urban services that should have been used in more productive sectors of the economy.[138] Perhaps most important, it created a seething lumpenproletariat within Latin America's urban boundaries — a rural people who lived in cities only as transplants whose supposed marginalization and anomie created a host of social ills, from family dissolution to vagrancy, alcoholism, and crime.[139] The migrants' very presence guaranteed a constant surplus labor supply, depressing wages and limiting social mobility, which contributed to a vicious circle of unmet expectations and social unraveling. "Marginality" was the peculiar fruit of urban underdevelopment, the fate of rural migrants who carried the backwardness of the Latin American countryside to the city, in the process fracturing the "folk" values that had given their lives structure and meaning and creating a stagnant urban underclass.[140]

In a pioneering 1959 conference on Latin American urbanization — cosponsored by the Economic Commission for Latin America, UNESCO, the Organization of American States, and the International Labor Organization — an international cohort of researchers portrayed shantytowns as the fruit of inadequate development and overly rapid rural-to-urban migration.[141] Drawing directly from Robert Redfield and Robert Park, Philip Hauser, a conference organizer, emphasized what participants viewed as fundamental differences between urban and rural peoples. Habit and tradition shaped the latter, while the former acted on the basis of individual initiative and rational analysis. Rural relationships were mainly primary, rural families were extended, rural political allegiances were local, and rural social status was ascriptive. In cities, by contrast, merit determined status, families became more nuclear, secondary, impersonal relationships assumed new importance, political participation broadened, and the "nation" became a meaningful category.[142] While both rural and urban mentalities were functional in their own contexts, anomie and urban social disintegration were the potentially devastating offspring of the uncomfortable coexistence of such "unsynchronized phases" of civilization: "Urbanization begets a new type of personality, that is, in a class of human being with a special attitude towards the world and his relations with the rest of mankind. The contrast between the rural and the urban mentality is the source of virtually all the difficulties attendant upon the urbanization process, especially when this takes place too rapidly."[143] Such views dominated both popular and academic examinations of Latin American urban poverty in the 1950s and 1960s. The reports of the Economic Commission for Latin America—probably the period's most important Latin American policy forum—regularly employed the language of rural marginality, as did urban-planning specialists from around the world.[144] Articles in publications such as the *New York Times Magazine* and the *Saturday Review* speculated that shanty settlements were the "core of local despair and disaffection" in the developing world, and that migrants were "a floating mass that [played] little part in the economy or the political life" of Latin American countries.[145] Ford Foundation official Sam Schulman lamented that "peasant dignity was buried in urban poverty's abyss" in one Colombian tugurio: "In the past two decades poor rural people have flocked to the cities, found no opportunities but stayed on in urban fringe shanty-towns squatting squalidly on the land. . . . Living almost like animals, the tugurio's residents are overwhelmed by animality. Religion, social control, education, domestic life are warped and disfigured."[146]

It mattered little that research systematically debunked such impressions. Investigations in a variety of countries concluded that many shantytown dwellers were often not even rural migrants, and these researchers joined critics of the culture of poverty school in affirming residents' capacities for family life, hard work, education, participatory citizenship, and community solidarity.[147] In Peru and Chile especially, scholars also anticipated by several decades Hernando de Soto's arguments about poor people's entrepreneurial élan and upwardly mobile ambitions.[148] Researchers also quickly exposed the conceptual weakness of the terms *rural* and *urban*—while these two ideal types shaped most debate, it turned out that neither had much descriptive value. Rural and urban forms varied greatly over space and time and were increasingly interrelated. Rural peoples were culturally, socially, and economically distinct from one another, both within and across national borders, and the idea that inadaptability was a principal hallmark of rurality proved deeply false. None of these conclusions should have been especially surprising—what Anthony and Elizabeth Leeds termed "the myth of urban rurality" was always something of a straw man—but they did expose the sterility of thirty years of debate.[149]

Brazilians read the international literature closely, but they were producers rather than consumers of "rural" and "urban" as significant categories of social distinction. In the early twentieth century, shantytowns were already understood as rustic enclaves. For some, mocambos and favelas evoked the barbarism of Canudos; for others, they conjured the African-tinged degradation of Brazil's rural past.[150] In Recife, mocambos could recall the grim misery of droughts in the sertão; in Rio, some drew on a more Edenic sense of the rural, depicting the favela as a rustic refuge for simple souls driven from Rio's cruel modernities.[151]

In the 1930s, the association between rurality and urban informality tightened, largely for concrete empirical reasons. Cityward migration from Brazil's rural districts and provincial towns intensified, which reduced the proportion of urban-born adults in the favelas and mocambos, and many rural natives brought aspects of their former lifeways to the informal cities.[152] Photos from the 1920s and 1930s suggest that many favelas and mocambos had an overwhelmingly rural appearance, their populations sparse enough to allow the cultivation of small agricultural plots and the keeping of chickens, pigs, and even cows and horses.[153] As Freyre took pains to point out in the 1930s, mocambos were virtually identical to their rural counterparts, as were many of the huts that constituted Rio's early favelas; the scarcity of urban conveniences also recalled the countryside.[154] In all of these senses, there was a certain commonsense logic to portrayals that marked shantytowns as rural places.

Yet, as before, categories of "rural" and "urban" were charged with more than literal meaning. Some conservatives—most notably Oliveira Vianna—longed for a restoration of an idealized rural, patriarchal past. But many other intellectuals followed in the footsteps of the legion of public-health officials who had explored the grim physical realities of the Brazilian interior in the 1910s and 1920s.[155] In their incipient conception, the countryside held the roots of Brazil's most intractable problems. It was in rural areas that slavery and heedless abolition had left Afro-descendants sick, malnourished, ignorant, and helpless. It was in the countryside where parasitical descendants of slave masters monopolized untilled land and yoked poor laborers into relationships of extreme political and economic dependence and exploitation. It was in the backlands where once-proud *sertanejos* (backlanders) were physically and psychologically devastated by drought, forced first into impossible exploitation in the sugar zones and finally reduced to haggard specters begging for food on the streets of Fortaleza or Recife.[156]

The purpose of most of this dystopic literature about the countryside was denunciatory; Brazilian intellectuals from a wide range of ideological backgrounds sought to establish firm links between latifundia, slavery, state neglect, and national backwardness. But the unintended consequence was to further stigmatize rural people as the sick, malnourished, ignorant, degraded, helpless victims of systemic violence. Blame for rural backwardness may have been societal, but the horrors of rural existence still tainted its victims, sometimes irrevocably.

In the 1940s and 1950s, the Vargas regime's failure to carry out agrarian reform, or to significantly incorporate rural peoples into the welfare state, exacerbated already extreme patterns of rural-urban inequality. This in turn contributed to some of the region's highest rates of internal migration, resulting in annual growth of well over 5 percent in many of Brazil's capital cities. At the same time, the decline of overtly racialized understandings of Brazilian backwardness made Brazilian intellectual and policy circles especially receptive to the use of "rural" and "urban" as categories of social differentiation, and the modernizing ideal of development took stronger hold in Brazil than anywhere else in Latin America. International trends reinforced these patterns, and by the late 1940s, "rural" and "urban" were firmly established as social categories denoting primitive and modern, sick and healthy, ignorant and educated, parasitical and productive, stagnant and progressive.

Brazilian politicians and journalists discussed the rural-urban divide incessantly, as legislators debated endless and fruitless proposals for agrarian reform, and the prevalence of rural *atraso* (backwardness) became an easy explanation for every failure in Brazilian society and politics. Chief among those perceived failures was overurbanization: the flooding of Brazilian cities with legions of supposedly unskilled, nutritionally deficient, country people who bore within their psyches the deep scars of slavery, exploitation, and drought-induced starvation.[157] Such people, it was thought, were incapable of contributing to the modern sectors of the economy, and their presence in cities — especially their demands for expensive urban services — was a source of political danger and an empirical drag on the development process. In an interesting parallel with abolition debates of the 1870s and 1880s, discussions of agrarian reform often placed more emphasis on the harm the agrarian crisis caused to modern and urbanized Brazilians than on the issues of need, social justice, and human dignity stressed by most rural activists.

The favelas and mocambos, thought to be the first point of entry for these helpless refugees, quickly became a powerful touchstone for those who would argue that the tentacles of the rural crisis had extended deeply into the urban milieu. The straw man was already established in Recife's campaign against mocambos in the 1930s, in which mocambo residents were sometimes depicted as ignorant country people drawn to Recife more by the ease of mocambo construction than by productive work opportunities.[158] Once in the city, they were said to become a "vegetative population."[159] "Deformed by the attraction of the city," they quickly lost their love of the land, wasting their spare hours in urban degeneracy and failing to cultivate the open land surrounding their homes. Only the "crab cycle" — whereby, in Josué de Castro's famous formulation, crabs built the flesh of men who then fed the crabs with their excrement — provided a perverse reminder of the once-proud link between these degraded workers and the natural world.[160]

In both Rio and São Paulo, observers added the stigma of slavery to the composite of urban rurality. By Florestan Fernandes's account, São Paulo's black population shifted after slavery. Urbanized black libertos — many of whom had been sold south during slavery — fled back to the Northeast after abolition, and the black rural migrants who came in their place were so degraded by the brutalizing conditions of rural slavery that they (and especially the men) became an anomic and unproductive underclass.[161] In Rio, oblique reference to the slave origins of favela residents was common; while slavery, and not race, was blamed for the favelados' degradation, the stigma remained.[162]

More generalized iterations of rural social and cultural marginality abounded. In Rio, the author of the 1949 favela census noted that "the immigrant, almost always native to rural zones, initially feels out of place in the tumultuous urban environment, but it doesn't take long for him to follow the path of least resistance to the most degraded dens of temptation typical of the big city."[163] Vitor Tavares de Moura, the head of social services in Rio, observed that migrants arrived in the cities "without resources, without orientation, without professional qualifications or good health, without military service or labor documents." Such destitution led them to construct shacks from zinc, tin cans, and scrap wood, where they lived "a life quite different, and considerably less human, than the life they lived in their state of origin."[164] In 1965 Carlos Alberto de Medina argued that the favela maintained its character as a rural redoubt because migrants sought the familiar during the shocking transition to urban life, to the point that they came to live a disorienting double existence, assuming urban ways in the workplace and abandoning them for the comfort of rural primitivism in the favela: "The favela thus represents the continuation of the 'natural environment' within the 'technological environment' of the city."[165] While rural continuities eased the rural-urban transition, Medina argued, rural mentalities prevented favelados from assuming the abstract modes of thought necessary for urban life and full participation in the urban political process.[166]

By the early 1960s, such notions of rural marginality were fully integrated into even some the most thoughtful favela studies. In one landmark article from 1960, the authors noted that migrant favelados, unlike European cityward migrants, were refugees from rural misery rather than the energetic surplus of a healthy and productive countryside. As a result, "this migrant, aside from possessing scant technical skills, carries to the city all of the sanitary and educational deficiencies of our rural milieu: worms, illiteracy, bare feet, the herbal bath, superstition, and messianism."[167] While the causes of the favela were far from residents' control—"as long as the latifundio and minifundio are allowed to dominate extensive regions of Brazil, the founts of national misery and underdevelopment will not be plugged"[168]—the rural origins of favela migrants rendered them a problem population in the popular imagination.

As in the rest of Latin America, the Brazilian straw man of rural marginality was toppled early and often; by the early 1970s, its empirical foundations were mostly shattered.[169] Yet this mattered little in a political context where the "rural question" was the great developmental dilemma of the age, and where the rural-urban transition had become an internationally fetishized topic. The ideal types were gripping not because they were real but because they were such intellectually and politically compelling ways of connecting favelas' dramatic conditions to the worldviews of outsiders, and because they were so critical to the concrete policies that would determine the shantytowns' fates. At least two generations of scholars thus spent considerable energy explaining why the idealized notions of rural and urban made little sense in relation to Brazil's informal cities.

These scholars' efforts—like those focused on debunking the myths of shantytown radicalism or the culture of poverty—did much to muffle the repressive policies that might have grown from a wholesale acceptance of antirural prejudice. Yet the opportunity cost of such unrelenting focus was the neglect of far more original modes of thinking about informal cities. Principal among these were the incipient but often marginalized literature about shantytowns and the law; social and family networks among the poor; questions of social mobility; the importance of local, informal institutional life; the shantytowns' porous boundaries and multiple interdependencies with the formalized world; the methodological complications involved in outsiders' apprehension of the shantytowns; and the settlements' rootedness in history. The boom generation of favela scholars saw and wrote about these phenomena, but they were nearly always subordinated to the political urgency of debunking the myths that drove consequential public debate. Among progressives, informal legal systems and community organizations were portrayed as havens of humble, egalitarian participation; communist influence in shantytown politics was minimized; any hint of negative cultural, psychological, and operational adaptations to poverty was dismissed; and the identifiably rural features of favela life were mostly ignored. Almost no one seriously delved into the settlements' heterodox history, which contained elements for all sides to cringe from; likewise, few saw fit to explore the idea that the formal, affluent urban sphere could develop cultures of inequality, which themselves precluded the bridging of economic, social, and legal divides. As a result, several decades of intense debate ended in a sterile impasse; the straw men on either side were cast off, but the workings of favela politics, society, and culture remained largely obscure.

POSTSCRIPT: AN ESCAPE FROM THE PRESENT TENSE?

In the late 1970s and the 1980s, informal cities faded somewhat from epochal ideological debates, even as they became the focus of steadily more-serious academic investigation within Brazil and Latin America.[170] Planners and policymakers grudgingly accepted the notion that the informal city *was* the city, shantytown growth accelerated once more during the "lost decade" of the 1980s, and the end of large-scale eradication campaigns led to significant infrastructural improvements. But the compelling international imperatives that had once lent glamour to favelologia had lost their sheen. In the wake of military brutality and stubbornly anti-ideological shantytown populations, neither revolutionaries nor reactionaries could imagine that informal cities would one day nurture radical social change. The culture-of-poverty debate had dwindled, as conservatives found other causes and progressives mostly observed a tacit accord to avoid the issue. And the rural-urban divide ceased to be so important as a political or social categorization, in part eclipsed by incipient identity politics and ideologies of citizenship, and in part made less relevant by the partial geographical decentralization of economic growth. Observers of favela life pursued any number of fruitful avenues of research during these decades, within Brazil and throughout Latin America: the dynamics of informal real-estate markets, the structure of informal rule making and enforcement, the development of social networks among slum dwellers, the associational culture of the shantytowns, the impact of state violence (both direct and systemic), and the racial and cultural dynamics of favela life. Without a compelling international agenda to grab onto, such writings attracted less attention outside the bounds of academic study, but they often brought a rich, ground-level perspective to issues that had been marginalized in years of more-politicized debate.

In the late 1980s and early 1990s, however, a new crop of gripping hemispheric and global phenomena revived broader interest in the informal city. The spread of democratization, the rise of neoliberalism, the intensification of drug and arms trafficking, the spike in urban violence, the growing significance of citizenship and legal dysfunction, the rise of identity politics and the Latin American "pink tide," and the diffusion of technological means capable of transmitting more directly the experience of urban informality: all of these have spurred a new boom in favela studies. This new wave is arguably both deeper and more diversified than that of the 1940s to the 1970s, less framed by the current buzzwords of social science and certainly more directly shaped by the residents themselves. In Brazil, Argentina, and Chile, one can even see the beginnings of a shantytown historiography that goes beyond the memories of living witnesses, connecting the settlements to broader histories of emancipation, citizenship, migration, populism, race relations, and popular culture.[171]

And yet, just as debates about communism, cultures of poverty, and the rural-urban divide overshadowed the most original midcentury production, one wonders if our own generation of hot-button issues is in danger of monopolizing the contemporary shantytown debate. Internationally, fears of terrorism, environmental catastrophe, neoliberal capitalism, economic leveling, and metastasizing global poverty certainly exert undue influence, as Mike Davis's book attests. In Brazil, questions of violence, land regularization, and racial politics seem to hold similar potential. Violence and the drug trade are by no means the only forces that have transformed Brazil's informal cities, but their drama overwhelms the rest: across the spectrum of observation—from informal residents to journalists to politicians to musicians to academics—armed violence outflanks quieter and subtler dynamics and often seems posed to entirely monopolize the outside world's understanding of informal cities and their residents. Land regularization— understood through the lens of Hernando de Soto's theories about the legal and bureaucratic sources of poverty—has come to be regarded as a kind of global panacea for the urban slum, and the fact that these theories demonstrate little understanding of the actual function of informality, and show no signs of doing much to end extralegal land tenure in most Brazilian cities, has not prevented them from dominating urban policy debates. And race, so problematically absent in midcentury shantytown writings, now frequently crowds out most other categorizations of social difference, giving the false impression that racism is the single factor responsible for the informal city's century of stigmatization and poverty.

Like their predecessors, all of these issues have the capacity to bind the realities of informal cities too closely to the present tense, to allow favelas and *villas miseria* (Argentine favelas) and colonias proletarias to be defined only by their most dramatic links to contemporary crises. For more than a hundred years, such presentism has served important political purposes. But it has also dimmed contemporaries' understandings of informal cities' functional roles, distorted policy choices, perpetuated normative discussions of the urban form, and obscured the favelas' broader historical significance. It may be that the sheer diversity and creativity of recent favelologia will guard against such pitfalls, and that the democratization of communication will allow poor residents' values and understandings to compete for precedence with sweeping global theories. But if the ongoing appeal of apocalyptic visions of shantytown life is any clue, informal cities are unlikely to emerge any time soon from their state of perpetual conceptual emergency.

NOTES

1. Mike Davis, *Planet of Slums* (London: Verso, 2006), 1, 19.
2. Davis, *Planet of Slums*, 201.
3. Davis, *Planet of Slums*, 198.
4. To give a few examples: Davis wrote that many "new urban immigrants" in 1940s Latin America were "indigenistas," mistaking the mostly white advocates of

an idealized Indian culture for the Indians themselves (one imagines Frida Kahlo, Diego Rivera, and José Vasconcelos diligently constructing their zinc-roofed huts) (Davis, *Planet of Slums*, 54). While linking shantytowns and environmental catastrophe, Davis conflated one Brazilian city with another, and mischaracterized entire neighborhoods and towns as "Dantesque district[s] of slums shrouded in pollution" (129). Davis confused the city of Cubatão with the city of São Paulo, and mischaracterized the neighborhood of Iztapalapa in Mexico City and the municipality of Belford Roxo in Rio de Janeiro state. Iztapalapa is one of Mexico City's sixteen delegations, an enormous area that contains huge parks and a wide range of industrial and residential areas, some degraded and polluted, some no more so than the rest of the city; Iztapalapa attracts hundreds of thousands of visitors annually because of its well-known enactment of Christ's Passion. From my own experience working in this area, most residents do not consider their surroundings "Dantesque," and most poor neighborhoods have actually received considerable upgrading in the past few decades (see Duhau, this volume). Belford Roxo, though part of Rio de Janeiro's metropolitan area, is its own municipality, one of the wealthiest in Rio state and home to a wide variety of residential and industrial areas. Other errors ranged from the petty (misspellings of the Brazilian president João Goulart's name, calling Lima's poor neighborhoods *barricadas* rather than *barriadas*) to the more significant (Goulart, for example, was credited with "an urban new deal" that neither he nor any of his contemporaries carried out or even proposed). Davis, *Planet of Slums*, 62.

5. For elaboration of these points in an international context, see Ananya Roy, "Slumdog Cities: Rethinking Subaltern Urbanism," *International Journal of Urban and Regional Research* 35, no. 2 (2011).

6. Richard Morse, "Recent Research on Latin American Urbanization: A Selective Survey with Commentary," *Latin American Research Review* 1, no. 1 (1965): 48. See also R. Douglas Cope, *The Limits of Racial Domination: Plebeian Society in Colonial Mexico City, 1660–1720* (Madison: University of Wisconsin Press, 1994), 10–11; and Cynthia E. Milton, *The Many Meanings of Poverty: Colonialism, Social Compacts, and Assistance in Eighteenth-Century Ecuador* (Stanford, CA: Stanford University Press, 2007), 54.

7. Asael T. Hansen, "The Ecology of a Latin American City," in *Race and Cultural Contacts*, edited by E. B. Reute (New York: McGraw-Hill, 1934), 130.

8. Morse, "Recent Research on Latin American Urbanization," 71, footnote 77, citing *Relaciones de los virreyes*, III, p. 90.

9. Miguel Samper, *La miseria en Bogotá y otros escritos* (Bogotá: Universidad Nacional, Dirección de Divulgación Cultural, 1969). Samper's term for the poor is the evocative *vergonzantes*, whom he describes as follows: "They close themselves off with their children in broken-down habitations, where they suffer the horrors of hunger and nudity. If it were possible to assemble a census of everyone in Bogotá who could be described as vergonzantes . . . the number would be terrifying and the imminent danger would be perceived" (9).

10. On Capelo, see Morse, "La Lima de Joaquín Capelo: Un arquetipo latino-americano," in Juan Capelo and Richard Morse, *Lima en 1900* (Lima: Instituto de Estudios Peruanos, 1973).

11. William Eleroy Curtis, *The Capitals of Spanish America* (New York: Harper and Bros., 1888), 386.

12. Curtis, *The Capitals of Spanish America*, 482.

13. James R. Scobie, "Buenos Aires as a Commercial-Bureaucratic City, 1880–1910: Characteristics of a City's Orientation," *American Historical Review* 77, no. 4 (1972): 1047. Though the famous *conventillos* (tenements) housed most poor European migrants,

> some of the poor and humble, particularly the native-born migrants from the interior provinces, also ringed the city's outskirts with their shacks and thus continued a pattern established in the colonial period. Swampy or frequently flooded areas, public domain slated for port works, and localities far removed from transportation facilities provided these squatters with land. The huts might vary according to location and time from straw-thatched roofs and mud-plastered walls to corrugated iron sheets and flattened oil cans, but they all shared remoteness from rent and tax collectors. . . . The graphic term of *cinta negra*, or "black belt," did not emerge until years later, but the description printed in the *Revista Municipal* in 1896 vividly suggests the environment of these outlying squatter settlements. The stream bed of Maldonado, the marshes of Flores, the slaughterhouse district, the Riachuelo stream, La Boca district, and the lagoons in the port zone surround the central city like a chain, the links of which are formed by morasses bogs, pools of stagnant water, and piles of garbage, reinforced by a rosary of workshops, small plants, and other establishments that have no means to dispose of their wastes without endangering public health.

14. Georges Clemenceau, *South America To-day: A Study of Conditions, Social, Political and Commercial in Argentina, Uruguay and Brazil* (New York: G. P. Putnam, 1911).

15. List partially drawn from Bernard J. Frieden, "The Search for Housing Policy in Mexico City," *Town Planning Review* 36, no. 2 (1965).

16. This topic was virtually unexplored before the 1990s, and my description relies greatly on previously unpublished historical research.

17. While shantytowns continued to be disproportionately populated by Afro-descendants throughout the twentieth century, favela observers at midcentury took pains to dispel the notion that they were racial ghettoes. José Alípio Goulart, for example, draws a sharp contrast between the days when favelas were only home to *pretos* (blacks) and highlights statistics demonstrating that there were in fact more "whites" than "blacks" in Rio's favela (with a plurality of residents classified as "brown"). José Alípio Goulart, *Favelas do Distrito Federal* (Rio de Janeiro: Ministério da Agricultura, Servico de Informação Agrícola, 1957), 35.

18. Gilberto Freyre, *The Mansions and the Shanties: The Making of Modern Brazil* (Berkeley: University of California Press, 1986), 194. Perhaps following Freyre, the author of the favela census of 1950 also suggested a link between freedom and barracos or mocambos: "Someone who studies more deeply this evolution and its influence on the social development of work will reasonably affirm that collective habitations such as 'cabeças de Puerco' and 'cortiços' (both types of tenements) are descendants of the slave quarters, just as barracos or mocambos correspond to the era of free labor in both rural and urban zones." IBGE (Instituto Brasileiro de Geografia e Estatística), Serviço Nacional de Recenseamento, *VI recenseamento geral do Brasil* (Rio de Janeiro: IBGE, Conselho Nacional de Estatística, 1954), 9.

19. For Gilberto Freyre's African etymology, see *Mucambos do nordeste, algumas notas sobre o typo de casa popular mais primitivo do nordeste do Brasil* (Rio de Janeiro: Ministerio da educação e saude, 1937), 20; see also José Tavares Correia de Lira, "Hidden Meanings: The Mocambo in Recife," *Social Science Information* 38, no. 2 (1999). For the association between freedom and mocambos, see Freyre, *The Mansions and the Shanties*, 170. For a racist association between mocambos and Africa, emphasizing the "savagery" and primitive cultural level of Africans, see Mário Lacerda de Melo, *Pernambuco: Traços de sua geografia humana* (Recife, Brazil: Jornal do Comercio, 1940), 150.

20. For the existence of "abolitionist quilombos" in Rio, Santos, Recife, and elsewhere, see Maria Helena Pereira Toledo Machado, *O plano e o pânico: Os movimentos sociais na década da abolição* (Rio de Janeiro: Editora UFRJ; São Paulo: Edusp, 1994); and Eduardo da Silva, *As camélias do Leblon e a abolição da escravatura: Uma investigação de história cultural* (São Paulo: Companhia das Letras, 2003), esp. 32. On hillside and backyard shacks, see Mary C. Karasch, *Slave Life in Rio de Janeiro, 1808–1850* (Princeton, NJ: Princeton University Press, 1987), chapters 5 and 10.

21. See Maurício de Almeida Abreu, "Reconstruindo uma história esquecida: Origem e expansão inicial das favelas do Rio de Janeiro," *Espaço e debates* 37 (1994); Jaime L. Benchimol, *Pereira Passos, um Haussmann tropical: A renovação urbana da cidade do Rio de Janeiro no início do século XX*, Biblioteca Carioca (Rio de Janeiro: Prefeitura da Cidade do Rio de Janeiro, Secretaria Municipal de Cultura, Turismo e Esportes, Departamento Geral de Documentação e Informação Cultural, 1990); Sidney Chalhoub, *Cidade febril: Cortiços e epidemias na corte imperial* (São Paulo: Companhia das Letras, 1996); Liliana Fessler Vaz, "Contribuição ao estudo da produção e transformação do espaço da habitação popular: As habitações coletivas no Rio antigo," MA thesis, Universidade Federal do Rio de Janeiro, 1985; and Liliana Fessler Vaz, *Modernidade e moradia: Habitação coletiva no Rio de Janeiro, séculos XIX e XX* (Rio de Janeiro: 7 Letras, 2002).

22. For a more detailed exploration of this process in Rio, see Brodwyn M. Fischer, *A Poverty of Rights: Citizenship and Inequality in Twentieth-Century Rio de Janeiro* (Stanford, CA: Stanford University Press, 2008), chapter 7. On similar phenomena in Recife, see Zélia de Oliveira Gominho, *Veneza americana x mucambó-*

polis: O estado novo na cidade do Recife (décadas de 30 e 40) (Recife, Brazil: Cepe, 1998); Ricardo Leite, "Recife dos morros e corregos," paper presented at the *Encontro Nacional de História Oral (X)*, Recife, Brazil, April 26–30, 2010; and "Vivendo na lama e comendo carangueijo: 100,000 párias devastados pela fome a padecer miserias nos 20,000 mocambos do Recife," *Folha do Povo*, October 23, 1935. For a fictional rendering, see A. C. Chagas Ribeiro, *Mocambos . . . romance* (Recife, Brazil: Mozart, 1935).

23. Arquivo Nacional, Rio de Janeiro, GIFI, 5C-500, letter written on behalf of Manuel Joaquim de Pereira Leite to the minister of the empire, August 6, 1884; the municipal council resolution is from February 9, 1884. This reference is nearly a decade earlier than that given by Vaz and Abreu as the founding point for the future favela of Santo Antônio. All translations are my own unless otherwise noted.

24. See Abreu, "Reconstruindo uma história esquecida"; Fischer, *A Poverty of Rights*; Vaz, "Contribuição ao estudo da produção e transformação do espaço da habitação popular."

25. This version of the story appears to have its origins in Everardo Backheuser, *Habitações populares: Relatório apresentado ao Exm. Senhor Doutor J. J. Seabra, Ministro de Justiça e Negócios Interiores* (Rio de Janeiro: Imprensa Nacional, 1906), and has become the iconic version of the favelas' origins. See Sonia Zylberberg, *Morro da Providência: Memórias da favela* (Rio de Janeiro: Prefeitura Secretaria Municipal de Cultura Turismo e Esportes, 1992).

26. Both journalistic articles printed during a campaign against mocambos in the late 1930s and a number of writings from a weaker initiative from the 1920s implied that a lack of political will was at the center of mocambo tolerance in Recife. In "Recife dos morros e corregos," in *Encontro Nacional de História Oral (X)* (Recife, Brazil: Pernambuco, 2010), Ricardo Leite suggests that Magalhães himself allowed mocambo settlement in some parts of the city even as he razed the huts in Recife's central neighborhoods.

27. Recife (Brazil), Eudoro Correa, and Alfredo Vaz de Oliveira Ferraz, eds., *Recenseamento realizado em 12 de outubro de 1913* (Recife, Brazil: Escolas Profissionaes do Collegio Salesiano, 1915), 83. Of 37,409 total *fogos* (hearths), 16,347 were classified as mocambos, and another 8,470 as houses of *taipa* (mud). Only 12,918 were made of brick.

28. Departamento de Saúde e Assistência, Inspectoria de Estatistica Propaganda e Educação Sanitaria [Pernambuco], *Recenseamento do Recife, 1923* (Recife, Brazil: Secção Technica da Repartição de Publicações Officiaes, 1924), 3.

29. Abreu, "Reconstruindo uma história esquecida," 37, citing *Correio da Manhã*, October 17, 1901.

30. *Jornal do Comércio*, December 11, 1913, cited in Abreu, "Reconstruindo uma história esquecida," 38. See also Licia do Prado Valladares, *A invenção da favela: Do mito de origem a favela.com* (Rio de Janeiro: Editora FGV, 2005).

31. Ministério de Agricultura, Indústria e Comércio, Directoria Geral de Estatís-

tica, *Recenseamento do Brasil, 1 de Setembro de 1920* (Rio de Janeiro: Tipografia da Estatística, 1924), vol. 2, part 3, 20–21.

32. Abreu, "Reconstruindo uma história esquecida," citing Mattos Pimenta, *O Globo*, August 15, 1927.

33. Ministério do Trabalho, Indústria e Commércio, Serviço de Estatística da Previdência e Trabalho [Brazil], *Estatística predial do Districto Federal, 1933* (Rio de Janeiro: Departamento de Estatística e Publicidad, 1935).

34. Preston James, "Rio de Janeiro and São Paulo," *Geographical Review* 23, no. 4 (1933): 295.

35. See, especially, Backheuser, *Habitações populares*.

36. On racial thought in Brazil's First Republic, see Lilia Moritz Schwarcz, *O espetáculo das raças: Cientistas, instituições e questão racial no Brasil, 1870–1930* (São Paulo: Companhia das Letras, 1993).

37. Paulo Barreto, "Os livres acampamentos da miséria," in *Vida vertiginosa*, edited by Paulo Barreto (Rio de Janeiro: Garnier, 1911), 143–52.

38. Licia do Prado Valladares, whose *A invenção da favela* is the best extant account of the favelas' place in the Brazilian social-science imagination, interprets this passage—indeed, the entire structure of Barreto's essay—as an extended evocation of Euclides da Cunha's *Os sertões*. The explicit linkage of favelas with Canudos can be traced back to Everardo Backheuser and is repeated periodically in Rio's shantytown literature. It is important to note, however, that the "sertão" was a much larger concept than Cunha's rendering of it; it could denote rusticity in a positive and nostalgic sense that would become quite common in conservative intellectual production; or it could evoke the opposite of urban in ways that didn't necessarily recall Cunha, who was using the concept even as he reinvented it.

39. Lira, "Hidden Meanings," 306–7.

40. Benchimol, *Pereira Passos, um Haussmann tropical*.

41. See Marcus André B. C. de Melo, "A cidade dos mocambos: Estado, habitação e luta de classes no Recife (1920/1960)," *Espaço e debates* 14 (1985).

42. Otavio Freitas, "Um século de medicina e higiene no Nordeste," in *O livro do nordeste*, edited by Gilberto Freyre (Recife, Brazil: Arquivo Público Estadual, 1979), cited in Marcus Melo, "A cidade dos mocambos," 47. Freitas was a demographer for Recife's hygiene inspectorate and the director of the Instituto Pasteur de Pernambuco.

43. Artur Orlando, *Porto e cidade do Recife* (Pernambuco, Brazil: Typ. do "Jornal do Recife," 1908), 139. Orlando quotes a very similar take on Rio from Backheuser, *Habitações populares*.

44. Amaury Medeiros, *Saúde e Assistência 1923–1926 doutrinas, experiências e realizações* (Recife, Brazil, 1926), quoted in Lira, "Hidden Meanings," 310.

45. Rui Ribeiro Couto, "Cartas de França," *A Provincia*, 1929, quoted in Lira, "Hidden Meanings," 311. Couto is also cited in Freyre, *The Mansions and the Shanties*, 406, for his more lyrical renderings of the shanties.

46. On leprosy metaphors in Rio, see Alfred Donat Agache, *Cidade de Rio de Janeiro: Extensão, remodelacão, embellezamento* (Paris: Foyer Brésilien, 1930); and João Augusto de Mattos Pimenta, *Para a remodelação do Rio de Janeiro* (Rio de Janeiro, 1926).

47. Agamenon Magalhães, "Triste Pregão," *Folha da Manhã*, July 15, 1939.

48. For excellent histories of early shantytown policies in Mexico, see Frieden, "The Search for Housing Policy in Mexico City"; on Chile, see T. Robert Burke, "Law and Development: The Chilean Housing Program," *Lawyer of the Americas* 2, nos. 2 and 3 (1970).

49. Luciano Parisse, *Favelas do Rio de Janeiro: Evolução, sentido* (Rio de Janeiro: Pontificia Universidade Católica do Rio de Janeiro, Centro Nacional de Pesquisas Habitacionais, 1969), 24. Neither of these surveys specifically targeted shacks located in favelas; in fact, they probably excluded some of the more isolated favelas entirely. In 1947–48 and 1950, surveys that only counted shacks in favelas (defined as groups of fifty or more shacks, located on illegally occupied lands) found 36,000 and 44,000 shacks, respectively. Departamento de Geografia e Estatistica [Federal District, Rio de Janeiro], *Censo das favelas* (Rio de Janeiro: Departamento de Geografia e Estatistica, 1949); and IBGE, *As favelas do Distrito Federal e o Censo Demográfico de 1950* (Rio de Janeiro: IBGE, 1953).

50. Comissão Censitária dos Mucambos do Recife [Pernambuco], *Observações estatísticas sobre os mucambos do Recife, baseadas no censo efetuado pela Comissão Censitaria dos Mucambos, criada pelo Dec. no. 182, de 17 de setembro de 1938* (Recife, Brazil: Impr. Oficial, 1939).

51. Josué de Castro, *A cidade do Recife: Ensaio de geografia urbana* (Rio de Janeiro: Livraria-Editôra da Casa do Estudante do Brasil, 1954), 151–53. This analysis is also present in his earlier works, especially *Geografia da fome: A fome no Brasil* (Rio de Janeiro: O Cruzeiro, 1946). A similar analysis of the motives for rural migration to Recife is in Daniel Uchoa Cavalcanti Bezerra, *Alagados, mocambos e mocambeiros* (Recife, Brazil: Instituto Joaquim Nabuco de Pesquisas Sociais MEC, Imprensa Universitária, 1965), 30–34.

52. Melo, *Pernambuco*, 157.

53. Concentration came in this era to be one of the defining features of the favela. The census of 1950 makes clear that housing akin to favela shacks was widespread in the city, but favelas only existed, for statistical and public-policy purposes, when they were concentrated in groups of fifty or more. IBGE (Instituto Brasileiro de Geografia e Estatística), *As favelas do Distrito Federal e o Censo Demográfico de 1950* (Rio de Janeiro: IBGE, 1953).

54. See Michael L. Conniff, *Urban Politics: The Rise of Populism, 1925–1945* (Pittsburgh, PA: University of Pittsburgh Press, 1981); Fischer, *A Poverty of Rights*; and Dulce Chaves Pandolfi, *Pernambuco de Agamenon Magalhães: Consolidação e crise de uma elite política* (Recife, Brazil: Fundação Joaquim Nabuco, Editora Massangana, 1984).

55. See Fischer, *A Poverty of Rights*; Gominho, *Veneza americana x mucambópolis*; Valéria Lima Guimarães, *O PCB cai no samba: Os comunistas e a cultura popular, 1945–1950* (Rio de Janeiro: Governo do Rio de Janeiro, Arquivo Público do Estado do Rio de Janeiro, 2009); Maria Lais Pereira da Silva, *Favelas cariocas, 1930–1964* (Rio de Janeiro: Contraponto, 2005).

56. For a fuller discussion, see Fischer, *A Poverty of Rights*, chapter 8.

57. All are depicted in Luiz Edmundo, *O Rio de Janeiro do meu tempo* (Rio de Janeiro: Imprensa Nacional, 1938), an evocation from 1930s of belle epoque Rio. See chapters 7–8.

58. Josué de Castro, *Documentário do nordeste* (Rio de Janeiro: J. Olympio, 1937), 15–16.

59. Freyre, *Mucambos do nordeste, algumas notas sobre o typo de casa popular mais primitivo do nordeste do Brasil*; see also Alde Sampaio, "A casa tropical," *Boletim de Engenharia* 3, no. 2 (1927).

60. See Bryan McCann, *Hello, Hello Brazil: Popular Music in the Making of Modern Brazil* (Durham, NC: Duke University Press, 2004); and Hermano Vianna, *O mistério do samba* (Rio de Janeiro: J. Zahar Editor, Editora UFRJ, 1995).

61. Comissão Censitária dos Mucambos do Recife, *Observações estatisticas sobre os mucambos do Recife, baseadas no censo efetuado pela Comissão Censitaria dos Mucambos, criada pelo Dec. no. 182, de 17 de setembro de 1938*.

62. See Fischer, *A Poverty of Rights*, chapters 1–2.

63. On Vargas and his rhetorical relationship with the working class, see Jorge Luiz Ferreira, *Trabalhadores do Brasil: O imaginário popular, 1930–45* (Rio de Janeiro: Fundação Getulio Vargas Editora, 1997); and Angela Maria de Castro Gomes, *A invenção do trabalhismo* (Rio de Janeiro: Instituto Universitário de Pesquisas do Rio de Janeiro; São Paulo: Vértice, 1988). On the overlap between rhetoric and practice, see Sueann Caulfield, *In Defense of Honor: Sexual Morality, Modernity, and Nation in Early-Twentieth-Century Brazil* (Durham, NC: Duke University Press, 2000); Adriano Luiz Duarte, *Cidadania e exclusão: Brasil 1937–1945* (Florianópolis: Editora da UFSC, 1999); Fischer, *A Poverty of Rights*; Alexandre Fortes, *Na luta por direitos: Estudos recentes em história social do trabalho* (Campinas, Brazil: Editoria da Unicamp, 1999); Alexandre Fortes, *Nós do quarto distrito: A classe trabalhadora porto-alegrense e a era Vargas* (Rio de Janeiro: Garamond Universitária, EDUCS, 2004); and John D. French, *Drowning in Laws: Labor Law and Brazilian Political Culture* (Chapel Hill: University of North Carolina Press, 2004).

64. On communists and mocambos in the 1930s, see Gominho, *Veneza americana x mucambópolis*; and Pandolfi, *Pernambuco de Agamenon Magalhães*; there is also substantial evidence of this involvement in the police files of the Pernambucan state archives, and a noted novel was written on the subject in 1935 (Ribeiro, *Mocambo . . . romance*).

65. *Folha da Manhã*, date unknown, 1939.

66. Vitor Tavares de Moura, who held a long series of jobs in Rio's social-service

divisions, had worked on Recife's Liga Social Contra o Mocambo before heading similar efforts in Rio. Moura, "Favelas do Distrito Federal," in *Aspectos do Distrito Federal*, edited by Academia Brasileira de Letras (Rio de Janeiro: Sauer, 1943).

67. Henrique Dias da Cruz, *Os morros cariocas no novo regime, notas de reportagem* (Rio de Janeiro: Grafica Olímpica, 1941).

68. Janice E. Perlman, *The Myth of Marginality: Urban Poverty and Politics in Rio de Janeiro* (Berkeley: University of California Press, 1976).

69. See José Campello, "Os aspectos sociais e económicos do mocambo," *Folha da Manhã*, July 30, 1939. For the theory that the availability of mocambos facilitated overmigration, see Agamenon Magalhães, "Concentração urbana," *Folha da Manhã*, July 18, 1939.

70. See Fortes, *Nós do quarto distrito*; Fischer, *A Poverty of Rights*; French, *Drowning in Laws*; Gomes, *A Invenção do trabalhismo*; and Wanderley Guilherme dos Santos, *Cidadania e justiça: A política social na ordem brasileira* (Rio de Janeiro: Editora Campus, 1979).

71. See, for example, John F. Kennedy, "Text of Kennedy Message to Congress on Latin Aid," *New York Times*, March 15, 1961. See also Leandro Benmergui, "The Alliance for Progress and Housing Policy in Rio de Janeiro and Buenos Aires in the 1960s," *Urban History* 36, no. 2 (2009).

72. David G. Epstein, *Brasília, Plan and Reality: A Study of Planned and Spontaneous Urban Development* (Berkeley: University of California Press, 1973); James Holston, *The Modernist City: An Anthropological Critique of Brasília* (Chicago: University of Chicago Press, 1989); and Alex Shoumatoff, *The Capital of Hope: Brasília and Its People* (Albuquerque: University of New Mexico Press, 1987).

73. These included academic studies, informal social-science surveys, investigative reports, and federal censuses. For the best bibliography, see Licia do Prado Valladares, Lidia Medeiros, and Filippina Chinelli, *Pensando as favelas do Rio de Janeiro, 1906–2000: Uma bibliografia analítica* (Rio de Janeiro: Relume Dumará, URBANDATA, 2003).

74. On the latter, see, especially, Raúl Prebisch, *Towards a Dynamic Development Policy for Latin America* (New York: United Nations, 1963). See also Philip Morris Hauser, *Urbanization in Latin America* (Liège, Belgium: UNESCO, 1961).

75. See Goulart, *Favelas do Distrito Federal*, 45–46; see also Anthony Leeds and Elizabeth Leeds, eds., *A sociologia do Brasil urbano* (Rio de Janeiro: Zahar Editores, 1978); José Artur Rios, "Favelas," in *Aspectos da geografia carioca*, edited by Associação de Geógrafos Brasileiros (Rio de Janeiro: Conselho Nacional de Geografia, Instituto Brasileiro de Geografia e Estatística, 1962), 213–24; and Luiz Antônio Machado da Silva, "O significado do botequim," *América Latina* 12, no. 3 (1969).

76. See, for example, Parisse, *Favelas do Rio de Janeiro*.

77. See, particularly, Carolina Maria de Jesus, *Child of the Dark: The Diary of Carolina María de Jesus* (New York: Dutton, 1962); Oscar Lewis, *The Children of Sánchez: Autobiography of a Mexican Family* (New York: Random House, 1961); and Oscar

Lewis, *La Vida: A Puerto Rican Family in the Culture of Poverty — San Juan and New York* (New York: Random House, 1966).

78. See, for example, Frank M. Andrews and George W. Phillips, "The Squatters of Lima: Who They Are and What They Want," *Journal of Developing Areas* 4, no. 2 (1970); Henry Dietz, "Urban Squatter Settlements in Peru: A Case History and Analysis," *Journal of Inter-American Studies* 11, no. 3 (1969); Frieden, "The Search for Housing Policy in Mexico City," 83–84; William Mangin, "Latin American Squatter Settlements: A Problem and a Solution," *Latin American Research Review* 2, no. 3 (1967): 87–88; Morse, "Recent Research on Latin American Urbanization," 53; John Powelson and Anatole A. Solow, "Urban and Rural Development in Latin America," *Annals of the American Academy of Political and Social Science* 360 (1965): 54–55; and Anatole A. Solow, "Housing in Latin America: The Problem of Urban Low Income Families," *Town Planning Review* 38, no. 2 (1967): 94–95, 100. For a popularized version, see "Latins Have 'Rebel' Slums," *Washington Post*, May 19, 1968. The direction of such proposals was already anticipated when President Kennedy spoke to Congress to request funding for Latin American social assistance, noting that the most effective way to improve housing was to give poor Latin Americans the materials and land they needed for orderly autoconstruction. See Kennedy, "Text of Kennedy Message to Congress on Latin Aid." Pilot programs along these lines were active in Brazil, Chile, Venezuela, Puerto Rico, and Mexico by the early 1960s. See Luis Muñoz Marín and Donald Robinson, "The Governor of Puerto Rico Tells How We Can Save Latin America from Castro," *Baltimore Sun*, December 16, 1961; "4 UN Units Help Latin Slum Plan," *New York Times*, December 26, 1961; Jacqueline Gross, "As the Slum Goes, So Goes the Alliance," *New York Times*, June 23, 1963. For global perspectives, G. A. Atkinson, "Mass Housing in Rapidly Developing Tropical Areas," *Town Planning Review* 31, no. 2 (1960): 87, 89, 96–97; John W. Dyckman, "Some Conditions of Civic Order in an Urbanized World," *Daedalus* 95, no. 3 (1966): 800–801; and "Venezuelan Town Honors Kennedy," *New York Times*, December 1, 1963.

79. See Benmergui, "The Alliance for Progress and Housing Policy in Rio de Janeiro and Buenos Aires in the 1960s"; Guida Nunes, *Favela, resistência pelo direito de viver* (Petrópolis, Brazil: Vozes, 1980); Perlman, *The Myth of Marginality*; and Licia do Prado Valladares, *Passa-se uma casa: Análise do programa de remoção de favelas do Rio de Janeiro* (Rio de Janeiro: Zahar Editores, 1978).

80. Milton Bracker, "Beneath the Ferment in Latin America," *New York Times*, February 13, 1949.

81. Emanuel de Kadt, "Religion, the Church and Social Change in Brazil," in *The Politics of Conformity in Latin America*, edited by Claudio Veliz (London: Oxford University Press, 1967). See also Nathan Miller, "Catholic Leaders Warn: Need for Basic Reforms Voiced in Latin America," *Baltimore Sun*, August 14, 1963.

82. "The Crisis in Our Hemisphere," *Life*, June 2, 1961.

83. C. L. Sulzberger, "A Tale of Too Many Cities — and Ourselves," *New York Times*, December 4, 1961.

84. "Shriver Says Reds Peril Latin America," *New York Times*, November 20, 1963.

85. Dyckman, "Some Conditions of Civic Order in an Urbanized World," 800. For a useful summary of other arguments about political radicalism in the shanty-towns, see Mangin, "Latin American Squatter Settlements," esp. 82–83.

86. Samuel P. Huntington, *Political Order in Changing Societies* (New Haven, CT: Yale University Press, 1968), 278, 283.

87. Prebisch, *Towards a Dynamic Development Policy for Latin America*, 23.

88. See Manuel Castells, *The City and the Grassroots: A Cross-Cultural Theory of Urban Social Movements* (London: E. Arnold; Berkeley: University of California Press, 1983); Howard Handelman, "The Political Mobilization of Urban Squatter Settlements: Santiago's Recent Experience and Its Implications for Urban Research," *Latin American Research Review* 10, no. 2 (1975); and Murphy, this volume.

89. See Arquivo Publico do Estado de Pernambuco, Departamento de Ordem Polícica e Social (DOPS) files, Prontuário 260, Arquivo 1, Fundo SSP no. 420, "Liga dos Proprietários da Vila São Miguel."

90. Ribeiro, *Mocambo . . . romance.*

91. Articles about the mocambos were steady fare in the communist daily *Folha do Povo*, both during its run in 1935 and during its longer continuous existence between 1947 and 1960.

92. The party was banned in the wake of these elections, and subsequent communist politics operated through shadow parties.

93. Agamenon Magalhães, "O ciclo do carangueijo," *Folha da Manhã*, July 6, 1939.

94. See Carlos Lacerda, "O Partido Comunista e a Batalha do Rio de Janeiro," *Correio da Manhã*, May 21, 1948.

95. In the late 1940s, for example, Vitor Tavares de Moura saw himself battling against "the permanent and intense action of some communist councilmen." Vitor Tavares de Moura Archives, Casa de Oswaldo Cruz, Parque Proletário e Favela, Caixa 1, "Relatório e balancete dos trabalhos executados pelo serviço de extinção das favelas até 4-10-1947." See also Rio's municipal council debates from 1947–64.

96. José Arthur Rios, "Operação Mutirão," *Cuadernos Latinoamericanos de Economia Humana* 6, no. 12 (1961): 254.

97. For a succinct expression, see "Favela política," *Jornal do Brasil*, December 24, 1964.

98. "Os casos dolorosos da cidade: Caso 956," *Diário de Notícias*, February 2, 1948.

99. See the political police documents on the Federação de Associações de Favelas do Estado de Guanabara, held in the Arquivo Estadual do Rio de Janeiro, Polícia Política, diversões 32, dossiê 3.

100. Mangin, "Latin American Squatter Settlements," 85–86; see also William Mangin and John C. Turner, "The Barriada Movement," *Progressive Architecture* 49 (May 1968); and John C. Turner, "Lima's Barriadas and Corralones: Suburbs versus Slums," *Ekstics* 112 (1965). This perspective also appears in Alejandro Portes, "Rationality in the Slum," *Comparative Studies in Society and History* 14, no. 3 (1972).

101. Eric Hobsbawm, "Peasants and Rural Migrants in Politics," in *The Politics of*

Conformity in Latin America, edited by Claudio Veliz (London: Oxford University Press, 1967).

102. This conclusion emerges most clearly and subtly in Castells, *The City and the Grassroots*.

103. See Robert Park, "The City: Suggestions for the Investigation of Human Behavior in the City Environment," *American Journal of Sociology* 20, no. 5 (1915): 611–12.

104. Aluísio Azevedo, *The Slum: A Novel*, translated by David Rosenthal (Oxford: Oxford University Press, 2000); Everardo Backheuser, "Onde moram os pobres," *Renascença: Revista Mensal de Letras, Sciências e Artes* 13, no. 2 (1905).

105. The clearest explanation of Oscar Lewis's version of the idea can be found in his introduction to *The Children of Sánchez: Autobiography of a Mexican Family* (New York: Random House, 1961).

106. See Oscar Lewis, "Urbanization without Breakdown," *Scientific Monthly* 75, no. 1 (1952).

107. Lewis, *The Children of Sánchez*, xxvi.

108. Lewis, *The Children of Sánchez*.

109. For an interesting comment on continuities with Redfield's "folk-urban continuum," see Richard Morse, "Trends and Issues in Latin American Urban Research, 1965–1970," *Latin American Research Review* 6, no. 1 (1971): 96.

110. For a journalistic example, see Gross, "As the Slum Goes, So Goes the Alliance." Widespread academic rejections included works such as Dietz, "Urban Squatter Settlements in Peru"; Leeds and Leeds, *A sociologia do Brasil urbano*; Mangin, "Latin American Squatter Settlements"; Perlman, *The Myth of Marginality*; and Portes, "Rationality in the Slum." For a rejection focused particularly on the issue of "informal" law, see Kenneth J. Karst, "Rights to Land and Housing in an Informal Legal System: The Barrios of Caracas," *American Journal of Comparative Law* 19, no. 3 (1971): 558.

111. Sam Schulman's "Latin American Shantytown," *New York Times*, January 16, 1966, rendered culture-of-poverty theory for a popular audience: "Living almost like animals, the tugurio's residents are overwhelmed by animality. Religion, social control, education, domestic life are warped and disfigured." For an account that claims that some, but not all, Latin American slums were characterized by a culture of poverty, see Alejandro Portes, "The Urban Slum in Chile: Types and Correlates," *Land Economics* 47, no. 3 (1971). For the argument that Lewis's notion granted shantytown culture too much coherence, see Sam Schulman, "Family Life in a Colombian Turgurio," *Sociological Analysis* 28, no. 4 (1967): 184.

112. Bengelsdorf, "Latin America Breeds Misery," *Los Angeles Times*, June 30, 1967; Gerald William Breese, *Urbanization in Newly Developing Countries* (Englewood Cliffs, NJ: Prentice-Hall, 1966); John Goshko, "Success Shatters a Dream in a Latin Slum," *Washington Post*, April 10, 1966; John Gunther, *Inside Latin America* (London: H. Hamilton, 1942).

113. Gordon Parks, "Shocking Poverty Spurs Reds," *Life*, June 16, 1961.

114. Parks was African American, the youngest of fifteen children born to tenant farmers in Kansas. In the late 1930s—broke, responsible for a wife and child, and ranging the country for work—he bought a camera inspired by Dorothea Lange's Farm Security Administration photos. Through sheer talent, he was soon taking his own pictures for the Farm Security Administration, especially in Chicago's segregated black belt; by 1942 he had already authored one of the most iconic images of American racial hypocrisy, *American Gothic*. In 1948, after a five-year stint at *Vogue*, Parks became *Life*'s only black staff photographer. There, in addition to becoming a superb interpreter of high fashion and the arts, he became an unparalleled chronicler of urban poverty and the civil rights era.

115. This was a purposeful, but not misleading, choice; somewhere around a third of Rio's shantytown population—and probably more of its informal dwellers— were "white" by census standards, most northeastern migrants like the Silvas.

116. For an account of the controversy in Brazil, see Fernando de Tacca, "O Cruzeiro versus Paris Match e Life Magazine," *Libero* 9, no. 17 (2006).

117. Departamento de Geografia e Estatistica. *Censo das favelas*, 10. In an interesting counterpoint, the federal favela census of 1950 pointedly countered such views, emphatically noting that *pardos* (browns) and pretos dominated the favelas because well-paid work was not easily accessible to them, and sticking to a rigorously deracialized analysis of the economic structures that had led to the favelas' growth. IBGE, *As favelas do Distrito Federal e o Censo Demográfico de 1950*, 20.

118. Waldemir Falcão, "O ministro do trabalho reafirma o seu apoio à campanha contra o Mocambo," *Folha da Manhã*, September 8, 1939.

119. Agamenon Magalhães, "O gusto pela habitação," *Folha da Manhã*, July 4, 1939.

120. Undated document titled "Habitação popular," from the Victor Tavares de Moura Archives, Casa de Oswaldo Cruz.

121. Speech to the Botafogo Rotary Club, January 8, 1957, from Vitor Tavares de Moura Papers, Casa de Oswaldo Cruz.

122. Bezerra, *Alagados, mocambos e mocambeiros*, 65.

123. Such letters can be found in the Lacerda archives at the University of Brasília and in the records of the secretariat of the president of the republic in Brazil's Arquivo Nacional, Rio.

124. Jesus, *Child of the Dark*.

125. See Fischer, *A Poverty of Rights*, part I; and Jane Souto de Oliveira and Maria Hortense Marcier, "A palavra é: Favela," in *Um século de favela*, edited by Marcos Alvito Alba Zaluar, 61–114 (Rio de Janeiro: Fundação Getúlio Vargas, 1998).

126. "Com Getúlio, isto não aconteceu," *O Radical*, May 20, 1949.

127. "Uma favela que começa em Botafogo e termina nas Laranjeiras," *O Globo*, May 25, 1949.

128. The residents of Jacarezinho, Turano, Santa Marta, Dendê, and Borel were especially notorious in Rio. In Recife, some of the best-known groups before the 1980s were Vila São Miguel and Brasília Teimosa.

129. Goulart, *Favelas do Distrito Federal*. Goulart took special pains to dismantle the line of argument that the physical structure and overcrowding of the favelas led to "promiscuity" and broken families, arguing that favelas gave residents less crowded conditions that were better matched to a stable family structure (37).

130. Boaventura de Souza Santos, "The Law of the Oppressed: The Construction and Reproduction of Legality in Pasargada," *Law and Society Review* 12, no. 1 (1977).

131. Perlman, *Myth of Marginality*.

132. Lacerda wrote frequently of favela residents' virtues, but always from a distance and with a paternalistic vision of social hierarchy. In one article from 1948, arguing against sending all favela residents back to the countryside, he began by stating that it was wrong "to categorize the favelados [favela dwellers], rigidly, as if they were all a single category of undesirables, a caste of untouchables whom it is necessary to run out of the city." But he hardly saw them as urban equals: "On the day they all went back, where could we find the cooks, the washerwomen, the mosquito killers, the drivers, the municipal workers, the infinitely varied and useful population that lives in the favelas?" Lacerda, "O Partido Comunista e a Batalha do Rio de Janeiro." Cavalcanti's claims were more grating. Though her often-violent removal campaigns spurred mass protest, Cavalcanti insisted that the revolt was simply the work of leftist agitators. As if it were a revelation, she exhorted readers of her autobiography to recognize that favelados were "our" "boys," servants, and employees, and recounted the experience that, she said, led her to abandon her prejudices against favelados: when a young, green-eyed (and presumably white) student in one of her elementary classes stopped attending, she went to the students' home in the Formiga favela and was surprised to find that it was possible for her to keep a clean family home in the midst of the slum. Cavalcanti also found it important to affirm that the favelas were in no way similar to the irredeemable poor ghettoes in places like Chicago. Sandra Cavalcanti, *Rio, viver ou morrer* (Rio de Janeiro: Editora Expressão e Cultura, 1978).

133. See Oscar Lewis, "Urbanization without Breakdown," *Scientific Monthly* 75, no. 1 (1952); Robert Redfield, "The Folk Society," *American Journal of Sociology* 52, no. 4 (1947); and Eric R. Wolf, "Types of Latin American Peasantry: A Preliminary Discussion," *American Anthropologist* 57, no. 3 (1955).

134. Particularly influential in Brazil was St. Clair Drake and Horace R. Cayton's *Black Metropolis: A Study of Negro Life in a Northern City* (New York: Harcourt, 1945).

135. This was, of course, a Marxist view as well as the capitalist and developmentalist one, and some of its most important articulations in Brazil came from the left-wing press. On the rise of development, see H. W. Arndt, *Economic Development: The History of an Idea* (Chicago: University of Chicago Press, 1987). For the classic anticommunist formulation of stages of modernization, see W. W. Rostow, *The Stages of Economic Growth, a Non-Communist Manifesto* (Cambridge: Cambridge University Press, 1960).

136. See Hauser, *Urbanization in Latin America*; following that volume, see

David L. McKee and William H. Leahy, "Intra-urban Dualism in Developing Economies," *Land Economics* 46, no. 4 (1970); Powelson and Solow, "Urban and Rural Development in Latin America"; Prebisch, *Towards a Dynamic Development Policy for Latin America*, 23; Solow, "Housing in Latin America." For a subtler reading, which places urbanization in historical perspective and relates it to the nature of city formation and mechanization in the countryside as well as to the rural-urban imbalance, see Morse, "Recent Research on Latin American Urbanization," 42–46.

137. On food shortages, see Powelson and Solow, "Urban and Rural Development in Latin America."

138. Hauser, *Urbanization in Latin America*, 37; McKee and Leahy, "Intra-urban Dualism in Developing Economies," 486–87.

139. These notions were deeply rooted in the Chicago School of sociology, and especially in the work of Robert Park and Louis Wirth; their articulation in Latin America had much in common with contemporary comment on the U.S. Great Migration.

140. The term *folk* was first used by Robert Redfield, with reference to Mexican rural peoples. Redfield's intention was to substitute a more "neutral" word for the pejorative terms that often came into sociological use. But his actual description of the "folk-urban continuum" tended to accept many of the same premises about "rural" and "urban" peoples that had long formed the basis of American urban sociology. In Redfield's words, a "folk" society "is small, isolated, nonliterate, and homogeneous, with a strong sense of group solidarity. The ways of living are conventionalized into that coherent system which we call 'a culture.' Behavior is traditional, spontaneous, uncritical, and personal; there is no legislation or habit of experiment and reflection for intellectual ends. Kinship, its relationships and institutions, are the type categories of experience and the familial group is the unit of action. The sacred prevails over the secular; the economy is one of status rather than of the market" ("The Folk Society," 293). Despite some differences, this vision of rural life did not differ all that significantly from that of Redfield's father-in-law and University of Chicago mentor, Robert E. Park, who at the cusp of the U.S. Great Migration was already writing about the difficulties that rural migrants had in adapting from a world of primary relationships to one of secondary relationships, from a world of norms to a world of laws, from group to individual identification (Park, "The City").

141. Hauser, *Urbanization in Latin America*, 76.

142. Hauser, *Urbanization in Latin America*, 48–50. Hauser was chair of the University of Chicago's Sociology Department.

143. Hauser, *Urbanization in Latin America*, 54, 25. Of the individual chapters in this collection, J. Matos Mar's on migrant communities in Lima provides the strongest support for Hauser's views of rural and urban mentalities. Mar writes: "It should be noted that the people who come from the rural areas into the cities bring with them their own way of life which is that of an underdeveloped people of peasant mentality, with the addition, in the case of those from the Andes region, of tra-

ditional 'Indian' cultural patterns. Thus, the migrants who come to settle at Lima, preferably in the barriadas, bring with them their traditional way of life and have to face an urban existence that proceeds at a different pace. The contrast between two ways of life leads to serious conflicts which are reflected in mental, social and economic maladjustment that militates against satisfactory integration." J. Matos Mar, "Migration and Urbanization—The Barriadas of Lima: An Example of Integration into Urban Life," in *Urbanization in Latin America*, edited by Philip M. Hauser (Liège, Belgium: UNESCO, 1961), 174.

144. See Atkinson, "Mass Housing in Rapidly Developing Tropical Areas," 86; ECLA, *Social Development of Latin America in the Post-war Period*, E/Cn. 12/66 (Mar del Plata, Argentina, 1963); and McKee and Leahy, "Intra-urban Dualism in Developing Economies," 488–89.

145. Juan de Onis, "Stevenson Saw Latins' Hardship," *New York Times*, June 25, 1961; and Barbara Ward, "The Uses of Prosperity," *Saturday Review*, August 29, 1964.

146. Schulman, "Latin American Shantytown."

147. See Dietz, "Urban Squatter Settlements in Peru," 353–70; William Finn and James Converse, "Eight Assumptions Concerning Rural-Urban Migration in Colombia: A Three-Shantytown Test," *Land Economics* 46, no. 4 (1970); Karst, "Rights to Land and Housing in an Informal Legal System"; Leeds and Leeds, *A sociologia do Brasil urbano*; Mangin, "Latin American Squatter Settlements," 68, 85–86; Mangin and Turner, "The Barriada Movement"; Bryan R. Roberts, *Cities of Peasants: The Political Economy of Urbanization in the Third World* (Beverly Hills, CA: Sage, 1978); and Turner, "Lima's Barriadas and Corralones." Alejandro Portes, Wayne Cornelius, and Larisa Lomnitz were just a few other scholars who reached similar conclusions in the 1970s.

148. See Dietz, "Urban Squatter Settlements in Peru"; and Mangin, "Latin American Squatter Settlements." See also Andrews and Philips, "The Squatters of Lima"; and Portes, "Rationality in the Slum." Hernando De Soto's ideas first gained global notice with *The Other Path: The Invisible Revolution in the Third World* (New York: Harper and Row, 1989).

149. See Anthony Leeds, "O Brasil e o mito da ruralidade urbana: Experiência urbana, trabalho e valores nas 'áreas invadidas' do Rio de Janeiro e de Lima," in *A sociologia do Brasil urbano*, edited by Elizabeth Leeds and Anthony Leeds (Rio de Janeiro: Zahar, 1977).

150. On Canudos, see Gilberto Hochman and Nísia Trinidade Lima, "Condenado pela raça, absolvido pela medicina: O Brasil descoberto pelo movimento sanitarista da Primeira República," in *Raça, ciência e sociedade*, edited by Marcos Chor Maio and Ricardo Ventura Santos (Rio de Janeiro: Fiocruz / CCBB, 1996); and Valladares, *A invenção da favela*. In relation to the shantytown's African associations, Freyre and others associated mocambos with freedom, but another view associated favelas with *senzalas* (slave quarters). The famous 1960 Sociedade de Análises Gráficas e Mecanográficas Aplicadas aos Complexos Sociais (SAGMACS) study argued that all kinds of "rustic" habitation in the favelas and the countryside

were "socially affiliated with the senzala of the times of slavery." SAGMACS, "Aspectos humanos da favela carioca," *Cuadernos Latinoamericanos de Economia Humana* 4, no. 12 (1961): 242.

151. The connection between drought and the mocambos appears most famously in the writings of Josué de Castro. For one example of the Edenic view, see *Correio da Manhã*, June 2, 1907.

152. This was certainly the conclusion of most statistical surveys through the 1950s, though the notion of rural origins came to be questioned in the 1960s. See, especially, Leeds, "O Brasil"; and Mário Lacerda de Melo et al., *As migrações para o Recife*, 4 vols. (Recife, Brazil: Instituto Joaquim Nabuco de Pesquisas Sociais, 1961).

153. The continuity between rural and urban mocambos, barracos, and *malocas* (another term for shacks) was noted repeatedly. See, for example, Geraldo de Menezes Côrtes, *Favelas* (Rio de Janeiro: Ministério da Educação e Cultura Serviço de Documentação, 1959), 8; Carlos Alberto de Medina, *A favela e o demagogo* (São Paulo: Martins, 1964), 50–51; and SAGMACS, "Aspectos humanos da favela carioca," 242.

154. This physically rural aspect was common in other parts of Latin America as well, most strikingly in Lima, Peru, where huts were often built of woven straw mats.

155. Gilberto Hochman, *A era do saneamento: As bases da política de saúde pública no Brasil* (São Paulo: Editora Hucitec, ANPOCS, 1998); Hochman and Lima, "Condenado pela raça, absolvido pela medicina"; and Nisia Trinidade Lima, *Um sertão chamado Brasil* (Rio de Janeiro: IUPERJ, Editora Revan, 1999).

156. This progression found its clearest expression in literature, especially the novels of José Lins de Rego and Rachel de Quieroz. Josué de Castro's *Geografia da fome* offers an interesting scientific parallel, as does his novel *Homens e caranguejos (romance)* (São Paulo: Ed. Brasiliense, 1967), and A. C. Chagas Ribeiro's *Mocambo . . . romance.*

157. For a definition and comparative discussion of overurbanization, see Dyckman, "Some Conditions of Civic Order in an Urbanized World." For criticism of the same notion, see Waldemiro Bazzanella, "Industrialização e urbanização no Brasil," *América Latina* 6, no. 1 (1963). The general argument that favela proliferation was due to unresolved rural problems was most apparent in the press flurries surrounding Agamenon Magalhães's Liga Social contra o Mocambo in the late 1930s in Recife and Carlos Lacerda's article "O Partido Comunista e a Batalha do Rio de Janeiro" in the late 1940s.

158. See Agamenon Magalhães, "Ainda o problema dos mocambos," *Folha da Manhã*, September 14, 1939.

159. José Campello, "Os aspectos sociaes e económicos do mocambo."

160. Agamenon Magalhães, "O pequeno agricultor," *Folha da Manhã*, July 1, 1939; Josué de Castro, *Documentário do nordeste* (Rio de Janeiro: J. Olympio, 1937), and *Homens e caranguejos (romance)* (São Paulo: Ed. Brasiliense, 1967).

161. Florestan Fernandes, *A integração do negro na sociedade de classes* (São Paulo: Dominus Editôra, 1965).

162. A typical example comes from Medina's *A favela e o demagogo*, when he blames the brutality of slavery for creating a class of slave descendants with no notion of family responsibility (94).

163. Departamento de Geografia e Estatistica, *Censo das favelas*, 18.

164. Moura, "Favelas do Distrito Federal," 268.

165. Medina, *A favela e o demagogo*, 50–53, 74.

166. Medina, *A favela e o demagogo*, 63.

167. SAGMACS, "Aspectos humanos da favela carioca," 240.

168. SAGMACS, "Aspectos humanos da favela carioca," 243.

169. These included, as elsewhere, the empirical question of rural origins; the supposed closed-mindedness, cultural rigidity, and superstition of rural people; the anomie that supposedly resulted from rural displacement in the city; the danger of political radicalism thought to grow from such anomie; the isolation of rural enclaves from the political, economic, and cultural networks of the metropolis; and the family disintegration that resulted from male migrants' inadaptability to urban life.

170. See Valladares, *A invenção da favela*.

171. See, for example, Lidia de la Torre, *Buenos Aires: Del conventillo a la villa miseria (1869–1989)* (Buenos Aires: Educa, Editorial de la Universidad Católica Argentina, 2008); Fischer, *A Poverty of Rights*; Gominho, *Veneza americana x mucambópolis*; James Holston, *Insurgent Citizenship: Disjunctions of Democracy and Modernity in Brazil* (Princeton, NJ: Princeton University Press, 2008); Edward Murphy, "A Home of One's Own: Finding a Place in the Fractured Landscape of Urban Chile," PhD dissertation, University of Michigan, 2006; M. Silva, *Favelas cariocas, 1930–1964*; Valladares, *A invenção da favela*; Alejandro Velasco, "A Weapon as Powerful as the Vote: Street Protest and Electoral Politics in Caracas, Venezuela before Hugo Chávez," PhD dissertation, Duke University, 2009.

TWO

In and Out of the Margins

URBAN LAND SEIZURES AND HOMEOWNERSHIP
IN SANTIAGO, CHILE

Edward Murphy

Academic debates about marginality in the Latin American city have come a long way since the 1960s, when the so-called marginality school dominated the literature and influenced policymaking. In an early criticism, scholars pointed out how the urban poor did not live in a culture disconnected from the dominant practices and structures of social life. Janice Perlman, in exposing "the myths of marginality," emphasized how low-income urban residents often shared values and political affiliations with other social classes. Such residents did not practice a distinct "culture of poverty" that condemned them to their marginal condition.[1] Others stressed how the urban poor, even though they have often been unemployed or underemployed in the legally sanctioned job market, provide sources of labor that have been crucial to socioeconomic reproduction.[2]

More recently, scholars have developed how the urban poor have successfully made claims to expand their rights as citizens, especially in their struggles to receive housing and services. The nature of this claims making has contributed to shaping the public sphere of politics and the possibilities of social mobilization.[3] All of this scholarship has helped to dispense with one of the most persistent myths of the urban poor: namely, that the informal socioeconomic relations that they have taken part in are pathological, necessarily destructive, and set apart from the rest of society. Instead, analysts have insisted that these relations have been central to processes of urban modernity, in Latin America and elsewhere.[4]

Yet even as criticisms of the marginality school have made crucial insights, many of the issues and debates that fueled questions about urban marginality remain unsettled. This has become particularly evident in the present as contemporary forms of urbanization in Latin America have tended to heighten socio-spatial segregation, informality, criminality, and violence. Marginality remains evident in the urban landscape, exacerbated by the effects of neoliberal economic restructuring. Work for low-income groups has generally become more flexible and less secure. Unemployment and underemployment have tended to rise, as the number of surplus and superfluous laborers in the legally sanctioned job market has often grown.[5] Inequality has increased, the spaces of the city have become more privatized and fragmented, and social mobilization has declined, cohering less around an organized working class.[6]

The persistence of obvious forms of urban marginality in Latin American cities serves as a reminder that the debates over its nature were never solely academic. These debates, after all, have raised vexing questions about the relationship between rapid urbanization, mass inequity, and such themes as social inclusion, governance, criminality, and market relations. These issues, in turn, have fueled popular protests, ideological struggles, and policy debates, not least during the moment of the marginality school's greatest political and intellectual influence in the 1960s. In much of Latin America at that time, transnational development organizations, state bureaucracies, social movements, and academic institutions focused unprecedented attention on the living conditions of the urban poor. In helping to shape reforms throughout the Americas, the marginality school was at the center of debates over urban modernity during an extraordinary period of bold policy initiatives and unparalleled popular activism.

This chapter returns to this moment, focusing on the question of urban housing. During this period, Santiago was the base of a research institute, El Centro de Desarrollo Social de América Latina (Center for Social Development in Latin America, DESAL), that was the intellectual home of the marginality school. The Christian Democratic government of Eduardo Frei Montalva (1964–70) sought to implement a number of DESAL's ambitious policy proposals. Many of these projects failed. Yet one of the primary objectives of DESAL's reforms, to provide housing for the urban poor and turn them into homeowners, was an important goal that animated actors across the sociopolitical spectrum. It remains so today. At the time, opponents seized on the inability of the Christian Democrats to deliver on the promise of secure housing in order to justify radical forms of activism, including an unprecedented number of urban land seizures. Involving some

400,000 Santiago residents between 1967 and 1973—about 14 percent of the city's population—these seizures eventually contributed to making property holders of the vast majority of Santiago's poor.[7]

In becoming homeowners, these squatters fulfilled not only a central objective of DESAL and the marginality school but also a foundation of order within liberal forms of state making. Yet in a seeming paradox, they primarily did so by transgressing legal frameworks and receiving organizational support and patronage from Chilean leftists, particularly the Communist Party. The land seizures became an important part of the era's revolutionary activism and symbolism. Squatters and housing-rights activists often violated the law and formed a powerful social movement that fired the imagination of the Chilean Left.

As they seized land, squatters tested the boundaries of legitimate action as they sought to deliver themselves from the margins of social life. Exploring the actions and goals of the squatters thus reveals important ways in which marginality was a central feature of both the urban fabric and sociopolitical struggle. As the squatters acted on the margins of the law in seizing land, they also operated on the margins of social power. Officials often dismissed the squatters as deserving of their harsh living conditions. Yet as they declared that they had a right to be property owners, squatters sought to come in from the margins and be recognized as citizens with legitimate grievances and claims.

Squatters did so by asserting that they had acted properly in demanding their right to homeownership. As recent studies on property have emphasized, persons asserting the rights of ownership assume that they should occupy a place in the social order appropriate to their standing. From this perspective, property is about understandings of propriety.[8] In the case of Chilean squatters, much of their success in gaining access to property depended on their ability to demonstrate that they were proper citizens who deserved certain living conditions. Through their actions, the squatters focused attention on the inability of the state to fulfill its promises of urban modernity to a vast segment of the Chilean citizenry. Acting as insurgents, the squatters ensured that a contradiction in state-citizen relations could be overcome.[9] Consequently, they altered the sociopolitical footing in Chile and helped to transform their social standing.

This was a dangerous game, however, as the squatters both continued to suffer from poor economic opportunities and often faced stigmatization, sanction, and repression, even after they became homeowners. Ultimately, the squatters came in and out of the margins of state frameworks, social acceptability, and economic relations as they struggled to improve their living conditions and find a stable place in the urban landscape. Uncovering this process underscores some of the central tensions and challenges that the poor have faced in Latin American cities as they have attempted to live in legally sanctioned homes since the 1950s.

During this period of rapid and often volatile urbanization, Latin American states have been unable to fully regulate and control the settlement of the urban poor. Yet squatters have tended to gain housing through de jure and de facto forms of land tenure.[10] Generally speaking, this has been an insurgent process in which squatters have successfully claimed a right to the city. They have gained access to forms of citizenship that had previously been denied them. In the shantytowns and informal settlements of Latin America, a significant struggle over the meaning and rights of citizenship has thus taken place. This has had important implications for state relations and socio-spatial development in the Latin American city as the urban poor have generally come to have homes of their own. Yet it is also the case that the acquisition of a home can be a limited gain, not fully responsive to a broader context that can still leave the poor in a precarious and marginal position.

In analyzing these dynamics, this chapter first reveals how certain normative assumptions about marginality and propriety helped to shape the ideological ground upon which reformers, revolutionaries, and housing activists in Chile acted. It then explores how, in one emblematic land seizure, these assumptions influenced not only state policy but also revolutionary mobilization and the gains that squatters could secure. Even as radical activism expanded the boundaries of the possible, coming in from the margins and becoming homeowners also meant conforming to what Paul Rabinow has called the "norms and forms of the social environment" and governance.[11] I conclude the chapter with a brief analysis of the present context, in which elements of marginality coexist with high levels of homeownership and social demobilization in Santiago's periphery.

Before proceeding, I should clarify how I treat the term *marginality*. Throughout the chapter, I attend to the effects that understandings of marginality had and, in certain key respects, continue to have. I thus treat *marginality* as a folk category, an active and consequential term that is embedded in historical relations. Yet I also adopt *marginality* as an analytical term. The creation of sociopolitical and economic margins is an unfolding process, in which the margins form a part of the whole. In his illuminating work on the relationship between the English countryside and city, Raymond Williams develops how this relationship has historically been one between a center and a periphery. But this hierarchical relationship has been obscured by the ways in which the multiple understandings and associations tied to the urban and the rural cast them as separate and independent social domains. In his analysis, Williams underscores how the formation of margins is central to the social relationships at play.[12] As Williams would argue, understandings about urban marginality have taken shape within "structures of feeling" that tend to mystify more than they reveal.[13] Yet such structures of feeling have themselves contributed to the making of marginality. Examining how the margins come into being thus casts a revealing light on dominant norms, practices, and ideologies. This is especially true of state frameworks and the dynamics of citizenship, as the struggles of Chilean squatters to receive a right to urban housing reveals.

Marginality is not limited to these domains though. If gaining a right to housing means coming out of particular sociopolitical and spatial margins, it does not follow that other forms of marginality are no longer at work. The urban poor may still assume marginal positions in other domains. The volatility of legally sanctioned labor markets and their inability to absorb potential workers, for example, has led to its own kind of marginality.[14] Gaining a right to housing for the urban poor has not directly addressed this issue, an important limit to the benefits of citizenship that they have received. In order to explore such limits and the contradictory processes of which they are a part, I focus in this chapter on the unfolding creation of margins. Such an approach stresses the successes that squatters have had as they have developed homes of their own during the past half century. But it also underscores the tense fault lines of power, hierarchy, and social suffering that have continued to mark the lives of the urban poor.

IDEOLOGICAL CONFLICT AND URBAN REFORM IN THE 1960S

The marginality school achieved prominence at a time when an increasingly intense ideological struggle was taking shape in the Americas. This competition linked particular national dynamics with transnational development paradigms and the priorities of the cold war. For policymakers in Washington and Santiago, Chile's Christian Democratic government represented an important opportunity: a chance to demonstrate that capitalist modernization was possible and that it could uplift the lower classes. As a moderate alternative to the Cuban Revolution, the Christian Democratic "revolution in liberty" held out the promise of creating fundamental change while building on Chile's liberal democratic tradition. Chile became a model for the U.S.-sponsored Alliance for Progress, a hemispheric-wide effort to implement reform, blunt the appeal of the Cuban Revolution, and support anticommunist militaries.[15]

Clearly, geostrategic interests helped to motivate the implementation of Christian Democratic reforms. Yet urban-planning and poverty-reduction efforts also gained traction because they tapped into a normalizing sensibility of development shared, at least in part, by a wide range of social groups and institutions. The marginality school was important sociopolitically because it followed widely accepted notions about the proper order of things and the place of low-income urban residents within that order. (Chileans generally referred to this group as *pobladores*, something that I will also do.)

In an initiative dubbed Popular Promotion (Promoción Popular), DESAL and Christian Democratic reformers explicitly sought to mobilize the lower classes.[16] They created or fortified a series of civic associations, providing funding, training, and legal status to neighborhood councils, mothers' centers, sports clubs, and youth groups. As the reformers did so, they entered into bitter conflicts with Marxists over how to involve such groups as the pobladores in political and social processes. During this period, Marxists and Christian Democrats claimed to both represent the popular classes and hold the keys to changing their position in Chilean society. Marxists and Christian Democrats each stressed that they needed to mobilize popular groups on a scale unprecedented in Chilean history. In the cities, they also emphasized that they should provide pobladores with proper housing and neighborhood resources, as rapid urbanization, poor economic opportunities, and inadequate government spending had exacerbated a housing shortage.

The intertwined goals of providing housing and mobilizing pobladores became wedge issues upon which Marxists, Christian Democrats, and their international supporters competed. In this respect, the ideological conflict between the Chilean political center and the Left played out, at least in part, on the assumption that deserving members of the urban poor should have access to appropriate housing. While there had long been a gap between expectations of a proper home life and living conditions for low-income Chileans, this was now an imminent and unavoidable public issue.

As had many presidents before him, Frei promised to resolve the problems of housing and urban order during his administration. But he committed an unprecedented amount of publicity and resources to realizing this vision. His government, moreover, cast Santiago's development as a pressing national problem. With much fanfare, Frei made the creation of the Ministerio de Vivienda y Urbanismo (Ministry of Housing and Urbanism, MINVU) a centerpiece of reform. As an indication of the international importance of this effort, MINVU and its programs received support and loans from the U.S. Agency for International Development, the Inter-American Development Bank, and even the American Federation of Labor.[17] In addition, many of Chile's programs became international models for programs in housing and poverty reduction.[18]

The programs were ambitious. Frei promised to resolve the housing crisis through an unparalleled effort to build 360,000 new housing units from 1964 to 1970.[19] Critics, especially leftists, pointed out that this would fall short of resolving Chile's housing problem, since the census of 1960 had identified a deficit of 488,000 units.[20] But the Christian Democrats countered that building sixty thousand units per year was far beyond anything the country had yet produced. Besides, officials asserted, government-subsidized housing would now be of a better quality. As Frei put it, the developments would not simply be a "row of houses on an unpaved street, but rather fully constructed neighborhoods where a family can develop with dignity."[21]

This kind of promise touched a nerve. In their dealings with government officials, pobladores often expressed how important the stakes were for them to receive dignified housing. In a plea to the minister of housing and urbanism in 1967, the directorate of one neighborhood committee pointed out how stigmatized and denigrated those without homes could be: "Señor Ministro, excuse our frankness, but when some families don't have a meter of their own land, people often say that they [these families] are naked, beggars, without any moral or patriotic honor. . . . [People say] that they walk like gypsies from one place to the next, like birds without nests."[22] Given such assumptions, having a proper place to live had potent status implications. If a Chilean was homeless, that person was on the margins of acceptability, stigmatized as morally reprehensible and unfit to be a part of the nation.

In the Chilean context, being homeless, or as it was literally put, "without a house" (*sin casa*), did not generally indicate that one lived in the street. It meant not having a proper home. This included living in the houses of extended family members or fictive kin, in addition to living in dilapidated housing without legal sanction in a squatter settlement. Ownership was crucial to this definition, as families who rented, especially low-income ones, were also homeless. The Christian Democratic housing reforms promised to help the homeless not only improve their living conditions but also overcome their troubling, marginal status.

These state programs, however, did not subvert the understandings that contributed to the stigmatization of the homeless. To the contrary, these programs used terms that reinforced the marginalization of the homeless, setting them up as an abnormal and pathological group. This occurred in the very categories that state technocrats used to administer their programs. In the national census of 1952, officials began to use the terms *campamentos* (encampments) and *poblaciones callampas* (a reference to a mushroom that grows uncontrollably at night) to classify what they called "irregular" neighborhoods that lacked property titles and services considered basic. In the first Chilean housing census in 1952, *callampas* and *campamentos* described areas that were built "clandestinely" and made from "scrap" materials.[23] While these terms were supposed to be only technical, they also marked campamentos and callampas as the most marginal and stigmatized of neighborhoods. This colloquial understanding bled into the categories of state and vice versa.

In order to transform the "irregular" and "unhygienic" campamentos and callampas, planners at MINVU sought (and continue to seek) to, in their word, *sanear* these spaces, a verb that simultaneously means "to sanitize," "to regulate," and "to make well."[24] To accomplish this task, state bureaucracies would need to provide the residents of these areas with both property titles and neighborhoods that would have the spatial and design qualities of modern planning. As such, the neighborhoods would include relatively uniform-sized housing lots designed for single-family homes, a street-grid pattern, and houses or apartments built of solid materials. The neighborhoods should also have urban services considered basic, including electricity, potable water, sanitation facilities, and paved roads, in addition to relatively close access to health clinics, police services, and schools. In many cases, officials only considered it possible to regulate, sanitize, and heal the campamentos by eradicating them, razing the neighborhoods and moving their residents to other areas of the city.

As medical metaphors, *sanitizing, healing,* and *making well* presume a normal and healthy bodily condition, outside of which lies pathology and illness.[25] The sensibility behind this metaphor impacted how officials approached the spaces of the city and also how they understood the city's inhabitants. One of the underlying assumptions of MINVU's housing policies was that nuclear families who lived in so-called hygienic neighborhoods would be better citizens. A basic MINVU principle stated that housing was a right of all Chilean families, and the conditions in the houses and the neighborhoods must be adequate to "permit the normal development of the family and . . . of the community."[26] A Christian Democratic deputy argued that MINVU's projects would develop "the necessary conditions of hygiene to prevent the promiscuity and degeneracy [that exists] in the campamentos, and resolve the misery of the workers."[27] This deputy assumed that the conditions in the campamentos produced marginal, destructive, and pathological behavior. But this would change in a hygienic environment, where nuclear families and appropriate personal conduct would be ensured.

Christian Democratic programs of Popular Promotion also assumed that low-income populations were abnormal and deviant. Planners designed these programs based on the supposition that pobladores were marginal to the economic and social structures of the nation. These officials argued that it was necessary for state projects to "integrate" the marginal so that they could become modern. This was why planners sought to foment the participation of pobladores through the creation of civic associations. According to government statistics, Popular Promotion programs helped to establish 21,917 organizations, with more than 660,000 participants, from 1964 to 1970 in Santiago alone.[28] These efforts reflected a firm belief in the virtue of existing social structures: the marginal needed to be brought into these structures so as to experience their benefits.

Officials granted MINVU an important role in Popular Promotion, seeing the creation of property owners and urbanized neighborhoods as crucial. In MINVU's Popular Savings Plan, the homeless would assume ten- to fifteen-year mortgages through a government-subsidized housing program. Marginal peoples would thus become enmeshed in the Chilean banking system, becoming consumers in the marketplace.[29] Once established in homes of their own, moreover, marginals would also become involved in neighborhood institutions, a process that would make them active citizens. Homeowners who paid mortgages and participated in civic associations were the norm, outside of which lay the marginal, a homogenous social group defined primarily by its deviance.

Reformers tended to misrecognize urban poverty as a pathological condition, unconnected to broader socioeconomic processes.[30] They did this even as the Christian Democratic platform sought to transform the Chilean economy through structural reforms. Such a problematic assumption fit within general understandings of modernization theory and its supposition that social actors (and societies) would follow a singular development path. If given the right tools — including such things as access to credit, education, homeownership, and community organizations — the marginal would be able to leave their impoverished and pathological condition behind. Yet even though some of these prescriptions could offer help to pobladores in their daily struggles, the prescriptions both ignored the formation of social inequality and reinforced hierarchical social relations.[31] Reports on marginality asserted, in line with long-standing stigmatizations of the urban poor, that the marginal were violent, lacked family structures, were uneducated, suffered from authoritarianism and fatalism, and were prone to crime. As a class, the urban poor possessed characteristics that, at least in part, were responsible for their own marginalization.[32] They were thus at the bottom of a hierarchical chain that assumed a middle- and upper-class norm.

Christian Democratic planners presumed that there were standards that governed how proper citizens should behave. Properly behaved citizens, in turn, would naturally live in certain conditions. Contemporary actors debated much about this understanding: Was pathology the result of socioeconomic conditions and a morally bankrupt political process, as the Left asserted? Or was it the result of the pathologies of the poor? Perhaps it was some combination of the two, as the overall Christian Democratic reform program seemed to recognize. Yet as impassioned and as important as these debates were, they took shape on the shared assumption that properly behaved citizens deserved living conditions commensurate with their status.

THE FAILURES OF REFORM

This understanding often posed a problem for the Christian Democrats, especially when their reform efforts in urban housing began to falter. In 1967 the Christian Democrats generally scaled back their ambitious social programs as the government faced budget shortfalls and rising inflation.[33] In the end, Chile produced a total of 228,398 housing units during Frei's six-year term. While this was a record for any six-year period, it still fell short of the original target of 360,000.[34] In low-income housing, Chile produced only 121,000 units, also below the original promise of 213,000.[35]

The budgetary problems that Christian Democratic officials faced were only part of the reason that low-income housing production was disappointing. The privately controlled Chamber of Construction and Chile's savings-and-loan institutions had very close relationships with MINVU. They effectively lobbied officials to build more middle-class housing in publicly financed programs than had been the initial intent. This process undermined efforts to provide low-income housing, as developers and credit institutions gained access to more lucrative real-estate deals for middle-class housing.[36] The effects of this were perverse, especially as immigration from the countryside and population increases continued to swell the size of Santiago. By the end of the decade, the Chilean housing deficit had actually increased, climbing to 585,000 units in 1970.[37] As housing became scarcer and as more of it was developed for middle- and upper-income sectors, it became considerably more expensive. Between 1960 and 1968, the average price of a square meter of housing tripled in Santiago and the average rent rose even more.[38]

Beyond these problems, MINVU developed low-income housing that maintained the socioeconomic segregation of Santiago. Middle- and upper-income neighborhood organizations would have it no other way. These organizations claimed that the construction of low-income housing near them would inappropriately undermine their property values and social status. As the leaders of one organization put it in a letter to the minister of housing and urbanism Andrés Donoso, a low-income housing development would put their families in "danger," since such an area would be a "center of infection and of delinquency."[39] Ultimately, MINVU's programs did not upset the socioeconomic segregation that existed in Santiago. Low-income, subsidized-housing projects were most often built on the outskirts of the city, in predominately poor areas.[40] These housing programs thus reproduced the mosaic of class distinctions that characterized Santiago's fractured urban landscape.

The shortcomings in the Christian Democratic programs meant that numerous housing applicants who had fulfilled the state's requirements were turned down. Leftists and housing-rights activists pointed to these kinds of problems when they defended the right of the homeless to seize land. Such arguments placed the Christian Democrats in an awkward position. While officials could plausibly condemn the land seizures as an illegal tactic that upset the state's housing plans, they nevertheless conceded that the demands the homeless made were legitimate. It was often difficult for them to adopt a hard-line against the land seizures.

If officials ordered the police to break up the land seizures, this would invariably lead to violent confrontations. Such an outcome contradicted the Christian Democratic goal of "popular promotion." The government's opponents could easily exploit police violence against pobladores for their own ends. This became particularly apparent in February 1969, when the police killed eleven homeless pobladores who had taken part in a land seizure in the southern city of Puerto Montt. The massacre provoked a national scandal that contributed to divisions among the Christian Democrats. Afterward, the police rarely broke up urban land seizures with force. This was the most important and immediate factor in the substantial rise in land seizures that occurred in 1969 and accelerated with Salvador Allende's election in 1970.[41]

On a deeper level, the rise in activism around housing demonstrated a central contradiction and dilemma of governance. Facing budgetary constraints and powerful private interests, overwhelmed reformers often fell well short of realizing the promise of transformation embedded in state programs. Yet pobladores continued to be inspired by visions of development and the possibility of fairness and propriety. These visions developed out of a fetishized understanding of the state as an impartial arbiter of justice and rights. As the case of urban housing makes clear, the state was neither impartial nor just. It was instead a set of diverse institutions weighed down by special interests and shot through with conflict. Political economic relations shaped the workings of the state.

Yet if pobladores and others could be well aware of the shortcomings of governance, the fetish of the state was nevertheless important.[42] Ideas of justice and fairness fueled action that ultimately contested the contours of state politics. Additionally, leftists celebrated the activism of homeless pobladores, and particularly the land seizures, as a symbol of a burgeoning revolutionary consciousness. Still, the normative power of state frameworks—including expectations of propriety in social relations—continued to matter as pobladores seized land and sought to become homeowners.

REVOLUTIONARY ACTIVISM AND EXPECTATIONS OF A PROPER HOME LIFE

The decision to seize land depended, in no small measure, on expectations of what homelife should be. Many homeless did not consider their individual living conditions to be in accord with their rights as proper Chileans as they came to see their lives through the gap between expectations and personal circumstance. This tension is evident in the way that Ana Valdés described her reasons for taking part in a land seizure in an interview.[43] When Valdés was nineteen, she was married and had two children. But Valdés and her husband were unable to buy their own house, lacking the income they needed to join a subsidized-housing program. Given this situation, Valdés was "homeless." She moved into her husband's family home, enduring circumstances that she considered to be unacceptable. Her family shared a three-room house with six others. They slept in a room that was barely large enough to fit the four of them, the kind of overcrowding that was a fairly common experience in the burgeoning shantytowns and run-down tenements that housed the urban poor in the 1960s.

Despite being married, and having her own children, Valdés occupied a marginal space, one that she felt was inappropriate to her status. She did not have the living conditions she needed in order to live in what Chileans referred to as a *well-constituted home*, a term that referred to both the moral comportment of a family and its housing conditions. As Karin Rosemblatt has pointed out, this notion was important politically. During Chile's period of state-led development, the state's social-welfare institutions, leftist political parties, and social movements each shared the goal of developing well-constituted homes.[44] This desire reinforced the normative sensibilities of homeownership: proper families should have living conditions in accord with their status.

For Valdés, this understanding led to a call for action because she felt that she legitimately deserved her own home. In early 1967, she joined Communist Party members in mobilizing the homeless of Renca, the municipality in which she lived. In building their movement, the Communist organizers built a large network, forming Committees of the Homeless in ten different neighborhoods. By 1969 approximately twelve hundred families had joined the committees, giving the umbrella organization, the Communal Command of the Homeless of Renca, a certain amount of clout and considerable responsibility. Nevertheless, by the end of April of that year, Renca's homeless had been unable to receive housing, despite the arduous planning and labor they had put into organizing more than six thousand people.

In an experience that was common throughout Santiago, Renca's homeless committees had negotiated with officials and had sought to comply with bureaucratic procedures and regulations for more than two years. But little had happened. On the morning of May 1, 1969, as a steady rain fell, Renca's homeless decided on a bold, if increasingly common, option. At dawn, several hundred committee members seized uncultivated land on a local vineyard. Through this action, they sought to establish, once and for all, proper homes. Rather than living as a "marginal in subhuman conditions"—the kind of expression commonly found in contemporary media reports and official speeches—Valdés would finally have the opportunity to live in a proper, well-constituted home.

As Valdés and her homeless neighbors organized their movement, their efforts to realize the dream of living in appropriate homes led them to bureaucracies inside MINVU. Such bureaucracies were often exasperating and slow moving. They were also potentially threatening for homeless pobladores.[45] The homeless, after all, could face sanctions as they dealt with state institutions, especially after they took part in such transgressive acts as seizing land. Yet if the homeless hoped to come in from the margins, access state benefits, and be included in the exclusive company of citizens, they had to work through state bodies.[46]

In approaching MINVU, the Communal Command of the Homeless in Renca often relied on the support and mediation of Communist politicians, especially Gladys Marín, a young parliamentarian who was making a name for herself as a leader of the Communist Youth and as an advocate of housing rights during the late 1960s. Marín's work with the homeless of Renca was typical of the actions of many politicians who provided a crucial link between citizen organizations and state bureaucrats. In sponsoring these claims, deputies and senators focused attention on the plight of specific homeless committees, recording their complaints in congressional records and often publicizing the inability of state bureaucracies to respond.

In working with Marín and the Communists, Renca's homeless committees joined forces with a party organization that had been prominently involved with pobladores and in many of Santiago's largest and most well-known land seizures since the 1940s.[47] As the Communist Party privileged the movement of the pobladores, it assigned the homeless movement an activist, heroic role that fit within the Left's general interpretation of Chilean society. The lack of appropriate housing symbolized the failures of the bourgeois state, while the homeless response expressed a class organization and militant consciousness that would help to develop a more just and humane society. By seizing land, pobladores ultimately took part in a struggle that would end in revolutionary transformation, encapsulated in the motto of many Communist-sponsored homeless committees: "from the seizure of land to the seizure of power."

In numerous public appearances, Marín publicly defended the cause of housing rights. In an event held shortly before the May Day land seizure of 1969, Marín addressed the Communal Command of the Homeless of Renca. In her remarks, Marín celebrated the "maturity of the consciousness of the pobladores." They had demonstrated tremendous resolve in their "long fight." Marín praised the pobladores for complying with state programs, noting how they had deposited monthly quotas into savings accounts with MINVU. In doing this, the homeless had demonstrated that they had the discipline needed in order to pay dividends. But while Marín praised the homeless for complying with legal requirements, she also recalled how other homeless committees had recently established exemplary neighborhoods by seizing land. For Marín, seizing land, while a revolutionary and illegal act, was also justified, because the pobladores had complied with state requirements.[48] Such a balancing act between transgression and legitimate propriety, revolution and respectability, marked the processes through which pobladores would establish neighborhoods throughout the period.

The Communist Party constantly worked in the marginal space between revolutionary activism and institutional processes. The party was committed, after all, to radically transforming Chilean society through existing legal frameworks. As the principal sponsor of the land seizures from 1947 until the late 1960s, the Communist Party provided pobladores who seized land with an impressive party apparatus that granted them critical logistical support, legal counsel, access to prominent legislators, and publicity. Through these activities, the Communist Party helped to publicly justify the land seizures and to establish new modes of activism. Most important, the party helped to ensure that the provision of minimally accepted housing conditions was understood as a right of citizenship and a central obligation of the state.

During the 1960s, this was often a revolutionary challenge, permitting pobladores to act outside of the law in their struggles to receive housing. By the end of the decade, groups of homeless pobladores increasingly went beyond the officially sanctioned channels of signing up for government programs, writing petitions to ministry officials, and seeking support from political party leaders. More and more, pobladores demonstrated in front of government buildings, took part in sit-ins, blocked traffic, and seized land. Through these tactics, homeless groups demanded, and often received, direct meetings with government officials.

Pobladores' memories of these meetings tend to stress how they could both voice their displeasure at government intransigence and demand respect from officials. The Committees of the Homeless of Renca, for example, were able to speak with the regional governor following a two-hour protest in front of his office. Eliana Parra remembered that during the meeting, the governor interrupted one of the committee members, shouting "¡cállate, pajarón!" ("shut up, idiot!"; literally, "shut up, big bird!"). According to Parra, she responded to the governor by saying, "We're not being arrogant, why do you have to come and insult a homeless *compañero* [comrade]? . . . More than anyone, you, as the *intendente* [governor], shouldn't treat us like that." For Parra, the exchange ended favorably, as the governor apologized and asked for forgiveness.[49] The homeless pobladores thus gained some measure of respect, even if, as in this case, they still weren't able to receive housing. Parra's narrative privileges the action of pobladores and their ability to confront officials. In its favorable ending, it satisfies a desire on Parra's part to be treated properly, with respect and dignity. For pobladores, long accustomed to being stigmatized and dismissed as marginal, insignificant actors, their activism had helped to transform the social footing on which interactions with state officials took place.

In the press, in song, and in the mass media, leftist narratives of this kind of activism connected efforts to be treated properly with the promise of revolution. These narratives, in fact, depicted pobladores as rebellious subjects who acted with singular resolve in assuming their class interests and transforming society. Communist newspaper reports depicted the land seizures as watershed events that represented the emerging consciousness of Chile's pobladores. Through their exemplary activism, pobladores would help to create a new Chile. While this understanding motivated supporters, it was not enough to ensure that pobladores could establish homes. If pobladores were to come out of the margins and receive legally sanctioned properties, they would also need to conform to the normative practices and expectations of propriety that existed at the very center of state frameworks and citizenship rights.

NEIGHBORHOOD ORGANIZATION AND THE (A)POLITICAL NATURE OF ACTIVISM

The activism of the homeless took shape within quite specific contours. Neighborhood and gender relations each played important roles in how the homeless could mobilize. It was only by organizing as a neighborhood that pobladores had the best opportunity to successfully negotiate with authorities. The claims of neighborhood organizations superseded those of individual families in attempts to gain access to housing programs.[50] In most cases, neighbors had to collectively assume payment plans and agree to take part in work teams that would help to "regularize" neighborhoods following land seizures.[51] According to the government, this was a way for pobladores to participate in the development of their own living spaces.[52]

This participation had its limits, however. Minimal expectations of what neighborhood development and homes should be framed the claims that pobladores could make. This framing fit within the goals of "sanitizing," "regulating," and "healing" the irregular campamentos. As such, the homeless could legitimately demand property titles, basic housing, and neighborhood services. The provision of these items would clearly improve the living conditions of many pobladores. Yet they also marked the boundaries of what pobladores could receive.

Somewhat paradoxically, the homeless could only successfully mobilize to receive housing if they presented themselves as apolitical, despite the fact that the popular sectors were central to the era's intense political mobilization. But having explicit political objectives, especially proselytizing the cause of the political parties, was not an effective means of mobilizing citizens in support of their housing rights. These rights, after all, were supposed to transcend narrow political interests. They were a part of the liberal contract of justice and fairness between citizens and the state.

Given this, homeless committee organizers in Renca claimed that they were only interested in the needs of the needy as they formed committees and signed pobladores up for housing programs. Parra recalled the long hours spent searching for Renca's homeless: "We were looking for people who didn't have their own house. We spoke with everyone; we didn't care if they were Catholics or Evangelicals, nor were we interested in what kind of politics they had. We didn't care about that; what we did care about was if they had a place to live, if they had a roof and if they had a place to shelter their children at night."[53] For an issue such as housing, all Chileans were expected to rise above parochial interests, not sullying the sanctity of the home with the rough-and-tumble of political life. Proper Chileans, no matter their politics, deserved an appropriate standard of living that the state should ensure.

Within this context, housewives played a particularly important role in organizing the homeless committees, since it was generally understood that they occupied the private, domestic sphere, an arena that remained largely cast as feminine and apolitical. These women emphasized their position as mothers who cared, above all else, about the well-being of their families. Women involved in the land seizures tended to argue that they had no other option than to mobilize in order to overcome hardship and fulfill their responsibilities as mothers. Given the transgressions of the state and the desperation and impropriety of their domestic situation, they simply had to enter the public arena.[54]

THE MAY DAY LAND SEIZURE

The leaders of the Homeless Committees in Renca found the symbolism of seizing land on May Day an important statement of solidarity. They hoped that the seizure would be received as a statement on working-class power and the possibilities of revolutionary activism. On the day of the seizure, the homeless pobladores carried Chilean flags with them, portraying the seizure as an act of patriotism. Two days earlier, in an attempt to rally support for continued mobilization, one pobladora invoked a saying credited to Manuel Rodríguez, a hero of the Chile's Wars of Independence: " 'We still have *patria* [fatherland] citizens.' We too are Chileans, and we have a right to live here. And there are lands here, and we should fight for them." [55]

Shortly after the beginning of the march, Communist elected officials, including a senator and Marín, joined the homeless pobladores. News of the seizure was broadcast on morning radio and television programs. Several dozen police officers, dressed in riot gear, encircled the pobladores. There were tense moments, but the police did not impede the pobladores, as they had evidently received orders to act with restraint. Once the pobladores were established in the land that they had chosen to occupy, the police immediately cordoned off the area, only permitting food, water, and temporary materials for shelter to enter. This uneasy standoff, where the police controlled any movement in and out of the new campamento, lasted for five days. During this period, the Communist Party organized a number of relief and solidarity efforts.[56]

In hopes of resolving the campamento's legal status, homeless committee leaders, with the support of Communist members of parliament, entered into negotiations with officials. The leaders defended what the squatters had done. They pointed out that the pobladores had money in the government's Popular Savings Program and that they had acted in a disciplined way. One pobladora commented to the press: "We aren't afraid. We're organized, we have rights, and we'll defend them, and we've done this seizure in an orderly manner, without provoking anybody. . . . If there's a fight, well, this wouldn't be the first time that some fall for the good of everyone else. Today we fight for tomorrow, for our children. . . . The struggle continues, and our children will have conquered a piece of land where they can live."[57]

In order to test the claims of the homeless, MINVU officials began a survey of the campamento.[58] Donoso, the minister of housing and urbanism, asserted that the survey would allow planners to understand the "true dimension of the housing problem" in Renca. According to Donoso, there were many squatters who legitimately had enough savings in government housing programs, but there were several others who did not. Some had even taken part in the seizure because they had been "pushed by political forces," while others already owned houses and were inappropriately trying to profit from the seizure.[59] But the survey would clear these issues up, allowing functionaries to determine whether or not the pobladores could legitimately establish the neighborhood. To accomplish this, the survey assessed if the pobladores had complied with the criteria normally demanded of housing applicants. It evaluated the living conditions that the pobladores had previously had, their ability to make dividend payments, if they owned other properties, and the nature of their families, including appraisals about comportment and hygiene.[60]

The squatter leaders did not object to this, as they viewed the survey as an opportunity to validate the propriety of their goals and actions.[61] They had, after all, already spent two years establishing the homeless status of committee members and enrolling them in government housing programs. In spite of this, negotiations between squatter representatives and officials were often tense and volatile. On May 6, however, the government permitted the pobladores to stay, following a lengthy series of meetings between Christian Democratic officials, neighborhood leaders, and Marín.[62]

If letting the pobladores establish sites for their new homes implicitly granted legitimacy to their demands, it did not necessarily resolve many of the practical concerns that the squatters had. Much planning remained to be done. Attempts to transform the campamento into an established neighborhood would drag on for years; it was not completed until well into the military dictatorship of 1973–90. The homeless committee leaders, now recognized as a neighborhood council, worked with architects and planners from MINVU to organize the neighborhood into lots and provide for basic services. By establishing security patrols and work teams, the neighborhood council sought to provide for the safety of residents and for the construction of a meeting hall, latrines, and footpaths. The council also arranged for the donation of medical supplies and building materials from Communist supporters and student groups.

Through 1969 and 1970, the residents of the campamento continued to negotiate with officials over what the government would eventually provide and how the neighborhood would be spatially organized. This was often a fractious process, including challenges from groups of pobladores sponsored by the Christian Democrats.[63] The most contentious issue to resolve stemmed from the fact that there was not enough room in the area to legally house all of the pobladores. To resolve this, the neighborhood council, Communist representatives, and officials agreed to two stipulations. First, MINVU would buy sections of a few adjacent properties to create more space. In exchange, residents agreed to provide work teams for infrastructure projects in the neighborhood, a kind of compromise that was common following land seizures.[64] Second, each committee had to identify a number of residents who would have to leave.[65]

Homeless committee leaders had considerable leeway to decide who these pobladores would be. They thus had the authority to act as state-like administrators. Inclusion in the newly formed community depended on expectations that the homeless committees themselves established. This was true not only in the May Day land seizure but also in committees that legally became a part of government-sponsored housing programs.[66] Yet even as these committees had the autonomy to make up their own minds about whom to include and exclude, they generally followed criteria that both the homeless and state officials shared. In doing so, they adhered to the ubiquitous norms and expectations of propriety in citizen relations.

Inside the new campamento, leaders stressed the importance of individual conduct in meetings with the pobladores. Parra remembered it this way:

> We explained to them . . . that each resident was going to live in the neighborhood as if they were in their own home, without making any scandals, without anyone who would get drunk, without people who

were looking for fights. . . . We also explained to them that the children should go to school, that the men had to go to work, and that the women should stay in and take care of their houses, keep everything clean. . . . When it was seen that people made scandals; that husbands arrived home to the campamento drunk or something like that, people would come look for the directive and call our attention to the bad behavior. On a number of occasions, I had to go speak to the people and some of them had to leave the campamento.[67]

Council leaders such as Parra thus attempted to regulate behavior, establishing codes of personal conduct that stressed appropriate comportment, including hygiene, family relationships, work, and relative abstinence from alcohol and fighting. Individuals had to demonstrate that they were capable of conforming in this way if they wished to stay.

Such efforts to police the behavior of residents were common in neighborhoods established by land seizures.[68] These efforts to order the neighborhood through the internal policing of residents reflect expectations of propriety in citizenship, class relations, and neighborly comportment. These expectations were a diffuse and yet critical part of the social landscape, influencing the plans of anyone who sought to develop a proper home sanctioned by state institutions. By demonstrating that they were responsible and disciplined, pobladores showed that they deserved, as citizens, to be homeowners who would have access to basic city services. Having these services and land titles was thus an important form of distinction, reflective of personal status. By gaining these benefits, the pobladores achieved a different state of being, in which they could demonstrate that they were full, not marginal, members of the imagined national community. In this context, local groups carried on state practices of inclusion and exclusion, as they decided who could shed the stigmas associated with being homeless and gain access to a home considered appropriate.

But the pobladores from the new neighborhood, now called the May Day Campamento, were far from having the homes that they hoped for, since they continued to live in a campamento. They thus busied themselves in the construction of their new neighborhood. MINVU organized the campamento into ten distinct sections, which eventually became city blocks. MINVU granted each individual housing lot approximately sixty square meters. Beyond this, however, MINVU provided little else when the pobladores first moved in, angering many. Ana Valdés recalled, "With everything that we had saved, Frei should have given us an urbanized neighborhood, with electricity, water, sewer services, the lots divided, and street lights, but he only gave us lots that were chalked off; I'll never forget how they were simply chalked off."[69]

The burdens placed on pobladores in this situation were onerous. Residents had to walk several blocks to wells for water or pay inflated prices for water drums.[70] They were also forced to dig their own latrines. In addition, the responsibility for the building of houses fell on individual households, although the pobladores received help from architectural students at the University of Chile and from Communist solidarity campaigns. In theory, a single family occupied each lot. However, extended family members or fictive kin often moved in, at times reproducing the kinds of cramped quarters that many of the pobladores had sought to escape.

Household and neighborhood designs were similar to those in place with low-income government housing programs. The kitchen was a small room where women tended to do the cooking, separated from the living room where meals were eaten.[71] As had happened in other land seizures, Communist neighborhood leaders debated organizing living spaces in more revolutionary forms. One proposal included the creation of a communal kitchen and eating area. However, this was ultimately rejected in favor of the prevailing norms and expectations of what domestic space should be. This happened in a number of cases. Following a different land seizure, a neighborhood leader explained why the homeless committees decided not to implement the communitarian option: "The integrity of the home and private life is fundamental. [We have] agreed not to have a common kitchen [olla común]. Each mother will prepare, as is the custom, the food for her children. . . . With good will, family intimacy can prevail."[72]

But despite general agreement among the campamento's residents about how the spatial development of the neighborhood should unfold and the effort that they had put into constructing it, they were unable to establish a neighborhood they considered acceptable. The government did not provide basic services for the campamento, prompting renewed activism on the part of the pobladores.[73] After Allende became president, government planners proposed apartment buildings as the way to transform the campamento. Nevertheless, the pobladores, as they did in several other cases, rejected this solution, preferring single-family homes. By the time of the military coup, the construction of the neighborhood's infrastructure had still not been completed.

LEGACIES AND IMPLICATIONS

Such an anticlimactic conclusion to the mobilization of the homeless pobladores in the May Day land seizure was not an isolated experience. While pobladores throughout Chile's urban areas became particularly visible actors on the national scene before the military coup, seizing, as one author has described it, their place,[74] they could neither entirely change the stages on which they acted nor the roles that they played. If they were able to ensure that state functionaries would listen to their demands for housing and urban services, they were nevertheless often stuck within a setting that did not let them realize their desire to leave the margins and act as full citizens. Government bureaucracies were not able to provide the services and infrastructure that the pobladores demanded, even if there was a general consensus that they should have.

In many cases, as in the May Day land seizure, the pobladores, rather than ceasing to be homeless, found themselves in unfinished settlements without property titles when the military dictatorship came to power on September 11, 1973. At that moment, the outpouring of militant activism among the pobladores of Santiago came to an abrupt end. For its part, the dictatorship targeted campamentos as both hotbeds of Marxist "subversion" and as areas that needed to be "developed" and "modernized" through the provision of property titles and infrastructure services. Pobladores would disproportionately suffer the human rights abuses of the dictatorship, particularly in neighborhoods known for leftist political activism.[75] In the May Day campamento, this kind of violence upset the tenuous cohesion and forms of solidarity that residents had established, as agents from the dictatorship arrested, tortured, and disappeared several neighborhood leaders and activists.

Yet even as the dictatorship violently altered the sociopolitical terrain, it sought to provide property titles and infrastructure services to residents in campamentos. In the May Day Campamento (renamed Huamachuco I after the coup), residents received basic urban services in 1981 as a part of what the military regime called "targeted" spending policies. The Inter-American Development Bank provided many of the funds for the project, an indication of the transnational support that the dictatorship's property-titling programs received.[76] Some of the dictatorship's efforts, in fact, have become models for neoliberal policies in poverty reduction. Importantly, the governments of the postdictatorship democracy have broadened these policies. Partially as a result of this, by 2000, more than 95 percent of the dwellings in Santiago had property titles and access to basic infrastructure services, when less than 70 percent did so in 1960.[77]

Such a transformation has taken place within Chile's vaunted economic "miracle" of the 1990s, but it is only partially due to the targeted spending policies and the uneven, if at times dizzying expansion of the neoliberal period. The insurgent activism among the pobladores in the late 1960s and early 1970s helped to ensure that urban homeownership was understood as a central obligation of the Chilean state. The celebrants of Chile's neoliberal policies in poverty reduction fail to recognize this legacy of collective action.

It is also the kind of history that proponents of property-titling policies, such as Hernando de Soto, overlook. In an odd, almost farcical echo of the marginality school, de Soto argues that legalizing the land tenure of the urban poor will bring them in from the margins of legal and economic structures. Making the urban poor homeowners will give them greater security and make both themselves and society at large wealthier. Through the formalization of their economic relationships and properties, the urban poor will suddenly have access to what de Soto calls "dead capital," wealth that is now kept off of the books.[78] Unlike the marginality school, de Soto does not stigmatize the negative personality traits of the urban poor. Instead, he rather simplistically celebrates their ingenuity and entrepreneurialism in developing informal economic relationships under strain and uncertainty.[79] In doing so, de Soto essentializes the urban poor as a singular kind of subject, making them out to be repressed capitalists. He thus represents a perspective attuned to the market-centered approaches of neoliberal development.

He nevertheless shares with the marginality school a normalizing vision that sees the creation of formalized socioeconomic relationships and property ownership as the ultimate path toward development. Furthermore, de Soto only partially embeds homeownership in broader socioeconomic and political relations, as he sees little in homeownership beyond its potential for generating wealth. He thus has little to say about the ways in which the volatility, disruptions, and speculative processes in market relations impact property holding. He has even less to say about the forms of subjectivity and power that property relations entail.

In developing a perspective that seeks to take these dynamics into account, this chapter offers a more cautionary, broader view of property holding and its relationship to the urban poor.[80] As the squatters in Chile struggled to gain access to housing and homeownership, they did, in certain respects, bring themselves in from the margins of citizenship and social acceptability. They came to have homes of their own, fundamentally altering patterns of settlement and residence in the city. They developed more-secure living conditions in which they were often better able to plan for the future. Yet the squatters were only successful if they conformed to the practices and expectations of propriety embedded in state frameworks and social relations.

The struggles that the squatters took part in were often tense and dangerous; they faced social sanction, state repression, and trying circumstances. Today pobladores still encounter a number of tensions and difficulties, in spite of their general success in gaining access to property. Living in one of the most inequitable countries in Latin America, pobladores generally remain a stigmatized social group, especially as the dictatorship's property-titling and slum-removal policies heightened socioeconomic segregation in Santiago.[81] To an important degree, pobladores are often still consigned to the margins of socioeconomic and political life. Pobladores tend to live in very particular, clearly demarcated areas of the city. They suffer from much higher rates of unemployment and underemployment than the rest of the Chilean population, particularly during periods of recession.

Pobladores also still face similar pressures to the ones that led them to break the law in the land seizures. I came to understand this more clearly after getting to know Alexi Martínez, an unemployed, thirty-year-old father of two.[82] Having been unable to afford his own home, Martínez lived with his in-laws in a legally sanctioned neighborhood with property titles. The neighborhood had first been established in 1973 through a land seizure sponsored by the Movimiento de Izquierda Revolucionaria (Movement of the Revolutionary Left). Martínez shared a small room and bunk bed with his wife and children. Six others shared the rest of the house: two bedrooms, a kitchen, a bathroom, and a dining and living room area.

Martínez often expressed frustration to me about the sporadic and insecure jobs he had been able to find. He had worked for some time as a landscaper and later he worked in construction. But he had broken his wrist while riding home on his bicycle from his construction job and, lacking health-care coverage, did not have his wrist set properly. He now found it difficult to do manual labor. After his injury, some friends of his approached him with a different opportunity for making money. Saying that they wanted to "look out for the people of the *pueblo* [town]," they asked Martínez if he'd like to join them in robberies in wealthier sections of Santiago. "They knew

I was unemployed and fed up [*choreado*] and that I had two kids," Martínez recalled. "They wanted to help me. They told me, 'You can make a lot of money and they're only the snobby rich [*cuicos*].'"

Martínez's acquaintances sought to justify their actions by making a moral argument. To a degree, their arguments were reminiscent of the ones that pobladores had used in taking part in the land seizures. These men claimed that they were ultimately trying to support people like Martínez, a young father who was struggling to provide for his family. According to this logic, Martínez had the right to transgress certain moral and legal frameworks because the socioeconomic context had not allowed him to properly care for his family. For Martínez, however, these arguments crossed a line. As a former soldier, Martínez had a rather firm sense of discipline and propriety. Taking part in this kind of criminal activity was an inappropriate way to support his family.

But Martínez remained unemployed, frustrated by his marginalization and living conditions. He was also homeless by Chilean standards, even though he lived in a home that, for several decades, had been a legally sanctioned property. Martínez had entered a subsidized-housing program, receiving priority because of his homeless status. But since he did not have a job, he had not been able to put together the savings needed to receive housing. He also generally did not have the option to join others to demand housing, because the forms of housing activism that had taken place before the coup had generally not reappeared. Martínez's ability to form a home that he considered appropriate seemed to be beyond his means.

Yet the pressure and the desire to do so were there, underscoring a tense gap between sensibilities of appropriate living conditions and actual experience. If hundreds of thousands of pobladores in Chile now live in legally established properties, they do not necessarily occupy homes and living conditions that offer full inclusion and fulfillment. For many, social suffering continues in the margins of urban life. Both the marginality school and contemporary proponents of property titling offer few edifying solutions to the kinds of circumstances that Martínez faces.

Yet even though the marginality school is now legitimately known for its errors and constricted vision, it did focus attention on the often troubled and tense margins of social life in urban Latin America. Roger Vekemans, one of the marginality school's most important figures, claimed that the study of marginality was, before anything else, an effort to overcome "misery" and unacceptable living conditions. To my knowledge, no critic of the marginality school has picked up on this imperative. But perhaps a better understanding of both the making and the consequences of urban marginality—in all of its guises—could offer a way to do just that.

NOTES

I dedicate this piece to Fernando Coronil, who died in August 2011. As part of his commitment to being a politically engaged scholar, Coronil developed an analytical approach that sought to expose forms of subalternity and social marginality in an effort to make their existence at once more intelligible and more intolerable.

1. See Janice E. Perlman, *The Myth of Marginality: Urban Poverty and Politics in Rio de Janeiro* (Berkeley: University of California Press, 1976); and Alejandro Portes, "Urbanization and Politics in Latin America," *Social Science Quarterly* 52, no. 3 (1971). Oscar Lewis famously coined the term *culture of poverty*, most explicitly spelled out in his article "The Culture of Poverty," in Oscar Lewis, *Anthropological Essays* (New York: Random House, 1970), 67–80.

2. See Manuel Castells, *The City and the Grassroots: A Cross-Cultural Theory of Urban Social Movements* (London: E. Arnold; Berkeley: University of California Press, 1983), 175–212; and Perlman, *The Myth of Marginality*. See also David Harvey, *Paris: Capital of Modernity* (New York: Routledge, 2003), 23–58. Harvey argues that failing to recognize informal labor power, including work in the home, is a fundamental "myth of modernity."

3. Brodwyn M. Fischer, *A Poverty of Rights: Citizenship and Inequality in Twentieth-Century Rio de Janeiro* (Stanford, CA: Stanford University Press, 2008); Daniel Goldstein, *The Spectacular City: Violence and Performance in Urban Bolivia* (Durham, NC: Duke University Press, 2004); and James Holston, *Insurgent Citizenship: Disjunctions of Democracy and Modernity in Brazil* (Princeton, NJ: Princeton University Press, 2008).

4. Rosemary Bromley, "Introduction: The Urban Informal Sector; Why Is It Worth Discussing?," *World Development* 6, nos. 9–10 (1978); Fischer, *A Poverty of Rights*, 219–52; Holston, *Insurgent Citizenship*; Alejandro Portes, Manuel Castells, and Lauren A. Benton, *The Informal Economy: Studies in Advanced and Less Developed Countries* (Baltimore, MD: Johns Hopkins University Press, 1989); Javier Auyero, *Poor People's Politics: Peronist Survival Networks and the Legacy of Evita* (Durham, NC: Duke University Press, 2001).

5. José Nun has discussed this theme since the 1960s. For an overview that emphasizes the present context, see José Nun, "The End of Work and the 'Marginal Mass' Thesis," *Latin American Perspectives* 27, no. 1 (2000).

6. Numerous scholars, working in Latin America and elsewhere, have pointed to these developments. For general views, see David Harvey, *The Condition of Postmodernity: An Enquiry into the Origins of Cultural Change* (Oxford: Blackwell, 1990); and Loïc Wacquant, *Urban Outcasts: A Comparative Sociology of Advanced Margin-*

ality (Cambridge, UK: Polity, 2008). For Latin America, see, among others, Teresa Pires do Rio Caldeira, *City of Walls: Crime, Segregation, and Citizenship in São Paulo* (Berkeley: University of California Press, 2000); Peter Ward, "Introduction and Overview: Marginality Then and Now," *Latin American Research Review* 39, no. 1 (2004). For connections between Latin America and the United States, see Javier Auyero, "Researching the Urban Margins: What Can the United States Learn from Latin America and Vice Versa?," *City and Community* 10, no. 4 (2011).

7. For a breakdown of these figures, see Edward Murphy, "A Home of One's Own: Finding a Place in the Fractured Landscape of Urban Chile," PhD dissertation, University of Michigan, 2006, 43.

8. Carol Rose, *Property and Persuasion: Essays on the History, Theory, and Rhetoric of Ownership* (Boulder, CO: Westview Press, 1994); Rachel Sturman, "Property and Attachments: Defining Autonomy and the Claims of Family in Nineteenth-Century Western India," *Comparative Studies in Society and History* 47, no. 3 (2005); and Katherine Verdery, *The Vanishing Hectare: Property and Value in Postcolonial Transylvania* (Ithaca, NY: Cornell University Press, 2003), 15–20.

9. On insurgent forms of citizenship, see Greg Grandin, *The Last Colonial Massacre* (Chicago: University of Chicago Press, 2004), chapter 5; Holston, *Insurgent Citizenship*.

10. My argument that the urban poor have developed legally accepted forms of land tenure in much of Latin America is based on a burgeoning number of cases in the region, although more work needs to be done in this area. See, however, Goldstein, *The Spectacular City*, 90–133; Holston, *Insurgent Citizenship*; Auyero, *Poor People's Politics*, 45–79; Edward Murphy, "Developing Sustainable Peripheries: The Limits of Citizenship in Guatemala City," *Latin American Perspectives* 31, no. 6 (2004); Skrabut, "Recognizing (Dis)order: Topographies of Power and Property in Lima's Periphery," in *The Housing Question: Tensions, Continuities, and Contingencies in the Modern City*, edited by Edward Murphy and Najib Hourani (London: Ashgate, 2013); and in this volume, Duhau, McCann, and Rodgers. It is important to stress, however, that this process is not inevitable and does not unfold in a linear fashion. Economic crises and neoliberal restructuring have also led to an increase in squatting and illegal forms of tenure, as Auyero, this volume, demonstrates in the case of Argentina.

11. Paul Rabinow, *French Modern: Norms and Forms of the Social Environment* (Cambridge, MA: MIT Press, 1989).

12. Raymond Williams, *The Country and the City* (New York: Oxford University Press, 1973). See also Julie Skurski and Fernando Coronil, "Country and City in a Postcolonial Landscape: Double Discourse and the Geo-politics of Truth in Latin America," in *Views beyond the Border Country: Raymond Williams and Cultural Politics*, edited by Dennis Dworkin and Leslie Roman (New York: Routledge, 1992).

13. Fischer, this volume, develops the importance of these misunderstandings in the Brazilian context.

14. See Javier Auyero, "'This Is a Lot Like the Bronx, Isn't It?': Lived Experiences

of Marginality in an Argentine Slum," *International Journal of Urban and Regional Research* 23, no. 1 (1999); Nun, "The End of Work and the 'Marginal Mass' Thesis"; and Wacquant, *Urban Outcasts*.

15. On Chile, the Alliance for Progress, and the Christian Democratic platform, see Jadwiga Pieper Mooney, *The Politics of Motherhood: Maternity and Women's Rights in Twentieth-Century Chile* (Pittsburgh, PA: University of Pittsburgh Press, 2009), 74–101; Paul Sigmund, *The United States and Democracy in Chile* (Baltimore, MD: Johns Hopkins University Press, 1993), 11–47; and Heidi Tinsman, *Partners in Conflict: The Politics of Gender, Sexuality and Labor in the Chilean Agrarian Reform* (Durham, NC: Duke University Press, 2002), 82–127.

16. For the assumptions and goals of Popular Promotion, see Centro para el Desarrollo Económico y Social de América Latina, *Aportes para un programa de promoción popular* (Santiago: Centro para el Desarrollo Económico y Social de América Latina, 1966); and Roger Vekemans and Ramón Venegas "Marginalidad y Promoción Popular," *Mensage*, no. 149 (1966).

17. See Peter Cleaves, *Bureaucratic Politics and Administration in Chile* (Berkeley: University of California Press, 1974), 201; Peter Cleaves, *Developmental Processes in Chilean Local Government* (Berkeley: Institute of International Studies, 1969), 55; and oficio 7763 in Archivo de la Administración, Ministerio de Vivienda y Urbanismo, Oficios con Antecedentes (hereafter ADA, MINVU OA), May/June/July 1966, Santiago, Chile.

18. Cleaves, *Bureaucratic Politics and Administration in Chile*, 217. On the overall importance of housing reforms in the Americas during the 1960s, see Leandro Benmergui, "The Alliance for Progress and Housing Policy in Rio de Janeiro and Buenos Aires in the 1960s," *Urban History* 36, no. 2 (2009).

19. "360,000 viviendas se construirán en seis años," *La Nación*, December 6, 1964, 15.

20. For one revealing example of the criticisms launched by leftists, see Orlando Millas's intervention in the Chamber of Deputies in Chile: Cámara de Diputados, *Boletín de las sesiones ordinarias* (Santiago: Congreso Nacional Cámara de Diputados), June 16, 1965, 1073–74.

21. "No se trata de crear hileras de casas a lo largo de una calle sin pavimento, sino de construir barrios donde la familia pueda desenvolverse con dignidad," *El Diario Ilustrado*, November 4, 1964, 35.

22. ADA, MINVU OA, January 1968, letter from J. Eduardo Truyol Díaz to the president of the directorate of the población Canihuante, Ovalle, January 5, 1968.

23. Secretaría General del Censo Dirección General de Estadística, *XII censo general de población y I de vivienda: Levantado el 24 de Abril de 1952* (Santiago: Instituto Nacional de Estadísticas, 1953), v–vi.

24. These three valences demonstrate how conceptions of health and cleanliness presume organization and regulation, a connection that Michel Foucault, in *The Birth of the Clinic* (New York: Vintage Books, 1975), develops. Richard Sennett,

Flesh and Stone: The Body and the City in Western Civilization (New York: W. W. Norton, 1994), 255–316, has explicitly analyzed this discursive formation in the case of modern urban planning and spatial practices.

25. In different contexts, Georges Canguilhem, *The Normal and the Pathological* (New York: Zone Books, 1991), and Susan Sontag, *Illness as Metaphor: AIDS and Its Metaphors* (New York: Doubleday, 1990), each analyze the social effects that these kinds of metaphors can have.

26. Cámara de Diputados, *Boletín de las sesiones ordinarias*, June 16, 1965, 1068.

27. Cámara de Diputados, *Boletín de las sesiones ordinarias*, June 16, 1965, 1069.

28. Departamento de Publicaciones Presidencia de la República, *Sexto mensaje del presidente de la República de Chile don Eduardo Frei Montalva al inaugurar el período de sesiones ordinarias del Congreso Nacional* (Santiago: Departamento de Publicaciones Presidencia de la República, 1970), 148. Arturo Valenzuela, in *The Breakdown of Democratic Regimes* (Baltimore, MD: Johns Hopkins University Press, 1978), notes these figures are probably overstated (33).

29. These efforts deepened efforts that Arturo Alessandri's conservative administration (1958–64) had already made to turn pobladores into homeowners.

30. Castells, *The City and the Grassroots*, 175–212, offers a synthetic critique along these lines.

31. Among others, Michael Latham in *Modernization as Ideology: American Social Science and "Nation Building" in the Kennedy Era* (Chapel Hill: University of North Carolina Press, 2000), criticizes the teleological assumptions of modernization theory. Arturo Escobar, in *Encountering Development: The Making and Unmaking of the Third World* (Princeton, NJ: Princeton University Press, 1995), and María Josefina Saldaña-Portillo, in *The Revolutionary Imagination in the Americas and the Age of Development* (Durham, NC: Duke University Press, 2003), 3–59, underscore the hierarchical sensibilities and forms of subjectivity embedded in modernization theory and discourses of development.

32. These suppositions overlapped with Oscar Lewis's ideas about a culture of poverty. Karin Rosemblatt, in "Other Americas: Transnationalism, Scholarship, and the Culture of Poverty in Mexico and the United States," *Hispanic American Historical Review* 89, no. 4 (2009), explores how the culture-of-poverty thesis traveled between the United States and Mexico.

33. Manuel Castells, *La lucha de clases en Chile* (México: Siglo Veintiuno Editores, 1975), 266.

34. Luis Bravo-Heitman, "Retrospectiva de 50 años de vivienda social," in *Chile: 50 años de vivienda social, 1943–1993*, edited by Luis Bravo-Heitman and Carlos Martínez Corbella (Valparaíso: Universidade de Valparaíso, Facultad de Arquitectura, 1993), 45.

35. Dirección General de Planificación y Presupuesto Ministerio de la Vivienda y Urbanismo, *Política habitacional del Gobierno Popular: Programa 1972* (Santiago: Editorial Universitaria, 1972), 23.

36. Rosemond Cheetham, "El sector privado de la construcción: Patrón de dominación," *Revista Latinoamericana de Estudios Urbanos Regionales (EURE)* 1, no. 3 (1971); and Cleaves, *Bureaucratic Politics and Administration*, 234–73.

37. Equipo de Estudios Poblacionales, Centro de Investigaciones del Desarrollo Urbano y Regional, "Reivindicación urbana y lucha política: Los campamentos de pobladores en Santiago de Chile," *Revista Latinoamericana de Estudios Urbanos Regionales (EURE)* 2, no. 6 (1972): 55.

38. Equipo de Estudios Poblacionales, Centro de Investigaciones del Desarrollo Urbano y Regional, "Reivindicación urbana y lucha política," 55. On the increase in rent, at least until 1966, see the September 28, 1966, letter in ADA, MINVU OA, October–December 1966.

39. See the correspondence between four neighborhood council leaders and the minister of housing and urbanism in ADA, MINVU OA, July 1969.

40. Homeless committees often complained about this tendency, as one did in a letter dated March 8, 1967, in ADA, MINVU OA, April 1967.

41. On the massacre in Puerto Montt and the ensuing scandal, see Mario Garcés, *Tomando su sitio: El movimiento de pobladores de Santiago, 1957–1970* (Santiago: LOM, 2002), 370–81.

42. For an important early statement on state fetishism, see Michael Taussig, "Maleficium: State Fetishism," in *Fetishism as Cultural Discourse*, edited by Emily Apter and William Pietz (Ithaca, NY: Cornell University Press, 1993).

43. Valdés's edited testimonial appears in Edward Murphy, *Historias poblacionales: Hacia una memoria incluyente* (Santiago: CEDECO, 2004), 39–65. (Further citations to this work also refer to testimonials I gathered in an oral history project.)

44. Karin Rosemblatt, *Gendered Compromises: Political Cultures and the State in Chile, 1920–1950* (Chapel Hill: University of North Carolina Press, 2000); and Karin Rosemblatt, "Por un hogar bien constituido: El estado y su política familiar en los Frentes Populares," in *Disciplina y desacato: Construcción de identidad en Chile, siglos XIX y XX*, edited by Lorena Godoy and Corinne Antezana-Pernet (Santiago: SUR / CEDEM, 1995).

45. Deborah Poole, "Between Threat and Guarantee: Justice and Community in the Margins of the Peruvian State," in *Anthropology in the Margins of the State*, edited by Veena Das and Deborah Poole (Santa Fe, NM: School of American Research Press, 2004), explores the importance of threat in processes at the margins of the state.

46. Many have developed how processes of inclusion and exclusion construct the boundaries of citizenship. Consult, among others, James Holston and Arjun Appadurai, "Cities and Citizenship," in *Cities and Citizenship*, edited by James Holston (Durham, NC: Duke University Press, 1999). It should be noted that this is an exclusion from the rights of citizenship, not from the reach of the state's power. Citizens excluded from certain rights are often the most vulnerable to the state's sovereign power.

47. For historical perspectives on urban land seizures between 1947 and 1970, see

Brenda Elsey, *Citizens and Sportsmen: Fútbol and Politics in Twentieth-Century Chile* (Austin: University of Texas Press, 2011); Vicente Espinoza, *Para una historia de los pobres de la ciudad* (Santiago: Ediciones Sur, 1998), 185–355; Mario Garcés, *Historia de la comuna de Huechuraba: Memoria y oralidad popular urbana* (Santiago: ECO, Educación y Comunicaciones, 1997); and Garcés, *Tomando su sitio*.

48. Marín's comments can be found in "Impresionante asamblea: Pobladores de Renca protestaron contra tramitación del Gobierno," *El Siglo*, April 29, 1969, 4.

49. Murphy, *Historias poblacionales*, 34.

50. Juan Hamilton, the minister of housing and urbanism, states this policy in a letter in ADA, MINVU OA, April 1967.

51. Oficio 345 outlines the stipulations in ADA, MINVU OA, April 1967.

52. See the legislation that established the neighborhood councils in the Biblioteca del Congreso, *Historia de la Ley 16.880, Ley sobre Juntas de Vecinos y demás Organizaciones Comunitarias*, 10–21.

53. Murphy, *Historias poblacionales*, 28. For similar statements, see the comments of a pobladora in the testimonial provided in Garcés, *Historia de la comuna de Huechuraba*, 90.

54. Female activism, whether leftist or reactionary, often followed this logic. Consult, among others, Mooney, *The Politics of Motherhood*; Margaret Power, *Right-Wing Women in Chile: Feminine Power and the Struggle against Allende, 1964–1973* (University Park: Pennsylvania State University Press, 2002); and Tinsman, *Partners in Conflict*.

55. "Impresionante asamblea: Pobladores de Renca protestaron contra tramitación del gobierno," *El Siglo*, April 29, 1969, 4.

56. "Pobladores de Renca se tomaron terrenos donde vivir," *El Siglo*, May 2, 1969, 3.

57. Ligia Balladares S., "Hablan los Sin Casa de Renca: 'No podemos seguir viviendo como perros,'" *El Siglo*, May 2, 1969, 7.

58. "Pobladores de Renca se tomaron terrenos donde vivir," *El Siglo*, May 2, 1969, 3.

59. "Encuestarán a pobladores que ocuparon terrenos en Renca," *El Diario Ilustrado*, May 3, 1969, 3.

60. "Encuestarán a pobladores que ocuparon terrenos en Renca," *El Diario Ilustrado*, May 3, 1969, 3. For a similar survey in another case, see Cleaves, *Bureaucratic Politics and Administration in Chile*, 293.

61. "Pobladores de Renca se tomaron terrenos donde vivir," *El Siglo*, May 2, 1969, 3. Homeless committees often asked that surveys be taken, as shown in the letter dated September 22, 1970, in ADA, MINVU OA, September/October 1970.

62. Behind the scenes, the housing minister agreed to buy the property from the landowners.

63. See "Comité de Pobladores de Renca pide nuevos sitios para vivir," *La Nación*, August 30, 1969, 2, and the June 17, 1969, letter in ADA, MINVU OA, March 1970.

64. See, for example, the March 3, 1970, letter in ADA, MINVU OA, March 1970.

65. Oficio 2262 in ADA, MINVU OA, March 1970. In this letter, an MINVU official explains how MINVU and local leaders had removed "the most serious cases" from the May Day Campamento.

66. Housing officials explain this policy in oficio 859, ADA, MINVU OA, September 1967; and oficio interno 485, ADA, MINVU OA, July 1967.

67. Murphy, *Historias poblacionales*, 33.

68. For other examples, see the testimonial in Ernesto Pastrana and Mónica Threlfall, *Pan, techo, y poder: El movimiento de pobladores en Chile, 1970–73* (Buenos Aires: Ediciones Siap-Planteos, 1974), 74–76; and Erika Cereño's testimonial in Murphy, *Historias poblacionales*, 101. Rosemblatt, *Gendered Compromises*, describes how leftist activists sought strikingly similar goals in the 1930s and 1940s.

69. Murphy, *Historias poblacionales*, 42–43.

70. As the oficio dated March 26, 1970, in ADA, MINVU OA, May 1970, discusses, bottled-water distributors often took advantage of the situation that pobladores in campamentos faced by overcharging.

71. For similar descriptions in other neighborhoods, both in the city and in the countryside, see Castells, *The City and the Grassroots*, 202; and Tinsman, *Partners in Conflict*, 186.

72. Virginia Vidal, "Toma de terreno de los Sin Casa de Barrancas: Operación dignidad," *El Siglo*, March 21, 1967, 7. For another similar case, see Equipo de Estudios Poblacionales, Centro de Investigaciones del Desarrollo Urbano y Regional, "Reivindicación urbana y lucha política," 64.

73. October 3, 1969, letter in ADA, MINVU OA, October 1969.

74. Garcés, *Tomando su sitio*.

75. A careful reading of National Commission on Truth and Reconciliation, *Report of the Chilean National Commission on Truth and Reconciliation* (Notre Dame, IN: University of Notre Dame Press, 1993) reveals this. See also Corporación José Domingo Cañas 1367, *Tortura en poblaciones del Gran Santiago (1973–1990): Colectivo de memoria histórica* (Santiago: Corporación José Domingo Cañas, 2005).

76. See Municipalidad de Renca, Dirección de Obras, *Antecedentes de Huamachuco I*.

77. For 1960, I have determined this number based on data in the second national census of housing, available in Dirección de Estadística y Censos, *II censo de vivienda 1960: Resumen país; Levantado el 24 de Abril de año 1952* (Santiago: Instituto Nacional de Estadísticas, 1960). For 2000, see Ministerio de Planificación y Cooperación, CASEN, *encuesta de caracterización socioeconómica nacional 2000* (Santiago: Ministerio de Planificación y Cooperación, 2002), chart 8.1. Note that these statistics refer only to the fact that the dwellings are legally owned. The occupants themselves are, in many cases, renters and do not have property titles.

78. Hernando de Soto, "Foreword," in *A Possible Way Out: Formalizing Housing Informality in Egyptian Cities*, edited by Ahmed Soliman and Hernando de Soto (Lanham, MD: University Press of America, 2004).

79. Hernando de Soto, *The Mysteries of Capital: Why Capitalism Triumphs in the*

West and Fails Everywhere Else (New York: Basic Books, 2000). For an insightful critique, see Timothy Mitchell, "The Work of Economics: How a Discipline Makes Its World," *European Journal of Sociology / Archives Européennes de Sociologie* 46, no. 2 (2005).

80. My approach to property draws on C. M. Hann's call to view property as embedded. See C. M. Hann, "Introduction: The Embeddedness of Property," in *Property Relations: Renewing an Anthropological Tradition*, edited by C. M. Hann, 1–47 (Cambridge: University of Cambridge Press, 1998).

81. Eduardo Morales and Sergio Rojas, "Relocalización socio-espacial de la pobreza: Política estatal y presión popular, 1979–1985," in *Espacio y poder: Los pobladores*, edited by Jorge Chateau (Santiago: FLACSO, 1987).

82. The name is a pseudonym.

THREE

Troubled Oasis

THE INTERTWINING HISTORIES OF THE
MORRO DOS CABRITOS AND BAIRRO PEIXOTO

Bryan McCann

The favela known as the Morro dos Cabritos (Hill of Goats) and Bairro Peixoto, the middle-class residential neighborhood nestled in the crook of that great curving hillside, have been tethered in an awkward three-legged race since the early twentieth century. For a brief moment in the late 1970s and early 1980s, they established a mutually acceptable rhythm and hit their stride. While some of the gains of that period linger, their subsequent return to an ungainly stagger reveals the extent of the larger challenges facing favela residents and their neighbors over the past decades. Even in this case, marked by unusual levels of goodwill and benign planning, larger forces dictating the separation between favela and *bairro* (neighborhood) have prevailed. The patterns of middle-class involution on one hand and increasing territorial control by criminal interest groups on the other have not been as drastic here as in many cases, but they not been absent. Residents of these neighborhoods share space, but they do so by following largely unspoken agreements about the limits to that sharing.

A new security strategy implemented by the state government in 2010 seeks to drive the drug traffic out of the Morro dos Cabritos, or at the very least to eliminate the drug gang's ability to control and exploit territory. The outcome of this new strategy is impossible to assess, but even in its early stages the program has revived both hopes of greater favela-bairro integration and trepidation about the consequences of that integration. Only a long historical assessment of the vexed relationship between these two adjacent neighborhoods can illuminate the current aspirations and anxieties.

ORIGINS OF FAVELA AND BAIRRO

For most of the nineteenth century, the only way to get to Copacabana beach from downtown Rio de Janeiro was to trek over the steep hills that form a natural barrier around Copacabana. The easiest pass was the Ladeira do Barroso, which led over the hill from Botafogo toward the midsection of Copacabana's long, curving waterfront. Beach going had not yet become a definitive aspect of everyday Carioca life, and Copacabana itself was largely unsettled. But the striking Atlantic exposure inspired a broad range of visitors to make the journey, including Emperor Dom Pedro II, who on several occasions was shuttled over the *ladeira* (incline) in an imperial carriage to survey the view of Copacabana.

Imperial visits helped generate further traffic, some commerce, and at least temporary settlements on the Ladeira do Barroso. Many current residents of the Morro dos Cabritos understand this to be the origination of the favela. Villa Rica, the name of the local *bloco* (Carnival parade band) was meant to allude to this imperial connection. While the place-name Villa Rica was indeed associated with this vantage point on the old ladeira well before the foundation of the bloco in the 1960s, there is no solid evidence of continued settlement from the days of the late empire.

Instead, the initial nucleus of homes built on the hill's flank dates from a more recent source, one typical of early favela growth. The demise of the empire in 1889 and the inauguration of the republic that followed initiated an era of rapid transformations in Rio de Janeiro. While the republican government initiated massive projects to reform downtown Rio de Janeiro—expanding avenues, clearing tenements, and constructing majestic civic buildings—private investors expanded settlement in outlying areas. A consortium of real-estate entrepreneurs and the owners of a trolley company opened a tunnel under the Ladeira do Barroso in 1892. The tunnel connected residential Botafogo with the still largely unsettled Copacabana, opening the region for real-estate development along a new trolley line (see map 3.1).[1]

The tunnel made the Ladeira do Barroso obsolete as a travel route but increased its practicality for development. Residential real-estate investment inevitably focused on the beachfront properties, leaving the hill available for other enterprises. In 1904 the Brazilian Navy opened a hospital on the site, designed primarily to treat sailors for beriberi. Informal settlement grew around the hospital, in a manner typical of Rio's large institutions in this period. Functionaries of the hospital were permitted to build shelters on

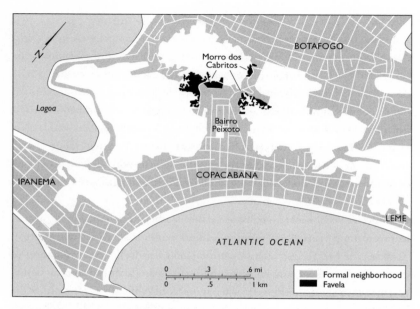

MAP 3.1 · The location of Bairro Peixoto and Morro dos Cabritos in the South Zone of Rio de Janeiro, surrounded by well-to-do neighborhoods.

surrounding grounds and used these to house themselves and their families in a process of slow but inexorable accretion. This was by no means worker housing of an organized sort—settlement was tolerated, not directed, but it obeyed the codes of institutionalized patronage and responded to the exigencies of a labor environment where subsistence-level wages required a workforce living in the immediate vicinity without paying rent.[2]

This nucleus of informal housing grew among extended families of hospital workers, and then among a larger network, spreading down a road that stretched behind the hospital and along the hill to the west. When the hospital relocated to the northern suburbs during World War II, it eliminated the initial source of local employment, but this decision also removed the only practical restraint on expanding settlement. By the 1940s, residents could look to the growing middle-class developments of Copacabana for employment in the service sector, and the Morro dos Cabritos grew in response to that demand.[3]

Meanwhile, formal housing and commerce grew along Rua Siqueira Campos, one of the avenues leading out of the tunnel. The blocks closest to the tunnel had the lowest value, and were not an immediate target for middle-class real-estate investment. Instead, merchants and service providers opened storefronts along this stretch. These were part of the formal urban grid, recognized on property deeds, bought and sold on the legal real-estate market. But the rear boundaries of the properties, on the east side of Siqueira Campos abutting the hill, tended to be poorly defined at best. Several property owners along Siqueira Campos opened *vilas* on their back lots—clusters of homes or a single, small tenement house designed for a working-class rental market. These vilas backed up on to the lower stretches of the old Ladeira do Barroso, which had become known as the Ladeira dos Tabajaras, for reasons not entirely clear—certainly no Tabajara Indians had inhabited the region for many decades. In some cases, administration of these vilas eventually passed on to third parties who claimed authority to extract rents from vila residents, even where their connection with legal titleholders along Rua Siqueira Campos was dubious to nonexistent. These rent-accruing *grileiros* (illegal land speculators) had every incentive to increase settlement within the zones where they effectively presided.[4]

By the early 1940s, then, there were two distinct generators of informal development on the slopes above Copacabana's broad midsection: the cluster of homes built by former employees of the Naval Hospital and their relatives, and the hillside vilas stretching out from the back of formal addresses on Rua Siqueira Campos and the Ladeira dos Tabajaras.

Meanwhile, middle-class Copacabana quickly outgrew its horizontal and vertical constraints. The opening of the Copacabana Palace Hotel in 1924 made the beach district fashionable and spurred development. Two-story bungalows along the beach gave way to multistory apartment buildings. By the late 1930s, the only significant stretch of unoccupied land in Copacabana lay directly west of Rua Siqueira Campos, in the valley flanked by the half-circle of the Morro dos Cabritos. A Portuguese dry-goods merchant and real-estate speculator by the name of Felisberto Peixoto had purchased these lands in the first years of the twentieth century, and he had leased the fertile stretches to truck farmers. Peixoto had no descendants, and in 1938 he donated the lands to five Catholic Church–affiliated charitable institutions.[5]

The terms of the donation required these institutions to pool their interests in a real-estate development comprising the entire area. Peixoto stipulated the sale of small lots and the construction of homes and apartment buildings of no more than three stories. The charitable institutions hired a planning team to draw up a development plan and submitted it to the city for approval in 1940. The municipal government rejected the plan primarily because it showed no specifications for a large lot at the center of the plot. City planners returned with their own design, based on the original submission, but specifying that the central plot remain undeveloped and protected as a plaza, and projecting an ingenious street grid designed to lead traffic away from the core neighborhood. According to this plan, traffic emerging from the tunnel heading toward the beach would be channeled either along Siqueira Campos on the eastern flank of the development or along Rua Santa Clara, flanking the development on its west side. The smaller streets between these avenues would have limited access to the surrounding traffic grid, and would be strictly residential, in buildings of no more than four stories — stretching the guidelines of Peixoto's original terms by one story.[6]

Development on the borderline avenues of Siqueira Campos and Santa Clara, as well as Rua Tonelero, which ran perpendicular to them on the south side of the neighborhood, would face no height restrictions. Over the next few years, the city extended another avenue, Figueiredo Magalhães, from the beach into the neighborhood. Figueiredo Magalhães ran close to Siqueira Campos and converged with it at the mouth of the tunnel. Development along Figueiredo Magalhães and the triangle between it and Siqueira Campos would also be unrestricted by height. This resulted in a core of small buildings around a protected central space, surrounded by speculative interests pushing for vertical growth.

Real-estate investors christened the new development Bairro Peixoto, and they sold almost all of its plots over the next few years. Construction moved more slowly, but by the early 1950s, most plots were developed, in styles ranging from single-family homes in ersatz Tyrolean architecture to modernist boxes on the concrete pillars known as *pilotis*. The pilotis left a space to be occupied by parked cars, rock gardens, and play areas, and required some tinkering with height limits — stilts added a story without adding residential density. By the early 1950s, the accepted limit on the streets surrounding the plaza was three stories of residential space, plus one story for garage and one for common space. Upward creep would become the defining issue in the middle-class neighborhood over the next two decades.

CONSOLIDATION

Neighbors up the slope faced a vastly different set of issues: they struggled for basic infrastructure and services. As a result of marked differentiation within the favela, this struggle was highly localized. The Ladeira dos Tabajaras began in Copacabana as a formal street, with well-defined property limits and urban services; climbed into a zone of increasing informality; and descended on the other side of the hill in Botafogo, another formal, middle-class neighborhood. Residents of the stretch of the Ladeira closest to the beach did not consider themselves to be living in a favela. They lived in stable structures, had satisfactory infrastructure, and paid monthly rent. Whether the landlords held legal property titles was irrelevant to their daily lives. Farther up the Ladeira, homes were more precarious and infrastructure was often absent. There was no clear boundary between formal and informal on the Ladeira, which created an ambiguity that proved persistent.

Near its crest, the Ladeira intersects with Rua Euclides da Rocha, the road initially created by the Naval Hospital and named for its first director, running west along the hill from the old hospital grounds. In the 1950s, this was a rough dirt road, subject to frequent washouts and not used to deliver any public services. The favela of Morro dos Cabritos spread out along this road. Dirt paths intersecting with Euclides da Rocha and either running up toward the crest or down toward Bairro Peixoto led into separate nuclei of informal housing. These separate nuclei were often home to extended families, and these intimate loyalties shaped the struggle for urban improvements. The nuclei closest to the intersection of the Ladeira were served sooner and better, a pattern that has largely endured. The bloco Villa Rica established its *quadra* (rehearsal space) at this intersection. The Capela, a nucleus that took its name from an abandoned chapel on the hill's flank near this intersection, became the most organized of these microcommunities, and the most successful at lobbying for services. Other nuclei were known by numbers, which indicated the address of the house within each nucleus closest to the street. Living in Euclides 376 was a significant step up from living in Euclides 11: 376 was on the upside of the hill close to the Capela, while 11 was on the downside farther along the slope.[7]

In contrast to many favelas, where the poorest sections are those farthest up the hill, in the Morro dos Cabritos the poorest areas were those below Euclides da Rocha, the odd-numbered nuclei. These were more vulnerable to floods and mudslides, and also faced a more immediate threat of removal. The poorest areas were in the backyards of Bairro Peixoto residents and did not seem likely to withstand the expanding real-estate boom.[8]

The extreme localism of this environment, and the minimal presence of public authority, facilitated the operations of criminal interests in the favela. The notorious burglar Micuçú frequently hid out in the Morro dos

Cabritos before he was gunned down by the police in the early 1960s in the nearby favela of Babilônia. Elizabeth Bishop's poem about the episode, "The Burglar of Babylon," captures many of the details of the uneasy coexistence between Copacabana's middle-class residents and their favela neighbors in the period. In Bishop's poem, the uneasy rich take refuge in their apartment blocks, spying through binoculars on the police operation to capture Micuçú on the hill. The police, disorganized, unprepared, and themselves of humble background, finish the job in violence, gunning down the burglar in view of his family. Throughout the chase, the hill echoes with the sound of children flying kites, the bleating of goats, and the conversation of drinkers at one of the favela's little bars.[9]

In the same years that Micuçú was availing himself of the hideouts of Morro dos Cabritos, residents of Bairro Peixoto had other worries. Carlos Lacerda, who lived just a few blocks away on Rua Tonelero, was the new governor of Guanabara, the city-state created when the federal capital was moved from Rio de Janeiro to Brasília in 1960. Between 1960 and 1975, Guanabara had its own governor, elected for most of the period from a narrow list of candidates approved by the military dictatorship. In 1975 Guanabara was fused with the surrounding state of Rio de Janeiro and ceased to exist as a political unit.

Lacerda was notorious among *favelados* (favela dwellers) for his removal campaigns, which razed several Zona Sul (South Zone) neighborhoods. But it was the residents of middle-class Bairro Peixoto who objected to his immediate development plans. Lacerda proposed construction of a school in the Praça Edmundo Bittencourt, Bairro Peixoto's central plaza. Construction and operation of the school would open the heart of the neighborhood to greatly increased traffic, and in particular to buses. And the school would eliminate the existing uses of the plaza for public leisure and sociability.

The residents of Bairro Peixoto organized to block Lacerda's plans.[10] There were several ironies to this campaign. Middle-class citizens rallied to oppose a politician generally perceived as the bastion of the middle class, himself a neighbor from a nearby apartment building. They did so to prohibit construction of a public school that would have served their own children, but also those of the neighboring favela. In the short term, this preserved the plaza as an implicitly exclusive space of middle-class sociability. But it also allowed for the harmonious cross-class use of this space that unfolded in the 1970s and beyond.

THE SANTA CRUZ YEARS

As in most of Rio de Janeiro, relations between the favela and the adjacent formal neighborhood were uneasy and circumscribed. Bairro Peixoto's residents relied on favelados from the Morro dos Cabritos as maids, cooks, and handymen but had little social contact with them. The one exception, here and elsewhere throughout the city, came in pickup soccer games, both on the beach and in Bairro Peixoto's plaza, where boys from the favela and the middle-class neighborhood mingled more or less freely. These pickup games, fondly remembered though they are, were not a strong enough basis for consistent conviviality, much less common cause.

That began to change in the 1960s, largely due to the arrival of Father Ítalo Coelho, a priest from northeastern Brazil. Like many Brazilian seminarians of his generation, Coelho had embraced the incipient ideas of liberation theology—the blend of gospel and work for social justice, strongly infused with Marxist principles of class-consciousness—taking root in the Brazilian church.

The parish of Santa Cruz da Copacabana in 1960, where Coelho was assigned, did not initially appear to offer a hospitable local environment for liberation theology. Santa Cruz was Latin America's first parish church to be built on top of a shopping center, the Shopping Cidade Copacabana, a three-story mall of swooping modernist curves, inaugurated in 1960. The investors behind the shopping mall had paid handsomely to build on church land and had funded the construction of a sleek chapel on the building's roof, a concrete half-shell with a glass front. The mall and its chapel stood on the corner of a busy intersection two blocks from Bairro Peixoto's quiet central plaza; technically, it was within the bounds of Bairro Peixoto, but the mall shared its character with the neighboring high-rises closer to the beach. Indeed, the chapel shared space on the mall's roof with a six-story apartment building. Everything about Santa Cruz's location and design seemed to orient it toward middle-class, acquisitive Copacabana.

The military coup in 1964 and the increasingly fierce anticommunism of the dictatorship that followed presented Coelho with a further challenge. He responded to these trials in the same way as many of Rio's social activists during the early dictatorship and subsequent generations: by going up the hill to Rio's favelas. In this case, that meant to Ladeira dos Tabajaras and Morro dos Cabritos.

Residents of these informal settlements did not necessarily perceive themselves as joined in common struggle. While the two favelas effectively abutted one another by the early 1960s, their conditions differed. The houses along the Ladeira tended to be in better condition, often made of brick, and were more likely to be occupied by renters who paid monthly sums to self-proclaimed property owners (whose legal claim to the land was, in fact, highly dubious). The houses in Morro dos Cabritos were more likely to be ramshackle structures of scrap wood and mud made by their own residents—although many of these residents paid low monthly rents for the use of the lot where they had built. Both favelas endured severe infrastructural deficiencies—limited or no plumbing, electricity only via an irregular connection with public lines, and no paved access roads. Services were largely nonexistent—no trash pickup, no public health care, no school in either favela, and only minimal access to schools in surrounding neighborhoods. Both faced the same uncertain future: rising real-estate pressures in Copacabana made their perch increasingly valuable, raising prospects of forced removal to make way for apartment buildings targeting middle-class buyers. But the favelas' residents had not previously joined forces.

Coelho understood joint community mobilization to be the fundamental requirement for fighting against removal and demanding greater investment in infrastructure and services. He set about training a staff of lay volunteers to lead this campaign. His tactics did not immediately endear him to favela leadership. Like many of Rio's favelas, the Morro dos Cabritos had a resident's association in the early 1960s that brokered deals with populist politicians, trading votes for concessions such as the installation of a single public water pump and the widening of the dirt access road. When the dictatorship put the brakes on community organizing in the late 1960s, the association largely ceased its activities, leaving in its place only a *comissão de luz* (light commission)—a self-appointed committee of prominent local residents who collected monthly dues from each household, ostensibly to maintain the irregular electric hookup. The members of the light commission were not inspired by Coelho's call for vigorous grass-roots mobilization. The Ladeira dos Tabajaras had no resident's association and initially resisted Coelho's overtures.

He looked to the only civil-society organization that effectively united the Morro dos Cabritos and the Ladeira dos Tabajaras, the Villa Rica samba bloco. By the late 1960s, a cohort of young composers and musicians in Villa Rica were eager to assert a more prominent role within the bloco and to use it as a forum for community discussion and an organ for community mobilization.[11] During the late 1960s and early 1970s, Coelho worked with several of the members of this cohort, bringing them into the activities of the Santa Cruz parish and joining forces with them to respond to needs in the favela. The neighborhood day-care center Cantinho da Natureza, inaugurated in 1973, was one notable result of this collaboration, providing free day care for dozens of working mothers in the community.

The collaboration between Coelho, his lay assistants, and the activists within the Villa Rica bloco also dramatically transformed one of Bairro Peixoto's most prominent civic rituals. Bairro Peixoto had been known for hosting the best *festas juninas* in Rio's Zona Sul since the 1950s. All over Brazil, these annual celebrations of St. John's and St. Peter's Days, usually in late June or early July, featured a romantic re-creation of Brazil's agrarian past, with bonfires, country music, and down-home treats, such as *queijo coalho* (farm cheese toasted on a stick over a charcoal brazier). In the 1960s, Bairro Peixoto's festas had served to knit friendships among the residents of that neighborhood, using the countrified amusements of the festa junina to stage a contrast between the relatively bucolic confines of the neighborhood's central plaza and the surrounding skyscrapers growing in Copacabana, its larger, enveloping district.

Beginning in the early 1970s, Coelho and his cohort invited residents from the Morro dos Cabritos and the Ladeira dos Tabajaras to sell food at the celebration, dedicating part of the profits to the day-care center and other projects. The young *sambistas* (samba musicians) from Villa Rica provided much of the entertainment. By the end of the decade, the famous festa junina was a joint venture between residents of Bairro Peixoto, the Villa Rica bloco, and the Santa Cruz parish church. The annual success of this venture enabled key members of the Villa Rica cohort to win office in a revived residents' association representing the Morro dos Cabritos — now representing the Ladeira dos Tabajaras as well. And Bairro Peixoto also formally organized a new residents' association, led by lay assistants from Santa Cruz. The festas juninas served as the catalyst, the principal fundraising activity, and the most prominent example of increasing cooperation between the middle-class community and its adjacent favela.

This collaboration yielded transformed understandings and uses of public space. Until the mid-1970s, residents of the favela had rarely availed themselves of Bairro Peixoto's central plaza. There was no overt social restriction on use of this space, but in practice its use remained limited to middle-class residents until the collaborative festas juninas became a defining feature of the neighborhood. Until the 1970s, Bairro Peixoto's central plaza was like ostensibly public spaces in much of the formal city—nominally open to all, but in practice open only to those deemed socially acceptable. In the nineteenth century, several downtown plazas had been off-limits to those without shoes, a clear and effective way to ban slaves, who were legally prohibited from wearing shoes. Following abolition in 1888, such overt restrictions disappeared, but unwritten social codes took their place. The poor, and in particular the residents of the favelas, were made to understand where they were not welcome through gestures, glances, and stage whispers. Spaces of middle-class leisure, such as plazas in well-heeled neighborhoods and certain stretches of Zona Sul beaches, were effectively delimited in this fashion for decades.

Those old codes began to break down in the 1970s and 1980s. The movement to bring the long military dictatorship to an end released pressures that undermined social, as well as political, hierarchies. All over the city, and in other parts of Brazil as well, social distinctions once accepted as basic features of everyday life gave way to new challenges. Where Bairro Peixoto seemed to stand out was in the harmonious nature of that process. In contrast to other neighborhoods in Rio de Janeiro, where the proximity of favela and middle class was increasingly uncomfortable, the rapid integration of Bairro Peixoto's plaza did not result in public conflict and left no obvious lingering resentment. Residents of both the Morro dos Cabritos and Bairro Peixoto celebrated this integration as a sign of increasing interdependence.

This difference arose from two factors, the relatively enclosed nature of Bairro Peixoto and the work of political persuasion and transformation undertaken by Coelho and his allies. Vehicular traffic through Bairro Peixoto remained minimal in comparison with surrounding Copacabana, owing to the neighborhood's original design and the vigilance of residents in restricting unwanted development. Residents knew that the integration they were witnessing was circumscribed by geography and happening between neighbors. The second factor was trickier, and sadly less enduring—it depended not only on the dedication of Coelho and the Villa Rica activists but also on the favorable context of redemocratization, when the political future of the nation and the city seemed to be up for grabs.

Subsequent governors of Guanabara and Rio de Janeiro were less overtly committed to favela removal than Lacerda, but they did not shy away from it. Residents of the Morro dos Cabritos had every reason to believe their number was coming up and began to organize to protect their stake. Coelho served as the catalyst for this campaign. Favela residents such as José Luiz Pires, better known as Chimbirra, helped persuade residents to join forces in support of Santa Cruz projects. Building an improved sewage ditch, building concrete stairways to replace dirt paths, and building the day-care center all met immediate needs, strengthened community bonds, and solidified the community's infrastructure, making it a less obvious target for rapid removal.[12]

Chimbirra and Villa Rica allies such as Jorge Marreco and Nelson Marcolino gave the projects the imprimatur of the bloco and made Santa Cruz's endeavors functionally indistinguishable from Villa Rica's for much of the 1970s. Coelho encouraged Chimbirra and his cohort to initiate the process of founding a new residents' association, one that would challenge and supersede the decadent light commission. Santa Cruz's lay assistants proved crucial to nurturing that process; they built the incipient Morro dos Cabritos residents' association into a strong representative body by the late 1970s, a key component in a broad favela association movement unfolding across the city.

In the late 1970s, Coelho won approval from the archbishop of Rio de Janeiro, Eugénio Salles — far from an adept of liberation theology himself, but strongly opposed to favela removal — to create the Pastoral das Favelas, which would minister specifically to the archdiocese's favela population. The Pastoral das Favelas had two wings, the community-mobilizing wing, staffed by lay pastoral assistants, and the judicial wing, staffed by lawyers. The Morro dos Cabritos was the nurturing ground for the first wing and one of the early venues of struggle for the second.

The judicial wing of the Pastoral das Favelas won its first major battle in 1978 by halting a removal of the Vidigal favela that was already in process. Vidigal, overlooking Leblon beach, was a fat target for real-estate investment, and plans for development of the property, postremoval, were already well under way. The pastoral's ability to fend off these powerful interests through political negotiations and savvy legal work made it the key body in the larger struggle to bring the age of favela removal in Rio to an end.

During the same period, the Pastoral das Favelas discovered that another real-estate consortium planned to remove much of the Morro dos Cabritos favela to make room for a massive apartment complex. The consortium included both private developers and Chicaer, the air force's mortgage and real-estate division that was created to provide housing and low-interest mortgages to air force personnel. Chicaer had great leverage within the military dictatorship, but by the late 1970s, redemocratization had already begun; the foundation of the new association in the Morro dos Cabritos, the victory in Vidigal, and the growth of the Pastoral das Favelas were all components of this movement. The pastoral took on Chicaer and its private real-estate partners as steadfastly as it had taken on the Vidigal investors.[13]

Pastoral lawyers used the doctrine of *usucapião* (adverse possession) to demonstrate that the Morro dos Cabritos had been consistently occupied for decades, giving it claims to permanence under Brazilian law. But only individual claimants, not communities, could file for title under the doctrine of adverse possession. The Pastoral das Favelas was reluctant to support the individualization of title in Rio's favelas, believing it would lead to gentrification and removal via the market instead of sudden removal via force. Instead, the lawyers from the judicial wing of the Pastoral das Favelas used the threat of adverse possession to fight off real-estate ventures, while pursuing other tactics of collective mobilization outside of court.[14]

In the case of the Morro dos Cabritos, the lawyers made no attempt to block the construction of the apartment towers, which were within the bounds of Bairro Peixoto, on Rua Henrique Oswald. Instead, they opposed only the plans for private leisure areas behind the apartment towers, on grounds then occupied by the poorest of the Morro dos Cabritos's nuclei. And they insisted that the vast majority of the favela was not close enough to the proposed towers to justify removal.

Chicaer and its partners proposed paying each family in the favela the approximate equivalent of one thousand dollars and giving them housing out in Queimados, in the distant northern periphery, in return for leaving the Morro dos Cabritos. The offer was relatively generous in comparison with those frequently offered by developers in similar circumstances. But in early 1979, the pastoral negotiated a much better deal. Rather than permitting Chicaer to pay off families individually, the deal required payment of a lump sum, to be invested in the community. More important, the deal required Chicaer to fund construction of new housing farther along Euclides da Rocha for all the removed families to make way for the towers and their leisure space. No residents would be driven out of Morro dos Cabritos, and the residents of the worst housing would be given access to new homes. The pastoral team worked with architects and engineers from three local universities to draw up plans for an ingenious complex of duplexes stretching up the hill, to be built through a combination of communal labor and professional help. The residents of these duplexes would then be granted legal title in a way that recognized both individual rights and communal restrictions. The Morro dos Cabritos seemed on the verge of nurturing a model experiment in favela upgrading.[15]

Little of this plan came to fruition. The Chicaer towers were built, but their planned leisure space was not. A few favela residents closest to the new towers accepted individual payments and relocated farther up the hill. Most families stayed put and struggled toward improved conditions largely on their own. The space projected for the chain of duplexes within the favela was cleared and then occupied by individual families who built their own homes, following no plan or project. The down payment that Chicaer and its private partners had initially paid to the residents' association disappeared. No explanation emerged, and no one pressed for such an explanation — at least not in public.

CHANGING CHARACTERS

For the residents of Bairro Peixoto, the construction of the Chicaer towers was clear evidence that their cherished height restrictions were vulnerable to political manipulation. Noting that the new residents' association in Morro dos Cabritos served as an effective defender of community interests, Bairro Peixoto's residents embarked on the same path. As in Morro dos Cabritos, lay assistants from Santa Cruz led the way, transforming the lapsed old Sociedade dos Amigos do Bairro into the more formal and vigorous Associação de Moradores de Bairro Peixoto (AMA-Bairro Peixoto), known to its participants as Oásis.[16]

Over the course of the 1980s, AMA-Bairro Peixoto mobilized community involvement in the struggle to enforce firm restrictions on development. Like their favela neighbors, members of AMA-Bairro Peixoto were able to exploit a brief favorable conjuncture. In 1985 Cariocas elected a mayor for the first time — during the dictatorship, and during Rio's prior history as national capital, the mayor had always been appointed by the federal government. They chose the socialist Roberto Saturnino Braga, with Jô Resende, a leader of a broad neighborhood-association movement, as his vice mayor.

Saturnino and Resende were both strong opponents of unchecked development. Pressed by the Bairro Peixoto association, Saturnino declared the heart of Bairro Peixoto a protected area, limiting new construction. The new regulations effectively made construction in Bairro Peixoto so bureaucratically laborious and expensive that real-estate speculators looked to greener pastures.

Partly through the actions of Santa Cruz, Bairro Peixoto acquired a reputation as an enclave of left-wing intellectuals and social workers; it remained a solidly middle-class neighborhood, but the kind of middle class that taught urban planning at the socially progressive Faculdade de Arquitetura da Universidade Santa Ursula or wrote for the arts section of the *Jornal do Brasil*. This reputation became self-fulfilling, as prominent members of Rio's intellectual Left started to move to Bairro Peixoto to take advantage of its pedestrian-friendly, socially engaged lifestyle. Fernando Gabeira, a former socialist revolutionary and left-wing politician, moved to Bairro Peixoto, as did Arturo Xexéo, a columnist for the *Jornal do Brasil*. Jacques Wagner, a union organizer and politician of the Partido dos Trabalhadores (Workers' Party), lived there for years. The psychoanalyst and novelist Luiz Alfredo Garcia-Roza lived there, and he used it as a prime location in his Copacabana detective novels, contrasting Bairro Peixoto's neighborly charms with the treacherous inferno of the surrounding district.

Bairro Peixoto also developed a reputation as a haven for young artists and comedians. Regina Casé, the star of *TV Pirata*, a late-night comedy show in the *Saturday Night Live* vein, lived just down the street, and she spent much of her youth at her grandfather's house in Bairro Peixoto. Cláudio Besserman Viana, better known by the nickname Bussunda, another *TV Pirata* veteran and the founder of the *Casseta Popular* satirical magazine, also spent much of his youth with his grandparents in Bairro Peixoto. For as long as they could insist on it, he attended its synagogue, where he shared space with Wagner. These prominent residents bolstered the reputation of the neighborhood as a space set apart from the surrounding zone of Copacabana.

For reasons not entirely clear, *O Planeta Diário*, a satirical newspaper of the mid-1980s, listed on its masthead a fictional character named "Carlos Maçaranduba, O Fodão do Bairro Peixoto," which can be roughly translated as "Charles Hardwood, the Big Fucker from Bairro Peixoto." In 1984, in the spirit of redemocratization, *O Planeta Diário* proposed a satirical constitution for a postdictatorship Brazil. Its provisions included the declaration that "National Security will be removed from the domain of the Armed Forces and will be made the responsibility of Mr. Carlos Maçaranduba, the Big Fucker from Bairro Peixoto, who will remain at the door of the Country organizing the entrance of invited guests."[17]

"O fodão do Bairro Peixoto" became popular slang for a powerful urban operator, the kind that could get you into snooty Zona Sul nightclubs without waiting in line. The moniker took on a different tone in the mid-1990s, when it was recast by *Casseta e Planeta Urgente*, the late-night television show created by the veterans of *Casseta Popular* and *O Planeta Diário*. At the time, so-called pitboys had become a media sensation and the scourge of the Zona Sul. They were heavily muscled, aggressive practitioners of Brazilian jiu-jitsu (a martial art first honed at the Academia Gracie in Copacabana, a block away from Bairro Peixoto). The pitboys, nicknamed after the breed of dogs they both favored and resembled, did not hesitate to use their skills on anyone who offended their highly sensitive notions of honor. *Casseta e Planeta* reinvented Carlos Maçaranduba, o fodão do Bairro Peixoto, as a steroid-pumping pitboy, matching him with a buddy named Montanha. In the long-running skit, Montanha and Maçaranduba roamed the streets of Rio looking for targets.

The image of rampaging pitboys ran directly counter to Bairro Peixoto's previous image of tranquility and engagement in the cause of social justice, but it was not simply invented by satirical television writers. A bare-bones fitness academy operating under the curious name of Ronald Gym, by the mouth of the tunnel on Siqueira Campos, became a favored pitboy workout site. And a small band of teenage pitboys calling themselves the Tatuís (sand crabs), began flexing their muscles around the neighborhood. They hung out at the juice bars in the Shopping Cidade Copacabana on Siqueira Campos, drinking concoctions spiked with weight-gain powder and supplements and looking for fights. Before long they were implicated in a quick string of burglaries along Siqueira Campos and its side streets. The Tatuís were mostly residents of Bairro Peixoto, with a few friends from the Morro dos Cabritos. Their cross-class conspiracy seemed to be the flip side of the collaborative social engagement of the late 1970s, one that reflected how much the city had changed.

The Tatuís looked tame in comparison to more nefarious forces creeping into the neighborhood. The Comando Vermelho, notorious in the city since the late 1980s, asserted greater control over local operations in Morro dos Cabritos beginning in the early 1990s.[18] Through the Comando Vermelho, the operators on the hill became hooked up with a vast network of local gangs loosely knit into a collaborative enterprise, but one where infighting between Comando Vermelho factions and within local gangs was a constant threat. Incorporation into the Comando Vermelho network brought far heavier firepower to hill. In the 1950s, Micucú's Taurus .45 was one of the only guns around. By the 1990s, the *donos do morro* (owners of the hill) had submachine guns, grenade launchers, and ranks of armed cadres.

The cross-class voluntarism that had characterized the late 1970s and early 1980s declined. Convincing gentle matrons from the church to walk a gauntlet of teenage *soldados do tráfico* (drug-traffic soldiers) in order to carry out charitable work on the hill was not easy. Coelho died in 1991, depriving the parish of its most able leader. Voluntarism within the community also declined. The mobilization of the 1970s and early 1980s had eliminated the threat of removal and secured basic services. By the 1990s, energies again focused on individual improvements.

Villa Rica diminished its involvement in local social projects. In 1990 Villa Rica made the juridical transition from bloco to samba school, participating in the official carnival competitions run by Liesa (Liga Independente das Escolas de Samba do Rio de Janeiro; the Independent League of Samba Schools of Rio de Janeiro). This transition made Villa Rica eligible for funding from Riotur, the state tourism agency, thereby increasing the leverage of its directorship, while inevitably distancing it from local residents. In recent decades, the president of the bloco has usually been someone who does not reside in the favela, and Villa Rica has had little involvement in communitarian projects.

As grass-roots mobilization declined, a professionalized social-service sector partially took its place. The Fundação Bento Rubião has been active in the Mangueira de Botafogo section of the favela since the late 1980s. It is named for one of the leading members of the Pastoral das Favela's judicial team, and was founded by Eliana Athayde, the most active pastoral lawyer. The Fundação Bento Rubião is essentially a remodeled version of the judicial wing of the pastoral, tailored for the age of NGOs. Its primary focus in Mangueira de Botafogo is on guaranteeing the permanence of the recent growth of the favela and on facilitating infrastructural improvements for these houses. Grass-roots community mobilization plays a much smaller role than in the old pastoral days.

The NGOs founded more recently, like Energia Olímpica, an after-school martial arts program, have created a new trend, offering targeted services designed to underpin the expansion of cultural and social citizenship, rather than legal or structural incorporation. Sponsorship of Energia Olímpica by the federally owned energy corporations Eletrobrás and Furnas is also typical of this recent trend — the state has an ever greater presence in centrally located favelas such as Cabritos, but that presence is often indirect, mediated by a civil-society organization contracted to provide services.

Municipal government did substantially increase its direct investment in the community in the late 1990s, under the auspices of Favela-Bairro, a massive slum-upgrading endeavor carried out in dozens of communities across the city, funded primarily by the Inter-American Development Bank. Favela-Bairro improved infrastructure along Euclides da Rocha, built concrete pathways and stairways higher up, and created a few public spaces within the favela.[19]

Although the program was explicitly designed to integrate the favela with the surrounding formal neighborhood, it failed to do so, for reasons evident in the Morro dos Cabritos. Favela-Bairro contributed to the expansion of the Morro dos Cabritos in two ways. By improving infrastructure along Euclides da Rocha, Favela-Bairro added to the rising value of rental property along that street. Some tenants who could not afford rising rates resettled in Mangueira de Botafogo, fueling expansion on the other side of the hill. And by facilitating pedestrian traffic higher up the hill, Favela-Bairro improved the conditions both for new construction and occupation in areas closer to Rua Vitória Régia, on the other side of the hill in the exclusive Lagoa neighborhood. Favela-Bairro failed to make any progress whatsoever toward its goal of granting title to favelados, guaranteeing that all the growth it facilitated would be informal.[20]

Favela-Bairro did not and could not confront the territorial authority of local criminal interests: as a municipally directed program, Favela-Bairro could not address problems of public security, under the purview of state government. Consequently, Favela-Bairro helped raise the value of property in the central part of the favela without loosening the grip of the local gang.

By the early twenty-first century, armed turf control — characterized by the strength of the *traficantes* (drug traffickers) in the favela and the increasingly prominent presence of private security guards in the streets below — had driven a wedge into the partnership between the residents of Bairro Peixoto and the Morro dos Cabritos, dividing the favela decisively from the middle-class neighborhood. Mutual suspicion became more common than collaboration.

Both middle-class and favela spaces were characterized by increased fortification, in different ways that yield similarly restrictive results. Middle-class gated condominiums, barred windows, armored cars, and private security guards shielded insiders from disruptive interaction.[21] Armed drug traffickers and their lookouts kept casual visitors out of the favela and restricted presence to those required to accept the political status quo. Within the favela, residents invested in fortification by enclosing previously open space in order to shield their families from shoot-outs among traficantes, or between traficantes and the police.[22]

From 2003 to 2005, an elderly resident of one of the middle-class apartment buildings that backs up to the Ladeira dos Tabajaras filmed and photographed the drug traffic on one of the favela stairways visible from her back window. Like the apartment dwellers in Bishop's "Burglar of Babylon," this resident had spent hours studying operations on the hill through binoculars. When her complaints to the police of ongoing drug sales on the Ladeira provoked no response, she took it upon herself to produce hard evidence. For two years she collected footage of gang members selling drugs and paying off low-ranking military police officers. She then gave the footage to reporters from the newspaper *O Globo* and the Globo television network—but not before selling her apartment and moving out of Rio de Janeiro.

O Globo gave the story extensive coverage, describing the amateur videographer pseudonymously as dona Vitória, and prompting a shamed police force to take action. In the wake of the dona Vitória scandal, nine police officers and several local gang members were imprisoned.[23] Point-of-sale operations temporarily moved across Botafogo to the Santa Marta favela, which has nurtured close criminal relations with the Cabritos crew since the early 1990s.[24] By late 2006, everything was back to "normal," and drugs were once again sold in open view at several locations in and around the Morro dos Cabritos.

THE UNIDADES DE POLÍCIA PACIFICADORA

In 2009 the government of the state of Rio de Janeiro, in partnership with the federal government, initiated a bold new security strategy to confront criminal turf control in Rio's favelas. The strategy hinges on establishing Unidades de Polícia Pacificadora (Pacifying Police Units, UPPs) in high-profile favelas, eliminating strongholds of the drug-trafficking network—and, to a lesser degree, those of the militias. The UPPs begin with a militarized police occupation that gradually gives way to strong community police presence and state-supported social projects. Santa Marta—the small but well-known favela across the Botafogo valley from the Morro dos Cabritos—was chosen as the first UPP site, initiated in 2009. The UPPs in the Morro dos Cabritos, along with a dozen other favelas—almost all of them in Rio's Zona Sul—followed in 2010. By the end of 2011, there were UPPs in twenty-one favelas, including a scattered few in the Zona Norte (north zone) and Zona Oeste (west zone). Drug-trafficking crews had previously dominated nearly all of these communities. Only one—the favela Batan, on Rio's west side—had previously been under militia control.

The UPP in the Morro dos Cabritos, like those throughout the city, has brought some tremendous improvements—along with some risks of its own. The UPP has dramatically transformed the experience of living in the favela. The armed drug traffickers are gone, replaced by a constant presence of police patrolling the favela. Following the initial, militarized phase of the operation, those officers have embraced a strategy of community police work. They are lightly armed, are constantly visible, and make an effort to recognize and engage with local residents.

This approach explicitly and deliberately revives a strategy of community policing pioneered by Colonel Magno Nazareth Cerqueira, an innovative state police commander of the mid-1980s. Nazareth Cerqueira's efforts failed, partly because of a lack of resources, partly because of a lack of broad societal support. The revived strategy has concentrated impressive labor force on a handful of pilot neighborhoods, taking pains not to stretch beyond available resources. And the strategy also counts both on far greater funding and much higher levels of societal support, both inside and outside the UPP favelas.

That support, if anything, has been somewhat exaggerated: the UPP has been trumpeted as a solution to Rio's crisis of urban violence. The UPP has made some crucial and welcome improvements, but it is not by itself a solution. To begin, there is an obvious difference between securing twenty, fifty, or even two hundred neighborhoods and securing the entire city. The theory behind the UPPs is that by taking the principal strongholds of the criminal networks, those networks will be mortally crippled, leaving them unable to retrench in other locations. Whether this turns out to be true will depend on a broader security strategy, as well as ever-expanding resources for the growing number of UPPs.

Other risks are less obvious, but as severe. The presence of the UPP has triggered rampant real-estate speculation within Zona Sul favelas, notwithstanding the lack of legal title that characterizes land tenure in these areas. In the Morro dos Cabritos, rents doubled and in some cases tripled in the two years after the inauguration of the UPP. Some longtime residents capitalized on this transition, renting rooms and building new rental units on top of or behind their own homes. Other residents, who were renting already, found themselves facing the difficult choice of either struggling to meet rising rents or moving to distant locations, far from their current work (and often in favelas as yet unvisited by the UPP). The UPP's promised social projects, meanwhile, have been minimal and—so far—largely ineffectual. At the same time, economic activity within the favela has increased substantially—partially the result of a generally booming economy in Rio, partially in response to the ways the UPP has lowered security costs and facilitated increasing circulation throughout the favela. The UPP has notably improved the quality of life within the Morro dos Cabritos, at the risk of driving out some of its less fortunate residents.

NEW COLLABORATIONS?

By eliminating the most obvious barriers to cross-class collaboration, the UPP has once again awakened aspirations of forging positive connections between the Morro dos Cabritos and the Bairro Peixoto. Far more residents of the middle-class neighborhood have taken to climbing the hill since the inauguration of the UPP—in some cases to volunteer at NGO social endeavors, but more frequently to see, at last, the interior of the neighboring community, perceived as off-limits for the previous two decades.

As in the 1970s, the Santa Cruz parish has served as one of the primary conduits of this exchange, albeit now in a new guise. While the modernist shell on top of the Shopping Cidade Copacabana continues to be the parish's nominal main church, early in 2007 the parish inaugurated a new, larger church on Rua Euclides da Rocha, within the Morro dos Cabritos. For the first three years of its existence, attendance at Mass and other church events was minimal and almost entirely from within the favela. Since the inauguration of the UPP, far more parishioners from Bairro Peixoto have chosen to attend Mass in the Morro dos Cabritos rather than in Copacabana. In keeping with the general revival of civic life in the favela, attendance among favelados has increased as well (see map 3.2).

The current parish priest, Father Enrico Arrigoni, has deliberately re-

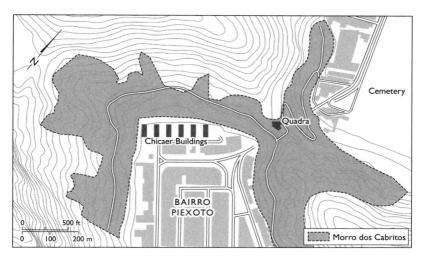

MAP 3.2 · Locations of key sites within Bairro Peixoto and the Morro dos Cabritos. This map gives a strong indication of the pattern of growth in the Morro dos Cabritos. The distinct original nuclei along the curve of the hill are still visible in the clusters of currently existing buildings.

taken the efforts of Coelho to unite favela and middle-class neighborhood—to a certain degree. In contrast to Coelho, he is not an adept of liberation theology. Like most of Brazil's current priests, he criticizes the liberation-theology generation for placing too much emphasis on social justice and not enough on spiritual growth.[25]

The success of the new church notwithstanding, as in most favelas, Pentecostal sects attract far greater numbers of residents, either to spare, one-room churches within the favela or to the megachurches in the city below. The Pentecostal churches within the favela are attended only by favelados, while those down in Copacabana are attended by a broad range of parishioners—but these churches are not typically engaged in the kind of social-justice endeavors that characterized Coelho's work.

Overall, relations between the Morro dos Cabritos and Bairro Peixoto are more peaceful and constructive than they have been in a generation. But they generally lack the kind of intention—the explicit drive to break down social divides and broaden access—that characterized the 1970s. By the early twenty-first century, the festa junina in Bairro Peixoto's plaza had largely been taken over by outside commercial interests. Both the parish and the neighborhood association cut ties to the party, and eventually helped to shut it down by communicating to the municipal government the growing local resentment against the commercialized celebration.

More generally, the plaza remains a space of relatively harmonious cross-class interaction and continues to stand out in this regard in a city notorious for its divisions. Unorganized activity in the plaza, including pickup *futsal* (hard-court soccer) on the sports court; chess, checkers, and cards on the concrete game tables; and play on the slides and swings, creates numerous daily opportunities for interaction between residents of the Morro dos Cabritos and of Bairro Peixoto. Organized activities sponsored by AMA-Bairro Peixoto, like capoeira, tai chi, futsal, volleyball, and dog-training classes, create a more formal structure for interaction, and the association gives preference to teachers from the Morro dos Cabritos for most of these classes.

But this only goes so far. Beyond the plaza and a few local bars and bakeries, opportunities for casual cross-class interaction are limited. The favela and the middle-class neighborhood remain linked economically, but perhaps not as extensively as in prior decades. Favela residents are now as likely to work anywhere in the Zona Sul and beyond as they are to work in Bairro Peixoto. And while the residents of Bairro Peixoto still depend on maids and handypersons, it is less likely that those working-class service providers will hail from the neighboring favela. In the 1970s, most school children from Bairro Peixoto attended public school, along with children from the Morro dos Cabritos. Today, almost all children from the middle-class neighborhood attend private schools. Residents of Bairro Peixoto are in many ways less likely to know a resident from the neighboring favela well than they were thirty years ago.

Coelho and his cohort tried to instill among the local population of both the Morro dos Cabritos and Bairro Peixoto the notion that the fates of the two neighborhoods were linked. This notion still has abstract appeal, but it appears to have little direct relevance in the daily lives of residents of either neighborhood. The favela and the bairro are symbiotic at a deep level, but the divisions that separate them are also enduring. As they enter a second century of uneasy coexistence, there are some indications that those divisions may become more permeable. But there is a long and difficult history that demonstrates that forging true collaboration and an acknowledgment of shared interest will be far more difficult.

NOTES

1. Maurício de Abreu, *A evolução urbana de Rio de Janeiro* (Rio de Janeiro: Instituto Pereira Passos, 1987).

2. For rich analysis of this pattern of favela development, see Brodwyn M. Fischer, *A Poverty of Rights: Citizenship and Inequality in Twentieth-Century Rio de Janeiro* (Stanford, CA: Stanford University Press, 2008).

3. Pastoral das Favelas, Morro dos Cabritos, pasta 1, Arquivo Pastoral das Favelas, 1979.

4. Pastoral das Favelas, Morro dos Cabritos, pasta 1, Arquivo Pastoral das Favelas, 1979.

5. Mário Aizen, *Bairro Peixoto: O oásis de Copacabana* (Rio de Janeiro: Prefeitura da Cidade do Rio de Janeiro, 1992), 39–46.

6. Aizen, *Bairro Peixoto*, 49.

7. Pastoral das Favelas, Morro dos Cabritos, pasta 1, Arquivo Pastoral das Favelas, 1979.

8. Since the 1980s, the growth of Mangueira de Botafogo — a subregion of the favela on the Botafogo side of the hill, largely behind the São João Batista cemetery — has displaced these downhill nuclei as the poorest area of the Morro dos Cabritos.

9. Bishop has been accused of holding a romantic view of Brazil, but her observation of the sad comedy of the showdown in the favela, ritualistic in its patterns but endlessly colorful in its details, was astute. She was ahead of the curve in identifying the increasing involution of both favela and bairro, notwithstanding the compelling attraction between them. Elizabeth Bishop, "The Burglar of Babylon," in *Elizabeth Bishop: The Complete Poems, 1927–1979* (New York: Farrar, Straus and Giroux, 1984).

10. Aizen, *Bairro Peixoto*, 65–70; Júlio César Ribeiro Sampaio, "Bairro Peixoto: A mobilização preservacionista da Associação de Moradores do Bairro Peixoto," BA thesis, Universidade Estadual do Rio de Janeiro, 1988, 15–19.

11. José Luis Pires, *Minhas verdades: Histórias e pensamento de um negro favelado* (Rio de Janeiro: Refluxus, 2004).

12. Pires, *Minhas verdades*, 24.

13. Pastoral das Favelas, Morro dos Cabritos, Chicaer documents, Arquivo Pastoral das Favelas, 1979.

14. Pastoral das Favelas, Morro dos Cabritos, Chicaer documents, Arquivo Pastoral das Favelas, 1979. For further analysis of the Pastoral das Favelas and issues of land tenure in the late 1970s and early 1980s, see Bryan McCann, *Hard Times in the Marvelous City: From Dictatorship to Democracy in the Favelas of Rio de Janeiro* (Durham, NC: Duke University Press, 2014).

15. Pastoral das Favelas, Morro dos Cabritos, Chicaer documents, Arquivo Pastoral das Favelas, 1979.

16. Sampaio, "Bairro Peixoto," 26–31.

17. "Consttuição da República Federativa do Brasil," *O Planeta Diário*, June 6, 1985, reprinted in Cláudio Paiva, *O Planeta Diário: O melhor do maior jornal do planeta* (Rio de Janeiro: Desiderata, 2007), 48.

18. Caco Barcellos, *Abusado: O dono do Morro Dona Marta* (Rio de Janeiro: Record, 2004), 169, 209, 526.

19. Favela-Bairro, *Morro dos Cabritos* (Rio de Janeiro: Instituto Pereira Passos), 2002.

20. For further detail, see McCann, *Throes of Democracy: Brazil since 1989* (London: Zed Books, 2008), 66–68. For a similar case on Rio's north side, see Mariana Cavalcanti, "Of Shacks, Houses and Fortresses: An Ethnography of Favela Consolidation in Rio de Janeiro," PhD dissertation, University of Chicago, 2008, 34–40, 216–20. For an insightful account of the strengths and weaknesses of the early stages of the program, see Roberto Segre, "Formal-Informal Connections in the Favelas of Rio de Janeiro: The Favela-Bairro Programme," in *Rethinking the Informal City: Critical Perspectives from Latin America*, edited by Felipe Hernández, Peter Kellett, and Lea K. Allen (Oxford: Berghahn Books, 2010).

21. For extensive analysis of the trend toward middle-class fortification and the attendant emptying of democratic public spaces, see Teresa Pires do Rio Caldeira, *City of Walls: Crime, Segregation, and Citizenship in São Paulo* (Berkeley: University of California Press, 2000).

22. For innovative analysis of this trend, see M. Cavalcanti, "Of Shacks, Houses and Fortresses."

23. See, for example, "Imagens de dona Vitória condemam mais um traficante de Copacabana," *O Globo*, October 19, 2006.

24. This strategic movement between Santa Marta and Morro dos Cabritos and Ladeira dos Tabajaras characterized the period from 1990 to 2010 more generally. See, for example, "Guerra assusta Zona Sul," *O Dia*, March 23, 2009.

25. Liziane Rodrigues, "Um sinal em Copacabana," *Passos* (Rio de Janeiro), September 2009.

FOUR

Compadres, Vecinos, and *Bróderes* in the Barrio

KINSHIP, POLITICS, AND LOCAL TERRITORIALIZATION
IN URBAN NICARAGUA

Dennis Rodgers

In a classic essay on urban anthropology, Anthony Leeds famously remarked that although there existed a long-standing disciplinary tradition
of exploring local community life in Latin American cities, the theoretical
repertoire concerning "the mechanisms which create and maintain" local
urban communities was not particularly elaborate.[1] Most studies, he argued,
either assumed a priori the existence of a given community or transferred
"traditional concerns from tribal experience" to the urban context, for example by highlighting "essential" social phenomena such as kinship relations as the primary vectors for the socio-spatial constitution of communities. The result, according to Leeds, was that most studies customarily
tended to view urban communities as self-contained, autonomous units,
with "larger society . . . treated as more or less an epiphenomenon."[2] While
such an approach clearly makes it methodologically easier to carry out research—since it "delimit[s], either directly or indirectly, the parameters of
action and relationship" to be studied to the internal characteristics of a
given community—it also means that the research produced will almost
inevitably portray urban communities as relatively static and straightfor-
wardly self-reproducing entities, and "fail to see the dynamics of the social
process and of change."[3]

This is something that is particularly problematic in relation to contexts
that have repeatedly experienced large-scale processes of social transformation such as regime change, for example, which has been a frequent feature
of many Latin American societies during the past three decades.[4] Nicaragua
is a case in point in this respect, and its trajectory from Somoza dictatorship

(1934–79) to Sandinista revolution (1979–90) to postrevolutionary liberal democracy (1990–) arguably poses a critical challenge to the coherent apprehension of the dynamics of everyday life in the country's cities, insofar as any "view from below" needs to capture the concrete local-level consequences of these transitions if it is to be truly revealing. This chapter seeks to address this issue by explicitly focusing on the impact that political and ideological factors have had on the evolution of what can broadly be termed processes of *local territorialization*—that is to say, the ways in which social agents reify the physical space they occupy and bind themselves socially to it—in urban Nicaragua.[5]

Drawing on my longitudinal ethnographic research conducted in a poor Managua neighborhood called barrio Luis Fanor Hernández in 1996–97, 2002–3, and 2007, the chapter begins by exploring how the wider Nicaraguan political context affected the character of *compadrazgo* (a form of fictive kinship akin to godparenthood) before, during, and after the Sandinista revolution.[6] The chapter then moves on to consider the impact on local community life of an explicitly ideological urban development project implemented in the neighborhood by the Sandinista revolutionary state during the early 1980s. This led to particular forms of local community mobilization, which subsequently declined due to regime change. After looking at the way that this ideological imagination has evolved over the past decade in a way that mirrors the country's broader political economy, the last part of the chapter traces the relationship between Sandinismo and the emergence of youth gangs as a vector for local territorialization in postrevolutionary Nicaragua.

THE VOLATILITY OF STRONG TIES

The classic anthropological study of the role that kinship can play in the socio-spatial construction of poor urban communities in Latin American cities is undoubtedly Larissa Adler Lomnitz's *Networks and Marginality*.[7] This book describes in extensive and vivid detail the efforts and ingenuity of the impoverished and marginalized inhabitants of the Cerrada del Cóndor shantytown in Mexico City to construct dense networks of reciprocal exchange with each other based on kinship links, compadrazgo, and *cuatismo* (a traditional form of male friendship). These various relationships were imbued with obligations of social and economic solidarity that allowed shantytown dwellers to broaden their resource bases, access otherwise inaccessible goods, engage in barter exchange, and recycle surplus and waste material toward their maximum utilization, thus counteracting the vicissitudes of shantytown dwellers' destitution and exclusion. At the same time, however, Lomnitz also describes how these different kinship-based networks not only provided the inhabitants of Cerrada del Cóndor with the means to alleviate their material predicament but also simultaneously constituted the primary institutional channels through which a sense of community emerged in the shantytown — the essential strength of kinship ties powerfully bound the settlement population into a definite group that inevitably became associated with a particular territorial space insofar as the majority of such relationships tended to occur locally, that is to say endogenously within the shantytown.

Very similar kin-based reciprocal exchange networks were observed by Roger Lancaster in the Managua working-class neighborhood barrio Erasmus Jiménez during the late 1980s. He particularly describes how compadrazgo relations were a key means through which inhabitants "coped with less" in the midst of economic crisis, facilitating "the perpetual exchange of goods and favors," such as "advice, food, supplies, clothing, and medicine," across as wide a (local) network of individuals as possible.[8] Lancaster argues that parents in Nicaragua customarily engaged in careful strategizing when deciding whom to choose as *padrinos* (godparents) for their children, traditionally selecting these from among "both social equals and social superiors and from those both close at hand and at various distances," in order to be able to engage in transactions of "generalized reciprocity" with the former, and forms of clientelism with the latter.[9] At the same time, however, he also notes how the Sandinista revolution had rendered relations with social superiors "more brittle and less common, forcing a more 'egalitarian' or lateral distribution of padrino choices," and suggests that this had led to the emergence of a form of compadrazgo that he denotes as "ideological," insofar as *compadres* (coparents) came to be principally chosen among one's *compañeros*: fellow Sandinista militants, local political organizers, or neighborhood activists.[10] In other words, ideological ties became inscribed in local social relations as a result of the revolution, a state of affairs that leads Lancaster to speculate that this might be one reason why "political memories are long in Central America . . . [, as] Nicaraguan cultural practices afford numerous mnemonic techniques for preserving, remembering, and binding people together in the face of adversity. . . . If the Sandinista position has remained stronger than many analysts predicted in the wake of its electoral defeat [in 1990], memory and resilience may owe more to compadrazgo than is immediately apparent. A revolutionary decade was more than enough for leftist political and ideological identifications to acquire the traditional form of an association of fictive kin."[11]

Lancaster's conjecture about the "mnemonic" link between compadrazgo and revolutionary political affiliation was certainly borne out by my own investigations in barrio Luis Fanor Hernández during the mid-1990s. Many of the interviews I conducted with neighborhood inhabitants in 1996–97 confirmed that the revolutionary period had seen a rise of ideological forms of compadrazgo in the barrio, very much along the lines that Lancaster describes, and that these had constituted important channels for the institutionalization of pro-Sandinista sentiments in the postrevolutionary context, as well as contributing to the construction of a sense of local community during the 1980s. My investigations also found, however, that this "ideological compadrazgo" had become a primary vector for a very divisive form of territorialization in the postrevolutionary period. Rising political tensions and the ideologization of personal conflicts during the first few years following regime change in 1990 saw many households in barrio Luis Fanor Hernández relocate closer to family and compadres within the neighborhood, for security reasons.[12] Kinship relations — and compadrazgo in particular — were clearly the key vector for this process of spatial reorganization, which ultimately led to the division of the neighborhood population into two spatially distinct groups between which there were almost no compadrazgo relationships. But these groups had definite political associations, with one group being predominantly made up of Sandinista sympathizers and the other predominantly associated with anti-Sandinistas.

I assumed in 1996–97 that emergent compadrazgo relations within the anti-Sandinista group would likely also be conditioned by political affiliations, namely to the dominant anti-Sandinista party, the Partido Liberal Constitucionalista (Constitutionalist Liberal Party), and I speculated that this would lead to increased political polarization in barrio Luis Fanor Hernández. This conjecture, however, overlooked the fact that mnemonic features such as compadrazgo are always cumulatively layered and that they can be associated with a wide repertoire of memories, which in turn will shape territorialization processes very differently, depending on which memory comes to the fore, as became evident when I revisited the neighborhood in 2002–3. In particular, certain elements from the community's prerevolutionary political history emerged as much more important explanatory factors than the revolutionary period for understanding the nature of the neighborhood's evolving postrevolutionary territorialization.

Barrio Luis Fanor Hernández was originally established as an illegal squatter community by rural-urban migrants in the early 1960s, one of many such informal settlements that mushroomed in and around Nicaraguan urban centers at the time, due to the disruption of Nicaragua's traditional agrarian society by the spread of agro-export capitalism. The new settlement—which became known as La Sobrevivencia (Survival) due to its extreme poverty—brought together two separate groups of squatters.[13] These groups had initially arrived as rivals in order to occupy fallow farmland on the outskirts of Managua, but they rapidly began to collaborate in the face of efforts by the authorities to expel them, as an original settler named Don Sergio described during an interview in November 1996:

> There was nothing here when we arrived, just grass. The land was part of one of [Anastasio] Somoza's farms, on the edge of the city, and easy to get to, which is why we were two groups. We all came as *paracaidistas* [parachutists, meaning illegal squatters], though, and when he heard about us, Somoza sent tractors to evict us irrespective of which group we belonged to. He sent the tractors three times, to destroy our shacks, both theirs and ours, but each time we rebuilt, helping each other, and we stayed. Then Somoza sent his goons to expel us, but we resisted again all together, everybody helping everybody else, and finally, Somoza decided to let us live here.

Although the two squatter groups collaborated to resist expulsion, and what had initially been two separate settlements rapidly coalesced into one, by all accounts there was not much in the way of social interaction between the two groups, to the extent that one of the primary characteristics of La Sobrevivencia was its division between *los de abajo* (literally, "those from below," meaning those on the west side of the settlement) and *los de arriba* (literally, "those from above," meaning those on the east side of the barrio). This territorial distinction reflected the settlement's dual origin but was further reinforced when the two groups became associated with different local-level political patrons and the predominantly vertical forms of compadrazgo of this period became highly group specific as a result. As Don Sergio described:

Somoza sent a woman called Mercedes Zúniga, to make us pay for the land and who promised to legalize our situation, but she was only interested in taking our money, and we never received land titles. She would hold meetings every week, and we'd all have to pay five pesos, but nothing ever came of it. Later, another woman called Raquel Herrera came and said that she would help us instead, and the community ended up divided between los de arriba who were led by Herrera, and los de abajo who were with Zúniga. You were linked to either one or the other, but not both.

This particular abajo-arriba pattern of socio-spatial segregation remained a key element of La Sobrevivencia's local territorialization until the Sandinista revolution, which led to a wholesale transformation of community dynamics. Such was the extent of the neighborhood makeover, though, that the abajo-arriba distinction lost its currency, and the distinction was rarely brought up by neighborhood inhabitants during my research in 1996–97, except in conversations about the past. When I returned to barrio Luis Fanor Hernández in 2002–3, however, it was on everybody's lips again, and by July 2007 it had effectively replaced the pro-Sandinista–anti-Sandinista political divide that had very tangibly permeated the neighborhood's territorialization in the early and mid-1990s, and which I had attributed to the emergence of mutually exclusive ideological compadrazgo networks.

In this respect, although the neighborhood was still made up of two separate groups that engaged in mutually exclusive compadrazgo networking, there now seemed to be little in the way of an explicitly ideological element to compadrazgo relationships. Indeed, both the quantity and quality of compadrazgo relations had changed radically. Partly as a result of the wider Nicaraguan context of ever-increasing poverty, exclusion, and destitution, there were less compadrazgo relations within both groups. Individuals were clearly seeking to minimize their obligations to others, in order to preserve their meager assets, and those relations that remained tended to be the oldest ones, mostly forged during the prerevolutionary period of La Sobrevivencia. Furthermore, whereas during the early and mid-1990s the vast majority of compadrazgo relationships had been principally lateral ones between equals, those that remained in barrio Luis Fanor Hernández in 2002–3 were predominantly vertical, between socioeconomically distant individuals (both within and outside the neighborhood), and were clearly increasingly taking on an explicitly clientelist nature when I revisited in 2007. In other words, these relationships' general structure corresponded quite closely to that of compadrazgo as it had existed in La Sobrevivencia before the revolution. And to this extent, the resurfacing of the old abajo-arriba distinction in the neighborhood arguably represented an instance of the compadrazgo territorializing mnemonic—no longer "remembering" the politics of the revolution but rather those of the prerevolutionary period.

IDEOLOGICAL NEIGHBORLINESS

The volatility of the political associations linked to local territorialization processes in barrio Luis Fanor Hernández also starkly emerged in relation to the implementation of a housing development project in the neighborhood by the Sandinista state during the early 1980s. This differed significantly from compadrazgo as a vector for local community territorialization insofar as it was very purposefully and exogenously imposed, but it was at the same time much more explicitly political in nature. Urban development was one of the major priorities of the Sandinista revolutionary junta that took power after overthrowing the dictator Somoza in July 1979.[14] Managua, the capital city of Nicaragua, had suffered a devastating earthquake in 1972, and—despite several hundreds of millions of dollars of international aid pouring into the country to help with its reconstruction that Somoza mostly pocketed—had not been significantly rebuilt.[15] The country's urban centers had furthermore suffered more than rural areas during the course of the Sandinista-led insurgency that brought down the dictatorship. Barrio Luis Fanor Hernández, for example, was attacked by Somocista (Somoza's) National Guard tank columns, as well as bombed by National Guard planes, to the extent that "after the insurrection, there were almost no houses left standing in the barrio, because they were all destroyed in the fighting," according to Don Sergio. In an interview in October 1996, however, he described enthusiastically how

> the triumph of the revolution changed everything, and gave us new houses, electricity, and water. A few months after Somoza was defeated, Daniel Ortega, who was the new president, came and told us that the revolution would help us overcome our poverty. He told us how the Cubans had donated prefabricated houses to Nicaragua, and that because we were the poorest neighborhood in all Managua, we

had been chosen to be the pilot project for a new Sandinista approach to urban development. We were all to get houses and build them ourselves. And that's how it was, we all worked together, to build our barrio, everybody, the whole community. The houses, the roads, the alleyways, the electricity, the water, the sewage, everything was built through the efforts of the inhabitants of the barrio, and nobody else!

This urban reconstruction project was clearly a critical event in the neighborhood's history. What had been an extremely poor informal settlement known as La Sobrevivencia—subsequently renamed barrio Luis Fanor Hernández to honor a local Sandinista martyr—was completely rebuilt in 1980–81 through a mutual aid self-help process, whereby local inhabitants were randomly organized into work teams and built their own houses, as well as basic neighborhood infrastructure, under the supervision of government-appointed civil engineers. The new housing was then distributed among local residents by lottery, which had the effect of mixing the population that had previously been segregated into los de abajo and los de arriba. In terms of territorialization, this process clearly forced neighborhood compadrazgo networks to become less spatially segregated than they had been previously. Moreover, the process facilitated the emergence of more ideological forms of compadrazgo, insofar as the distribution of relatively uniform housing to all neighborhood inhabitants constituted something of a leveling of their (physical) capital asset portfolios, so to speak. But the urban reconstruction project also explicitly sought to implement a very definite political agenda, linked to the revolution's aim to foster a "new socialist man."[16] An official Ministry for Housing and Human Settlements (Ministerio de la Vivienda y Asentamientos Humanos) document describes the underlying logic of a similar program to the one implemented in barrio Luis Fanor Hernández very well:

> The 45 years of oppression to which the recently overthrown dictatorship subjected the popular strata of this country's population have resulted in the emergence of individualistic activities and behaviors, of competition and mistrust among in particular much of the urban population. This has impeded the full expression of the creative potential inherent to the solidarity and cooperation that characterize Nicaragua's population, especially regarding the development of community life. Now that we stand on the threshold of a new revolutionary era, which will open the floodgates to popular participation

at all levels of society, it is essential to devise and make use of specific systems, techniques, and methods that will act as means of promoting or channeling these positive energies among urban populations, with an aim in particular of achieving the collective realization of an improvement in their living conditions. . . . Housing projects will therefore build upon the methodology of Construction by Mutual Aid, which not only teaches communities to work together collectively but also shows them that by means of a serious and well-structured effort they can relieve themselves of the frustrations that the past has engendered, and fully grasp the opportunities offered by the historical moment we are now living.[17]

Apart from "providing access to basic housing for families with low incomes," the aims of the housing project also included: "serving as a means of promoting popular participation, social cohesion, and organized community development, through cooperation and collective action"; "establishing the foundations for a wide-ranging process of educating the country's population in relation to notions of public responsibility, civic behavior, and social participation"; and "serving as a means of promoting and developing the self-managing capacities of communities, based on cooperation and collaboration between families, in such a way as to permit the organization of future collective action in relation to the task of community development."[18] The extent of this veritable social engineering enterprise came out very clearly during the course of an interview with an inhabitant of barrio Luis Fanor Hernández, Doña Yolanda, in May 1997, when I asked her whether she had actively participated in the reconstruction of the neighborhood. "Absolutely," she exclaimed:

I worked liked everybody else, that's what Mutual Aid was all about. Everybody in the barrio worked, women like men. Men mixed the cement and set the bricks, which women would pass to them. Those who couldn't work because of their age would prepare fruit juices or lemonade, and the children would bring them to us. Everybody did something! We'd work every weekend, from 2 p.m. to 5 p.m. on Saturdays, and 7 a.m. to 5 p.m. on Sundays, with an hour for lunch, between 12 p.m. and 1 p.m. We'd also work whenever we'd have free time, especially those who were unemployed. A schedule was drawn up when the project began, the authorities noted down when this and that person had free time, and you had to go and help with the building.

"So it was all very well organized?" I asked.

"Of course!" interjected her eldest daughter, Adilia, who had been listening to us talk:

Listen, the barrio reconstruction project happened like this. After Daniel Ortega came to tell us that we were all going to get new houses, in October 1979, a woman called Carmen Rodríguez came from the Ministry of Housing to do a census of the barrio, to see how many families there were, and how many houses needed to be built. She went to all the households in the neighborhood, and asked how many people there were in each, how many families, how many members each family had, how many children there were. This was to determine how many families there were, because the project was to be done so that there would no longer be three or four generations living under the same roof. Each family—the mother, the father, and the children—was entitled to its own house, she told us, so that there would be no more overcrowding, like there was before the revolution. A family of two adults and two or three children would get a house with two rooms, while one with more would get a house with three rooms. Every house was planned with a toilet, water, electricity, everything!

Doña Yolanda continued:

There were two types of houses, one in wood and one in concrete, "miniskirt" style [with concrete foundations and wooden walls]. The concrete houses cost more, 35,000 *córdobas* [Nicaraguan currency], while the wooden one cost 25,000 córdobas, but both had to be paid back over a period of twenty-two years, at an interest rate of 3 percent. You signed a contract with the Ministry of Housing, whereby on the fifteenth of every month, you had to pay them an installment. For the first two years, the installment was 100 córdobas a month, then for the next five years, 150 córdobas a month, and so on until a maximum of 350 córdobas a month. Once you had finished paying the installments, the house was legally yours.

"But there were also a number of special clauses in the contract," Adilia added, "which said that you couldn't sell the house without the permission of the ministry, or rent out rooms. These were against speculation, so that people wouldn't use what the revolution was giving them the wrong way."

"After Carmen Rodríguez finished the census, a team of technical experts came from the ministry to help us organize ourselves," Doña Yolanda explained. "They held a meeting to ask how many carpenters there were in the barrio, how many masons, and then they divided us into groups of twenty families, each with a carpenter and a mason. Each group then built its block under their direction, tearing down one house at a time and then building the new one, until everybody had a new house. Those who lived in the houses that were torn down went to live with other families in the barrio until their new house was ready."

"How long did it all take?" I asked.

"The last house was finished in December 1981," Doña Yolanda answered. "There was a big celebration, and Daniel Ortega came to congratulate us, and told us how we had done something incredible, that through our own efforts we had changed our lives, and that we should continue to help each other, to cooperate, and that we should now organize ourselves to manage the continued development of our community all together, by organizing a Sandinista Defense Committee [Comité de Defensa Sandinista, CDS]."

The organization of a barrio CDS was in many ways supposed to represent the institutionalization of what might be described as a generalized "ideology of neighborliness." As Don Sergio described during an interview in March 1997:

> Through the CDS, we were to coordinate *vigilancia* [crime watch], health, employment, food distribution. Each block was to have its subcommittee, and each one would have a health representative, who would coordinate the vaccination campaigns, and there would also be a vigilancia representative, to would establish a rotation for the men of the block to spend at least one night a month patrolling the block, to make sure that we wouldn't be robbed. The barrio CDS was also to coordinate the cutting of the grass in the public areas of the neighborhood every weekend, or the stockpiling of food supplies to be distributed to people. It was also to organize a rotary fund, which everybody would contribute to, and which people would then be able to use to buy material to help them build an extension for their houses when their families grew, for example.

Don Manuel, another longtime resident of barrio Luis Fanor Hernández, linked this collective action directly to the reconstruction of the neighborhood and highlighted the action's fundamentally ideological nature during an interview in November 1996: "All the neighborhood inhabitants participated in reconstructing the barrio, and then afterward in the CDS and the organization of vigilancia. *Todos hacían el rojinegro* [literally, 'everybody did the red and black,' which are the Sandinista colors; the expression is used here to denote mobilizing for communal activities], because this barrio would be nothing without the revolution. It gave us everything—our houses, water, electricity, everything! Without Sandinismo, we'd still be living in our cardboard houses of La Sobrevivencia. . . . Because of all this, people here are Sandinista in their blood, and always will be!" Seen in this light, the urban reconstruction project can be said to have constituted an instance of top-down territorialization, which sought to impose an ideologically specific form of local community organization that would mobilize grass-roots support for the revolution.[19]

By the time I first arrived in barrio Luis Fanor Hernández in 1996, however, the CDS has disappeared, collective mobilization had completely collapsed, and the oft-repeated motto of many in the neighborhood was now "each to their own."[20] As Don Sergio—who had run the neighborhood CDS—described during an interview in April 1997: "The houses are falling apart, the electricity's been cut off because nobody can afford it. Nobody cares about cleaning up the public areas of the barrio; nobody does anything for the upkeep of the neighborhood. The streets are dark because none of the lights work any more, the sewers are blocked, and the roads are potholed. Nobody does anything for the good of the community any more; they only act for themselves, according to their self-interest. We're eating one another, as they say in the Bible." On one level, this situation could clearly be related to the dire economic circumstances that Nicaragua has suffered since the late 1980s. Doña Ursula, a staunch local Sandinista activist, explained during an interview in March 1997: "People are apathetic, they don't have the will to mobilize. . . . The economic crisis has caused people to stop mobilizing because everybody has become preoccupied with their unemployment, their poverty, their hunger. . . . We're in a critical situation, people are demoralized, and therefore don't mobilize anymore, and so there's no solution." Omar Pineda, another inhabitant of barrio Luis Fanor Hernández, offered a different analysis of the situation during an interview in May 1997, however, which explicitly brought ideological factors back into the equation. He suggested that

> the reason why people mobilized was because of the houses. Nobody had proper houses here before the revolution; it was a shantytown,

the poorest in Managua. The revolution changed our lives in a concrete manner by giving us the houses. . . . This organization continued after we finished building the houses, because people were still paying for the houses. . . . But after the Sandinista defeat [in 1990], people began selling their houses and others began to rent rooms in their houses, even though these were not allowed because of the antispeculation clause in their contracts signed with the Ministry of Housing. . . . But because the Sandinistas were no longer there to enforce the contracts, people just went ahead and did whatever they wanted, as it was not something that the new government was ever going to enforce. . . . All this completely changed the barrio. . . . There's no unity, no community here anymore. People don't help each other—they hardly even say hello to each other—because they have nothing in common. There's nothing that connects them, as the houses used to.

In other words, regime change in 1990 led to the rebuilt houses losing their currency as indices of the particular—Sandinista—politics associated with the mass collective mobilization that the neighborhood had known in the 1980s. As houses were sold, or rooms rented out, the sense of neighborliness that the process of reconstruction of barrio Luis Fanor Hernández had fostered dissipated, to the extent that by the mid-1990s it existed as little more than a lingering sense of nostalgia.

ROUGH LOVE

This nostalgia was largely sustained in barrio Luis Fanor Hernández by an unlikely social phenomenon during the mid-1990s, namely the local youth gang. This was not completely surprising, as there was arguably a direct relationship between the rise of contemporary Nicaraguan youth gangs and the Sandinista revolution. Although the phenomenon has roots that can be traced back to the 1940s, it only emerged as a significant social issue in the early 1990s, following the demobilization of thousands of young men from the ranks of the Sandinista Popular Army (the age of military conscription was sixteen).[21] Gang members from this period systematically mentioned three basic reasons for joining a gang. First, the change of regime in 1990 led to an abrupt devaluation of their social status, which, as conscripts defending "the nation," had previously been very high, and becoming gang members had seemed a means of reaffirming themselves vis-à-vis a wider society that seemed to rapidly forget them. Second, becoming gang members had been a way of recapturing some of the dramatic, yet almost addictive, adrenaline-charged experiences of war, as well as of comradeship and solidarity that they had lived through as conscripts, and that were rapidly becoming scarce commodities in postwar Nicaragua. Third, but perhaps most important, becoming gang members had seemed to many a natural continuation of their previous role as conscripts. The early 1990s were highly uncertain times, marked by political polarization, violence, and spiraling insecurity, and these youths felt that they could better "serve" their families and friends by joining a gang than attempting to "protect" them as individuals.

By the mid-1990s, however, what could perhaps be characterized as an incipient form of vigilantism had institutionalized into a full-blown process of local territorialization based on semiritualized forms of gang warfare, which, through their ritualized nature, provided a sense of predictability for local inhabitants within a wider context of chronic insecurity. The first battle of a gang war typically involved fighting with fists and stones, but each new battle involved an escalation of weaponry, first to sticks, then to knives and broken bottles, and eventually to mortars, guns, and AK-47s. Although the rate of escalation varied, its sequence never did — that is, gangs did not immediately begin their wars with firearms. The fixed nature of gang warfare arguably constituted something of a mechanism for restraining violence, insofar as escalation is a process in which each stage calls for a greater but definite intensity of action, and is therefore always under actors' control. Gangs also provided local neighborhood inhabitants with an early-warning system, such that gang wars could be conceived as scripted performances that offered local communities a means of circumscribing what Hannah Arendt famously termed the "all-pervading unpredictability" of violence.[22]

The motivation offered by gang members for this particular behavior pattern was imbued with a definite political ideology. All those I interviewed in 1996–97 actively and repeatedly claimed to be "the last inheritors of Sandinismo," contending that they had joined the gang and engaged in violence due to their love (literally, *querer*) for their local neighborhood. "That's how we are, us gang member brothers [*así somos, nosotros los bróderes pandilleros*]; we show our love for the neighborhood by fighting other gangs," a gang member named Miguel claimed, while another, Julio, told me that "you show the neighborhood that you love it by putting yourself in danger for people, by protecting them from other gangs. . . . You look after the neighborhood in that way, you help them, keep them safe."

A conceptual parallel can be made here with the "love" that Che Guevara saw as the mark of "the true revolutionary."[23] At the same time, however, Guevara was referring to an abstract "love of the people," while gang members were clearly motivated by a much more narrow, localized form of affection. This emerged very clearly one morning in October 1996, when I chanced across Julio during a stroll around the neighborhood. He was cleaning up graffiti from the 1980s, which extolled the virtues of the Sandinista youth organization, that a person or persons unknown had crudely painted over in bright red—the colors of the anti-Sandinista Partido Liberal Constitucionalista—the night before. As Julio angrily berated the "sons of seventy thousands whores" (*hijos de la setenta mil putas*) who had done this, I initially assumed that this was just one more example of his overt Sandinista sympathies, but it quickly became apparent that he saw this act of vandalism less as an attack on Sandinismo and more as a desecration of a material manifestation of barrio Luis Fanor Hernández's past: "Those *jodidos* [assholes] don't respect anything in the neighborhood, Dennis, nothing! Okay, so they don't like Sandinismo, that's how it is. I don't like their politics either, but this is more than just a Sandinista *pinta* [graffiti]; it's a part of the neighborhood history. *Our* history, *bróder* [brother]! It's something that belongs to the community, to all of us; it shows us who we are, where we come from, how Sandinismo built our houses and made us into a community. It shows what the neighborhood is, and people should therefore respect it, whatever their political opinions."

To this extent, the barrio Luis Fanor Hernández gang members' Sandinista sympathies can arguably be said to have reflected the neighborhood's particular historical associations with Sandinismo rather than the political ideology per se. Certainly, gang members' discourses tended to invoke the neighborhood reconstruction project instead of any of the numerous national-level achievements of the Sandinista revolution,[24] and they frequently directly compared their violent "care" for the neighborhood with the rebuilding of the neighborhood in the 1980s and the sense of community it had fostered, maintaining that they were all that was keeping the neighborhood together in the face of the atomizing impulses of economic crisis and political polarization in postrevolutionary Nicaragua. As such, it can be argued that there was a clear link between the territorialization process that they embodied and that which had been generated by the reconstruction project. At the same time, however, gang dynamics changed dramatically between the mid-1990s and the early 2000s. As I have described in detail elsewhere, the barrio Luis Fanor Hernández gang evolved from being motivated by a sense of social solidarity with the local community to an exclusive and predatory institution focused on regulating a local cocaine-based drug economy to the exclusive benefit of its members, who dominated the drug-dealing labor market.[25]

Although drugs were by no means unknown to barrio Luis Fanor Hernández gang members in the mid-1990s, the main drug of choice at the time was marijuana, and gang members had not been involved in any regular form of trafficking. Cocaine dealing developed in the neighborhood from mid-1999 onward—initially on a small scale involving just one individual but rapidly expanding into a three-tiered pyramidal drug economy solely involving gang members and former gang members by mid-2000.[26] The potential rewards of the drugs trade were substantial at all levels of its pyramidal economy, ranging from around US$450 per month at the lowest street-selling level to upward of US$1,100 per month for the middle level, and clearly much more for the top tier, about which I have less precise information. In a local neighborhood context where about half of the economically active population was unemployed, a further 25 percent underemployed, and where those who did work earned a median monthly income of about US$105 in 2002–3, such sums were extremely significant, as a gang member called Kalia made clear during an interview in February 2002: "What the fuck do you do when you don't have any food and there's no work to be had? You have to find some other way to look out for yourself, that's what! That's where the drugs come in. It's the only thing that's worthwhile doing here in the barrio."

Overall some 40 percent of barrio Luis Fanor Hernández households seemed to be benefiting either directly or indirectly from the drug trafficking. Most obviously, many of the previously ramshackle, mainly wooden, washed-out, monochrome houses had undergone a very visible process of infrastructural amelioration, with a significant proportion now bigger, rebuilt in brick and concrete, often painted in bright pastel colors, and in some cases even two-stories high (a rarity in earthquake-prone Managua). The changes inside many of these houses were just as impressive and extensive, as they now displayed tiled instead of dirt floors, fitted kitchens instead of gas burners, and (local) designer instead of secondhand furniture, as well as luxurious appliances such as wide-screen televisions with cable services, megawattage sound systems, Nintendo game consoles, and in one particularly surreal case a broadband-connected computer with Skype (which subsequently gave a whole new meaning to the notion of "virtual ethnography"). The inhabitants of these new houses generally wore better-quality, often brand-name, clothes than had been the norm; displayed ostentatious jewelry and expensive watches; had the latest model mobile phones — in a neighborhood where only a dozen households had had landlines in the mid-1990s — and ate imported food that they often bought in supermarkets rather than the local open-air market.

At the same time, however, the drug economy in barrio Luis Fanor Hernández was violently regulated by gang members who frequently brutalized local neighborhood inhabitants in order to precipitate a generalized state of terror and ensure that their dealing could occur unimpeded. Doña Yolanda described this during an interview in February 2002, specifically contrasting the situation with the mid-1990s, when the gang had an ethos of social solidarity:

> Before, you could trust the gang, but not any more. . . . They've become corrupted due to this drug crack. . . . They threaten, attack people from the neighborhood now, rob them of whatever they have, whoever they are. . . . They never did that before. . . . They used to protect us, look out for us, but now they don't care, they only look out for themselves, for their illegal business. . . . People are scared, you've got to be careful what you say or what you do, because otherwise they'll attack you. . . . We live in terror here, you have to be scared or else you're sure to be sorry.

Despite this clearly very different relationship with the wider neighborhood, gang members nevertheless continued to invoke barrio Luis Fanor Hernández's historical association with Sandinismo in order to justify their actions. Indeed, during an interview in February 2002, in his plush new home built with drug money, a former gang member turned mid-level dealer named Bismarck directly compared the drug trafficking to the neighborhood-reconstruction program of the 1980s:

BISMARCK: So, Dennis, how do you see the barrio now? It's been what, almost five years since you were last here? Things have changed, haven't they? What do you think of my house? Do you remember how it used to be a wood shack with cardboard instead of window panes?

DR: Yes, I mean, wow, it's absolutely incredible how it's changed, Bismarck! All this concrete, this brick, these tiles, and this electronic equipment. . . . It's all because of drugs?

BISMARK: That's right! You wouldn't believe how much money you can make selling that shit!

DR: Well, it's certainly impressive, I have to admit. I never thought I'd see anything like this; last time the barrio seemed to be almost regressing back to being La Sobrevivencia again.

BISMARK: So it was, but now it's been rebuilt like after the revolution, except that instead of Sandinismo, it's the market that's been helping us!

DR: I guess you could put it that way, Bismarck, but don't you think there's also a big difference between Sandinismo and the market? I mean, the drugs aren't helping everybody, are they? Sure, there are lots of nice, new houses in the barrio now, but some of these new houses are better than others. Yours is much nicer than Kalia's next door, for example, although he also sells drugs, and there are also many houses in the barrio that haven't changed at all since I was here last. There's lots of inequality now, which wasn't the case before, and that can't be a good thing.

BISMARK: Well, you can't help everybody, you know. Life is hard here in Nicaragua, Dennis, and you've got be clever and try to survive by hook or by crook. Kalia's just plain dumb; he uses his profits from selling drugs to smoke up, and then loses his head and can't sell properly. And those who don't have the drugs to sell, well, that's just the luck of the draw. It's like the lottery that attributed the houses in the rebuilt barrio to everybody. Some people got bigger and better-located houses than others, but nobody complained because it was all random, and everybody had the same chances to start off with.

Drug trafficking in barrio Luis Fanor Hernández in the early 2000s was not just the luck of the draw, however, as not everybody had the same opportunities to participate, insofar as drug dealers were all gang members or former gang members, whose monopoly over the use of violence in the neighborhood was what enabled them to sustain and regulate drug dealing. As such, the barrio Luis Fanor Hernández gang in 2002–3 arguably still represented a form of territorialization, but one that is plausibly associable with a process of localized "primitive accumulation," whereby gang members violently constituted themselves as a nascent local narco-bourgeoisie, that made money within a context of otherwise extreme poverty and limited opportunities for capital accumulation.[27] Although very different from the socio-spatial organization promoted in the 1990s, the gang remained a form of territorialization that—despite the continued comparison of gang members' actions to the Sandinista revolutionary regime's reconstruction of the neighborhood—now embodied an ideology that clearly mirrored Nicaragua's post–broader revolutionary political economy of ever-increasing levels of inequality and iniquitous governance.[28]

CONCLUSION

The fact that local urban communities are inevitably embedded within, and shaped by, wider social, political, economic, and cultural structures is clearly critical to take into account when investigating these communities, but this reality is often difficult to demonstrate concretely. There are specific ways in which broader structural factors can impact local circumstances, particularly the ways in which changes at the broader level can be experienced at the local level. My exploration of the evolution of three processes of local territorialization in the poor Managua neighborhood barrio Luis Fanor Hernández, including compadrazgo relations before, during, and after the Sandinista revolution; the implementation of an urban development project during the revolutionary decade; and the youth gang phenomenon in the postrevolutionary period, links the emergence of these processes to broader political processes. Changes that occurred on a structural level transformed the nature of these local-level practices, including, in particular, the ways they reflected broader ideological factors. Each form of territorialization clearly displays its own specific dynamic, which is partly the consequence of the different aspects of everyday life that the different forms relate to, but also stems from their own intrinsic qualities. These interrelate with a changing political imagination.

At the same time, however, an overarching insight that emerges is that as important as political factors may be in shaping the everyday processes of territorialization, there comes a point in their respective evolutions and interrelations with broader structural factors where the influence of the political is clearly superseded by impact of the economic. There are two potential ways of conceiving of this situation. The first is to assume that ultimately even processes of socio-spatial territorialization are subject to Karl Marx and Friedrich Engels's "iron law" of materialism, whereby "life is not determined by consciousness, but consciousness by life."[29] The second is to follow Roger Lancaster, who suggests — citing Marx's contention that "*all* human relations and functions, however and in whatever form they may appear, influence material production and have a more or less decisive influence on it" — that instead of conceiving of everyday processes (such as the local forms of territorialization) in terms of "base and superstructure," it is better to think of them as constituted through "plural modes of production."[30] Seen in this light, rather than attempting to get down to the bottom of things by establishing "a series of determinations," it becomes more important to describe how different "practices of power and resistance are intertwined" in order to better highlight the real lived experience of individuals.[31] In both cases, however, the question of how to concretely relate broader structural factors with local-level lived experience remains key, and ought to be the starting point of any investigation of local urban life.

NOTES

1. Anthony Leeds, "The Anthropology of Cities: Some Methodological Issues," in Anthony Leeds, *Cities, Classes, and the Social Order*, edited by R. Sanjek (Ithaca, NY: Cornell University Press, 1994), 234.

2. Leeds, "The Anthropology of Cities," 235.

3. Leeds, "The Anthropology of Cities," 237, 234. Although there are still many anthropological studies that continue to offer fine-grained, detailed ethnographic accounts of local urban life in the manner critiqued by Leeds (albeit often adding a final chapter or epilogue that discusses the importance of large-scale processes — such as neoliberalism, for example — but generally in a broad-brush and disconnected manner), his essay sparked the emergence of a significant and increasingly dominant strand of research within the field of Latin American urban anthropology that has explicitly attempted to tackle the fact that local communities are embedded within, and shaped by, wider social, political, economic, and cultural structures. Notable examples for instance include Javier Auyero, *Poor People's Politics: Peronist Networks and the Legacy of Evita* (Durham, NC: Duke University Press, 2001); Daniel M. Goldstein, *The Spectacular City: Violence and Performance in Urban Bolivia* (Durham, NC: Duke University Press, 2004); Roger N. Lancaster, *Life Is Hard: Machismo, Danger, and the Intimacy of Power in Nicaragua* (Berkeley: University of California Press, 1992); Nancy Scheper-Hughes, *Death without Weeping: The Violence of Everyday Life in Brazil* (Berkeley: University of California Press, 1992); and

Michael Taussig, *The Nervous System* (New York: Routledge, 1992), among others, and this chapter explicitly positions itself within this vein of work.

4. See Guillermo O'Donnell, *Counterpoints: Selected Essays on Authoritarianism and Democratization* (Notre Dame, IN: University of Notre Dame Press, 1999).

5. I borrow this notion of *local territorialization* from geography, where it is used to describe the way that "territory is not; it becomes, for territory itself is passive, and it is human beliefs and actions that give territory meaning." See David B. Knight, "Identity and Territory: Geographical Perspectives on Nationalism and Regionalism," *Annals of the Association of American Geographers* 72 (1982): 517. *Local territorialization* is, in other words, a term that points to both the organization and the imagination of space.

6. On godparenthood, see Sidney W. Mintz and Eric Wolf, "An Analysis of Ritual Co-parenthood (Compadrazgo)," *Southwest Journal of Anthropology* 6, no. 4 (1950). Barrio Luis Fanor Hernández is a pseudonym, as are the names of all interviewees and most places mentioned in this chapter.

7. Larissa Adler Lomnitz, *Networks and Marginality: Life in a Mexican Shantytown* (New York: Academic Press, 1977).

8. Lancaster, *Life Is Hard*, 63.

9. Lancaster, *Life Is Hard*, 66.

10. Lancaster, *Life Is Hard*, 67.

11. Lancaster, *Life Is Hard*, 68.

12. See also Lancaster, *Life Is Hard*, 294–96, for a parallel process in barrio Erasmus Jiménez.

13. As Don Sergio vividly described:

> The barrio was called La Sobrevivencia [Survival] then, because we were so poor that all we ever managed to do was survive. Whenever you asked anybody in those days how they were, they'd always answer, "Well, surviving . . . [*pues, sobreviviendo . . .*]." Life was very, very hard then. The government never helped anybody — in fact, it actively persecuted us instead — and people had to do almost anything they could in order to make a living — wheel and deal, rob, scavenge on the streets and in the rubbish dumps, looking for anything that could be sold as scrap, recycled, or reused. Old cans, bottles, paper, food, anything. . . . Even our houses were made of whatever we could scavenge — bits of wood, scrap metal, plastic, cardboard. . . . We were known as *los sobrevivientes* [the survivors], because there was so much poverty here that you would surely die under normal circumstances! We didn't always eat, and there was lots of malnutrition, and many children and sometimes even adults died of disease and hunger.

14. See Roberto Chavez, "Urban Planning in Nicaragua: The First Five Years," *Latin American Perspectives* 14, no. 2 (1987).

15. See Julio César Godoy-Blanco, "El proceso de estructuración urbana de Managua: 1950–1979," PhD dissertation, Universidad de Costa Rica, 1983.

16. See Donald C. Hodges, *Intellectual Foundations of the Nicaraguan Revolution* (Austin: University of Texas Press, 1986), 288.

17. MINVAH, *Programa Integral de 2,800 Viviendas para Managua* (Managua: MINVAH, 1980), 3–4, my translation.

18. MINVAH, *Programa Integral de 2,800 Viviendas*, 168–69, my translation.

19. Barrio Luis Fanor Hernández in fact ended up being just one of a small handful of slum-upgrading projects that were actually carried out in Sandinista Nicaragua. The diversion of public funds to finance a war of defense against U.S.-sponsored counterrevolutionary forces known as the Contra from 1981 onward meant that funding for the revolutionary regime's ambitious urban development plans rapidly dried up.

20. See Dennis Rodgers, "Each to Their Own: Ethnographic Notes on the Economic Organization of Poor Households in Urban Nicaragua," *Journal of Development Studies* 43, no. 3 (2007).

21. Demobilized Contra youths were also involved, albeit to a much lesser extent, and were generally concentrated in a few specific neighborhoods only.

22. Hannah Arendt, *On Violence* (New York: Harcourt Brace, 1969), 5.

23. Ernesto Guevara, *Venceremos: The Speeches and Writings of Che Guevara* (New York: Simon and Schuster, 1969), 398. This is an analogy that is all the more relevant considering the strong associations between Sandinismo and the Cult of Che. See Roger N. Lancaster, *Thanks to God and the Revolution: Popular Religion and Class Consciousness in the New Nicaragua* (New York: Columbia University Press, 1988), 132, 185.

24. This idea of localized political association is implicitly further supported by the fact that not all Managua gang members are pro-Sandinista. The increased political polarization that followed the elections of 1990 led to a spatial reorganization of the city's population. New neighborhoods emerged and coalesced, some pro-Sandinista and others pro-Contra (the postelectoral return migration of refugees also greatly contributed to the formation of the latter). The gang members in barrio Enrique Bermúdez (who was the commander of the Contra Northern Military Front during the war in the 1980s) are in no way sympathetic to Sandinismo, for example. Instead, this particular gang's solidarity is grounded in identification with the historical experiences of the barrio Enrique Bermúdez population's opposition to the Sandinista regime, just as the Luis Fanor Hernández gang members were discursively pro-Sandinista as a result of their neighborhood's local historical association with Sandinismo.

25. See Dennis Rodgers, "Living in the Shadow of Death: Gangs, Violence, and Social Order in Urban Nicaragua, 1996–2002," *Journal of Latin American Studies* 38, no. 2 (2006); and Dennis Rodgers, "When Vigilantes Turn Bad: Gangs, Violence, and Social Change in Urban Nicaragua," in *Global Vigilantes*, edited by D. Pratten and A. Sen (London: Hurst, 2007).

26. For details, see Dennis Rodgers, "Managua," in *Fractured Cities: Social Exclu-*

sion, *Urban Violence and Contested Spaces in Latin America*, edited by K. Koonings and D. Kruijt (London: Zed, 2007).

27. Alternatively, this process can also be seen as a microlevel example of "accumulation by dispossession." See David Harvey, *The New Imperialism* (Oxford: Oxford University Press, 2003).

28. See Dennis Rodgers, "A Symptom Called Managua," *New Left Review* 49 (January–February 2008).

29. Karl Marx and Friedrich Engels, "The German Ideology," in *Karl Marx, Selected Writings*, edited by David McLellan (Oxford: Oxford University Press, 1977), 164.

30. Karl Marx, *Capital*, vol. 4 (Moscow: Foreign Languages Publishing House, 1963), 280; Lancaster, *Life Is Hard*, 281.

31. Lancaster, *Life Is Hard*, 281.

FIVE

The Informal City

AN ENDURING SLUM OR A PROGRESSIVE HABITAT?

Emilio Duhau

The current specialized literature about the informal city shows two main concerns. The first one is linked to the issue of property rights and the advantages and shortcomings of property-regularization programs and land titling. The second concern turns around negative *place effects* of informal settlements, such as social exclusion, spatial segregation, territorial control exercised by drug-trafficking gangs, and so on. But besides the rather indecisive results of research concerning the property-regularization issue, and the gloomy landscape usually depicted by those addressing informal city place effects, it is worth considering an alternate experience, characteristic of Mexico in the twentieth century: what kind of urban space results when a rather permissive and mostly clientelistic government approach converges with lasting property-regularization programs and public investment? This chapter will address this latter issue by considering the scope and limits of the informal city's ability to gradually improve over time, a trait that I call *progressiveness*.

INFORMAL SETTLEMENTS AND THE MEXICAN REGULARIZATION MODEL

Unlike policies that addressed informal settlements all over the developing world during the sixties and the seventies, current public policies follow two main orientations: in situ housing-settlement improvement and land-tenure regularization.[1] Nevertheless, Latin American land-tenure-regularization programs follow different national models, and many times the adopted model varies between regional-provincial political subdivisions and cities within a given country. In any case, the armature of each model shows that most share the common assumption that informal settlements are a rather irreversible fact and an enduring feature of Latin American cities. But they differ not only in the scope and continuity of policies and programs but also in the ideas that orient public intervention in the informal city, in the model of informal settlements that functions as a main reference for public intervention, and more generally in the definition of the issues surrounding the informal city.

The Mexican model, a pragmatic one, developed over several decades and reached its maturity toward the eighties. Since the thirties, when conflicts and reclamations about low-cost subdivisions first emerged in Mexico City, the Mexican federal government and local authorities have resorted to different measures, among them land expropriation and government-promoted subdivisions, in order to appease popular mobilizations and to incorporate neighborhood organizations in Mexico's official party.[2] Although the Federal District government fought irregular subdivisions and land invasions within the capital during the fifties and part of the sixties, they spread out in adjacent municipalities, giving place to the first large-scale informal city, Nezahualcóyotl, which in the sixties comprised about 150,000 housing plots. It was there, ten years after the foundation of Nezahualcóyotl municipality in 1963, that federal and state governments applied the first large-scale regularization program, through the creation of a trusteeship integrated by the estate government, Nacional Financiera (a federal financial institution), the representatives of developers, and settlers (*colonos*).[3]

It was precisely at the beginning of the 1970s that the Mexican federal government put in motion a number of initiatives involving housing, irregular settlements, and urban planning. These included the creation in 1973 of a federal agency for the regularization of irregular settlements created in *ejidal* land, the enactment in 1976 of the Human Settlements General Act, and the foundation of a few federal social-housing institutions.[4] In addition, from that time forward, the governments of the state of Mexico and the Federal District have operated through their own land and popular-housing agencies to address issues concerning tenure regularization in irregular settlements on private and public lands.

It is important to say that when all these initiatives were carried out, there was a deep concern among federal and provincial authorities about land-tenure and housing conflicts, and about the sometimes-violent demonstrations and actions promoted by organizations pertaining to the so-called *movimiento urbano popular* (popular urban movement).[5] In some cases, as in the city of Monterrey, these groups went as far as founding an autonomous large squatter settlement, Tierra y Libertad (Land and Liberty). Not incidentally, Nuevo León's state government responded by creating Fomerrey, a trusteeship dedicated to developing publicly managed self-help housing subdivisions.[6]

In addition, policymakers were concerned that the operation of the already-developed, irregular, low-cost land market was characterized by various forms of cheating and buyer frustration. Sellers frequently offered to introduce urban services and grant property deeds only after a buyer had completed all payments, and sellers often sold the same plot to several buyers. Thus, the problem involved not only irregular transactions but also fraud. The case that exemplifies this on the largest scale is Nezahualcóyotl.

It is fair to state that since their beginnings in the 1930s, government policies addressed at self-help neighborhoods (then called *colonias proletarias*, or proletarian settlements) aimed to intervene in conflicts and claims regarding low-cost land subdivisions in order to politically incorporate and control the urban poor.[7] Since then, for the same reasons, these policies have had a rather pragmatic orientation, despite attempts to impose various planned alternatives to the *colonias populares* (self-help urban settlements) in the 1970s and 1980s. These usually involved the institutionalization of land-tenure regularization programs, various public initiatives concerning formal low-cost subdivisions, and self-help housing programs (such as those carried out by Fomerrey in Monterrey). These initiatives, however, were always overwhelmed by the massive character of irregular urbanization processes and the rationale of local urban management and governance, which were based on clientelistic partisan politics.

These governmental initiatives, programs, and agencies largely managed to appease popular land and housing mobilizations. During the eighties they extended as far as to put the movimiento urbano popular's organizations and their leaders to orderly work as government partners in the execution of self-managed housing projects, under the label of "housing-applicant organizations."[8]

Given this outcome, it is not coincidental that in 1989, when Carlos Salinas, Mexico's president, put in motion Solidaridad (the main social program of his term), it had as its main components land-tenure regularization and urban improvement in colonias populares.[9] In fact, it was during Salinas's presidency (1989–95) that the implementation of tenure-regularization programs attained its maximum speed.[10] In any case, by the time Salinas launched Solidaridad, what had until the seventies been a turbulent, irregular low-cost housing land market had already become a rather quiet one. That is, the market had become one in which transactions are carried out beyond the reach of planning, and land property laws, but that are transparent with regard to their real character. This means two main things: (1) buyers know that neither services nor property deeds will be delivered by the seller, and that the introduction of services and facilities will be an issue to be addressed step-by-step, by settlers themselves, in dialogue with municipal authorities; and (2) settlers realize that getting property deeds depends on becoming beneficiaries of a regularization program, something that is a likely event despite being situated in an indefinite future.

In sum, we can conclude from the evolution of government intervention in Mexico's colonias populares that a steady application of land-tenure-regularization programs, in conjunction with an equally steady public investment in upgrading colonias' infrastructure, has resulted in the normalization of the informal housing land market, as well as the conversion of the informal and progressive production of a large part of Mexican cities into a natural and generally accepted urban process.[11] This outcome can be interpreted as the result of a pragmatic intervention model because, so far and as a whole, government intervention in informal settlements has remained within a legal framework that defines land-property regularization as "of public benefit," therefore allowing public authorities to implement settlement-regularization and upgrading programs. But there are neither norms that oblige public authorities to regularize irregular settlements or introduce scarce public facilities and services nor clear-cut settlers' rights concerning these issues. Nonetheless, regularization programs continue to be implemented, sometimes as a routine endeavor, sometimes as a government priority; and provisions for services and facilities go forward at a rhythm that seems more rapid nowadays than it was two or three decades ago. This process leaves aside only those settlements whose problems go far beyond property irregularity and the lack of permits for legal subdivision.

THE INFORMAL LAND MARKET AND THE PRODUCTION OF THE INFORMAL CITY

The 1980s was when the last large-scale informal developments under the form of colonias populares took place within the sociopolitical framework previously depicted. There was a general logic of the informal housing land market that can be summarized as follows.[12] Land supply was facilitated by the incorporation of property on the urban outskirts for popular-housing use. Obviously enough, the spatial location of informal subdivisions has changed over time and comprises areas under different kinds of property regimes, although ejidal lands have historically played a prominent role. More recently, during the last two decades, besides colonias populares, the informal city has been significantly fueled by the unregulated expansion of rural villages that are currently engulfed by the metropolitan conurbation. The lands concerned are those surrounding each village; they are usually composed of a large number of, but rather scattered and diversely sized, plots.

It is difficult to compare land prices in the formal and the informal markets because there are not currently, in the Mexico City Metropolitan Zone (MCMZ), formal subdivisions that offer low-cost, urbanized, vacant housing plots.[13] In any case, it is clear that price levels in irregular subdivisions are jointly determined by their location, their lack of urban services and facilities, the private nature of land transactions, and the housing density and level of urban upgrading achieved by any given settlement. In general terms, informal developers' profitability is determined by the fact that investments in land development are almost nonexistent and because the lands that are sold could not be allocated to more-profitable alternatives.[14]

The supply of housing plots adapts to the buying power of potential customers through low prices and also by avoiding formal transaction costs and giving buyers flexible payment conditions. In the same subdivision, plots may be selling in a variable number of installments, and credit is granted without resorting to the guarantees and requisites applied in formal credit transactions. In my view, this last point is a critical factor in the feasibility of this kind of transaction, which involves households that are mostly excluded from formal credit. It is also one of the main explanations for the success of firms such as Elektra, which specialize in selling home furniture, appliances, and electronics to low-income households through very expensive but easy-to-obtain loans. In this regard I agree with Erhard Berner when he states that "residents of extra-legal subdivisions may pay just as much money per square meter as those in legal ones, or sometimes even more. The major benefit lies in the possibility of incremental development and building improvement which leads to a spreading of the costs: 'Ultimately, the difference between the two systems is probably not the price limit per se but the way low-income families phase their expenses for housing.'"[15]

Buyers are mostly families in the early phase of their vital cycle (young couples with or without children) who acquire a plot of land in order to build their own homes as an alternative to rental housing or a dwelling shared with relatives. The model that has been described for the municipality of Valle de Chalco applies to the great majority of colonias populares currently in the making.[16] According to a survey from 1993, families' arrivals to Valle de Chalco usually coincided with events linked to the early vital cycle of nuclear families: couple formation, 6.5 percent; birth of a child, 50 percent; couple formation and birth of a child, 10.2 percent.[17] On the other hand, according to another survey carried out in 1990, the great majority of Valle de Chalco inhabitants (93 percent) came from some metropolitan municipality or a Federal District ward, mostly an adjacent one, and only 7 percent from outside the MCMZ. Additionally, 90 percent of this population was composed of families that were not housing owners before arriving in Valle de Chalco: 60 percent were tenants, 12 percent inhabited a borrowed dwelling, and 15 percent shared a dwelling with relatives.[18]

As a whole, the kind of informal city that results from this informal land market is based on a customary house-building know-how and a simplified version of the formal low-cost subdivision model common in Mexico City and metropolitan municipalities until the 1980s. This simplified model, as far as land topography and the size of subdivided parcels allow it, comprises a regular street layout that sometimes includes one or more main streets, as well as standard-sized housing plots of around 150–200 square meters. All in all, the emerging urban space usually shows several characteristic traits.

Public spaces are mostly reduced to streets and narrow sidewalks (though sometimes there are no sidewalks) and can include public leisure and open facilities (a small plaza, a basketball field, and so on) introduced by local authorities who take advantage of small chunks of land unallocated for whatever reason to housing or other private uses.

Dwellings are built and improved step-by-step, depending on household savings and informal loans, and often in response to changes in family size or the incorporation of another, related household unit (usually formed by a male child). In this latter case it is common to build a small new dwelling on a still-free portion of the original plot. Many times, housing incorporates commercial or workshop uses, or the original household builds one or more rooms or small rental apartments at ground level or on a second story. In fact, the combination of housing with commercial, service, or workshop uses, or with the production of rental units, is one of the main factors responsible for the improvement of average socioeconomic conditions in the informal city over time. Other explanatory factors include access to high school and college for many of the initial inhabitants' children and the gradual arrival of better-off households as the colonia upgrades.

Besides housing, new land uses are gradually incorporated in response to growing demand for retail commerce, consumer services, and public facilities (grocery stores, churches, schools, medical clinics, and so on). The spatial distribution of these activities is usually oriented by the emergence of some local commercial districts, mostly corresponding to one or more main streets and to the paths followed by public transport.

In spite of the rather low quality and reduced variety of most public spaces, they are usually intensively used and traversed, most of all by housewives buying staples and bringing their children to and from school, or by kids and teenagers playing and socializing. This markedly contrasts with what we can observe in the formal city, where, with the exception of some areas of the old central city, most people avoid public walking as much as possible, and kids are usually not allowed to stay and play in public streets. Additionally, in many colonias populares, local streets are from time to time the scenes of family parties, where neighbors usually are welcome if not expressly invited. And one or more wider streets are converted into a weekly market place, where a *tianguis* (street market) is set out, and people from the colonia or nearby ones not only buy a wide range of goods but also, especially during the weekends, go for a stroll, eat popular dishes at *antojitos* (snack) stalls, and socialize. The other side of the coin is that the uses of public spaces are regulated by customs of urbanity that suppose, in order to avoid neighborhood conflicts, the acceptance of different kinds of mishandlings concerning the uses of the streets and sidewalks.[19]

COLONIAS POPULARES AS A PROGRESSIVE HABITAT

Let us go now to a quantitative characterization of the informal city as it has evolved under the guise of colonias populares. Such a characterization, by tracing a number of socio-demographic indicators and their changes across time, shows what I call the *progressiveness* of the informal city. Up to just under two decades ago, the general evolution of the MCMZ informal city had to be based on case studies or gross comparisons of whole capital districts or metropolitan municipalities. This lack of finer general data was in part corrected by Jan Bazant, who characterized the evolution of a group of sample cases over twenty-eight years (1967–95), using both aerial photography and field observation.[20] Among other things, Bazant's research showed that the colonias populares he studied reached a gross housing density of fifty dwellings per hectare three decades after their beginnings. At this time, public facilities, commerce and services, workshops and small manufacturing plants, and street networks, occupied 2.1, 1.7, 1.7, and 21.2 percent, respectively, of the urbanized area. A shortcoming of the analytical model developed by Bazant is that he applied it to areas composed of a number of colonias founded at different moments during the period he studied. Therefore, the resulting data concerning land use, save perhaps the information corresponding to street networks, do not reflect land-use evolution for *each* settlement, which to my mind implies an underestimation of the density not used for housing in the older settlements — that is, those that were established at the beginning of the relevant period.

I rely on data obtained through the exhaustive classification of the MCMZ urban area at the census tract level for 1990, 2000, and 2005 by types of urban contexts, as defined in table 5.1. The evidence discussed from here on has allowed me, along with my colleagues at the Urban Observatory of Mexico City (Observatorio Urbano de la Ciudad de México), to get an overall physical, social, and demographic picture of the informal city in the MCMZ.[21] I try to characterize the informal city's role in the production of metropolitan urban space, as well as the scope and limits of the informal city's progressiveness, based on a number of selected indicators.

Table 5.2 displays census tract data concerning colonias populares' participation in the production of urban space up to 2005 (see map 5.1), as well as their role in metropolitan population growth between 1990 and 2005. A brief review of table 5.2 allows us to state a few points. First, during the last decade of the twentieth century, informal production of urbanized space, including originally rural villages that became part of the conurbation, accounted for 72.2 percent of population growth, of which more than 80 percent was concentrated in colonias populares (51.8 percent of total metropolitan population growth). Second, 60 percent of colonias populares' population growth took place on urban census tracts that did not register inhabitants in 1990, or whose population increased 50 percent or more between 1990 and 2000. In other words, the expansion and densification of colonias populares were in full effect during this period, and therefore the informal expansion of urban peripheries continued to be a popular housing alternative. But it seems that by the 1990s the phase of large irregular developments was over.

TABLE 5.1 · Types of Urban Contexts in the MCMZ

Older City	The portion of Mexico City composed of urban census tracts corresponding to its urbanized area up to 1929. The portion includes three different kinds of urban contexts.
	Colonial city: the area containing the so-called perimeters A and B of Mexico City's historical center.
	Central city: the area forming the center of Mexico City according to the cadastral map of 1929.
	Administrative headquarters (cabeceras conurbadas): former urban localities situated outside Mexico City in 1929.
Formal City	The part of the metropolitan urban area formally developed since 1929. It includes three types of urban contexts.
	Housing projects: urban census tracts concerning public or private developed large housing estates. There are two main generations of housing projects. The first one includes those developed since the 1970s up to the early 1990s, mostly composed of a number of apartment buildings (towers). The second corresponds to the so-called urban projects (conjuntos urbanos).
	Formal subdivisions (middle and low cost): urban census tracts concerning formal subdivisions developed from 1930 to the early 1990s. Subdivisions (fraccionamientos) were, for six decades, the procedure established for land urbanization. Mexico City's first Subdivisions Act (Ley de Fraccionamientos) was enacted in 1934, and the state of Mexico's act concerning metropolitan municipalities was passed in 1959.
	Upper-class subdivisions and projects: urban census tracts regarding high-profile subdivisions and contemporary residential projects oriented toward the well-to-do.
Informal City	The part of the current metropolitan urban area originated under three main kinds of informal settlements.
	Colonias populares (popular settlements): urban census tracts originated as different kinds of informal neighborhoods, sometimes initiated as squatter settlements but mostly consisting of informal subdivisions.
	Within conurbation villages: urban census tracts corresponding to originally rural villages currently engulfed by the metropolitan conurbation.
	Outside conurbation villages: urban census tracts corresponding to originally rural villages that in 2005 were not yet part of the metropolitan conurbation but were in the territory of a metropolitan municipality.

TABLE 5.2 · MCMZ: Dwellings Distribution by Types of Metropolitan Urban Contexts, 1990, 2000, 2005

DWELLINGS

Type of Urban Context	1990		2000		1990–2000	2005		2000–2005
	N	Share (%)	N	Share (%)	Growth Share (%)	N	Share (%)	Growth Share (%)
Urbanized Area Until 1929								
Colonial City	15,629	0.5	12,236	0.3	-0.4	10,446	0.2	-0.3
Central City	339,265	10.6	323,464	7.8	-1.7	353,525	7.6	5.5
Old Administrative Headquarters	73,228	2.3	99,577	2.4	2.8	88,862	1.9	-2.0
Sum Older City	428,122	13.4	435,277	10.5	0.8	452,833	9.7	3.2
Formal City								
Housing Projects	458,380	14.3	636,089	15.4	19.0	835,272	17.9	36.7
Formal Subdivisions	327,334	10.2	362,113	8.8	3.7	373,801	8.0	2.2
High Profile Developments	50,833	1.6	64,134	1.6	1.4	74,730	1.6	2.0
Sum Formal City	836,547	26.2	1,062,336	25.7	24.1	1,283,803	27.5	40.8
Informal City								
Colonias Populares	1,516,196	47.4	2,001,523	48.4	51.8	2,171,380	46.4	31.3
Inside Conurbation Villages	245,155	7.7	345,244	8.4	10.7	403,359	8.6	10.7
Outside Conurbation Villages	121,193	3.8	212,574	5.1	9.7	255,023	5.5	7.8
Sum Informal City	1,882,544	58.9	2,559,341	61.9	72.2	2,829,762	60.5	49.8
Other	52,822	1.7	81,090	2.0	3.0	100,013	2.1	3.5
MCMZ	3,195,491	100.0	4,133,050	100.0	100.0	4,676,276	100.0	100.0

Source: Elaborated with OCIM-GIS data.

Note: "MCMZ" (Mexico City Metropolitan Zone) refers to the 16 Federal District wards (*delegaciones*) and 59 municipalities of the Valley of Mexico.

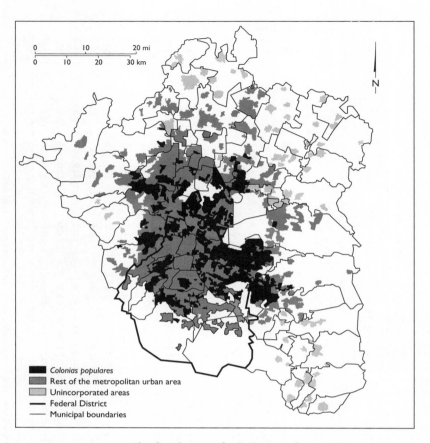

MAP 5.1 · The distribution of colonias populares in the
Mexico City Metropolitan Zone.

As table 5.3 demonstrates, this process went hand in hand with the introduction of urban services. By 2000 in the MCMZ, 96.4 percent of inhabited
dwellings had access to the potable water network, but only 68.7 percent of
them had tap water inside their homes. This difference indicates a significant degree of housing precariousness in the informal city and shows that
colonias populares' urban improvement currently seems to go ahead of residents' ability to improve their individual homes.

Table 5.3 also displays some housing and socio-demographic indicators
that compare different subsets of colonias populares census tracts within
the MCMZ as a whole and housing-projects census tracts. This table allows
us to observe the overall improvement of colonias populares between 1990

TABLE 5.3 · MCMZ: Housing Projects and Colonias Populares, Selected Socio-demographic Indicators—1990, 2000, 2005

| Indicators | MCMZ | Housing Projects | COLONIAS POPULARES | | | | |
			Mature by 2000	Consolidating in 1990–2000	Without Population in 1990	Without Population in 2000	All Colonias Populares
Gross demographic density (by hectare)							
1990	78.1	156.6	233.4	46.5	NA	NA	130.2
2000	84.7	183.0	213.0	101.7	70.0	NA	146.8
2005	84.7	164.4	NA	NA	NA	45.1	143.9
Average inhabitants per dwelling							
1990	4.8	4.7	4.9	5.2	NA	NA	5.0
2000	4.4	4.3	4.3	4.8	5.1	NA	4.5
2005	4.0	3.9	ND	ND	ND	4.4	4.2
% of dwellings with piped water							
1990	63.7	88.7	59.7	21.9	NA		47.7
2000	68.8	93.1	70.6	38.7	14.5		56.7
2005	76.6	90.2	ND	ND	ND	23.1	70.1
% of dwellings with one computer							
2000	16.9	20.0	12.8	5.5	1.7	NA	9.5
2005	30.1	37.2	NA	NA	NA	7.6	22.1
% of population earning more than 5 x minimum wage 2000	16.0	21.2	12.0	6.0	4.2	NA	9.5

Source: Elaborated with OCIM-GIS data.

Notes: "MCMZ" (Mexico City Metropolitan Zone) refers to the 16 Federal District wards (delegaciones) and 59 municipalities of the Valley of Mexico. Colonias populares are "mature"; that is, census urban tracts classified as colonias populares show a stagnant or a decreasing population between 1990 and 2000. "Consolidating" means census urban tracts registering between 1990 and 2000 a population growth up to or less than 50 percent. "Without population in 1990" means census urban tracts classified as colonias populares in 2000 that did not register inhabitants in 1990. "Without population in 2000" means urban census tracts classified as colonias populares in 2005 that did not register inhabitants in 2000.

and 2005, which shows a general urban-ecological process that exhibits a number of significant patterns. First, the social heterogeneity of colonias populares increases gradually and persistently. Though they usually begin populated only by poor households, as time passes *colonias populares* gain a growing proportion of better-off families, including a number of middle-class units. Second, colonias populares show a steady improvement in urban services and housing quality. And third, the colonias populares population shares some common trends with the average metropolitan population — for instance, an improvement of average formal education level over time, as reflected by the percentage of those eighteen and older that achieve some higher education. In fact, the gains obtained regarding this third indicator by the four subsets of colonias populares between 1990 and 2005 are larger than those concerning all the other metropolitan urban contexts.

In sum, colonias populares show an average trajectory that always begins in the lowest extreme of metropolitan urban and social conditions, and that trajectory usually ends when colonias populares arrive at their maturity, near to the metropolitan average. Colonias populares' maturity arrives about two to three decades after the first — usually precarious — dwellings are built in a given area, and that maturity is expressed in a stagnant or decreasing population (although the number of dwellings may be still increasing).

During the period 1990 to 2005, colonias populares improved their social indicators at a faster rate than either the MCMZ as a whole or the housing projects, and these indicators improved most rapidly when the rate of colonias populares' population growth was also the highest. It seems, however, that there are limits to colonias populares' housing and social improvement. For example, by 2000 only 70.6 percent of mature colonias populares dwellings had inside running water, which of course indicates widespread poverty even in mature colonias populares. But at the same time this lack shows that colonias populares, even as they gain nonpoor households, *retain* poor ones.

All in all we can state, based on census data, that MCMZ's informal city, and probably many of Mexico's other informal cities, generally functions as a progressive habitat and as a socially heterogeneous one in the medium and long term. Yet we cannot ignore three main hard facts. First, such progressiveness implies that *pioneer* households — those that arrive in a given informal settlement during its first stage — have to deal with very hard material conditions for a good number of years. Second, the informal production of the inhabited urban space is one of the main expressions of a highly unequal society, and it is one of the main vehicles through which that society and its still-underdeveloped forms of citizenship are reproduced. Third, there exists an irredeemable portion of the informal city. That portion consists of an indeterminate number of informal settlements that, for different reasons, do not evolve as a progressive habitat. So far, we mostly speculate about what the reasons are, usually pointing to highly adverse environmental or legal conditions. In any case, assessing the size and localization, and explaining the causes of this *nonprogressive informal city*, is a task that requires much undone fieldwork.[22] If anything, the informal settlements that form this nonprogressive informal city probably exhibit the kind of urban marginality described by Javier Auyero in the case of Villa Paraiso, largely because they do not become socially heterogeneous over time. Instead they tend to keep the poorest population without facilitating social mobility or attracting better-off new settlers.[23]

CONCLUSIONS: THE FUTURE OF THE INFORMAL CITY

Colonias populares continue to be one of the main housing delivery systems in Mexican cities, but it seems that things are quickly changing. Since the second half of the 1990s, the reform of public-housing institutions is yielding a growing supply of formal housing, under the guise of large (sometimes gigantic) housing projects, which account for an increasing share of the metropolitan (and national-urban) housing stock's growth. In table 5.2 we can see how between 1990 and 2000 and 2000 and 2005, housing projects were quickly assuming a prominent role in the growth of the metropolitan housing stock, outweighing that of colonias populares in 2000 to 2005. But housing projects' increasing role is still smaller than that of the colonias populares combined with villages. As we can observe from table 5.3, colonias populares and villages have increased their share of the metropolitan housing stock's growth since the 1990s.

These two converging tendencies raise some tricky issues concerning housing-stock evolution and the future of the metropolitan informal city. It is likely that lands situated on the outskirts of the metropolitan conurbation (which until the early 1990s would have been expected to become incorporated sooner or later into the informal housing market) now have a greater possibility of being incorporated into the formal housing market through their acquisition by large formal-housing developers. Therefore, the owners of this land, mostly small landholders and *ejidatarios*, are currently either negotiating the land's sale to formal developers or waiting to do that. In contrast, village landholders have no such options for two main reasons. On the one hand, their properties, though locally recognized, are usually irregular given that current holders have inherited or received land from an older relative, but they don't have a property deed in their names. On the other hand, villagers' land is usually composed of many rather small pieces randomly scattered on areas surrounding the villages' original layouts. These conditions imply that in order to sell their land, village landholders can only operate in the informal, low-cost housing land market.

If I am right, the converging conditions outlined here had several consequences. The possibility of access to credit for acquiring a low-cost dwelling in a housing project means that formal housing tends to comprise an increasing portion of metropolitan households, including many that previously had to resort to acquiring a housing plot in the irregular market under the former prevailing conditions. Conversely, the supply of informal land through the formation of new colonias populares has been contracting. At the same time, and it seems for the same reasons, the informal housing land market in the villages has been expanding since these new conditions became apparent.

But what are the meanings of these new conditions in regards to the future of the (metropolitan) informal city? First, if current tendencies persist for an extended-enough period (let us say the next fifteen to twenty years), and (as has been announced) formal housing credit continues expanding in order to include poorer households earning up to three minimum wages, the growth of the informal city will slow considerably.[24] At the same time, the remaining informal new housing production will mostly serve the housing needs of the poorest.

Second, large or gigantic housing projects will lodge many more socially homogeneous populations (ranging from low- to lower-middle-income households, each one according to the market niche it is oriented to fit) than those currently inhabiting mature and consolidating colonias populares. Compared to these, housing projects have the advantage of apportioning serviced—but not always finished—dwellings from the start. In fact, as the current housing policy includes a wider and poorer clientele, dwellings are delivered as "basic" structures. These consist of roofed surfaces of twenty-five to thirty square meters and are defined as "progressive" because they can be extended independently by the owners. In fact, even in those housing projects where dwellings are larger (about fifty to sixty square meters) and

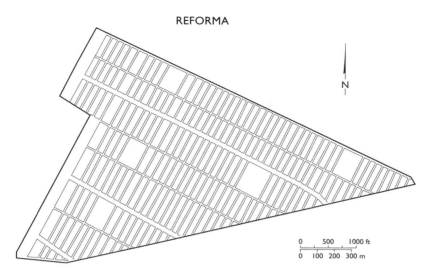

REFORMA

N

| 0 | 500 | 1000 ft |

| 0 | 100 | 200 | 300 m |

FIG. 5.1 · The street layout of Reforma, a consolidated colonia popular
in the municipality of Nezahualcoyotl.

supposedly finished at delivery, it is possible to observe over a short span
of time the proliferation of irregular additions. These additions usually fill
the small back- or front yards envisioned as natural lighting and ventilation
buffers, or these additions are built on an unplanned second floor.

We are witnessing the diffusion of a new low-cost housing urban context, whose management will impose, in my view, severe burdens on what
are often rather incompetent and partisan municipal administrations. What
we can foresee is that, regardless of the precise future scope of this rapidly
expanded new type of low-cost formal housing, the majority of the already
existing colonias populares will remain as a main component of the metropolitan built environment for the next several decades. Therefore, the overall fate of the metropolitan inhabited space will depend not only on the
problem-ridden evolution of new large and gigantic housing projects but
also on the evolution and progressive transformation of currently mature
and consolidating colonias populares.

Large-scale examples such as that of Nezahualcóyotl clearly show that
this progressive transformation is a likely possibility. In fact, unlike large
housing projects or the large walled condominiums and developments currently in vogue, colonias populares constitute a highly malleable built environment. In this respect they function much like the central city (the urban

AMPL. SAN PEDRO XALPA

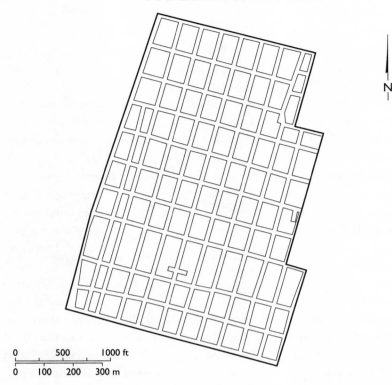

FIG. 5.2 · The street layout of Ampliación San Pedro Xalpa,
a consolidated colonia popular in Azcapotzalco, D.F.

area built before the 1940s) and the formal subdivisions that were developed between the 1940s and the 1980s according to the regular grid model. That is, as long as colonias populares have a layout based on this model and their streets and other open areas are part of the public domain, their original housing plots can be rebuilt, eventually merged, and destined to other urban uses besides self-help housing, including new types of housing (condominiums, blocks of flats), commerce, community and private services, offices, and so on. This is an evolution, by the way, that we currently can observe in a great number of consolidated colonias populares, and it is equally observed in central city neighborhoods and old formal housing subdivisions.

Therefore, what can we expect regarding the future metropolitan role of colonias populares? They will likely deliver an ever-contracting proportion of new housing stock during the next fifteen to twenty years. But we are facing a metropolitan urban-scape where distant and probably decaying housing projects, along with colonias populares, already compose by far the largest part of the housing stock. We can guess that mature and more or less well-located colonias populares, "some [of which] have become over the years extremely nice places to live," together with some well-located and rather nice villages, will represent an increasingly attractive residential alternative for middle-class households.[25]

Another story has to be told about the future of the *nonprogressive* informal city. Extreme manifestations of the four main disadvantages usually attributed to informal settlements can probably be found in these places: precarious housing tenure, unsuitable location, lack of a planned layout, and the poor urban population's susceptibility to political control and appeasement. In this case we are roughly talking about settlements with a very unfavorable topography and location, which have resulted from highly hazardous and fragmented land-subdivision processes. As long as many settlers' basic needs satisfaction depends on the good will of government bureaucracy and officials, there is a fertile ground for clientelistic practices. That being the case, we can hope that the nonprogressive informal city, unlike the progressive one, will be a transitory urban reality that will be replaced, along with Mexico's development, by a more suitable form of popular habitat.

NOTES

1. See Alain Durand-Lasserve and R. Lauren Royston, *Holding Their Ground: Secure Land Tenure for the Urban Poor in Developing Countries* (London: Earthscan, 2003); and Edésio Fernandes, "Regularizing Informal Settlements in Brazil: Legalization, Security of Tenure and City Management," paper presented at the ASF-N Aerus Workshop, Brussels, May 23–26, 2001.

2. The Institutional Revolutionary Party (Partido Revolucionario Institucional) and its predecessor, the National Revolutionary Party (Partido Nacional Revolucionario) ruled the nation for seventy years, but the Institutional Revolutionary Party was displaced in 2000 from the presidency by the National Action Party (Partido de Acción Nacional).

3. Martha Schteingart, *Los productores del espacio habitable: Estado, empresa y sociedad en la Ciudad de México* (Mexico City: El Colégio de México, 1989), 82–98.

4. The ejidal land is the main outcome of the agrarian reform carried out after

the Mexican Revolution. The ejido was a means for distributing land to peasants and—given that it was forbidden to sell, lease, or rent ejidal land—for avoiding the re-creation of latifundia. Up to now, ejido's land roughly composed a half of the national territory. These institutions are the Institute of the National Fund for the Worker's Housing (Instituto Nacional del Fondo de la Vivienda para los Trabajadores) and the Housing Fund for the Government Workers' Housing (Fondo de la Vivienda para los Trabajadores al Servicio del Estado).

5. See Antonio Azuela, *La Ciudad, la propiedad privada y el derecho* (Mexico City: El Colégio de México, 1989); and Ann Varley, "Clientelismo o tecnocracia? La lógica política de la regularización de la tierra urbana, 1970–1988," *Revista Mexicana de Sociologia* 56, no. 4 (1994).

6. María de los Ángeles Pozas, "La burocracia y la acción estatal en Monterrey," *Medio Ambiente y Urbanización* 7, no. 24 (1988).

7. Antonio Azuela and María Soledad Cruz, "La institucionalización de las colonias populares y la política urbana en la ciudad de México (1940–1946)," *Sociologica* 4, no. 9 (1989).

8. See Emilio Duhau, "Politica habitacional para los sectores populates en México: La experiencia de Fonhapo," *Medio Ambiente y Urbanización* 7, no. 24 (1988).

9. Emilio Duhau, "La política social y la gestión estatal de la pobreza," in *Dinámica urbana y procesos socio-políticos*, edited by René Coulomb and Emilio Duhau, 235–53 (Mexico City: OCIM, UAM-A, CENVI A.C., 1993).

10. Emilio Duhau, "La regolarizzazione dell'habitat popolare in México," *Storia Urbana* 23, nos. 88–89 (1999).

11. Land-tenure-regularization programs are a kind of policy that has been characterized as *self-defeating* because it inevitably promotes what it aims to eliminate. See Erhard Berner, "Informal Developers, Patrons and the State: Institutions and Regulatory Mechanism in Popular Housing," paper presented at the ASF-N Aerus Workshop, Brussels, May 25–26, 2001.

12. In the case of the MCMZ, a complete characterization of irregular urbanization processes would require taking into account, along with colonias populares, another kind of informal settlements. These settlements resulted from the housing densification and extension of old rural villages that were already engulfed by the metropolitan conurbation or, though not yet engulfed, were affected by the metropolitan dynamics.

13. The MCMZ is composed, according to an official definition, of the Federal District, divided into sixteen wards and fifty-nine municipalities situated in the Valley of Mexico. The data shown in tables 5.1, 5.2, and 5.3 concern all the urban census tracts located within this delimitation. Urban census tracts concern localities with more than 2,500 inhabitants.

14. There are some researchers that hold that land prices in irregular settlements are higher than in formal low-cost subdivisions. Yet, in my view, these researchers' claims are not supported by any systematic evidence. See, for example, Alfonso Iracheta, "Políticas e instrumentos de generación de suelo urbanizado para pobres

por medio de la recuperación de plusvalías," in *Los pobres de la ciudad y la tierra*, edited by Alfonso Iracheta and Martim Smolka (Toluca, Mexico: El Colegio Mexiquense, 2000).

15. See Berner, "Informal Developers, Patrons and the State," 12.

16. Valle de Chalco is an area to the southeast of Mexico City, where the last large-scale informal development in the MCMZ is situated.

17. Alícia Lindón, *De la trama de la cotidianidad a los modos de vida urbanos: El Valle de Chalco* (Mexico City: El Colegio de México, El Colegio Mexiquense, 1999), 105.

18. Daniel Hiernaux, "Ocupación del suelo y producción del espacio construído en el valle de Chalco, 1978–1991," in *Espacio y vivienda en la ciudad de México*, edited by Martha Schteingart (Mexico City: El Colegio de México, 1991), 187–88.

19. For instance, one abuse is the use of the sidewalks and the streets as de facto workshop extensions. Emilio Duhau and Angela Giglia, "Espacio público y nuevas centralidades: Dimensión local y urbanidad en las colonias populares de la ciudad de México," *Papeles de Población*, no. 41 (2004).

20. Jan Bazant, *Periferias urbanas: Expansión urbana incontrolada de bajos ingresos y su impacto en el medio ambiente* (Mexico City: M.A. Porrúa, UAM-A, 2001).

21. In the 1990s, R. Coulomb and I, with the participation of other colleagues forming part of the UAM-A's team of urban sociologists and the Center for Housing and Urban Studies (Centro de la Vivienda y Estudios Urbanos), launched the Urban Observatory of Mexico City, which in recent years has been coordinated by Priscilla Connolly. A main Urban Observatory of Mexico City product has been a geographic information system for the MCMZ, based on census tracts classified by *tipos de poblamiento* (types of urban contexts).

22. Priscilla Connolly, *Urban Slum Report: The Case of Mexico City* (Washington, DC: Habitat-UN, 2003).

23. Javier Auyero, "'This Is a Lot Like the Bronx, Isn't It?': Lived Experiences of Marginality in an Argentine Slum," *International Journal of Urban and Regional Research* 23, no. 1 (1999).

24. Federal authorities and developer representatives have stated that during the six years of the former federal administration, the majority of housing credits will be given to households earning up to three minimum wages. Currently, the Mexican minimum wage is equal to US$140.

25. Connolly, *Urban Slum Report*, 13.

SIX

The Favelas of Rio de Janeiro

Photographs by Ratão Diniz
Captions by Bryan McCann

FIG. 6.1 · A consolidated favela in Rio de Janeiro. Homes are made
entirely of brick and concrete; several are three or four stories tall, streets
are paved, and electric wires and water tanks indicate basic infrastructural
development. The *lajes* (flat roofs) provide both space for sociability
and the possibility of vertical expansion.

FIG. 6.2 · Young residents of the favela Parque Maré play
ping-pong on a narrow alleyway known as the Rua da Alegria.
During tranquil periods, the *becos* (alleyways) of Rio's favelas serve
as crucial sites for sociability, particularly at night.

FIG. 6.3 · The stairways of Providência, one of Rio's oldest favelas, serve the same purpose as the becos. Multiple generations share space, turning the stairway into a community meeting ground.

FIG. 6.4 · Skateboarding has grown in popularity as Rio's favelas absorb and transform global urban culture. Basketball has also become a favela mainstay, with several tournaments bringing together teams that represent favelas across the city.

FIG. 6.5 · Soccer remains the most popular pastime, and the one best adapted to the vacant lots and marginal spaces on the peripheries of consolidated favelas. The balustrade on the home at left, with a *birosca* (combination bar and all-purpose store) on the ground floor, shows the mix of commercial and residential and the rising material fortunes of many favela lots.

FIG. 6.6 · This favela home is pockmarked with bullet holes and protected by a window grate and a steel door, with a graffiti mural proclaiming peace. The air conditioner in the window indicates rising material fortunes in the midst of urban violence.

FIG. 6.7 · "Our pain is commemorated as an indicator of police efficiency." A family from the favela protests police violence—in this case, the death of another favela child in a shoot-out between police and suspects of drug trafficking.

FIG. 6.8 · Commerce has expanded dramatically in Rio's favelas. Often that commerce, such as this beloved restaurant in Vigário Geral, depends entirely on the sweat equity of its locally rooted owners and the cultivation of a loyal neighborhood clientele.

FIG. 6.9 · The *quadra* (community multipurpose court) is at the center of community life—used for soccer, basketball, samba, forró (a Brazilian dance), funk dances, rallies, birthday parties, and more. Effective control over who uses the quadra and when is equivalent to tremendous leverage over community life.

FIG. 6.10 · The physical beauty of the favela—its density, complexity, and organic energy—continues to draw the attention of artists, architects, and authors from Brazil and abroad, inspiring both utopian and dystopian depictions of favela life.

FIG. 6.11 · Graffiti has transformed the surfaces of consolidated favelas in recent years. Among other possibilities, it offers an opportunity for the proclamation of individual creativity and identity in spaces that the official city considers to be marginal and uncultured.

FIG. 6.12 · The sprawling favelas of the Complexo de Maré were founded by fishermen and their families, and a few older residents still ply that trade in the murky waters of the Guanabara Bay. The concrete seawall and promenade are the result of a city project, delivered after years of community activism.

FIG. 6.13 · "Your trajectory makes the line that invades my life."
The graffiti reminds commuters driving by on the busy Red Line highway
in Rio's North Zone of the existence of the adjacent favela, while the
bunkered and heavily armed swat-team officer shows evidence
of a different and more dangerous invasion.

FIG. 6.14 · The boxing school in Maré has been one of the most
successful of the many NGOs that have arisen in Rio's favelas in recent
decades—one that addresses the everyday violence of favela life, particularly
among young, unemployed men—and seeks to transform the city into
something more disciplined, civic, and hopeful.

FIG. 6.15 · Vibrant graffiti, paved roads, steel gates, barred windows, a profusion of irregular electrical hookups, three-story painted homes pocked with bullet holes, advertising, and sociability on the concrete stairways: the consolidated favela.

SEVEN

Informal Cities and Community-Based Organizing

THE CASE OF THE TEATRO ALAMEDA

Sujatha Fernandes

"Good evening, residents of San Agustín. We're meeting today, trying to commemorate a little of those times, of the Grupo Madera. Because for those who remember, we lost the Teatro Alameda, but we realized a dream on April 13, 2004, when we took it over and created the Casa Cultural Alameda. And in a joint program with the Cinemateca Nacional, we're going to have a cycle of Cinema under the Stars. Bring your chairs, your girlfriends, and your popcorn, and we'll provide the film."

In March 2005, some local coordinators in the Caracas parish of San Agustín had set up a projector outside the Casa Cultural Alameda (Alameda Cultural Center) to show Jacobo Penzo's film *El Afinque de Marín* (1980). Penzo, a documentary filmmaker, had come to barrio Marín of San Agustín in the 1970s wanting to shoot a film about musicians in Caracas. His visit to Marín coincided with the vibrant historical moment of the local radical cultural musical ensemble Grupo Madera. His documentary chronicled its attempts to create spaces of community resistance. Some people from the Casa Cultural Alameda had organized the screening of Penzo's film as a way of linking their occupation of the abandoned theater on April 13, 2004, with the history of revolutionary cultural movements of San Agustín. San Agustín is a relatively established popular parish in Caracas, Venezuela, located close to the city center. The Teatro Alameda had ceased functioning in 1965 and was recuperated by the residents in 2004 as a community cultural center.

Residents from sectors and barrios across the parish had turned out for the showing: older people and small children, couples and families, men and women. As the film began, the silence and darkness were punctuated only by the occasional passing cars and the soft glow of light emanating from the screen. During the film, people whispered to each other and pointed at the screen. They laughed, nodded silently, and smiled as they recalled some forgotten memory, and some had tears streaming down their faces.

The film begins with a tribute to the residents of San Agustín: "In 1971, it was announced that certain barrios of the parish San Agustín would be demolished to construct a park. Thanks to their active resistance, the residents of El Mamón, El Manguito, La Ceiba, La Charneca, Hornos de Cal, Negro Primero, and Marín stopped the destruction of the old Caraqueño communities. This documentary is intended as a homage to those barrios and a recognition of the dignity and cultural vitality of their residents." The images on the screen are a testament to the vitality and strong sense of community in San Agustín of the 1970s. A young man sporting a black tracksuit and short Afro cruises through the streets of the barrio on a motorbike, two congas strapped on either side of his bike. He waves at people, stops for a chat, and taps lightly on the congas as he weaves his way through the lanes and narrow streets. A group of men stand talking animatedly on a street corner in their tight jeans, broad lapel shirts, and aviator sunglasses. The musical legend Mandingo appears in a pair of striped orange sweat pants, giving a demonstration of drums such as the *culo 'e puya* and the *mina*. A youthful Alejandrina Ramos, a silver star pinned to her Afro, talks about the importance of music in the life of the community.

Scenes from the film capture something of the extraordinary musical crucible that San Agustín has been historically. In a series of continuous shots, a young girl and boy sit talking, while in the background a man works out dance steps. A group of men sit on a front stoop and one of the men plays pianos chords on his legs. A woman stands in the street fixing the rollers in her hair. A small boy perches on the hood of a car, smiling and playing imaginary congas. A group of children come running down a set of concrete stairs, and some slide backward down the iron railings. The film conveys a sense of community presence in the streets and public spaces of the barrio, and the beat of the *tambores* (drums) that underlies the rhythm of life.

The occupation of the abandoned Teatro Alameda in San Agustín on April 13, 2004, represented a taking back of community spaces that had been lost through decades of social decline, government neglect, and privatization. At the base of this action was the historical memory of the Teatro Alameda, the musical life of the parish, the vibrant years of Grupo Madera, and the dignity that the Teatro and the musical group represented for ordinary residents, as well as the multiple losses suffered by the community. The date of the takeover was symbolically linked with the coup against the leftist president Hugo Chávez two years earlier. Residents involved in the takeover made constant references to the Bolivarian constitution as giving them the right to take over spaces that are not being used and convert them into centers for the community.

But over the course of the following year, the Teatro Alameda became the subject of bitter disputes, as rival factions in the barrio — partly the result of state and party intervention — fought to align these symbols with their own projects. The institutionalization of the space by the state and the emergence of a small clique within the leadership eventually led to an abandonment of the space by the residents. How can we understand the failure of the theater to embody the hopes of the residents? Why did the theater succumb to the control of a small faction of local elite interests, excluding broader participation? What can this example tell us about the promise and the limitations of urban social movements in a Chávez era?

This chapter looks at new trends of popular protagonism emerging in urban centers of Venezuela that aim to revitalize public spaces and reassert community control over these spaces. But I argue that the localism at the heart of the Alameda seizure also paved the way for parochialism and entrenched interests to take over, leading to the failure of a transformative agenda. Unable to build strong connections with preexisting social movements, the Alameda project became too easily drawn into maneuvering by political parties and strategies of incorporation by the state. Localism and informality have been a hallmark of contemporary urban movements not based in factories, union halls, or traditional sites of collective action. But unless these informal movements can tie into organizational structures of democratic practice and accountability, they remain vulnerable to being absorbed by the dominant praxis. The case of the Teatro Alameda indicates the potential of Chavismo to activate new lines of community-based participation, but it also demonstrates a downside to informality — the lack of mediating bodies that could strengthen and sustain local movements.

URBAN SEGREGATION AND SOCIAL MOVEMENTS

San Agustín is one of the older parishes of Caracas, located close to the city center. The census of 2000 lists a population of some 39,175 residents in the parish, although this is an estimate. The actual numbers are probably somewhat higher than what is recorded in the census due to the difficulty of accurately counting highly dense urban populations with a large number of squatters.[1] San Agustín del Sur is divided off from the more prosperous area of San Agustín del Norte by the river Guaire. Walking along the main avenue of San Agustín del Sur, one encounters a series of small bodegas selling groceries, cleaning products, and baked goods; small religious shops with statues of saints and other mementos in the windows; and auto-repair shops. Men sit outside on makeshift boxes, beer bottles in hand, laughing and making jokes. The pavement is jammed with a steady stream of pedestrians and street vendors selling small snacks. Moving east along the avenue, there is a large basketball court on the left, and on the right is the Teatro Alameda. A lane behind the theater, littered with trash and syringes, and reeking of urine, leads to a small square known as the Afinque de Marín, at the heart of barrio Marín. Several houses face the square and there is a basketball hoop to the right. On one wall of the Afinque, life-size murals of the original members of the Grupo Madera give a sense of the cultural history of the sector.

Barrio Marín is unique among Caraqueño barrios for its old-style colonial houses with inner courtyards, decorated with ornate grills and pastel colors; its wide stone streets; and street lights that begin to glow in the early evening. Some residents have the means to preserve these colonial houses, but most have watched their homes deteriorate in the humid climate, because they are unable to pay for repairs. Between the tall façades of the houses, one sees the ranchos in the hills behind. The more precarious ranchos are made with wood or recycled materials, and they have zinc roofs and earth floors, while the consolidated ranchos may be multistory with brick walls, tiled roofs, and electricity. Leaving Marín and climbing several long, concrete staircases, one reaches the *cerro* (upper barrios of the sector), such as Charneca, El Mamón, and La Ceiba. Interspersed among the precarious ranchos are rich vegetation, papaya trees, and overgrown grass; public water amenities for residents of the sector; a makeshift basketball court; and bodegas, where residents sell malt, pasta, toothpaste, and soap from small windows of their dwellings. Salsa musicians gather in dark rooms to practice. Occasionally the clash of a snare or the rumble of a conga can be heard coming from a rancho. Reggaeton blares from small radios. The climb up to the cerro reveals views of large city skyscrapers, the Hotel Caracas Hilton, the downtown Parque Central district, and San Agustín del Norte.

In San Agustín, community-based activism emerged during the 1970s in response to government plans for urban remodeling. In his program of governance, the Christian Democrat Rafael Caldera offered to build 100,000 houses in order to provide a solution to housing problems.[2] In 1972 the area of Parque Central was created, which affected those in the barrios of San Agustín del Sur.[3] The government demolished Saladillo, a barrio well-known for its musical traditions of Gaitera.[4] Caldera promoted a housing program known as The New San Agustín, which proposed to eliminate the ranchos and to build houses in the lower and middle ranges of the cerros, while the higher ranges of the cerros would become public gardens, uniting the botanical gardens and Parque los Caobos.

Through a state agency known as the Centro Simón Bolívar (csb), the government expropriated the lower and intermediary territories of the barrio Hornos de Cal and relocated the displaced to the Urbanización La Yerbera. But for the other residents who were to be displaced, the government intended to send them to Valles del Tuy, which would isolate them from their work and schools.[5] Young promoters from the csb came to the barrio in an attempt to win support for their urban remodeling projects through social activities. These promoters involved people from the parish in baseball teams, choirs, and musical groups, such as the San Agustín Popular Choir. They helped barrio youths edit a newspaper known as *La Realidad*, and they organized spiritual retreats.[6] One leader from San Agustín, Jesús "Totoño" Blanco, recounts: "It was a form of getting into the community, so that the people would soften up, sell their houses, and leave." Then the government could demolish their houses and organize their project." But as barrio residents realized that the activities of the csb were part of a program to displace them, they began to organize on their own.

A group of radical youths from San Agustín del Sur, inspired by Che Guevara, Ho Chi Min, and Víctor Jara, formed the club Wilfredo Carrillo, also known as the Comité contra los Desalojos (Committee against Displacement). The committee began in the premises of an abandoned bodega, known as La Palma, which the young people occupied, cleaned out, and painted.[7] Residents across the parish became involved in the activities of the young people, and they raised money through raffles and games. The committee proved that the price being paid for each square of land was not that indicated by the Oficina Municipal de Planificación Urbana (Municipal Office of Urban Planning). Nevertheless, the csb continued demolishing sections of La Charneca and Hornos de Cal, and it constructed two buildings, which were not available to barrio residents due to their high prices. The committee continued to protest, and finally the work of the CSB was paralyzed, leaving mutilated barrios, open sewers, water shortages, and ruins. One of the biggest casualties of this urban remodeling was the industrial sector north of the main avenue. The CSB had purchased the businesses and sawmills of this sector, which were later abandoned.[8] The remodeling plan was a disaster, and it betrayed the hopes of those who had hoped for positive change.

Carlos Andrés Pérez from Acción Democratica (Democratic Action) came to power in 1974 and in his V Plan of the Nation he continued his predecessor's plans for urban remodeling and displacement of barrio residents.[9] But during this period of the 1970s, community resistance in San Agustín grew stronger, and it was based around the movement El Afinque de Marín, which was started by the Grupo Madera in 1977. The members of the Grupo Madera were musicians from different barrios of San Agustín del Sur, who worked in salsa orchestras and other musical groups. The members began to investigate the black movement in Venezuela, and some went back to their place of origin in Barlovento to carry out research on the African slave trade, and the distinct places in Africa from where slaves were brought to Venezuela. Others carried out research on salsa music and other musical genres in Venezuela. Members of the group went to the library of the Universidad Central de Venezuela (Central University of Venezuela) to research fiestas and popular traditions. The group began to perform and create fusions of these autochthonous Venezuelan traditions, from *guaguancó* (a percussive rumba) to Yoruba chants.[10] The Grupo Madera was part of a vibrant cultural revival; similar groups were also started in other barrios of Caracas, such as the Grupo Autoctono, founded by Williams Ochoa in barrio Carmen of La Vega in 1974. The Grupo Madera was symbolically associated with the small plaza of barrio Marín, where the group would practice, hold jam sessions, and perform large concerts for barrio residents. At that time, Jesús Blanco, Totoño's father, noted: "Look how these kids *afincan* [get down]."[11] From this phrase came the name El Afinque de Marín for the small plaza and by extension of the political movement that formed around the Grupo Madera.

Grupo Madera was a radical cultural movement that was concerned with building solidarity and unity among the members of the barrio, and with other groups nationally. According to Nelly Ramos, one of the surviving members of the group, the members of Grupo Madera wanted to create an artistic project of quality and dignity, as well as "forge an ideological consciousness[,] . . . above all, to give incentive to all the participants to define their corresponding role as the protagonists of a cultural response that was emerging in the heart of the community."[12] The Grupo Madera created a free school for children of the parish, known as Maderita. They made all decisions related to their work in popular assemblies, and at the same time, their music garnered national and international attention.[13] They were part of a broader current of socially committed music, or protest music during this era, which included the *nueva trova* of Silvio Rodriguez and Carlos Varela in Cuba, the *nueva canción* of Victor Jara and Violeta Para in Chile, and the civil rights song movement in the United States.

Vibrant social movements in the barrios suffered some setbacks in the early 1980s under the administration of Luis Herrera Campíns. In August 1980, several of the members of Grupo Madera died in a tragic boat accident, which many believed to be a deliberate act of negligence on the part of the government. The Grupo Madera had been invited to come to the Amazonas by the Ministry of Youth in the Amazonian Federal Territory. As the boat crossed the Orinoco River during a turbulent storm, it sank, leading to death by drowning for eleven members of the group. The journalist Alexis Rosas confirmed the suspicions held by many community activists of government involvement in the accident. Rosas says that there were too many indicators of negligence for the accident to be fortuitous: the captain of the ship was drunk, and during the accident he abandoned the ship rather than organizing a rescue, and the life vests were locked up in compartments. With the knowledge that crossing the Orinoco in winter required a captain with expertise, the ministry had put the lives of the group in the hands of an inexperienced sailor.[14] After the accident, the president of the Ministry of Youth, Charles Brewer Carías, protected the captain by concealing his identity. For the residents of San Agustín del Sur, this was a sad moment. The Madera tragedy marked a moment of decline for some sectors of urban popular movements, and they would not be reinvigorated again until the mid-1990s.

This trajectory of community-based organizing in San Agustín is somewhat similar to trends in poor barrios and parishes across the city. In recent years, the barrio has emerged as a central site of working-class politics. From being a temporary residence that housed rural workers who came to Caracas in search of work; to being a step on the ladder to greater social mobility as opportunities expanded during the industrial development of the

1940s and 1950s; and then to becoming a sign of the city's chaos, poverty, and decline following the debt crisis of the 1980s, the barrio has increasingly come to be seen as the space of belonging and the source of identity for new social actors. Barrio movements claim distinct genealogies that include the clandestine movements against the military regime of the 1950s, the post-transition era of guerrilla struggle in the 1960s, movements against urban displacement in the 1970s, and the cultural activism and urban committees of the 1990s. These movements asserted the political presence and power of the urban poor, differentiating them from the state and middle-class sectors. The barrio itself came to be a symbol of urban life and struggle, as barrio residents fought for dignity, respect, and recognition.

The rise of barrio-based movements must also be understood in the context of histories of segregation and marginality in urban centers across Latin America. An important body of scholarship emerged in the 1960s to document and understand the problematic of urban segregation presented by the shantytowns. Some scholars sought to challenge what they saw as the "myth of marginality," debunking the idea that the shantytowns were peripheral and marginal to urban life.[15] Shantytown dwellers, they argued, were integrated into the life of the city and national politics through clientelist networks guaranteeing service provision in exchange for political votes and the struggles of neighborhood associations to improve their standard of living.[16] Contrary to notions of shantytowns as marginal zones or "cultures of poverty," these scholars argued that the urban poor were capable of social mobility, entrepreneurship, and political participation.[17]

Revisiting these classical theories of marginality four decades later, a new generation of scholars reflected that the conditions of marginality that earlier scholars sought to challenge may indeed be being realized in contemporary societies.[18] Structural adjustment and neoliberal policies of the 1980s and 1990s produced classical features of marginality such as unemployment, a growing informal sector and barter economy, and social exclusion and violence.[19] In addition to producing the *conditions* of marginality, with the advance of neoliberal restructuring, the *idea* of marginality has reemerged in the social imaginary of Latin American urban societies.[20] Intensified rural immigration to the cities, growing poverty and segregation, and rising insecurity have led to the criminalization of poorer sectors, which are seen as disrupting the order and health of the city.[21] In Caracas, both wealthy and poorer sectors refer to the barrios as the *barrios margina-*

les (marginal barrios) or *zonas marginales* (marginal zones). Understanding this new geography of power and marginality in the city is crucial to understanding how it may also be the site for a new kind of politics.

Cities have played a major strategic role in contemporary processes of social change in Latin America, especially given the concentration of the population in cities. Saskia Sassen argues that the city emerged as an important terrain for new conflicts and claims by both global capital and disadvantaged sectors of the population, which are concentrated in urban areas.[22] As emerging elite classes became increasingly powerful and transnational under processes of neoliberal restructuring, the urban informal working class has become the fastest-growing class on the planet.[23] Disconnected from the formal economy, lacking structures of unionization or access to social welfare, and stigmatized by the middle classes, the "new cities of poverty" are important sites for political organizing. But the social-movement organizations that have taken shape under conditions of informality have sometimes been weakened by their lack of mediating structures that can help them navigate strong executive power in the hands of states and ongoing efforts by partisan interests to intervene in their affairs.

FROM THE TEATRO ALAMEDA TO THE CASA CULTURAL ALAMEDA

I remember when the entry used to cost twenty-five centavos, and we'd go to see artists like Pedro Infante, María Félix, Andrés Soler, Sonia López, and Sonora Matancera live. Apart from this, we went to the theater to see movies like *Los peligros de Nioca* and *El tesoro de la isla misteriosa*. . . . When I was eleven years old, the entry cost fifty centavos. . . . The theater was visited as much by musicians as by artists and journalists; there was Vitas Brenner, who just died in Germany; Jerry Well; Cheo Feliciano; Ismael Miranda; Larry Harlow; Ray Barreto.[24]

I remember that I would take my children when they were small. They showed children's movies; we paid one bolivar. They were silent movies; they were very fast to watch. Many artists of high status came. They still have photos of this.[25]

After the presentations of Pedro Infante, we'd go to the Bar Cuba, very close to the theater, to celebrate with a glass of clear *caña* [rum].[26]

"El Morocho del Abasto," "La Novia de América," Libertad La-Marque, el Azúcar de Celia Cruz, the performance of "La Tongolele," the flavor of "Bárbaro del ritmo," Benny Moré, the grace of Virginia Lopéz, Jorge Negrete.[27]

I remember that my father used to say that when the artists presented there (I was very young at the time), you'd see great cars there in San Agustín; there were, well, the Cadillacs of the time, Pontiacs, and all those cars that were in style at the time.[28]

After a presentation, we'd go to a party close by to the theater. It was in the house of Jhony Pérez, also a musician by profession, who became a good friend. So much so that I baptized one of his girls.[29]

It was Sunday April 19, 1963. It was 2:45 p.m. There were 15 minutes until the start of the film, "The Robot versus the Aztec Mummy." From all sectors of the cerro, young people and children came down, in their Sunday clothes and best shoes on their way to stand in line at the ticket booth to buy the ticket of 75 centavos, which was the price of a matinee from 3 to 5 p.m.[30]

The quotes from residents of San Agustín indicate the centrality of the Teatro Alameda in the cultural and social life of the barrio. The Teatro Alameda was founded in 1944; it was the third theater to be built in Caracas, after the Teatro Nacional and Teatro Municipal in the city center.[31] The Teatro Alameda functioned as both concert hall and cinema hall during the 1940s and 1950s. It acted as a magnet for musicians, orchestras, and big-name performers from around Latin America and the Caribbean. Pedro Infante, Celia Cruz, Daniel Santos, Yolanda Montes "Tongolele," Benny Moré, Jerry Well, Mauricio Silva, Joel Ramírez, Cheo Feliciano, and Jorge Negrete all performed there. These artists interacted with barrio residents in the many bars and clubs that surrounded the theater during this time and contributed to the cultural vibrancy of the barrio. As the local historian Antonio Marrero observed, "The kids who grew up in this era seeing Pedro Infante, seeing Jorge Negrete, seeing Daniel Santos in their community, they began to rub elbows with them, and this helped them to define their own artistic sensibility." At the same time, the theater played an important role in regional musical trends, it "began to give a new light to the shape of Latin American music," as artists formed relationships with one another and created enduring musical ensembles.[32]

The theater also screened a variety of films, such as *Tarzan, Beauty and the Beast, Battle of the Titans, Snow White and the Seven Dwarfs,* and *Captain America,* as well as the films of Mexican comic actors Cantinflas, Tin-Tan, Resortes, and Viruta y Capulina.[33] Like other cinemas in the barrios, such as the Cine Dupuicito in La Vega, residents would go to the movies on Sundays as a form of recreation. Mexican cinema was especially popular in that time, as "El Gordo" Edgar recalls: "Mexican cinema has more to do with our culture even if it's very machista [chauvinist], but at least we had Cantinflas, who is an expression of the political situation in Latin America. We could see Pedro Infante in *La escuela de vagabundos.* All of that expressed a way of life that exists in Latin America."[34] At between twenty-five centavos and one bolivar, the cinema was relatively affordable for most barrio residents.

During the movement against the dictatorship in the 1950s, the theater played a political role in supporting the insurgency. The prodemocracy activist Carmen Veitia recalled: "We carried out assemblies in the salons of the Teatro Alameda, we had sessions of collective lectures, discussions, and seminars."[35] However, once the dictatorship was overthrown and the Acción Democratica came to power, the theater, which was owned by the corporation Cines Unidos, ceased functioning in 1965 and was turned into a depository of films. Since then, several groups have declared their intentions to rescue the theater. As part of their plan for urban remodeling in the 1970s, the government-sponsored CSB proposed to buy the theater and convert it into a great cultural center for the community.[36] This was not realized, and when the CSB was expelled from the community and the Grupo Madera began their cultural work, it also proposed to recuperate the theater. In 1977 there was one attempt to occupy the theater, but the residents were removed forcibly by the national guard.[37]

The theater remained closed for thirty-seven years. During the 1970s and 1980s, the three other cinemas in San Agustín were also shut down, along with cinemas in many barrios that were all centrally owned by Cines Unidos. This elimination of entertainment venues coincided with a period of deindustrialization that left the urban landscape bereft of public and community spaces. People became afraid to leave their houses after dark or even to be in the streets for fear of being attacked by delinquents or security forces. Cinema complexes were built in malls in middle-class neighborhoods, such as the Centro Sambil in Chacao, and cinema became accessible only to the middle and upper classes, who could afford the high prices of film tickets.

After being a symbol of the cultural life and internationalism of the people of San Agustín in the 1950s, the disrepair and shabbiness of the theater was a testament to years of social dislocation, neglect, and the loss of public spaces suffered by barrio residents. In the humid climate, the films rusted and produced noxious chemical fumes. The outside façade of the building gave an indication as to its interiors. Windows were smashed in and bricked up. The outside ledges were overgrown with moss, and the original green tiles were painted over with patches of white paint and gray cement. The sign centered over the front doorway that used to read "Alameda," was missing the A and the l, and the d dangled upside down from the base of the sign.

On April 13, 2004, an assembly of 278 residents from San Agustín del Sur met in the Afinque de Marín to decide on whether to occupy the theater. For eight months prior to the takeover, various groups in the parish had been proposing it, and they formed a coalition known as the Comisión General de Grupos Organizados de la Parroquia San Agustín (General Commission of Organized Groups of the San Agustín Parish). The date was symbolically linked with the coup against Chávez two years earlier, although, as one of the leaders, Nelson, relates: "This night was by coincidence Tuesday, April 13; the rescue of the president happened on April 13, so the rescue of the Teatro Alameda was this same day, but of this year."[38] The date of April 13 provides a symbolic reference point for the actions of the residents. During the assembly, community leaders explained to a nervous but jubilant crowd their proposal to take over the theater. There was a vote and the residents decided unanimously to occupy the theater.

When the residents arrived at the theater, the metropolitan police were blocking the entrance, but the leaders began to speak with the police, and eventually the police stepped back. "They spoke to us politely," said Nelson, "because they realized that this was a cultural occupation supported by the people, by the community." The residents went into the theater and others stayed outside, placing banners over the entrance that read: "San Agustín occupies its spaces," "The Alameda is ours," "Culture for the People," and "The community supports the occupation." As some of the residents entered the back rooms where the reels were kept locked up for many years, they were assaulted by the overpowering stench of the rusting films, and several of the leaders were ill for more than a month from breathing in these fumes.

The next morning, April 14, musicians played the tambores in front of the theater to indicate that the theater now belonged to the community.

Several of the leaders signed an act, which declared: "We, the undersigned, on the aforementioned date and at 9:00 a.m., after an extraordinary assembly of 278 people in the Afinque de Marín, behind the Teatro Alameda, decided unanimously to take over the installations of the old Teatro Alameda. The conditions in which we found the theater are recorded on video film, on the same date. The aim of the takeover is the total recuperation of the structure for the creation of a cultural complex for the parish of San Agustín." A month later, there was a visit from one of the owners of Cines Unidos. As another leader, Héctor, recalls: "They were never against us, but they wanted to know why and for what reasons we did what we did."[39] Héctor and others told the owners that they wanted to write new statutes so that the theater would be administered, cared for, and organized by the community. Barrio residents sought to negotiate with the owners and the state, because, as Nelson told me, "if you make a mistake here, you're a dead man."

Residents involved in the takeover made constant references to the constitution, claiming that it gave them the right to take over spaces that are not being used and convert them into centers for the community. José Luis said, "When we did this occupation it was peaceful, by the norms of the constitution." I searched the constitution for such a clause, but this does not exist, and I realized that they were broadly interpreting Article 70, which states: "Participation and involvement of people in the exercise of their sovereignty in political affairs . . . and in social and economic affairs: citizen service organs, self-management, co-management, cooperatives in all forms, including those of a financial nature, savings funds, community enterprises, and other forms of association guided by the values of mutual cooperation and solidarity."[40] The mention of participation and protagonism in the constitution has provided the impetus for these kinds of occupations, which have also taken place in other parishes such as La Vega and 23 de Enero. On April 13, 2002, when Chávez was restored to power after a coup attempt, the residents of La Vega briefly occupied a police module. In the sector La Cañada, of 23 de Enero, the militant organization Coordinadora Simón Bolívar organized residents to take over the local unit of the metropolitan police. After years of harassment, repression, and abuse by the local police, it was an empowering act for the residents of La Cañada to take over this locale and turn it into a cultural center. The takeovers are not expropriations, in the sense that it is the people rather than the state who are occupying the installations. But nevertheless, the occupations happened mostly with the implicit support of the state and particularly Chávez, who encouraged this activity. The residents felt that there was more space available under the Chávez government than previous governments to carry out these kinds of acts, but some worried about the impact of too much state presence. Totoño, a long-term leader in the barrio and founder of Tacusan, a culture workshop in San Agustín, warned from the start that "they need to be responsible for the space, for what will happen to it."[41]

The theater began operating as the Casa Cultural Alameda almost immediately after the takeover. The leaders formed an organizing council that consisted of coordinators and personnel in charge of security, finances, and general services. One reason for the creation of these posts was to give the leaders greater legitimacy before state institutions. For instance, when I went with one of the local organizers, Cástor, to the state institution Fundarte, I noticed that he pulled out an official-looking badge with his name, personal identification number, and "Casa Cultural Alameda" written underneath. He introduced himself as a member of the board of directors of the Casa Cultural Alameda and asked to see someone in the office. The badge seemed to be a way of signaling the authority and presence of the residents in their dealings with institutions.

The organizing council of the Casa Cultural Alameda did not want to wait for institutions to provide grants or money toward the recuperation and rehabilitation of the space; rather, the members began to devise their own means of fundraising. Many people from the community volunteered their services and labor in the recuperation of the space, but, as Cástor said, they still needed money to buy cement, paint, and other building materials. The council members organized courses in dance, percussion, and painting as a way of raising some money. They also opened up a concession stand on the premises to sell snacks and drinks. Through the volunteer labor of the residents in cleaning out the premises, teaching classes, and making donations, the Casa Cultural Alameda was functioning in a short time.

There was a renewed vibrancy around the Casa Cultural Alameda for many months in the wake of the occupation; it became a central meeting place for residents of the parish. The Casa Cultural Alameda was integrated into the community work of groups in the sector, with meetings of the government-sponsored land committees, health committees, and literacy courses, as well as classes, music workshops, and an eye clinic, which gave free eye examinations and prescription glasses to residents who needed them. Every day around 6:30 p.m., after work and school, residents would come to the Casa Cultural Alameda to participate in meetings, or just to socialize with the other residents. In the evenings, the rooms would be full of people having their meetings. The general congregation of people in the open meeting spaces would spill out onto the streets. The Casa Cultural Alameda hosted two exhibitions, one on the architecture of the Central University of Venezuela, and a second on historic and contemporary photos of San Agustín. They organized bolero concerts, comedy nights, and theater and dance performances, among other events.

From the start, the organizing council faced the problem of how to relate to state institutions and the Chávez government. As they tried to apply for funds from state institutions, council members came up against problems of bureaucracy and corruption. "They haven't helped us as they should," the finance director Wendy complained initially. "We have submitted projects, we've gone to all the institutions, we've done a million things and we've not had any response."[42] Given the long time it took for institutions to respond, Freddy Bernal, the mayor of the Libertador municipality, gave four million bolivares (US$1,905) worth of construction materials. The city council also guaranteed certain basic services such as water and electricity for the Casa Cultural Alameda.[43] The leadership combined these funds with the volunteer labor of the community and fundraising activities to support the initial functioning of the theater.

When barrio-based organizations mobilized in August 2004 to defend Chávez in the opposition-initiated recall referendum that sought to oust him from power, the Casa Cultural Alameda became an organizing nucleus for the Comando Maisanta, the electoral units working in the barrios toward Chávez's victory. One of the local organizers, José Gregorio Ruiz used the metaphor of a trampoline to describe the strategic alliances with the state: "The project of the Alameda depends on the persistence of the community and our links with the state, which is the trampoline for organized groups."[44] The residents distinguish this kind of support from traditional clientelism, where local groups are dependent on the state for resources and are not organized autonomously.

THE TAKEOVER WITHIN THE TAKEOVER

Within six months of the Casa Cultural Alameda being functional, there had already emerged a small elite within the leadership who sought to establish control over the organization's direction. From the broad coalition of community leaders and groups that had carried out the takeover, many long-term leaders such as Totoño had been edged out of the running of the theater. One of the members of the small and entirely male clique who retained control of the Casa Cultural Alameda expressed the situation to me in the following gendered terms: "The theater is like a beautiful woman. You've got her and others want to dress her, claim her as their own, but she is your wife." This statement revealed the notions of male dominance guiding the small elite; the theater is conceived of as an object of exchange and ownership, as women's bodies are.

Differences began to emerge between this small clique and the community groups such as the health committees and land committees meeting in the theater. On one occasion, a woman from a health committee came into a room of the Casa Cultural Alameda and asked two leaders if they could carry out their business in another room so that her committee could hold their meeting. One of the leaders responded: "We're all in this revolution together; we can share this room." When she left the room, the other leader remarked: "She's not a real revolutionary like us." The divisions opening up in the theater seemed to be gender based, with the emerging clique consisting of all men and the committees consisting of nearly all women. By disparaging the woman leader as "not a real revolutionary," the male leader was creating a hierarchy between the community work being carried out by mainly women residents and political militancy, as supposedly represented by this leadership.

By the middle of 2005, the year following the takeover, the Casa Cultural Alameda had ceased to be a central hub of activity for barrio residents. Besides a few classes and meetings that took place there, it was fairly quiet. The concession stand had fallen into disuse. At the same time, the government had created an information center in the Casa Cultural Alameda, was using the rooms of the theater to house various international guests, and was giving money for further renovations of the restrooms and facilities. The notion of self-financing seemed to have been relinquished. During the local municipal elections of July 2005, the small clique managing the theater used it as a base to run an electoral campaign, promoting themselves as candidates for local parish council. They had joined the Tupamaros party, and the walls of the Afinque de Marín and other prominent walls were covered in murals advertising their candidacies. The political party Tupamaros is loosely connected to the militant underground movement of Tupamaros that originated in the parish of 23 de Enero in the 1980s. After Chávez came to power, the party was formed in order to contest elections. Although the

Tupamaros party saw itself to the left of Chávez's Movimiento V República (Fifth Republic Movement), it retained a hierarchical and vanguardist orientation like the other parties. Running on a Tupamaros ticket in the local elections was a logical extension of the clique's growing concentration of power in the Casa Cultural Alameda. The decision of the clique to affiliate with the Tupamaros was surprising to many residents of the barrio, since the Tupamaros had never had a base in San Agustín. Totoño said that what was happening was an example of *politiquera* (politicking), because the small group of elites was mainly interested in seeking power and not in advancing the interests of the community. He explained that none of the members of the clique had a history of organizing work in the community, other than their leadership of the occupation. Totoño countered the masculine, hierarchical logic of party militancy with an appeal to feeling and emotion, stating: "Real politics comes from the heart, not from the pursuit of power."

There was widespread disappointment and a sense of betrayal among residents of San Agustín, although no one felt empowered to confront the elite openly. In the spaces of everyday life and community gatherings, people expressed their criticisms. At a funeral for an older woman from Marín, the women present at the funeral were more interested in talking about the politics of the theater than the passing of their friend. "The Teatro Alameda is being taken over by a small group and they are very corrupt. Just last week, the government sent televisions and VCRs to the theater, to be used in educational instruction for the older people who can't make it to the Missions [the literacy classes]. One of the leaders took the equipment for himself and distributed it among his family," said one woman. "Now he's running for alderman, and it will be terrible if he wins, because he'll have access to even more resources," responded another. One woman suggested to the others that they make an official complaint, but they were too scared. "Anyway, the current aldermen and councilpeople are also corrupt and alcoholic, so what difference will it make?" responded one. Later that week, a number of women were gathered in the kitchen of a friend in San Agustín and they began talking about collecting testimonies and signatures from all of the women to present to the head of the literacy mission in San Agustín. But as one said, "What good would that do? She herself is corrupt and has eliminated the scholarships for a number of students in order to keep the money herself." The degree of corruption that emerged in the state-sponsored programs in San Agustín, with the theater itself at the center of the scandal, was an indication of the weakness of community networks and the dominance of male-centric politicking.

A few weeks later, the community organized a homage to the Grupo Madera in the Afinque de Marín on the anniversary of its tragic accident. On the same night, the new Grupo Madera, a group created by Noel Márquez, one of the original members, was performing in the Poliedro for the closing of the International Youth Festival. There was a sense of bitterness among the residents that the current Grupo Madera was capitalizing on the name of the original group and that they had become government spokespersons; indeed their hit song "Uh ah Chávez no se va" (Uh ah Chávez won't go) had become the anthem of the Chavista movement. People used the event as a platform to make their denunciations of Márquez and the current Grupo Madera. Felipe Rengifo Mandingo, a member of the original group living in Germany, sent a recorded message reclaiming the Grupo Madera as cultural patrimony of the country: "Why should Noel Márquez, who is not a native of Marín, nor of San Agustín del Sur, direct an institution as sacred as the group and the Foundation Madera, which is patrimony of the country?" Mandingo accused Márquez of using the name of Madera to enrich himself personally through state subsidies, rather than creating spaces of social participation for the community. He went on to say that Márquez was corrupt and a drug addict.

After the recording finished, others climbed onto the stage to voice their agreement. At times, the situation bordered on farce. One woman from the audience got up and said that all these people making accusations were themselves drug addicts. People whispered in the audience that this woman would know, as she herself was a drug dealer and supplied drugs to most of them. Even as the concert began, the women of the barrio were grouped together in small circles recounting and discussing the issues, like the day in the funeral home. Some argued that this was just clashes of ego between male leaders of the parish, while others disagreed, saying that it did relate to the struggles of the community. One of the surviving members of the original Grupo Madera, Nelly Ramos, stood quietly watching the events. She leaned over to me and commented: "This is all a form of catharsis. It is the way we have of relieving tensions and speaking to the grief and the divisions that exist within our community."

The historic symbols of the community of San Agustín—the Grupo Madera and the Teatro Alameda—had become contested sites among various factions in the community, each laying claim to a distinct vision of what role these played in the community. As David Harvey has argued, places are sites of collective memory that hold the possibilities for different futures. But such heterotopic spaces are also susceptible to being absorbed by the dominant praxis: "The production of space and place is shot through at every moment with the dynamics of indeterminate social struggles whose outcomes depend upon the shifting currents between social groups."[45] State and party intervention fed the internal divisions existing in the community to convert the theater and the memory of the Grupo Madera into instruments for political incorporation. The conditions of informality that had enabled the takeover of the theater also made the theater activists vulnerable to hierarchical and corporatist interests, as they lacked enduring institutions that could sustain and build momentum.

The occupation and the homage to Grupo Madera brought to the fore a series of oppositions through which people located themselves: male or female, politickers or community, and politics from the heart or politics in pursuit of power. While it seems that over time a particular community-based vision was defeated and relegated to the informal channels and microspaces of the community, at the end of that day of the concert, the vision seemed to be revived for a moment. After the various musical groups left the stage, the organizers of the event played the song "Canción con todos" (Song with all), by the original Grupo Madera: "From this barrio has emerged my feeling and my expression that I show you now / . . . Share your pain, and also your happiness, to the strong beat of the drum." There was silence in the Afinque, and then slowly the older men and women came up to the front to dance. Young children placed a wreath of flowers at the foot of the Grupo Madera mural. An old man with a soft white Afro and a cane smiled as he stepped into the spotlight and moved his hips in time to the music, winking at two elderly women dancing near him. On the corner, a group of young boys tapped out the drum rhythms of the song—da-da, da-da-da. The *cofradía* (brotherhood) brought out live drums and began playing along to the song, and after it was finished they continued playing until late in the night.

CONCLUSION

The occupation of the Teatro Alameda represented a taking back of community spaces that had been lost through decades of social decline, government neglect, and privatization. It is one example of a broader trend of popular protagonism that aims to revitalize public space and take back the streets for the community. At the base of this action was the historical memory of the Teatro Alameda, the musical life of the parish, and the vibrant years of the Grupo Madera and the dignity and pride that it represented for ordinary residents, as well as the multiple losses suffered by the community. While the community could never reverse the painful defeats and losses of the past few decades, the residents could try to take control of their present. As they renamed the theater as their culture house and reclaimed it as collective cultural patrimony, the residents linked their collective memories to the hope for a different kind of future.

The subsequent takeover by a small internal leadership, and state occupation of a space left dormant by the community, points to the fragility of this community-based vision. A self-appointed leadership marshaled the resources of the theater for their own personal benefit as they sought to win political office. Early on in the occupation, leaders such as Totoño were warning that the residents needed to take responsibility for what would happen to the space. But it was precisely the absence of strong organization structures, linked to popular assemblies and other forums for accountability and deliberation, that facilitated the rise of an undemocratic current within the leadership. The story of the Teatro Alameda produces questions about the potential for local and sometimes fragmented community-based movements to launch a challenge to broader structures of power. While mobilizing the "power of place" can be an important political strategy, argues Harvey, the politics of localism is not an answer to the ever-present threat of reactionary and exclusionary dangers.[46]

Building a new form of coalitional politics has become the most urgent task facing urban social movements in the contemporary era. Rumor, murmurings, and gossip act as a vigorous leveling mechanism that holds in check the emergence of new class and status stratification, but they may also act as a safety valve to channel discontent rather than bring about change.[47] Social movements united around specific tasks such as the election of Chávez, defeating the coup against Chávez, and the recall referendum, but they have faced greater difficulty in sustaining a common agenda to represent their own interests as a collective. Rather, a functioning substantive democracy may depend on the ability of social movements to build broad-based coalitions, especially across the urban-rural divide.

NOTES

Thanks to Brodwyn Fischer, Bryan McCann, and Javier Auyero for their guidance and comments on various drafts. I also appreciate all of the commentary provided by the participants of the "Informal Cities" conference held at Northwestern University. The research was carried out with support from Princeton University faculty grants and PSC-CUNY research grants. All translations from Spanish to English are my own. I have used pseudonyms for anyone identified by a single name.

1. Gobierno del Distrito Federal, República Bolivariana de Venezuela, *Anuario Estadístico de la Gobernación del Distrito Federal* (Caracas: Gobierno del Distrito Federal, República Bolivariana de Venezuela, 2000).

2. Antonio "Pelon" Marrero, *San Agustín: Un santo pecador o un pueblo creador* (Caracas: Fundarte, 2004), 20.

3. Alejandra Ramos and Jesús Quintero, "Relato de una experiencia: Grupo Madera," in *Seminario Nacional de Investigación Participativa* (Caracas, 1980).

4. Author interview with Totoño, San Agustín, January 2005.

5. Marrero, *San Agustín*, 20.

6. Rafael Quintero, "La lucha contra el desalojo del Centro Cultural Simón Bolívar," in Rafael Quintero, *Vivir en Marín*, accessed April 14, 2007, http://www.nodo50.org/alameda/lalucha.php.

7. Quintero, "La lucha contra el desalojo del Centro Cultural Simón Bolívar."

8. Marrero, *San Agustín*, 20–24.

9. Felix Baptista and Oswaldo Marchionda, "¿Para que afinques?," BA thesis, Universidad Central de Venezuela, 1992.

10. Author interview with Antonio Marrero, local historian, San Agustín, July 2005.

11. Felipe "Mandingo" Rengifo, "Embajador de San Agustín en Alemania," in *San Agustín: Un santo pecador o un pueblo creador*, edited by Antonio Marrero (Caracas: Fundarte, 2004), 162.

12. Nelly Ramos, "Trabajadora cultural a tiempo completo," in *San Agustín: Un santo pecador o un pueblo creador*, edited by Antonio Marrero (Caracas: Fundarte, 2004), 176.

13. Rafael Quintero, "El Grupo Madera," in Rafael Quintero, *Vivir en Marín*, accessed April 14, 2007, http://www.nodo50.org/alameda/madera.php.

14. Alexis Rosas, *Objectivo Chávez: El periodismo como arma* (Caracas: Editorial Texto, 2005), 123–25.

15. Janice E. Perlman, *The Myth of Marginality: Urban Poverty and Politics in Rio de Janeiro* (Berkeley: University of California Press, 1976).

16. On clientelism, see Susan Greenbaum, "Backgrounds of Political Participation in Venezuelan Barrios," BA thesis, University of Kansas, 1968; and Talton Ray, *The Politics of the Barrios of Venezuela* (Berkeley: University of California Press, 1969). On struggles to improve living standards, see Larissa Adler de Lomnitz, *Networks and Marginality: Life in a Mexican Shantytown* (New York: Academic, 1977).

17. See Oscar Lewis, *La Vida: A Puerto Rican Family in the Culture of Poverty — San Juan and New York* (New York: Random House, 1966).

18. Mercedes González de la Rocha, "From the Marginality of the 1960s to the 'New Poverty' of Today," *Latin American Research Review* 39, no 1 (2004): 183.

19. Peter Ward, "Introduction and Overview: Marginality Then and Now," *Latin American Research Review* 39, no 1 (2004): 186.

20. Daniel Goldstein, *The Spectacular City: Violence and Performance in Urban Bolivia* (Durham, NC: Duke University Press, 2004), 12.

21. Goldstein, *The Spectacular City*, 13–14.

22. Saskia Sassen, "Whose City Is It? Globalization and the Formation of New Claims," in *Globalization and Its Discontents*, edited by Saskia Sassen (New York: New Press, 1998).

23. Mike Davis, *Planet of Slums* (London: Verso, 2006), 178.

24. Author interview with Angel Ramirez, barrio Marín, San Agustín, June 2004.

25. Author interview with Graciela Suárez de Robles, barrio Marín, San Agustín, July 2004.

26. Juanita Linares, cited in Jennifer Molina, "El Alameda cuenta la historia de San Agustín," *Parroquia Dentro* 3, no. 17 (2004): 3.

27. Merlina La Rosa, cited in Molina, "El Alameda cuenta la historia de San Agustín."

28. Author interview with Marrero.

29. Cruz Mijares, cited in Molina, "El Alameda cuenta la historia de San Agustín."

30. Rafael Quintero, "Teatro Alameda," in Rafael Quintero, *Vivir en Marín*, accessed April 14, 2007, http://www.nodo50.org/alameda/teatro.php.

31. Author interview with Carlos Villegas, Teatro Alameda, San Agustín, May 2004.

32. Author interview with Marrero.

33. Molina, "El Alameda cuenta la historia de San Agustín"; Rafael Quintero, *Vivir en Marín*, accessed April 14, 2007, http://www.nodo50.org/alameda/vivir.php.

34. Author interview with El Gordo Edgar, La Vega, January 2004.

35. Cited in Fania Petzoldt and Jacinta Bevilacqua, *Nosotras también nos jugamos la vida: Testimonios de la Mujer Venezolana en la Lucha Clandestina: 1948–1958* (Caracas: Editorial Ateneo de Caracas, 1979), 275.

36. Marrero, *San Agustín*, 21.

37. Author interview with Irma Hypolite, San Agustín, July 2004.

38. Interview with Nelson (pseudonym), San Agustín, July 2005.

39. Cited in "La Alameda: Abre sus puertas una casa cultural en San Agustín," *Agencia Bolivariana de Noticias*, April 15, 2005, accessed April 14, 2007, http://www.nodo50.org/alameda/espacio_aniv2.php.

40. "Constitution of the Bolivarian Republic of Venezuela (in English translation from the original legal text)," http://www.venezuelaemb.or.kr/english/Constitution oftheBolivarianingles.pdf.

41. Quoted in *La Alameda de los sueños*, a documentary produced by Consejo Nacional de la Cultura (CONAC) (María Laura Vásquez, dir., Caracas, 2005).

42. Cited in Olafo Montalbán, "Autogestión comunitaria en la Venezuela Bolivariana," accessed April 14, 2007, http://www.nodo50.org/alameda/autogestion .php.

43. Author interview with Carlos Villegas, Teatro Alameda, San Agustín, May 2004.

44. Cited in "La Alameda."

45. David Harvey, *Cosmopolitanism and the Geographies of Freedom* (New York: Columbia University Press, 2009), 56.

46. Harvey, *Cosmopolitanism and the Geographies of Freedom*, 59.

47. Roger Lancaster, *Thanks to God and the Revolution: Popular Religion and Class Consciousness in the New Nicaragua* (New York: Columbia University Press, 1988), 144–51.

EIGHT

Threshold Markets

THE PRODUCTION OF REAL-ESTATE VALUE BETWEEN
THE "FAVELA" AND THE "PAVEMENT"

Mariana Cavalcanti

In early twenty-first-century Rio de Janeiro, the opposition between favelas and *bairros* (formal city neighborhoods), or favelas and the "pavement"
(i.e., the "formal" city), can prove an elusive perspective for unpacking the
relations between the so-called formal and informal cities. It is not just that
even the most affluent bairros contain favelas within their territorial boundaries. As part of the increasing formalization of the city's consolidated favelas, a few large communities have been recognized by the state as bairros.
Thus Rocinha (which is known as Latin America's largest shantytown) is
classified in data published by Rio de Janeiro's city hall as the city's twenty-
seventh administrative region that contains a single bairro—Rocinha. But
Rocinha also figures as a favela in the city hall's Sistema de Assentamentos
de Baixa Renda (System for Low Income Settlements, SABREN), in which
one finds data on the city's favelas and irregular *loteamentos* (allotments).[1]
Similar slippages occur in two of Rio's largest favela complexes (agglomerations of several favelas), such as the Complexo do Alemão (composed of
thirteen distinct favelas) and the Complexo do Maré (composed of fifteen
favelas and housing projects). Both constitute administrative regions and
are considered bairros, but the subunits composing them (the favelas) also
figure in the SABREN.

Perhaps more important, no one in the city questions the fact that for
practical purposes these so-called bairros are unequivocally favelas, for two
reasons. The first has to do with the favelas' legal standing and property
status. Rocinha, Maré, and the Complexo do Alemão are among the hundreds of favelas that have been declared "special social interest areas," the

legal device that places certain favelas under more flexible urbanistic rules than the formal city, thus creating the legal conditions for further infrastructural upgrades and the concession of legal property titles.[2] The second reason why no one questions that these are favelas rather than bairros is the fact that daily life here unfolds under raging drug wars between rival drug gangs (factions) or between drug dealers and the police.[3] These conflicts have endured since the late 1970s and have become entrenched in the daily routines of Rio de Janeiro's inhabitants, not only in the favelas but also in the pavement, in the form of stray bullets and the sound of constant shoot-outs.

Since December 2008, however, the push toward favela formalization has gained momentum with the beginning of the state government's favela Pacification program. The climax came in November 2010, when Rio de Janeiro's military police stormed the Complexo do Alemão in an unprecedented war operation involving the army, navy, and the civil police. Armed with tanks, trucks, and helicopters, more than two thousand men took over what had been for more than thirty years the stronghold of the city's oldest criminal faction, the Comando Vermelho. More than a territorial gain, the occupation of the complex was heralded as a victory comparable to D-day in the media.

Yet there was something anticlimactic in the media coverage of the takeover: it lacked images of live conflict. Like the most recent alleged "pacification" efforts, the press coverage of the occupation of the complex minimized violent confrontations.[4] The portrayal of the conquest highlighted, instead, the invasion of the drug lords' "castles," or, as the media called them their "mansions." Over the course of the next week, color pictures and moving images of the interior of the mansions uncovered by the forces of law and order were featured on every network and in newspaper, and then redistributed online through blogs, social networks, and YouTube.

The "mansions" in question were three-story constructions that were fairly unremarkable in the general favela landscape from the outside, but comfortably equipped inside with flat-screen televisions, low-cast ceilings with expensive lighting schemes, and hot tubs in the bathrooms. The top floors of the houses, with swimming pools (with the golden initials of their owners on the bottom) and elaborate *churrasqueiras* (barbecue fixtures), were swiftly dubbed penthouses rather than being portrayed as a more luxurious version of the typical favela *laje* (itself a characteristic favela feature best known for its double valence as recreation area and space for a possible future conversion into an additional story).

Though bizarre, the media field day with the alleged "mansions" of the drug lords is not entirely surprising. It could easily be attributed to decades of systematic decontextualization of the favela as an urban formation, in which the term *favela* has functioned more as shorthand for "drug-trade territory" than as a social form or mode of dwelling in the city. In short, the reporters saw "mansions" in the tackily decorated three-story brick constructions because they expected to see wooden shacks with dirt floors and scarce furnishings. That is, the reporters saw the buildings through the lens of what is increasingly recognized in the scholarly literature as ideal (stereo) types associated with the favelas in Rio de Janeiro's public imaginary. In this stereotyped (but resilient) imaginary, favelas are defined by the illegal occupation of land (most often on hillslopes), the poverty of their residents, and the lack of access to public services. Yet countless studies in the past ten years or so have countered such commonsensical knowledge, demonstrating, beyond any question, that none of these features are exclusive to the city's favelas.[5]

Still, the pervasiveness of such stereotypes and the stubborn refusal to see permanent homes in the brick-and-mortar constructions is not entirely absurd. Much of the public discourse on the favelas—and it seems there has never been so much public discourse on the favelas, in particular by emerging favela subjects who claim the authority and legitimacy to speak for themselves—emphasizes their material distress and demands for urgent investments, denouncing an alleged absence of the state. But the undeniable fact is that public investments and spending on favelas have steadily risen since the 1980s, and especially from the 1990s onward, and access to basic services, such as electricity, sewage systems, and water-distribution networks, has expanded considerably.[6] While isolated favela-urbanization programs date back to the 1950s and the large-scale removal programs of the 1960s and 1970s coexisted with a few urbanization efforts, it was only in the 1980s that infrastructural upgrading became a systematic policy. In the 1990s, under the aegis of the Favela-Bairro program, favela urbanization became a hegemonic public policy with the aim of incorporating favelas into the formal city.[7] The 2000s witnessed the continuation of the Favela-Bairro program and new initiatives, such as the federal government's Programa de Aceleração do Crescimento (Growth Acceleration Program). The program's favela-urbanization component sedimented favela urbanization with a normative aim of granting legal land tenure to residents. That is, in the past decade, policy has retained the Favela-Bairro program's basic tenets, but now these tenets are applied in the context of increased investments in strategic planning for the city in order to prepare for the World Cup in 2014 and the Olympic Games in 2016. In late 2010, the Rio de Janeiro's city hall announced its intention to conclude the full urbanization of all of the city's favelas by 2020, under the auspices of the Morar Carioca Program.[8]

Despite the endurance of stereotypical representations of the favelas as agglomerations of precarious shacks on hillsides, the fact is that decades of infrastructural upgrading have radically transformed the favela landscape. And that is only part of the story. As I have argued at length elsewhere, favela consolidation is not just the work of state investments.[9] The impressive changes in the materiality of the favela are also the product of countless small interventions by residents themselves, in the public and private spaces of their communities and their homes. Perhaps their homes are not as ostentatious as the drug lords' alleged mansions, but they are occasionally decorated with elaborate finishes and carefully laid out adornments. All these processes have been unfolding since the mid 1980s; they were expedited many times over in the context of President Luís Inácio Lula da Silva's policies of economic growth and income distribution and an overall reduction in inequality levels in Brazil.

Favela housing markets, even before so-called Pacification, had also become not only increasingly dynamic but also more regulated, institutionalized, and valued.[10] Thus, favela consolidation has also brought about an increasing formalization of property, albeit under the special legislation regulating special social interest areas. Urbanistic interventions have set particular parameters and standards for calculating property values that take into account not only built structures but also the housing-market values of each favela. Transactions are mediated by the residents' association, which recognizes property ownership in each community. While not fully formal, these markets increasingly connect to their "pavement" counterparts (i.e., in the so-called formal city).

One such connection concerns me in this chapter: at the time this research was conducted, in certain areas of the city, particularly in middle-class neighborhoods closely bordering favelas, there was virtually no difference in the market value of properties located in the favela and those on the "pavement." The devaluation of formal property as a function of its proximity to favelas, coupled with the unrelenting valuation of properties in consolidated favelas, produced a particular, and perhaps fleeting, socio-spatial arrangement that I provisionally refer to as a "threshold" effect upon real-estate markets. It is a zone of indeterminacy, where the constant symbolic rearrangements of the favela-pavement divide inevitably depend on one's perspective.

The idea of a threshold effect reminds us that the favela-pavement boundary in question is neither spatial nor physical but an essentially symbolic construction. It offers a privileged perspective for capturing how these areas are inhabited, as well as the intersection of physical and subjective spatialities that make the monetary equivalence of these two allegedly distant social worlds possible. Recognizing this convergence of monetary value does not mean assuming that the historical, social, symbolic, or spatial boundaries between the "favela" and the "pavement" have been erased or even blurred; it merely inaugurates a connection (or, depending on one's perspective, a passage) between the "favela" and the "pavement" that would have seemed incongruous only twenty years ago. The emergence of this passage, in and of itself, is part of an ongoing reconfiguration of symbolic, spatial, and social boundaries of the city's favelas that preceded the "Pacification" program but was also severely altered by it. If I am right, the exploration of this threshold effect upon real-estate markets shows how socially productive the favela-pavement boundary is, and how it is experienced and constructed by different subjects.

This chapter is therefore an initial exploration and conceptualization of this (possibly transient) social phenomenon. It aims to explore the analytical possibilities opened by the idea of a threshold effect upon real-estate markets as a means of illuminating the concrete, empirical connections between the "favela" and the "pavement." I begin to unpack some of the challenges involved in qualitatively describing this zone of indeterminacy between the "formal" and "informal," then elaborate the conditions in which this research unfolded, and discuss the conceptual need to differentiate between property bordering favelas in general from property under the threshold effect. The latter, I argue, captures a more specific socio-spatial configuration than proximity to favelas. I examine the social construction of the threshold effect upon real-estate property through three distinct but complementary perspectives. I describe the trajectory of what can be read for my purposes here as an archetypical site under the favela threshold effect: a building directly facing the favela of Bela Vista, to which former favela residents have been moving in a steady trickle over the past decade. The second perspective I explore is that of a longtime favela resident who moved into the outer border of the threshold, at a moment when its effect was quite extended as a function of decades of shoot-outs and steady spill-overs of violent episodes. I look at how real-estate agents talk about, represent, and attempt to sell such threshold real estate. In articulating these three complementary perspectives, I attempt to move the gaze away from the space itself and into the social relations that constitute, imagine, and inhabit it. Finally, I spin a few concluding remarks that draw on field research conducted more recently, with some exploratory remarks on the effects of the "Pacification" process in the city's favelas, and the consequent contraction (but not erasure) of the threshold effect.

CONCEPTUALIZING THE THRESHOLD EFFECT

Capturing the extent and implications of the dynamic I have been referring to as a real-estate threshold effect is challenging. In many ways the processes at stake here are too fragmented in space and too subject to local singularities to be understood by the usual type of scholarly work on real-estate markets. While these studies constitute a consolidated field of inquiry in urban studies, the way the field is structured tends to reproduce the formal-informal dichotomy. The so-called formal market constitutes a central source of information for quantitative studies of internal migration patterns in the city and of large-scale social processes, such as the economic restructuring of the past decades, the emergence of strategic planning as a key feature of urban governance, real-estate speculation, and land-usage policies.[11] There is also considerable knowledge accumulated on the internal workings of so-called informal cities, particularly in Latin America: studies of housing strategies and daily tactics that reproduce the favelas, *villa miserias, colonias proletarias*, and so forth, as well as quantitative and qualitative data on the urban crisis, housing deficits, and evaluations of infrastructural-upgrading programs. Yet the endeavor to construct a comprehensive picture of large-scale patterns does not capture the subtleties of the social relations engendered by fear of crime and victimization, the impact of the favela upon the visual landscape, and daily conflicts over the use of space. More-qualitative case studies of real-estate values and valuations tend to conceive of real-estate markets as composed of two mutual sectors, the formal and the informal.[12] The same is true of business-oriented studies that have already attempted to construct models to systematize and describe the effect of favela vicinity upon property values.[13]

In this attempt to think through the spatial and subjective interstices of the "favela-pavement," or "formal-informal," divide, I draw on one of the most promising directions in urban studies — namely the attempt to theorize informality not in opposition to the formal city but as a way of life.[14] These studies draw on settings and research objects as distinct processes wherein refugee camps metamorphose into city-camps: the new connections between the illegal, the informal, and the irregular; the new intermediaries of the unskilled labor market; and the process of favela formation.[15] The common thread in these studies is a shared assumption of urban informality as an "organizing logic, a system of norms that governs the process of urban transformation itself," or as a "series of transactions that connect different economies and spaces to each other."[16]

In this sense, conceiving the real-estate market as a social phenomenon makes it possible to venture a hypothesis: once the monetary equivalence between the "favela" and the "pavement" is produced, one can glimpse other registers of value production that shape the ways in which city dwellers imagine, use, and represent urban space, rendering legible the very complexities of value-producing mechanisms in cities marked by sharp inequalities and shaped by long-standing informalities.[17] Thus the threshold effect as an analytical construct opens an ethnographic perspective that inquires into the practices and routines that continuously reproduce the spatio-social figures of the "favela" and the "pavement," in space and in the imagination.

For this talk of threshold effects to make sense, it is necessary to clarify the conceptual need for this term. A threshold effect is not necessarily inscribed in physical space in any visual way, as a border region might be. Proximity to the favela constitutes a necessary condition for the constitution of threshold real-estate markets, but these do not emerge, as a rule, on the outskirts of just any favela. The threshold requires a more particular social and spatial constellation for a connection between markets to form. Ideally, the threshold effect arises in a built environment designed before the drug trade and its association to the favelas became widespread, and in regions where the social contrast between the "favela" and the so called formal city may be marked but not necessarily sharp. That is, threshold real estate — rather predictably, one might add — tends to form more readily in middle- and lower-middle-class regions. The vicinity of the Complexo do Alemão is one case in point; entire apartment blocks and formerly modestly prosperous streets and well-built houses have come to suffer the same dynamics as the favelas surrounding them. Before the November occupation, entire portions of neighborhoods in Ramos, Bonsucesso, and Penha, to name a few, had deliveries—from pizza to postal services to home utilities—refused because of their location in so-called risk areas. While legally considered "formal," considerable portions of the city have, in practice, become neither fully "favela" nor "pavement."

In contrast, in areas where the social gap between the favela and the formal city is overly sharp—that is, in upper-class neighborhoods—the threshold effect does not form. Even though one finds both conditions of possibility of the threshold effect here (that is, valuation in the favela and a decrease in property in the "formal" city), the convergence in property values is not enough to connect the "favela" and the "pavement" through real-estate transactions. An obvious example can be found in the neighborhood of São Conrado, the archetypical (and by now cliché) illustration of the city's sharp social contrasts. São Conrado, which was planned to provide the city's elites with an idyllic neighborhood of gated condominiums, shining high-rise buildings, and plentiful recreation areas with breathtaking views, very swiftly became a visual aid in describing the city's inequities: the glass towers with large balconies against the backdrop of the favela of Rocinha spilling over the hill to one side, and the shining beach to the other.

The luxurious, four- or five-bedroom apartments that face Rocinha directly have not become incorporated into the favela markets. Rather, properties in the formal city tend to withdraw from a commodity state, to borrow Igor Kopytoff's provocative suggestion: no longer a source of economic value, nor of status, they are momentarily removed from the commodity sphere.[18] The maintenance fees and property taxes charged in these high-end buildings and condominiums render the formation of the threshold impossible: favela residents might somehow afford to buy these units, but they cannot afford to live in these buildings. Those who can afford the fees, taxes, and extra expenses have little desire to live with a view of a favela, though bulletproofing can provide an affordable solution. Thus, many of these apartments get boarded up or shut down, often accumulating debts with city taxes and maintenance fees.

Finally, a word regarding the ethnographic present of this chapter. I stumbled upon what I came to develop as the idea of this threshold effect on real estate while conducting ethnographic fieldwork in 2004 and 2005, in a favela I refer to here as Bela Vista. This chapter draws on data collected during that time, in which I undertook my doctoral fieldwork, but also on continued visits and observations of this and other favelas and their surroundings up until early 2011. Hence, many of the social situations explored here unfold in very different contexts. Since April 2010, the favelas of the region have been permanently occupied by the police, under the aegis of the state government's favela Pacification program, the Unidades de Polícia Pacificadora (Pacifying Police Units, UPPs). The UPPs spearhead the current public-security program implemented by the Sergio Cabral administration of Rio de Janeiro state under the public-security secretary José Mariano Beltrame. In theory, the program draws on the ideal of community policing, but in the UPP version, the community is necessarily a favela and it must be permanently occupied.

In practice, the "Pacification" process works like this: the special police forces initially occupy the favela and undertake special operations of armed confrontation and tactical dismantling of the drug-trade networks, thus clearing the path for their replacement by specially trained and recently graduated military police who set up a station, usually at the hilltop.[19] The police occupy the strategic areas of the favela and stand guard permanently. Along with the UPP comes the city government's *choque de ordem* (shock of order), in which pirate transportation systems, cable TV, and commerce are increasingly subjected to regulation and formalization.

Under the UPP regime, favela residents are still constantly exposed to the presence of men at surveillance spots bearing arms; the UPP police tend to keep watch in the same geographically strategic points. But there is one aspect of the process that transforms every single aspect of daily life, for the better: the end of shoot-outs. So while there is still plenty of criticism of the UPPs, voiced in the same quiet tones that once talked about the drug lords, everyone is mainly relieved about the end of the sound of shots ringing through the valley.

With these changes, many of the arguments and descriptions elaborated in the pages that follow no longer apply to these particular sites. But I am confident that they are reasonably accurate for many other regions in the city, in particular the parts of the northern suburbs where the drug trade — and control over the territories of poverty — remain up for grabs and constantly motivate armed confrontations between drug dealers and the police. Moreover, while the UPP shares many features of the previous community-policing attempts, the fact is that it remains a consensually approved policy (hence Cabral's easy reelection in 2010) that has only increased in breath and scope, and it has consolidated over time.[20]

This is an exercise in a historical anthropology of the present, with the potentialities and shortcomings that the effort entails. I must therefore re-

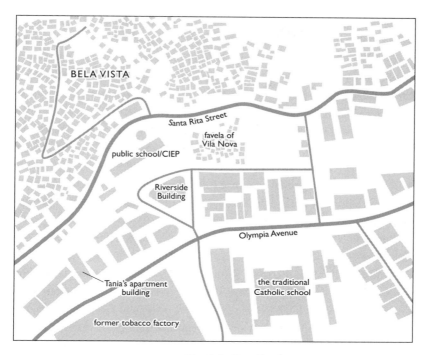

MAP 8.1 · The Bela Vista favela.

construct some of the conditions that made the social processes I describe possible. In order to do so, I must contextualize the field in which this ethnography unfolds (see map 8.1).

ON THE THRESHOLD: THE RIVERSIDE BUILDING, GREATER TIJUCA, RIO DE JANEIRO

Bela Vista is one of twenty-nine favelas spread throughout seven formal city neighborhoods in the region of Rio's northern zone that I shall refer to as Greater Tijuca.[21] The area is inhabited by 367,005 people, according to the National Census of 2000, of which 13 percent—nearly fifty thousand citizens—lived in favelas, roughly twelve thousand of them in Bela Vista.[22] Despite harboring considerable social and economic heterogeneity, the region shares a common history of urbanization, development, and recent socioeconomic decline—a trajectory connected to the region's natural landscape. The area is overwhelmed by the Tijuca Massif, an awesome mountain ridge on the slopes of which the region's favelas are now located. Back at the end of the nineteenth century, this was one of the most exclusive neighborhoods in the city because of its cool temperatures and awesome green views. The first massive modernizing urbanistic intervention in the city—the Passos remodeling—signaled a turn to the coast, thus creating the conditions for the invention of the marvels of the south zone.[23] But Greater Tijuca's views and shade still fared well, rivaling the southern zone in terms of services, infrastructure, and real-estate values for most of the century. The 1970s saw the emergence of the neomodernist urbanistic project that led to the urban development of Barra da Tijuca and the western zone. The juxtaposition of this new urbanistic model (and the ideology of safety) with rising apprehensions about crime and criminality in the 1980s led to Greater Tijuca's sharp decline in socioeconomic status and property values.

Part of this decline derived from the very geographical features that dictated Greater Tijuca's rise in the first place: the sense of being nestled against the forest that cooled the elites before air conditioning in a sweltering city was suddenly recast into a threat in the form of shots and stray bullets from drug-trade-infested hillside favelas. In several areas of Greater Tijuca, the favelas loom above the streets on horseshoe-shaped plains. Where streets run close to the mountain ridge, the rear of high-rise buildings face the favelas directly, no farther apart than two buildings across a narrow street. While such spatial arrangements are common throughout the city, the south zone included, long-standing violent conflicts between Tijuca's neighboring favelas exacerbated the sense of insecurity.

Bela Vista is located at one such juncture. Within its sight—and hence within shooting distance—there are four other medium-sized favelas, split between three different drug factions. Until the establishment of a UPP in the region, these conflicts emerged in the form of nightly shoot-outs that fluctuated in intensity and violence but never fully subsided. As the bullets traveled across the valley, many left imprints on the favela dwellings and also on the formerly elite buildings that face them directly.

It is thus not surprising that the 1990s and 2000s were times of an elite flight from the region, inaugurating a cycle of abandonment, divestment, and further population flight. According to Rio's city hall, Greater Tijuca began to lose residents in the mid-1980s, and the trend extended well into the 1990s. Between 1991 and 1996 the region lost 7.16 percent of its population. According to the same study, 58 percent of Greater Tijuca's residents named violence as the region's main problem. Among those who considered moving out of Greater Tijuca, once again violence was pointed out as the main repelling factor for 48 percent of interviewees.[24]

All these processes—though largely determined by a combination of geographical and social factors—have become inscribed in the forms and uses of space, and its reappropriations over time. In the late 1990s one found, fully functioning and in the vicinity of Bela Vista, a renowned private hospital; one of the top traditional, private Catholic schools in Rio and another large private school not so elitist nor traditional but also Catholic; and a large supermarket, owned by a multinational chain, that stood in the former site of a major tobacco factory. In the adjacencies there were also a film-dubbing studio and a large car-retail outlet. Since then, the car dealership and the supermarket have shut down, the studio has limited its activities, and there are constant rumors that the traditional school will move to a fortified space in Barra da Tijuca (in the wake of many of the region's wealthiest residents). The other Catholic school has experienced a considerable drop in its enrollment and a diversification of the activities within its grounds, with the charity work of a foundation linked to the school. Consequently, the proliferation of large, decayed spaces has precipitated further abandonment and unfolded the sense of insecurity associated to the favelas many times over.

Yet all this description of desolation and abandonment seems absurd to anyone standing at the entrance to any of the region's favelas. Ethnographically and experientially, the vicinities of the favelas, by day at least and except in the case of a period of prolonged conflict or an ongoing police incursion, are anything but desolate or cold. Quite the contrary: one could argue that few places in Greater Tijuca are as vital as the entrance to the favelas of Bela Vista and Vila Nova, a space residents refer to as "the foot of the hill."

Though they are as variable as the favelas themselves, each and every community has its own "foot of the hill." Even in flat favelas, the mixture of commerce and local sociability that characterizes the foot of the hill tends to form wherever formal public transportation (the official city bus lines) and the favela's internal transportation systems (the Kombi and motorcycle taxi) meet. The foot of the hill functions as the favela's central plaza, market, and space for and of social encounters.

The main traffic corridor in Greater Tijuca is Olympia Avenue, and the passage to the main pedestrian access to the favela is on Santa Rita Street. The entire city block between these two roads has become a highly dynamic open-market space, with stalls lining any and every available sidewalk. Right in the middle of this open market, bus station, and sociability node is a large building. I shall refer to it as the Riverside building, which can be read, for my purposes here, as an archetypical threshold space. This value constellation becomes even more striking in the light of the fact that the Riverside building was initially built to face Santa Rita Street. My pseudonym attempts to maintain something of the visual imagery evoked by the building's actual name, which means, in one of the native Brazilian languages, "singing river." Indeed, back in the late 1960s when it was erected, the building stood on a rather idyllic piece of land, right by a clean river and also near the forest and the green Greater Tijuca views.

In the 1980s and early 1990s, with the development of the Kombi transportation system, the construction of a public school meant to cater to the favela children, and the growth of the favela of Vila Nova just next door, the market value of property in the building dropped considerably.[25] As Gabriela, a schoolteacher I interviewed just months after her move to the Riverside building, recalls:

> They say it was a mess back then, right? I witnessed it because I had a friend who lived here. . . . People would just come and go, there was no doorman. No, I guess there was a doorman but there were all these rumors that people from Vila Nova used to come and break into the apartments. They say! We don't know whether it's true. But yes, there were all these people coming and going with no control. That's why when the shoot-outs got more intense, the value of apartments here dropped so much. That's when people from the morro started to move here.

In the mid-1990s, with nightly shoot-outs already established as part of the region's routine, tenants—a majority of whom were still working and middle-class people, "pavement" born and bred—organized a major remodeling with the intent of reversing the building's accesses: the rear became the front, and the former front turned into a service entrance. The makeover included fortification of the building's walls and the construction of a cabin with dark windows wherein a security guard could survey the images from several security cameras installed in the building's interior and accesses. "Like Big Brother!" as Gabriela put it.

I interviewed Gabriela just a few months after she moved to the Riverside building, in 2005. There were still unpacked boxes in the corners, but her tone and demeanor already expressed a marked distance from—and a wistful nostalgia for—the *morrão* (big hill), as she now referred to Bela Vista.[26] Her narrative about the move already crystallized a sense of a "return to her origins" rather than an accomplishment:

> I keep a good relationship with the morrão, with the people there, not the least because I taught there. But in the beginning, when we moved there, relations were not so tight and people didn't exactly welcome us, right? I guess they noticed that we came from a different background, were more educated, different.... And when you live in a place like a favela, that causes an estrangement. [When we moved to Bela Vista from the neighboring favela of Ribeira] my sister was in high school and I was already going to the university, and fourteen years ago it was very rare for *favelados* [favela dwellers] to go to university. Particularly a public one.[27]

The usage of the term *morrão* indexes how Gabriela constructed the move as the entry into a different world, unrelated to the favela. In crossing over to the "pavement" side of the threshold, she no longer hesitated to ask people over to her house because she did not feel the constraint of asking them to enter a favela. Living in the pavement is a coming home of sorts for a Rio de Janeiro State University graduate and public school history teacher.

Gabriela's home can be placed on the most expensive side of an apartment building in which market values vary considerably and accordingly provides an interesting glimpse into how property values are produced on the threshold.[28] There are more than one hundred apartments in the Riverside building, with two-bedroom units occupying the façades that face both Santa Rita Street and Olympia Avenue; there are fewer three-bedroom units, which have a side view only of the favela. The apartments facing Santa Rita Street are composed of a small living room, two bedrooms, a comfortable kitchen, and a view of the public school and Bela Vista. In 2004–5 the units were going for the same price as houses on the other side of the street, in Bela Vista, about 35,000 reais. Now the homes on the Bela Vista side of the street are not houses in the sense of detached or single-occupancy homes. They rise up to six stories, often with distinct units occupying separate floors. In each case, space is scarce, and both the Riverside apartments and the houses in Bela Vista could be estimated at roughly sixty square meters. An apartment on the other side of the Riverside building, also a two bedroom with a similar layout but not facing the favela, was sold for

45,000 reais at roughly the same time. The math is simple: avoiding the line of fire costs 10,000 reais. It is worth noting that most of the transactions I observed over the course of the past years went swiftly. That is, none of these properties were on the market for very long. Quite the contrary—in all cases buyers were extremely aware of the competition, and ensuring a quick transaction was a central concern.

These dynamics arguably incorporated the Riverside building into the favela housing market. This happened to such an extent that for many residents considering moving out of Bela Vista, the Riverside building has ceased to be a "pavement" option. They consider it an integral part of Bela Vista and therefore not distant enough to make the investment worthwhile. That is the case of the young manager of a Blockbuster video store, whose mother's residential trajectory is my next concern. And I have frequently heard similar opinions in the last few years. In 2009, under the federal government's Programa de Aceleração do Crescimento urbanization works, several families received financial compensation after being displaced from one of the favela's poorest regions. Most took the compensation to buy property in other parts of the favela; others made a down payment on houses in other parts of the city or in the vicinity of Bela Vista. All contemplated, no matter how briefly, the possibility of finding housing in the Riverside building.

SACRIFICE AND WINNING

The increasing valuation and formalization of favela properties has engendered in longtime favela residents a sense of upward social mobility. Many of those who now approach their retiring age marvel at the material improvements of their surroundings, at the increased offer of all sorts of services in their communities. They recall the old days when stucco shacks and muddy alleys dominated the favela landscape and laughingly tell of the hassles they suffered every day in attempting to make it downhill to work without being covered in mud, and they constantly remind their children that they have a comparatively easy life. Tania's residential trajectory tells one among many similar stories.

Tania left Barroso, a small town in the state of Minas Gerais, for Rio de Janeiro in 1974. She followed the lead of her elder sister, Telma, who had arrived in Rio two years earlier to work (and live) in a *casa de família*, that is, as a live-in domestic worker. The address—Olympia Avenue, number 737—

spelled affluence. Back then, property values in the Greater Tijuca region rivaled those of Ipanema; but while the latter's residents still had to resort to Copacabana for entertainment, leisure, and many services, Tijuca stood as a consumption and service hub, drawing the prosperous from all neighborhoods of the northern zone and the metropolitan region. So when Tania got off the bus from Barroso, her destination was Tijuca, where her sister had already secured her a job, also in a casa de família, just a few blocks away from Telma's workplace.

For two years Tania hardly left her employer's home. She stayed there on holidays and weekends to minimize expenses, but her mother's health back in Barroso deteriorated quickly, necessitating that Tania bring her mother to Rio where the sisters could care for her. In short: they needed a home of their own. They found a wooden shack for rent in a lower part of the favela of Bela Vista, one of the Greater Tijuca's largest. It cost more than they could readily afford, but living farther uphill was prohibitive given their mother's failing health. In order to have more free time than a regular live-in maid would, Tania quit her job after securing another one as a cleaner in the large, private, elite hospital just a couple of hundred meters away from Telma's workplace on Olympia Avenue, a less than ten-minute walk from home.

Like many employers of live-in domestics in the 1960s and 1970s, Telma's bosses helped her to buy the little wooden shack by giving her a substantial portion of the shack's value. Added to the savings that Telma and Tania had accumulated since coming to Rio, they covered the full amount asked and left a little to be used in "improvements" to the rather precarious structure. The shack, according to Tania, was "real ugly," with a dirt floor, and required quite a bit of refurbishing and finishing, issues to which they tended over the course of the next decade (see figure 8.1).

In the meantime, their mother died, and Tania met her husband-to-be one rare afternoon taken off for leisure. They met in the Saens Pena Square, which was Tijuca's cultural, consumption, and entertainment core in the 1970s. By the time she married, in 1977, Tania had already quit her job at the hospital and gone back to working as a domestic in yet another upper-middle-class home, also walking distance from Bela Vista. But now she no longer slept on the job, unless her employers paid her overtime (which she gladly took, and saved) to service the many dinner parties they hosted. In her spare time she made a little extra cash by ironing clothes, usually in the late evenings, after her husband had retired to bed. Her husband, José, also

FIG. 8.1 · The Riverside building, viewed from Tania's former favela house on Santa Rita Street. The favela constructions are in the favela of Vila Nova. Photo by Mariana Cavalcanti, 2010.

worked two jobs for all of his life. His routine was to leave for work at 4 a.m. to begin his first shift as a messenger at the Banco do Brasil, then move on to a second shift as a cleaner in different firms.

By saving the meager leftovers from these four jobs, they managed to buy another shack a few alley bends upward from the original house, where Telma now lived on her own. Their newly acquired house was considerably better than the first shack they had bought (which they had transformed into a modest masonry home). They continuously invested in and improved on the new home for the next twenty-three years. In the meantime their son was born in 1980. There was never any question that Renato would be an only child. As Tania put it: "Since I was a very, very poor person, to the point that we had nothing to eat back in the *roça* [hinterlands], I only had one child so I could give him the best I could."

In the late 1990s, with Renato past his teen years, Tania and José bought what they then perceived as their definitive home. This house was even more carefully finished over the years; Tania and José took their time re-modeling it one room at a time, spreading out payments over the years and carefully planning each new step of the process. Located a short flight of steps off the pavement of Santa Rita Street, the house occupied the first and second floors of a typical six-story favela building composed of four differently laid-out housing units. Tania and José owned two of these: halfway up the steps leading to the main house there was a separate entrance to a room equipped with its own bathroom. This separate apartment belonged to Renato. Tania and José had figured that this arrangement would keep Renato close to them for years to come.

But Renato saw things differently. Years of studying in private schools, of socializing in middle-class circles, had only fueled his lifelong wish to move out of the favela. He dreamed of an apartment where his *Tijucana* (from Tijuca, meaning from the "pavement") girlfriend or colleagues at Blockbuster would not think twice about visiting for fear of the nightly shoot-outs and violent drug dealers. It is hardly surprising that Renato was the first person to call Tania's attention to the fact that they could afford to buy an apartment in the "street." He reasoned that—with his parents' impending retirements from two of their jobs and his own savings since his promotion to manager at the Blockbuster branch—they could well buy a two-bedroom apartment in the streets bordering Bela Vista. He simply did the math, knowing they could reasonably expect to collect 30,000 reais on the sale of the house—it was, after all, located in the most valuable spot of the favela. His own separate room went for 8,000 reais, paid for up front, with less than one week on the market. They needed to scrape together about 40,000 reais. With both parents collecting the benefits of formal employment and his own savings added, the whole enterprise became feasible.

I met Tania during her last days living in the favela. She had just become the happy owner of an apartment located on Olympia Ave, number 735. The building was next door to the one Telma had first worked in when she ventured out to Rio de Janeiro so many years before. With its spacious closets and custom-made kitchen and bathrooms, the place very much resembled the homes that Tania had cleaned for most of her life.

For Tania it is all a matter of collecting just dues; hard work and sacrifice have made her a winner—not in the sense of opposing winners to losers as Americans would have it, but in the sense of claiming a just reward for decades of *lutas* (struggles):

> I married, got pregnant, and had my son. My mom stayed at home with him, until she got so sick she died, so what did I do? I left my job at the hospital; I asked them to fire me so I would get my compensation, took it, and saved it. Then I went to work in *casas de família* because I could

bring him along. But it was a big sacrifice because I brought him along with me, got things started, and then at about quarter of noon I had to stop whatever I was doing so I could take him to school. . . . Then I went back, finished things off at work, then came home to take care of my own house, to take care of him, cook for the next day. . . . You know, it was a big struggle, but I have faith in God and all the faith I have in God, and I think I am winning. I have not won yet, but I am managing to win. My husband also works hard; he holds two jobs, he battles. For you to have an idea, he leaves the house every day at around quarter of four in the morning and he only comes back at 10 p.m.

For Tania and so many other favela residents, winning, or collecting just rewards, is a direct function of hard work, and specifically hard work in a context of general hardship; hence the constant references to *battling* and *struggling*. All these terms constitute and express the work ethic of the *trabalhadores pobres* (poor workers) analyzed by Alba Zaluar in her classic study, and are reinforced in systematic efforts to differentiate themselves from the *bandidos* (bandits).[29] Tania's transition from being a trabalhadora, as well as a *batalhadora* (battler) and *lutadora* (fighter), to a retired woman who works by her own choice, and from a resident of a favela community to the owner of an apartment indiscernible from the ones she cleaned for most of her working life, materializes the rewards of a life of "hard work." It also highlights how this work ethic hinges on a notion of subjective value grounded in sacrifice: as Georg Simmel noted long ago, "sacrifice not only increases the value of the desired object but actually brings it about."[30]

The threshold effect allowed Tania to objectify this subjective sphere of value—in that all the sacrifice and postponed rewards of a lifetime were rendered visible, tangible, and materialized in the form of landed property in the formal city. It is striking that the different social worlds that Tania inhabited over the course of nearly thirty years—from live-in servant to stucco shack dweller to high-end favela house to legal owner of formal property in the city—occurred in less than one square kilometer.

THE VOID

A careful reading of real-estate classifieds reveals a series of ways of addressing the favela-proximity concern, particularly in neighborhoods where favelas are nearly omnipresent:

Um quarto aberto para sala. Sala 3 ambientes.Varandão vista para o mar. Próximo ao Fashion Mall. Ótimo condomínio (S. Conrado Green). Local seguro. *Próximo à praia e longe do túnel.* Tratar com o porteiro do Ed.Torrigiani.

(One bedroom converted into the living room. 3 living rooms. Large balcony with ocean view. Near the Fashion Mall. Excellent condominium [S. Conrado Green]. Safe place. *Near the beach and away from the tunnel.* Inquiries to the doorman of the Torrigiani Building.)

TIJUCA R$119,999. Próximo S. F. Xavier / UERJ! Já pensou morar cobertura? Prédio com infra clube!! Terraço panorâmico *s/comunidade* c/churrasqueira.

(TIJUCA $119,999. Near S. F. Xavier/UERJ [Rio de Janeiro State University]! Have you considered living in a penthouse? Building with leisure club infrastructure! Panoramic roof, *no community*, barbecue area.)

TIJUCA R$235.000 Superlar Imobiliária (Largo 2ªFeira) *s/morro* varandão salão 3 dorms suíte copa-coz c/armários dependências duas garagens ótima localização Tel.2208–0625 REF.3016.

(TIJUCA R$235.000 Superlar [Lgo 2a feira] Real Estate *no hill*, large balcony, living room, 3 bedrooms en suite, kitchen and dining room furnished with cupboards, two parking spots, excellent location. Tel.2208–0625 REF.3016.)[31]

In order to vouch for the advantage of a "panoramic roof," it is necessary to attest that there is no "community" in view. Or, as in the first case, the property is so fabulous because it is close to the beach *and* far from the tunnel (which cuts across the very hill the Rocinha spills over). The repetition of similar expressions week after week naturalizes them as objective components in the production of real-estate value. The very standardization of the abbreviation *s/morro* for *sem morro* (without hill) (more common than its variants *longe morro* [away from hill] or *livre morro* [hill free]) indexes the centrality of this feature, particularly in neighborhoods such as Greater Tijuca, Santa Teresa, São Conrado, and Rio Comprido, where the favelas are a marked presence in an otherwise middle-class landscape.

When I initially designed the field-research methods for this project, one of my goals was to inquire into how agents might present real estate in middle-class regions bordering favelas to potential clients. I suspected that

I would find a complex repertoire of evasion on the subject of the favela, or that the very danger might be deconstructed so as to avoid the theme of risk areas or shoot-outs. I thus developed a strategy, loosely inspired by the housing audits conducted by the U.S. Department of Housing and Urban Development in the 1960s and 1970s in order to verify whether the civil rights legislation, in particular the Fair Housing Act of 1968, was being duly observed. In the audits, researchers were paired up according to similar levels of income and family makeup, and they expressed the same preferences to real-estate brokers. The only difference was that the auditing pair was composed of one white member and one member of a minority. These studies found that white potential buyers were systematically offered more and better housing options than members of the minorities in question. The ultimate goal of the audits was the production of quantitative data to track patterns of racial or ethnic discrimination. My appropriation of this method was limited to provoking a potential sale situation in order to assess how such property was portrayed and objectified in practice. In short, I replicated the encounter between the agent and a fake potential buyer in order to assess how agents might attempt to present threshold real estate to possible customers.[32]

My original intention was to confront data collected in the audit-inspired visits with both formal and informal interviews with agents in their own offices. Surprisingly enough, I found no significant difference in the form or content of these narratives. Indeed, in the view of agents, real estate bordering favelas is a long-recognized problem. They do not avoid talking about it; they avoid dealing with it altogether.

When encumbered with the task of setting up apartment viewings with realtors, my assistant, Marcella Carvalho, wrote, with some exasperation:

> The agent asked me four times whether I knew where the apartment was. First she asked if I knew where the building was. I said yes, Santa Rita Street, but I did not know the number. She asked if I knew where Santa Rita Street was. She asked me if I knew it was near Rua Branca. I said yes. Finally she asked if I knew it was right by Bela Vista. Once again, I said yes. Only then she said she would call the owner to find out whether the place was still on sale. She later called back to let me know the place had been sold.

That was not the first, or the last, time that real-estate agents attempted to avoid showing houses in threshold areas. Often realtors denied having placed the ad or discouraged the potential client from the outset by saying that the property in question is near this or that favela. When asked about real estate in the vicinity of favelas in informal interview settings, each and every agent replied with some version of "time is money": what is the point in wasting time, gas, and the effort to take customers to unsellable properties? Yet another practice crystallized in advertisements: say it up front.

> V. Isabel. R$55.000 (Sta. Isabel), vista comunidade, sala, 2dorms, cozinha, banheiro condomínio barato, desocupado, bom apartamento.

> (Vila Isabel, R$55.000 (Sta. Isabel), view to community, living room, two bedrooms, bath, cheap building fees, unoccupied, good apartment.)[33]

When agents actually agree to show threshold property to potential buyers, they simply admit to the fact that threshold properties are second-rate real estate that suffers a structural and unavoidable problem: there is absolutely no room for bargaining on the grounds of favela proximity, and the buyer is responsible for the choice of even considering the option. In this sense, the agents treat the property as if it were not even worth spinning.

This second-rate real estate is a hard social fact for agents, and they define it as being produced by any combination of three factors: views of favelas, proximity to favelas, and locations near pedestrian routes to favelas. View matters because these are "risk areas," and the risk is that a stray bullet from the conflicts between police and rival drug gangs might end up in one's living room or bedroom. The line of fire and the reach of police officers' and traffickers' weaponry are quite extensive, and this produces the threshold effect upon entire blocks and streets. In relation to proximity, the issue is the spillover effect of violent crime in the favela from hijackings and holdups to fake checkpoints and body dumpings, as well as the subjection of threshold dwellers to forced "mourning" periods when drug bosses are arrested or killed. Likewise, even in cases where the favela is neither visible nor that close, the fact of being in the path to the favela also produces lost value, as is made evident in the assessment of city property taxes.[34]

One particular apartment visit is quite illustrative of agents' resignation in the face of these threshold spaces. The apartment in question was an eighty-square-meter, two-bedroom apartment in a gated condominium composed of two high-rise buildings, equipped with playgrounds, a swimming pool, a gym, and plenty of communal spaces. The agent identified himself on the phone as a resident of nearby Branca Street, and since he was free at home, he agreed to see us at once. As we met him at one of the side entries to the condominium, he warned us that the apartment had a "slit" of favela view. He hardly mentioned the apartment's many advantages: well-kept hardwood floors, custom-made kitchen, wardrobes and shelves in the smaller bedroom, all tastefully designed. A thick glass provided an additional barrier between the favela and the apartment, both on the balcony off the living room and on the bedroom window through which the slit was apparent. I asked whether the glass was bulletproof. He promptly called the owner, who explained that it was soundproof glass, because of the noise of the *bailes funk* (funk parties) in the favela. The agent said that the problem with the apartment was its "low liquidity"; he in no way pushed it, or even encouraged me to close the deal. As we were walking out, already on the common grounds, he showed us a rather well-kept playground, with brand-new toys. There was no sign of recent usage, which is not surprising since it was located exactly in the no man's land that separated Bela Vista from Ribeira—that is, in one of the neighboring areas most likely to be a target of stray bullets, flying from both sides of the conflict that raged between rival drug gangs on the two hills. The agent seemed to be at a loss for words. He opened his arms, as if to take in the breadth of the line of fire. With an ironic shrug, he finally suggested that we "might as well" take a ride up the elevator to see the swimming pool on the roof.

Entering the pool area was an impressive experience: the glare of the sun reflected many times over in the favela windows. The houses on the steep hill rose like a wall of haphazardly connected blocks and bricks. I was overwhelmed by the precise layout of alleys and bends on the streets, the detailed view of people's lajes and glimpses of the intimacy of individual homes through opened doors, all just across a two-lane street. Once again the agent opened his arms: "I would never bathe in this pool!"

It seems that no one does. Like the playground below, the overall impression that these spaces convey is typical of unsuccessful planning—there is no senses of placeness. It was simply an utterly deserted swimming pool, with no chair or bench to sit, no sign of water on the borders or in the surrounding area. Just a sparkling swimming pool on a hot concrete roof, without the slightest resemblance to a place of leisure.

As we parted with the agent, he gently steered us to the bus station farther away from Bela Vista. I asked him how bad the shoot-outs were. He then inexplicably lied for the first time: "No, I can barely hear them."

Yet another agent enacted a "graph" to describe real estate along Olympia Avenue, one of Greater Tijuca's main traffic arteries. He began by pointing to his shoulder, then dropped to his waist in what he called "the void"—the cluster of favelas around Bela Vista—then recovered some, but not fully—after all, he explained, those who lived beyond the "void" had to pass through it on a daily basis.

What the experiment with real-estate agents makes plainly visible is that entire portions of the city have all but withdrawn from the logic and circuits of the formal real-estate market. Homemade "for sale" signs seem to be more effective in reaching their appropriate audience, and the profits and resources at stake are scarce, making hiring intermediaries futile. Thus, while powerful in relativizing the dichotomy between the "formal" and "informal" sectors, threshold real estate simultaneously bears witness to the centrality of the favela-pavement dichotomy as a symbolic construction in the daily life of Rio de Janeiro residents. It is, however, a symbolic construction that allows for different spatial referents: regions that are considered too close to the favela to remain as pavement for longtime Tijucanos or real-estate brokers can instead be perceived as firmly anchored in the "pavement" for a longtime favela resident like Tania. The production of this zone of indeterminacy that I call the threshold effect shows that formal and informal real-estate markets are not mutually exclusive spheres. While one man's void is also one woman's opportunity for being a "winner" in life, the fact is that a qualitative reading of the logic of this real-estate market reveals how the favela-pavement dichotomy powerfully organizes the inhabited and imagined worlds of city residents.

CLOSING REMARKS FROM POST-SHOOT-OUT GREATER TIJUCA

One Tuesday afternoon in September 2010, a group of about fifty realtors, real-estate agents, and community and neighborhood leaders gathered at the traditional, elite tennis club in Tijuca for the "First Security and Real-Estate Forum," promoted by the Greater Tijuca section of the Regional Council of Real Estate Agents of Rio de Janeiro. At a glance, one might understandably infer that the purpose of the event was to discuss rising crime rates, alternative forms of policing, crime-mapping technologies, and tips for ensuring secure housing, or to provide an overview of the latest releases in surveillance gadgets for the home. But none of that was the case.

According to the chairman's introductory speech, the event's main goal was to provide an opportunity for agents to better understand the UPPs, so as to help them incorporate the forces' advantages to their sales pitches. He showed colorful graphs of the range of automatic rifles around the favelas' borders, emphasizing entire streets and city blocks that had ceased to contain risk areas. The UPPs, he said, reflected the impact of public security on the real-estate market, "promoting both the realtor's personal safety and the increase in real-estate values," consequently making what had seemed a "difficult" increase in property prices now "easy." Approving nods everywhere. The highlight of the evening was a speech delivered by Captain Amaral, the commander of the first and largest UPP in the region.

The affair resembled a thanksgiving ritual, performed to express the overwhelming collective gratitude for the blessing recently bestowed on the Tijuca community in the guise of the Pacification program. From the opening statement acknowledging "the most important presence in the event" — that of God — to the collective prayer before the concluding coffee break, the event all but named the UPP a miracle.

This is not surprising: greater Tijuca was the city region that experienced the quickest real-estate valuation in 2010 in Rio, and this was in a context of massive increases across the city. According to the Sindicato de Habitação (Union Housing), properties registered an increase of 51 percent in their market values and a 27 percent increase in rental agreements.[35] The buildings in the area surrounding Bela Vista have experienced even higher spikes, in some cases more than 100 percent. The threshold effect is temporarily suspended.

This threshold effect may well have been a brief moment in favela consolidation, one that will not repeat itself and is not subject to generalization. If so, I can only marvel as to having witnessed the emergence and demise of a social phenomenon so decisive to the imagined and inhabited worlds of those who shared it. But there is another possibility in the making: with the increasing formalization of favela property and the steady increase not only in property values but also in the fixed costs of living that go with formalization, perhaps a different type of threshold effect — from the pavement to the favela — may form. While it is too early to speculate on whatever contours such a context might assume, an ethnography of housing markets remains a vibrant source for thinking through the many transformations Rio de Janeiro is undergoing and will continue to endure in the light of the speculation, investments, and creative destruction that the Olympic Games of 2016 are bound to leave as their legacy.

NOTES

This chapter draws on fieldwork conducted in 2004–5 as part of my dissertation research, funded by the CAPES Foundation within the Ministry of Education, and by the Foundation for Urban and Regional Studies. The chapter also presents the initial results of research conducted in 2009–10, which was funded by the Conselho Nacional de Desenvolvimento Científico e Tecnológico (National Council for Scientific and Technological Research) and by the Fundação Carlos Chagas de Amparo a Pesquisa no Rio de Janeiro (Carlos Chagas Foundation for Support of Research in Rio de Janeiro).

This chapter has benefited from the comments of Brodie Fischer; Bryan McCann; my colleagues at the Nucleo de Estudos em Cultura e Economia, in particular Federico Neiburg, Benoît de L'Estoile, and Fernando Rabossi; and my friends at the ANPOCS Cities Working Group, particularly Cristina Patriota. I am extremely grateful to all these people and collectives. I also thank the generous reviewers at Duke University Press.

Names of people and places have been changed in order to protect the anonymity of my informants. I have translated their interview excerpts and the real-estate adds.

1. These data are available at http://portalgeo.rio.rj.gov.br/portalgeo/index.asp. According to the urbanist Luciana Correa do Lago, "two correlating criteria define a popular settlement as a 'loteamento,' independently of its legal situation: the [initial] purchase of the plot and hence the existence of a market, and the presence of an economic agent (the 'loteador') who is responsible for the enterprise." She notes, however, a convergence in the settlement of new favelas and the production of loteamentos in the periphery. See Luciana Correa do Lago, "Favela-loteamento: Re-conceituando os termos da ilegalidade e da segregação urbana," paper presented at the 10 Encontro Nacional da ANPUR, Belo Horizonte, Brazil, May 2003, accessed May 13, 2006, http://www.observatoriodasmetropoles.ufrj.br/download /anpur2003_lago.pdf.

2. Declaring low-income communities as special social interest areas is an instrument created by the city's Organic Law of 1990 and regulated by the Master Plan of 1992. Special social interest areas allow the state to set special parameters for urbanization, zoning, and construction in the areas. This makes the full formalization of favelas, housing projects, and irregular loteamentos possible, even though their incorporation into the formal city remains differentiated because of the more flexible urbaninistic rules that apply to the areas.

3. These are not the only sources of armed conflict in the city. Particularly in the more-remote favelas of the western zone, but also in the north of the city, the past decade has witnessed the emergence of paramilitary armed groups composed of retired police officers and firefighters that first expel the drug trade from the favela in question and then reproduce their territorial routines and armed surveillance of boundaries while making a profit out of selling "protection" to residents and store-owners, overtaxing the sale of gas vessels, and providing pirated cable television.

These groups also partake in shoot-outs with the police and any group of drug dealers that might attempt to take back control of the area.

4. The day before, however, Globo Network broadcast from a helicopter on live television the shocking image of dozens of dark-skinned young men running under rifle fire in a desperate attempt to escape the police takeover of the nearby favela of Vila Cruzeiro.

5. For example, Licia do Prado Valladares, *A invenção da favela: Do mito de origem a favela.com* (Rio de Janeiro: Editora FGV, 2005); Mariana Cavalcanti, "Of Shacks, Houses and Fortresses: An Ethnography of Favela Consolidation in Rio de Janeiro," PhD dissertation, University of Chicago, 2007.

6. The Mutirão Remunerado (Collective Effort Paid) program of the 1980s was highly experimental and notoriously underfunded. I have not been able to find data on its estimated or actual costs. The Favela-Bairro program, according to city hall estimates, consumed 1.1 billion reais in its first two phases (1994 and 2000), and an additional 700 million reais in its third phase (2008). The program targeted 143 favelas. In 2007 the federal government announced an additional 1 billion reais earmarked for the Programa de Aceleracao do Crescimento urbanization works in the Complexo do Alemão, Complexo de Manguinhos, Rocinha, and Cantagalo-Pavão-Pavãozinho. Finally, the Morar Carioca has recently begun in early 2011, with a budget of 8 billion reais. These (and other) figures can be found at the Agencia de Notícias das Favelas (News Agency of Favelas) website: http://www.anf.org.br/.

7. For historical accounts of these and other government policies vis-à-vis the city's favelas, see, for instance, Marcelo Burgos, "Dos parques proletários ao Favela-Bairro: As políticas públicas nas favelas do Rio de Janeiro," in *Um século de favela*, edited by Alba Zaluar and Marcelo Burgos (Rio de Janeiro: FGV, 1998); Mariana Cavalcanti, "Do barraco à casa: tempo, espaço e valor(es) em uma favela consolidada," *Revista Brasileira de Ciências Sociais* 24, no. 69 (2009); and Américo Freire, Feire Medeiros, and Mariana Cavalcanti, *Lu Petersen: Militância, favela, urbanismo* (Rio de Janeiro: FGV, 2009).

8. The program included an open contest of ideas for architectural projects for favela urbanization. There were forty selected projects, which the competition drew from the city's main architectural firms as well as young, recent graduates.

9. Cavalcanti, "Of Shacks, Houses and Fortresses."

10. In my doctoral dissertation, I describe this process as the transition from wooden shack to masonry house. See Cavalcanti, "Of Shacks, Houses and Fortresses."

11. See, for instance, in the case of urban Brazil, Pedro Abramo, "A dinámica do mercado de solo informal e a mobilidade residencial dos pobres," *Coleção Estudos Cariocas*, no. 3 (2003); Luciana Correa do Lago, *Desigualdades e segregação na metrópole: O Rio de Janeiro em tempo de crise* (Rio de Janeiro: Revan FASE, 2000); and Lícia Valladares, *Repensando a habitação no Brasil* (Rio de Janeiro: Zahar, 1983).

12. See, for instance, Osvaldo Luiz de Souza Silva and Alice Brasileiro, "Avaliação de imóveis no Rio de Janeiro: A depreciação do valor de imóveis circumvizinhos aos

assentamentos habitacionais espontâneos e o tratamento de políticas públicas para essas áreas," paper presented at the VII Seminário Internacional da Latin American Real Estate Society, São Paulo, 2007.

13. Fernando José de Lacerda Carvalho Jr. and Celso Funcia Lemme, "O impacto da violência criminal urbana no preço dos imóveis residenciais na região da Tijuca, cidade do Rio de Janeiro: um estudo exploratório," *Cadernos EBAPE.BR* 3, no. 3 (2005).

14. Nezar Alsayyed, "Urban Informality as a 'New' Way of Life," in *Urban Informality: Transnational Perspectives from the Middle East, Latin America, and South Asia*, edited by Ananya Roy and Nezar Alsayyed (Lanham, MD: Lexington Books, 2004).

15. Michel Agier, "Between War and City: Towards an Urban Anthropology of Refugee Camps," *Ethnography* 3, no. 3 (2002); Cristina Patriota de Moura, "As trajetórias de formalização: Condomínios horizontais em Brasília," paper presented at the 32º Encontro Anual da ANPOCS, São Paulo, October 27–31, 2008; and Vera da Silva Telles and Robert Cabanes, *Nas tramas da cidade* (Paris: IRD; São Paulo: Associação Editorial Humanitas, 2006).

16. Ananya Roy, "Urban Informality: Toward an Epistemology of Planning," *Journal of the American Planning Association* 71, no. 2 (2005): 148; for the case of Brazilian cities, see also Cavalcanti, "Do barraco à casa"; Brodwyn M. Fischer, *A Poverty of Rights: Citizenship and Inequality in Twentieth-Century Rio de Janeiro* (Stanford, CA: Stanford University Press, 2008); and Telles and Cabanes, *Nas tramas da cidade*.

17. I am drawing here, of course, on John Logan and Harvey Molotch's by now classic suggestion of the real-estate market as a social phenomenon. See Logan and Molotch, *Urban Fortunes: The Political Economy of Place* (Berkeley: University of California Press, 1987).

18. Igor Kopytoff, "The Cultural Biography of Things: Commoditization as Process," in *The Social Life of Things: Commodities in Cultural Perspective*, edited by Arjun Appadurai, 64–91 (Cambridge: Cambridge University Press, 1986).

19. The hilltop here refers, of course, to hill favelas. These tend to concentrate in the southern zone and near the northern zone of the city. In the western zone new favelas continue to spring up on flat lands. The UPP geography maps onto the social geography of the city, in that the southern and near-northern zones have high concentratations of both income levels and UPP units.

20. The Grupamento de Policiamento em Áreas Especiais (Grouping of Special Areas Policing) constituted an initial experiment in community policing for special areas (i.e., favelas dominated by the drug trade). It began in 1999 and targeted small favelas of the southern zone and the city center. While it reduced conflicts in a few token favelas (notably the Pereirão in Laranjeiras), the program was short-lived.

21. Defining Greater Tijuca as a scale of analysis is a strategic and methodological move. Strategically it lets me refer to tangible historical processes inscribed in the space of the city while providing a scale of analysis vague enough to protect the anonymity of my informants. Methodologically, it allows for a more con-

crete ethnographic portrayal of the relations between Bela Vista and its surrounding neighborhoods.

22. Cecília Maria Neder Castro and Miriam D'Ávila Calvacanti, "Plano Estratégico 2001/2004 — Retrato das Regiões: Tijuca e Vila Isabel: Uma planície entre o maciço e a floresta," in *Plano Estratégico II*, edited by the Prefeitura da Cidade do Rio de Janeiro (Rio de Janeiro: Prefeitura da Cidade do Rio de Janeiro, n.d.), 6.

23. The remodeling occurred between 1902 and 1906, during Francisco Pereira Passos's appointment as mayor of Rio de Janeiro. It occurred as part of an effort to modernize (in a vision of modernity marked by the Haussmann remodeling of Paris) the old colonial city that harbored violent epidemics of yellow fever, tuberculosis, and many other diseases. The remodeling is also largely believed to be connected to the spread of favelas on hillsides bordering central or middle-class areas as an alternative for low-income housing, because the remodeling privileged the demolition of old slum tenements in the downtown area with no provision for housing for those displaced. While many of the displaced poor also set up residence in the northern suburbs, these displacements are often cited as important in triggering the generalization of favelas in the cityscape. See, for instance, Jaime L. Benchimol, *Pereira Passos, um Haussmann tropical: A renovação urbana da cidade do Rio de Janeiro no início do século XX* (Rio de Janeiro: Prefeitura da Cidade do Rio de Janeiro, Secretaria Municipal de Cultura, Turismo e Esportes, Departamento Geral de Documentação e Informação Cultural, 1990); and Nicolau Sevcenko, *Literatura como missão: Tensões sociais e criação cultural na Primeira República* (São Paulo: Companhia das Letras, 2003), to name only two.

24. Castro and Cavalcanti, "Plano Estratégico 2001/2004," 7. While the establishment of several UPPs in the region has stalled the cycle of decay and decline in market values, and these effects are largely tangible in the daily lives of those in the Greater Tijuca region, it is too soon to argue for a full reversal of the dynamics here described.

25. The school is a Centro Integrado de Educação Pública (Integrated Center for Public Education), built in the context of the democratic opening in the 1980s, in Leonel Brizola's term as state governor (1983–87). The centers spearheaded the attempt of an inclusive educational politics of the anthropologist Darcy Ribeiro, who was then state secretary of education. The architect Oscar Niemeyer designed the armed standard, easily recognized concrete buildings that housed the centers. The standard building, however, soon came to be associated with schools for the poor. See Helena Bomeny, "Salvar pela escola: Programa especial de educação," *Sociologia: Problemas e Práticas*, no. 55 (2007).

26. As used by Gabriela, *morrão* denotes an affection and nostalgia for the past.

27. In Brazil, public universities are, as a rule, more prestigious than their private counterparts. The admission exams for federal and state universities are notoriously competitive. As a result, private school students are most likely to achieve the highest scores, in a process that reproduces the country's deeply unequal social structure.

28. I describe these dynamics based on a series of transactions I observed back in 2004–5. While values have changed — steadily rising — the mechanisms remain the same, given that the effects of the UPPS are not yet fully discernible.

29. Alba Zaluar, *A máquina e a revolta: As organizações populares e o significado da pobreza* (São Paulo: Brasiliense, 1985).

30. Georg Simmel, *The Philosophy of Money* (London: Routledge, 2004), 87.

31. These are real-estate advertisements from the brokers Coutinho Imóveis and Superlar, as well as classified ads in *O Globo*, ranging from 2006 to 2009. Italics mine.

32. See, for example, Rose Helper, *Racial Policies and Practices of Real Estate Brokers* (Minneapolis: University of Minnesota Press, 1969); Douglas Massey and Nancy Denton, *American Apartheid: Segregation and the Making of the Underclass* (Cambridge, MA: Harvard University Press, 1993); and Juliet Saltman, "Housing Discrimination: Policy Research, Methods and Results," *Annals of the American Academy of Political and Social Science*, no. 441 (1979).

33. *O Globo*, classifieds section, April 4, 2009, 14.

34. In the course of my research, I found that in Greater Tijuca, the city property tax can drop by half, sometimes from one city block to the next. Official inquiries to city officials yielded no results on the logic of such taxes, and formal requests to recalculate the taxes due from my assistant (who lived in a threshold region) were denied on the grounds that there is no tax reduction because of proximity to risk areas. But inquiries in the field demonstrated many cases in which the taxes charged in threshold regions were lower than those regions distant from the favelas. One additional lead this research has yet to follow is many mentions of entire gated condominiums and buildings, as well as individual property owners, that are in the process of suing the government for the loss of their property values.

35. "Tijuca de volta aos holofotes," *O Dia*, September 5, 2012, http://odia.ig.com .br/portal/imoveis/tijuca-de-volta-aos-holofotes-1.438824, accessed June 29, 2013.

NINE

Toxic Waiting

FLAMMABLE SHANTYTOWN REVISITED

Javier Auyero

Three decades of neoliberal economic policy have generated massive dislo-
cations and collective suffering in Argentina. Beginning in the early 1990s
and up to the early 2000s, impoverishment of the middle- and low-income
sectors was driven by the disappearance of formal work and the explosion of
unemployment levels. After the economic recovery that began in 2003, poor
people's material and symbolic conditions were deeply affected by the sustained decline of income levels in the lower ranks of the job market and the
growth of informal employment. The most dramatic physical manifestation
of this generalized degradation in the lives of the dispossessed can be found
in the explosive growth of the population living in informal settlements:
villas (shantytowns) and *asentamientos* (squatter settlements).

In particular, there has been a rapid increase in "informal settlements"
in the metropolitan area of Buenos Aires, which is composed of the city
of Buenos Aires and the twenty-four bordering districts known as Conurbano Bonaerense (Greater Buenos Aires).[1] By 2006 there were 819 informal
settlements—363 shantytowns, 429 squatter settlements, and twenty-seven
unspecified urban forms—with approximately one million residents.[2] This
represents 10.1 percent of the total population of the metropolitan area. This
figure was only 5.2 percent in 1991 and 4.3 percent in 1981.

Between 1981 and 2006, the total population in the Conurbano Bonaerense grew by 35 percent, while the population in shantytowns and squatter
settlements in the same region increased by 220 percent. If we look at the figures since the economic collapse of 2001, we see that most of the total population growth took place in informal settlements. Between 2001 and 2006,
for every one hundred new residents in the Conurbano Bonaerense, sixty

are found in informal settlements (ten for every one hundred between 1981 and 1991, and twenty-six for every one hundred between 1991 and 2001).[3]

The proliferation of shantytowns and squatter settlements is a concrete geographical expression of the fragmentation of Buenos Aires's metropolitan space, one that in turn reflects and reinforces growing levels of social inequality.[4] During the last three decades, there has been a steady decline in income in the country as a whole and a mounting disparity between Argentines. In 1986 9.1 percent of households and 12.7 percent of people lived below the poverty line in Greater Buenos Aires. In 2002 these figures were 37.7 percent and 49.7 percent, respectively.[5] In other words, whereas a little more than one in ten *bonaerenses* (Buenos Aires residents) was poor twenty years ago, at the dawn of the new century, one in two is living below the poverty line. The Gini coefficient, a standardized measure of inequality, went from .36 in 1974 to .51 in 2000.[6]

Overall poverty rates seem to have been declining since 2003.[7] The GDP has been growing at an annual rate of 9 percent, and unemployment and poverty rates have decreased to the mid-1990s levels. Still, 34 percent of the total population lives below the poverty line, and 12 percent subsists under the indigence line.[8] Despite the slowing of downward trends, economic and social disparities have become inscribed in urban space. Gated suburban communities (*barrios privados*), which have been referred to as "corridors of modernity and wealth," have been mounting alongside enclaves of deprivation.[9] These barrios privados, the villas, and the new asentamientos are the visual evidence of the growing extremes of poverty and wealth that characterize contemporary Argentina.

Slums, shantytowns, and squatter settlements are, in Argentina and elsewhere, closely associated with environmental risks and unsanitary living conditions, and their deleterious health effects have been noted repeatedly.[10] A significant proportion of the shantytown growth in Buenos Aires took place along the highly contaminated banks of the Riachuelo, the river that flows through the southern part of the metropolitan area. A recent count by the federal ombudsman office reports that thirteen shantytowns are located on the river's banks.[11] According to the Pan American Health Organization, this river receives huge amounts of heavy metals and organic compounds owing to the discharge of industrial waste.[12] Tons of toxic sludge; the diluted solvents dumped by meat-packing plants, chemical industries, tanneries, and households; cadmium; and lead are routinely tossed into the Riachuelo's dead stream.

Villa Inflamable (Flammable shantytown) is home to approximately five thousand inhabitants and sits on the southern banks of the mouth of the Riachuelo. Between 2004 and 2007, the anthropologist Débora Swistun (who was born in Flammable and at the time was still living there) and I conducted team ethnographic fieldwork and wrote a book that examines residents' experiences of environmental suffering.[13] In one of the last chapters of the book, we use the mythical image of Tiresias to describe one of the defining and most striking features of the lives of shantytown dwellers: like the Greek seer, they are forced to become "mere onlookers of happenings beyond their control."[14] Shanty residents *are always waiting for something either good or bad to happen.* As we show in the book, those poisoned outcasts live in a time oriented to and manipulated by powerful others. We argue that domination works through a forced yielding to the power of others; and it is experienced by the shantytown dwellers as waiting time. They are perpetually waiting, becoming first hopeful and then frustrated, for others to make decisions over their lives, and in effect surrendering themselves to the authority of others. In ways we did not expect, we found many similar to Tiresias among contemporary shantytown dwellers. The destitute and poisoned Tiresias of the shanty world is living in a time oriented to others, which is an alienated time. This person is obliged, as Pierre Bourdieu so eloquently puts it, "to wait for everything to come from others."[15]

This chapter draws on a combination of new data from an ethnographic revisit (carried out in December 2009 and January 2010) and reanalysis of the previous fieldwork (carried out between 2004 and 2006). I go back to Flammable to chronicle some of the events that took place since we published our book. Although a few changes did occur in the neighborhood (one of the families of the original study, along with two dozen others, was relocated to a new housing complex), the general state of the barrio's dwellers could be summarized using the words of one of the old-timers: "We are still waiting." This experience of waiting dovetails with a certain experience of politics.

WAITING AS POWERLESSNESS

The manifold ways in which human beings think, feel about, and act on time have been the subject of much scholarly work in the social sciences. This work ranges from general treatments to more empirically informed reports, many of them based on ethnographic work.[16] The relationship between the *workings of power* and the *experiences of time* has also been the object of many social scientific analyses. Time, for example, has been examined as a crucial dimension in the workings of gift exchanges and in the operation of patronage networks.[17] In both these cases, the objective truth of these usually unequal exchanges needs to be *misrecognized* or veiled so that the exchanges can function smoothly.[18] Time, these analyses demonstrate, is responsible for the veiling.

As these historical and ethnographic works illustrate, temporality is malleable. It can be the object of an incessant process of bargaining, as Julius Roth shows in his insightful ethnography of the ways in which patients and doctors jointly structure the passage of time in a TB hospital.[19] It can be the object of frantic "marking," as Stanley Cohen and Laurie Taylor examine in their phenomenology of the security wing of an English prison.[20] Time can also be the target of a constant onslaught, as Paul Willis illustrates in his dissection of British working-class lads' rejections of the school's arduously constructed timetable.[21] Or it can be the medium through which discipline is imposed and negotiated, as E. P. Thompson demonstrates in his classic analysis of the changes in the inward notations of time at the early stages of industrial capitalism.[22] Collective time senses are deeply intertwined with the workings of and potential resistance to social domination. These works show that time is the locus of conflict and also, and as important, of acquiescence.[23]

Waiting, as a particular experience of time, has not received the same scholarly attention. Highlighting the ubiquity of this experience, the essayist Edna O'Brien writes: "Everyone I know is waiting." Hinting at the sense of powerlessness that comes with waiting, she continues: "And almost everyone I know would like to rebut it, since it is slightly demeaning, reeks of helplessness, and shows we are not fully in command of ourselves."[24] *Pace* O'Brien, waiting does not affect everybody in the same way, nor is it experienced in a similar fashion by everyone. Waiting is stratified, and there are variations in waiting time that are socially patterned and that respond to power differentials.[25] The unequal distribution of waiting time tends to correspond with that of power.

To be kept waiting, Barry Schwartz asserts, "especially to be kept waiting an unusually long time, is to be the subject of an assertion that one's own time (and therefore, one's social worth) is less valuable than the time and worth of the one who imposes the wait."[26] Schwartz established the basic contours of a sociological study of waiting. Since then, however, the experiences of unequally distributed waiting time and the activities that go with it have received little empirical attention and no systematic treatment.

Though scant, the research on the subject does show that extensive waiting periods "weary people" or act as obstacles in the way of access to particular programs.[27] If frequent contact with long queues molds people's subjectivities, how is that, to quote from Bourdieu, the "interested aiming at something . . . modifies the behavior of the person who 'hangs,' as we say, on the awaited decision?"[28] If delays are not only suffered but also interpreted, what meanings do those who are routinely forced to wait attribute to the waiting? And, if waiting makes the waiter feel "dependent and subordinate," how does waiting produce these subjective effects of dependency and subordination?[29] In other words, how does objective waiting become subjective submission?

Writing precisely about the absence of systematic accounts of waiting as a way of experiencing the effects of power, Bourdieu asserts that we need to "catalogue, and analyze, all the behaviors associated with the exercise of power over other people's time both on the side of the powerful (adjourning, deferring, delaying, raising false hopes, or conversely, rushing, taking by surprise) and on the side of the 'patient,' as they say in the medical universe, one of the sites par excellence of anxious, powerless waiting."[30] This chapter makes a first step toward the construction of such a catalogue by focusing on poor people's waiting experiences and the way in which these experiences become entangled with a shared understanding of politics. Both waiting and politics are lived as profoundly disempowering processes. These two lived experiences tend to reinforce each other, generating the shared perception that the motor or the initiative of transformative action lies elsewhere. From the residents' point of view, reconstructed through interviews, real outcomes are not and cannot be generated by the residents. They are rather produced by those who, in their own words, seldom "come down" to the neighborhood. Politics, that "thing" that takes place "up there," will determine their fate. This shared understanding—typical among residents in other neighborhoods of relegation in contemporary Buenos Aires—is one key effect of domination. Most people we talked to do not see themselves as agents capable of modifying their own conditions of existence, which are in Flammable's case polluted.

KAFKA IN FLAMMABLE

One could begin a revisit of Flammable (see figures 9.1 and 9.2) with an analogy to the opening scene of Kafka's *The Trial*.[31] Someone must have slandered the neighborhood's residents, because one morning, without having done anything wrong, they find themselves waiting. They are waiting to be relocated or evicted; waiting for the results of a new blood or urine test that would let them know whether or not they are "contaminated" (*para saber si estamos o no contaminados*); and waiting for the courts to rule on a lawsuit that would grant them a dreamed indemnification for health damages. Much like Josef K., they are not waiting alone. The waiting is interrupted by officials' promises that routinely begin anew and lawyers' sporadic references to progress on a certain lawsuit. Different from K., however, this waiting is disrupted by the occasional distribution of concrete benefits, such as new homes for a few selected residents. These rewards demonstrate to the neighbors left behind that their waiting is not totally in vain, and yet further ensnare them in the waiting process.

After "engaging" his lawyer, K. keeps "waiting expectantly for [the lawyer] to take action."[32] Like K., Flammable residents are lured with vague hopes (a court-ordered indemnification, a new home) and tormented with unclear threats (eviction is about to happen). Like him, they continue to wait for someone to take action on their behalf. In my brief update on the state of Flammable, I reconstruct residents' points of view on waiting and on politics and present evidence that attests to their imbrication in dwellers' schemes of thought.

. . .

FLAMMABLE IS SURROUNDED by a hazardous-waste incinerator, by an unmonitored landfill, and by one of the largest petrochemical compounds in the country (the Polo Petroquímico y Puerto Dock Sud). The compound houses the Shell oil refinery, three plants that store oil and its derivatives (Petrobras, Repsol-YPF, and Petrolera Cono Sur), several plants that store chemical products (TAGSA, Antívari, and Solvay Indupa among them), one plant that manufactures chemical products (Meranol), one dock for containers (Exolgan), and one thermo-electrical plant (Central Dock Sud). Most of these plants and storage facilities have been in operation for fifty years or more. The soil, air, and water in Flammable are highly polluted with lead, chromium, benzene, and other chemicals.[33] According to an engineer who works for Shell, the area is "unfit for human residence."[34]

One epidemiological study compared a sample of children between ages

FIG. 9.1 · Flammable and the Petrochemical Compound, 2006.

FIG. 9.2 · Flammable and the Petrochemical Compound after a heavy rain, 2010.

seven and eleven living in Flammable with a control population living in another poor neighborhood with similar socioeconomic characteristics but lower levels of exposure to industrial activities. In both neighborhoods, the study found, children are exposed to chromium and benzene, both known carcinogens, and to toluene. But high blood levels of lead, identified as "the mother of all industrial poisons[,] ... the paradigmatic toxin [linking] industrial and environmental disease," distinguish the children of Flammable from the rest.[35] Fifty percent of the children tested in this neighborhood had higher-than-normal levels (against 17 percent in the control population).

Defined by the United Nations Environment Programme (UNEP) and the United Nations Children's Fund (UNICEF) as a "scourge," lead is a neurotoxin or nerve poison that is easily absorbed into the bloodstream and bones. Children are the most susceptible to the harmful effects of lead poisoning. "Exposure to excessive levels of lead," reads the UNEP/UNICEF report titled *Childhood Lead Poisoning*, "is harmful to the health and intellectual development of millions of children and adults, in almost all regions of the world."[36] At low levels, lead poisoning in children causes "reduction in IQ and attention span, reading and learning disabilities, hyperactivity and behavioral problems, impaired growth and visual and motor functioning, and hearing loss." At high levels, it causes "anaemia, brain, liver, kidney, nerve, and stomach damage, coma, convulsions, and death."[37]

Predictably, the epidemiological study conducted in Flammable found lower than average IQs among the Flammable children and a higher percentage of neurobehavioral problems. The study also found strong statistical associations between frequent headaches and neurological symptoms, learning problems, and hyperactivity in school. The children in Flammable reported more dermatological problems, such as eye irritation, skin infections, eruptions, and allergies; more respiratory problems, such as coughs and bronchospasms; more neurological problems, such as hyperactivity; and more sore throats and headaches.

Figures 9.3–9.6 are taken by the neighborhood's elementary schoolchildren in a photography workshop we organized in the second semester of 2009. They portray a few of the residents' homes, the barrio's general landscape, and the compound's smokestacks as seen from Flammable.[38] As reported in our original study, shantytown children still see themselves as living in the "midst of garbage and poison."[39] Back in June 2004, residents told us that their relocation was imminent. "By early 2005, nobody will be living here," we heard repeatedly. As proof of the forthcoming relocation,

FIG. 9.3 · Living in the midst of garbage and poison.
Photo by Daniel, fourth grader.

FIG. 9.4 · Luciana's swamp/backyard. Photo by Luciana, fourth grader.

FIG. 9.5 · Shantytown home. Photo by Agustina, fourth grader.

FIG. 9.6 · The Polo Petroquímico. Photo by Tamara, fourth grader.

residents pointed to a census that municipal agents were conducting to establish the exact number of families living in the neighborhood. As we highlight in the book, relocation or eviction was a sort of Damocles's sword always hanging above residents' heads. The threat of removal was a defining feature of their lives.

Four and a half years later, in December of 2009, we went back to the neighborhood and found out that another census had being recently carried out by municipal agents. The sword of eviction or relocation was still hanging. The flyer announcing the agents' visit read: "Census' Objectives: To define the number of families in the neighborhood. . . . To know the residents' opinions about the possibility of a relocation plan in order to propose a program that will resolve the neighborhood's needs." The government was once more raising neighbors' expectations and the local-improvement association was once again calling for meetings with neighbors to discuss the possibility of relocation raised by state officials. Old-timers, however, were skeptical. They complained that "nobody comes down, nobody informs us anything, and we keep hearing the same old story." They also expressed skepticism:

> I don't believe what the government is saying. If it were true, they would come down to the neighborhood and give us the information. (Alberto)

> I've lived here for twenty-eight years, and since the beginning they've been saying they were going to relocate us. I don't think so. (Mario)

> It's been thirty years since I moved here, and they always told us that we had to move out. But they never proposed anything specific. (Carlos)

> Agents come around, they ask questions, but nothing ever happens. (Celina)

Disbelief notwithstanding, neighbors acknowledged that some families (twenty-five, according to most) have been relocated. Their relocation demonstrated that something positive might, eventually, happen to them. Homes are being assigned and will be, sooner or later, allocated to a few; and this also demonstrates the value of waiting. Without occasional rewards that randomly disrupt the long waiting period, the waiting would not make much sense.

One of the relocated families was María Soto's. We met her in 2005 when she was living in a precarious wood house whose garbage-filled backyard sloped downward into a filthy swampland. María's daughter, Luisa, was tested for the lead study in 2003. By then, her lead levels were 18.5 micrograms per deciliter, far above what is now considered to be a nontoxic blood level of lead (10 micrograms per deciliter). At the time, María and Luisa were awaiting the allocation of a unit in a housing project that the federal government was building in nearby Wilde. Those who are "the most contaminated," María believed, "will leave first." I was quite incredulous, but, to my surprise, in early 2008 she received notification that she had been granted a unit. After months of anxious waiting—and of stating repeatedly, "Until I have the key in my hand, I won't celebrate!"—on May of that same year María and Luisa moved to their new home.

Surrounded by toxic hazards and right across from the petrochemical compound, María's old shack is still standing. One of her relatives is now living there, which proves that what neighbors told us is indeed true. According to Mario, "For every other one who is relocated . . . more people move into the neighborhood." Neighbors also believe that who moves in and who moves out, and who waits and who does not, is determined by "politics": Carlos says, "They moved some out, but more come in. . . . It's all political." And Isabel corroborates, "The new homes are given to those families who are in politics." As far as we can tell though, María was not granted a home because of her political connections. Her family was identified in the epidemiological study as one of those with an urgent need for a new home. But we should take seriously the fact that neighbors believe that it is only through politics, as something carried out "up there" by those who "never come down to the neighborhood" (*nunca bajan al barrio*), that waiting can be interrupted. Neighbors are convinced that during political times (i.e., close to an election) things (i.e., relocation) could get done. Politics, in this shared understanding, is a possible accelerator that can reduce the waiting time.

As we see through a series of ethnographic vignettes, politics for Flammable residents invokes neither a joint capacity to make positive changes nor a collective struggle for resources. Even less so does it invoke a process through which a specific policy is agreed upon and carried out. Politics, as the activity that can put a halt to residents' endless waiting, and politicians, as its main actors, loom above their lives and intermittently come down to the neighborhood. As an activity beyond residents' control, politics implies something profoundly disempowering. Thus, it is pretty much like waiting.[40]

ELSA, EUGENIO, ISABEL, GARCÍA, AND MARGA

Rewind to June 2004. The first people we interviewed while doing the research for our book were Eugenio, Isabel, and Marga. Understandably so, they were the leaders of the neighborhood's improvement association, Sociedad de Fomento Pro Mejoramiento de la Costa (Development Society for the Improvement of the Coast), and they showed great interest in our study. The day we met them, Isabel and Marga were coming back from presenting a petition to the welfare office at the local municipality. "Municipal agents are carrying out a census," they told us, "in order to relocate people, because of all the contamination, . . . but some neighbors say that it is not because of the contamination but because one of the compound companies needs to expand its operations and it bought all this land." As we examined in our study, rumors about what this or that company was about to do ran rampant during the course of our original fieldwork.[41] Isabel and Marga anticipated what we would repeatedly hear from many if not most residents. During this more recent visit, however, Isabel, Marga, and Eugenio told us that officials at the municipality had informed them that "eradication" of the neighborhood was going to proceed. These same officials were sending agents to conduct the census because, as Isabel told us, "they already have the authorization from the federal, state, and municipal governments to eradicate all the people from Flammable."

In June 2004, talk of relocation was constant in the neighborhood and triggered by the census and by meetings with officials. Yet neighborhood leaders were doubtful about the form it was going to take. After all, they were property owners and not squatters like most residents of Flammable. Isabel says, "What are they going to do with us, property owners? I pay taxes; I have all the proper documentation. I agree that we have to leave because of all the contamination, but this is not a gift. I want a similar property elsewhere, or the money so that I can buy something." Isabel reactivates a previously existing boundary between them (owners) and others (squatters).

"Did these officials tell you where they are going to relocate the neighborhood?" we asked. "No, they don't have the land yet; they don't have anything. . . . It's all idle talk [*chamuyo*]. They say they are conducting a census, but . . ." answered Eugenio, and Marga skeptically added: "Since I was a little kid they have been talking about eradication. This is a topic that has been going around for the longest time but never became reality. . . . I think the eradication is still green. But, who knows? Maybe one day, all of a sudden, they come and they tell us that we have to leave. But nobody knows what's going to happen, because nobody informs us." Still, municipal officials notified residents that "census and eradication" was the official policy, and they believed something was going to happen. The reasons behind the policy were, again, the subject of incessant rumors: "Apparently, the companies made a deal with the mayor. They gave money to the mayor so that he removed the people from here. The land is very valuable here." All the neighbors we talked to at the time conveyed their sense of uncertainty and powerlessness, a shared sentiment that the future was not in their hands. This sentiment was perhaps best captured by García, another old-time neighbor, when he said: "Now we have to wait until Shell or someone else, maybe the municipal government, expels us from here. . . . Since 1982 there are rumors that we will be evicted."

At that time, Eugenio and Isabel were also awaiting the decision of the courts on a lawsuit against Central Dock Sud. They were demanding 350,000 pesos (at the time, US$113,000) in compensation for the damages caused by the installation of a high-voltage wire line that runs on top of their homes. "It's three years now since we've been in this thing," Marga told us. She continued, "[I don't know] how the lawsuit is coming along because nobody called me yet, nobody called me. . . . It's been many years now. They [the lawyers] said that they will let us know when they have news. The lawsuit takes a long time, many years." Teresa concurred with her, and in a series of long conversations pointed out:

> Yes, we are part of a lawsuit [against Central Dock Sud] but we don't really know anything. It's been three years, and we don't know anything. The lawyer showed up at the very beginning. She told us that she would come back to inform us, but she never came back. . . . We called her several times and she is never in the office. We left messages but she never called us back. . . . [The lawsuit for indemnification] is quite difficult, but you need to have hope on something. I don't know how money much the lawyer asked for; she does everything, but does not inform us. We know nothing.

Finally, García expressed in one statement both his optimism and cynicism: "The lawsuit will begin to move forward this year. . . . We began with it three or four years ago. A lawyer from the company came but we didn't reach an agreement. We signed some papers and she left. It takes a long time. . . . I have a pending lawsuit for my pension and it's been ten years and I still haven't seen anything."

. . .

FAST-FORWARD TO DECEMBER 2009. During this visit, Isabel told us that a month ago municipal agents were conducting "another census." "Census workers were asking about the number of people living in each home, the number of rooms. They also asked us about what we wanted for the new neighborhood. Do we want a health center? A school? I say: 'I am not moving to a housing complex.' They [the new buildings where twenty-five families were relocated] look like birdcages." Isabel and Eugenio told us that in October 2009 they had a meeting with the mayor, and he told them: "All the people here are going to be relocated. And . . . the property owners are going to be expropriated. . . . But they [residents] don't really know anything. Nobody came here to inform us!"

This time, Eugenio and Isabel were accompanied by Elsa, Débora Swistun's mother. As recorded in our book, *Flammable*, over lunch one day she ironically portrayed herself in the distant future as an old toothless lady with a cane, her voice trembling, happily stating: "We are about to be relocated!"[42] Elsa and Eugenio concurred that for every family that the government is relocating, new families are moving in. "This is crazy," they agree, "this is not a place for a human being to be living!" And Eugenio adds: "I don't think anybody is going to be relocated. . . . This is all a game, they kick the ball forward, and they don't do anything." Regarding the lawsuit, Eugenio and Isabel were less hopeful than the time we first met: "The lawyer came by last year and told us to be patient."

In another conversation, Elsa told me that census workers have raised "the possibility of relocation." But she says, "There are so many versions, so many versions. . . . I really don't know." I ask her if she personally knows someone who has recently moved out of the neighborhood. Her answer encapsulates what, after all these years of waiting, may be the central narrative for Flammable old-timers: "The only people I know who left are those who went up, to heaven. . . . They died."

MARIANA

In Flammable the uneventful waiting is disrupted by random promises and initiatives such as the new census that was carried out in late 2009 or lawyers' visits, and also by concrete feats such as the occasional relocation of a small group of residents. These episodes demonstrate to neighbors that something is happening and that their waiting is not totally futile.

One last story, Mariana's, illustrates well the haphazard interruption of the waiting process. Far from an isolated and idiosyncratic account, Mariana's story portrays "a social universe dominated by [an] absolute and unpredictable power, capable of inducing extreme anxiety by condemning its victim to very strong investment combined with great insecurity."[43] The story also encapsulates residents' shared understanding of their waiting as something with intimate connections to the political world, which is a world located high up and in which they have no say. In Mariana's account we also see power at work through the constant deferment and the routine raising of false hopes, as elements that characterize the rhythm of collective life in the neighborhood as a site of anxious, powerless waiting. Last but not least, Mariana's story also shows, by way of example, that the social world described in Kafka's *The Trial* "could be simply the limiting case of a number of ordinary states of the ordinary social world or of particular situations within this world."[44] After the epidemiological study that identified a lead-poisoned cluster, "they [the government] said that there was going to be a treatment for the kids," says Mariana, whose own son suffers from chronic asthma.

> They said that there was going to be a follow-up, . . . that they were going to distribute aid. . . . Nothing happened. . . . There are lots of kids with lead in their blood, and we don't really know, because in the future that might bring you trouble, some kids might even die. . . . Officials use us; . . . they make promises and they never do anything. . . . Tons of times they have said that there was going to be a relocation, but nothing happened. . . . Now we are waiting for them to remove us, . . . because this land has been sold. Most of the people here are going to be evicted, but who knows, they said that same thing so many times. . . . I have my doubts. I really don't know because a couple of neighbors received an eviction letter because some of this land has an owner. But I didn't receive anything. There is no property record for this particular piece of land where we live. Apparently, nobody should be living here because this is an industrial area, but nobody comes here to inform us, nobody shows up. I heard that four hundred families will be relocated, . . . but there are so many families here and there is a school, a kindergarten, a church; it won't be easy for politicians to remove us. A neighbor sent a note to the politicians so that they come down and meet with us, but nobody showed up. . . . Offi-

cials told us that they are too busy, that they would come later, that they would schedule an appointment. . . . Nothing happened. Nobody wants to come down; they wash their hands. . . . *We are waiting to see if they, the politicians, come down and give us an answer.* (Emphasis added)

REASONS TO HOPE?

In July 2004, a group of residents joined forces with physicians, psychologists, and nurses from the Hospital Interzonal de Agudos Pedro Fiorito and, led by Dr. Mendoza, brought forth a lawsuit against the federal government, the government of the province of Buenos Aires, the government of the city of Buenos Aires, and forty-four companies. Many of these companies were located inside the petrochemical compound that sits adjacent to Flammable. The case was *Mendoza Beatriz Silvia y otros contra el Estado Nacional y otros por daños sufridos* (*Mendoza Beatriz Silvia and Others v. the National State and Others Regarding Damages Suffered*; i.e., injuries resulting from the environmental contamination of the Matanza-Riachuelo River). Breaking with former precedent, the lawsuit was received by the National Supreme Court in June of 2006.[45] The judges divided the claim in two parts: they declared the lack of original jurisdiction with respect to the claim aimed at redressing damage to the individual plaintiffs' assets as an indirect result of aggression toward the environment, but the judges affirmed their competence with respect to damages to the environment.

In its first ruling, the Supreme Court determined that the object of the lawsuit was the protection (*tutela*) of the common good and ordered the national government, the Province of Buenos Aires, the City of Buenos Aires, and El Consejo Federal de Medio Ambiente (Federal Environmental Council) to present an integrated plan that "addresses the area's environmental situation, control over anthropogenic activities, an environmental impact study of the defendant-businesses, an environmental-education program, and an environmental-information program."[46] Months later, the Supreme Court took two further actions. First, it accepted the federal ombudsman office and a group of NGOs, including the Fundación Ambiente y Recursos Naturales (Environment and Natural Resources Foundation), the Centro de Estudios Legales y Sociales (Center for Legal and Social Studies), and Greenpeace, as third parties in the lawsuit. Second, it included the Coordinadora Ecológica Area Metropolitana Sociedad del Estado (CEAMSE), which is the authority in charge of landfills in the metropolitan area, and fourteen municipal governments that have been defendants because of incidents in the Matanza-Riachuelo basin.

Over a period of three years, the Supreme Court held four public hearings in what, according to the Fundación Ambiente y Recursos Naturales director Andrés Napoli, was a "complex process that required the hard work on the part of the Supreme Court and in which the various involved parties participated actively."[47] On July 8, 2008, the Supreme Court's ruling established that the federal government, the Province of Buenos Aires, and the City of Buenos Aires were responsible for the prevention and restoration of the collective environmental damage existing in the Matanza-Riachuelo basin. The ruling mandated a series of obligatory actions to accomplish this goal and created a broad system of control for the enforcement of the sentence, including the imposition of fines to state authorities.

In the ruling, the Supreme Court understood claimants as "victims of the environmental contamination of the Matanza-Riachuelo river basin" and asserted that "the restoration from and the prevention of environmental harm requires the issuance of urgent, definitive, and effective decisions."[48] The Court, furthermore, delegated the execution of the decision to a "federal court of first instance, in order to ensure swiftness of future court decisions as well as effective judicial control over compliance."[49] The thrust of the decision is found on page 10 of the sentence where the Court mandates that the Autoridad de la Cuenca Matanza Riachuelo (River Basin Authority) complete a program with three simultaneous objectives: "(1) Improvement of the quality of life of the river-basin inhabitants; (2) the environmental restoration of all of the river basin's components (water, air, soil); (3) the prevention of reasonably foreseeable harm." The document then lists a series of specific objectives with regards to public information, industrial pollution, cleanup of landfills, cleaning riverbanks, expansion of the potable-water network, projects of storm drainage and sewage sanitation, and an emergency health plan. On page 11, under the heading "Industrial Pollution," the sentence mandates "the public presentation, detailed and well-founded," of a project for the reconversion and relocation of the petrochemical compound in Dock Sud.

The ruling gave residents of Flammable and environmental activists a newfound optimism for a state-led change. Whether through relocation of the neighborhood or through relocation of the compound (now ordered by the Supreme Court), new winds were blowing into the neighborhood and giving residents reasons to hope.

What has happened since then? A report published in December 2009 details the actions taken and not taken by state authorities on each one of the mandates produced by the Supreme Court.[50] The report concludes that no significant advances were made since the July 2008 ruling. Regarding the relocation of the petrochemical compound, which would have the most direct impact on Flammable's livability, the report expresses "concern about the authorities' delay in the implementation of the relocation and industrial reconversion of the Dock Sud petrochemical compound" and clearly states that the orders of the Supreme Court have not been heeded.[51]

NO ONE WRITES TO FLAMMABLE

Shit is the last word in Gabriel García Márquez's moving novella *No One Writes to the Colonel*. The colonel is replying to his wife, who impatiently wants to know what they will eat while he awaits the outcome of an upcoming cockfight. As the owner who has been feeding and training the animal, the colonel will be entitled to 20 percent of the winning bet. The colonel refuses to sell the rooster to pay for food and asks his wife to wait forty-four more days and to place her trust in the rooster that "can't lose."

The colonel's reply, *mierda*, can be read as a foul response to an anxious and demanding wife. Yet the meaning of that answer transcends Márquez's narrative. The colonel feels "pure, explicit, and invincible," Márquez tells us, because he is articulating his feelings after so many years of suffering, disappointments, frustrations, and endless waiting for a government pension to which he is entitled "after risking [his] neck in the civil war."[52] For fifteen years, the colonel has been expecting the pension. Every Friday, after visiting the postmaster, he realizes that "no one writes to the colonel." While his expectations for the pension barely sustain him, and while his and his wife's difficulties in making ends meet accumulate, he hangs his hopes on the rooster's victory.

Márquez's emotive tale can be read as a realistic and illustrative narrative of many of Latin America's defining features. The region has suffered governments that fail to deliver promised protection to their citizens, represented in the story by the pension that never arrives, but these governments are swift in delivering terror against dissenters, illustrated by the colonel and his wife's loss of a son to state repression. The story also expresses the region's poverty, suffering, and political instability, captured in the following passage: "Just think about it, [in the last fifteen years] there have been seven

Presidents, and each President changes his Cabinet at least ten times, and each Minister changes his staff at least a hundred times."[53] Yet the novella can also be read as a highly perceptive account of the meanings and feelings at work in the experience of waiting. *No One Writes to the Colonel* chronicles the endless waiting from the point of view of the colonel and his wife, and masterfully describes the changing import of that waiting time — from the hopefulness of the beginning to the resignation of the end. The nameless-ness of the main characters not only increases their insignificance in the light of bureaucratic indifference ("those documents have passed through thousands and thousands of hands, in thousands and thousands of offices, before they reached God knows which department") but also, and more im-portant, points to the fact that anybody can be the colonel.[54] Never-ending waiting, sometimes hopeful, other times resigned, characterizes the lives of the destitute and defines their identity, much like that of the colonel, who becomes "a man with no other occupation than waiting for the mail every Friday." The poor may, like the colonel, stubbornly defend their dig-nity while they retain hopes for a better future. But in their daily lives, "it is always the same story"; they are forced to wait for powerful others to make good on their promises.[55]

Most people in Flammable were interested in sharing their experiences because they wanted us and others to know what they were going through and because they wished to talk about their perceptions of what authorities should and should not do about residents' problems, what was right and wrong, and what was fair and unfair. People such as Eugenio and Mariana jumped at the opportunity afforded by the interview to describe a state of affairs and broadcast some standard of justice. They would simultaneously talk about morality and politics, and view us, accordingly, as both witnesses of their plight and advocates of their cause.

Moral standards are usually expressed as outrage at something perceived as deeply manipulative (i.e., "they use us") or irresponsible (i.e., "they allow people to move into this poisoned area"). These moral standards also ap-pear to be profoundly intertwined with state politics; and politics seems to permeate understandings of the causes of and possible solutions to every-day problems. Politics, in other words, is perceived by the poor of Flam-mable as the source of the injustice, unfairness, and arbitrariness that per-vades their everyday lives. Though politics powerfully determines their life chances, it is a distant and unfathomable source; and it is perceived as an arena and an activity in which poor of Flammable are not agents.

Flammable is a "strategic research site" that can be used to dissect the links between the experiences of time and waiting and the experiences of politics.[56] Once we ethnographically till the soil of residents' subjective representations, we realize that both waiting and politics are lived as phenomena that escape these residents' control. Further, even if the particular—and to a certain degree extreme—relationship between waiting and politics in the midst of toxic suffering is peculiar to Flammable, I believe that this relationship is a general phenomenon applicable to all those who live in territories of urban relegation. Powerless waiting, in other words, is a recurring and almost modal experience among the destitute.

NOTES

1. While shantytowns are the main form of informal settlement in Buenos Aires, squatter settlements predominate in the Conurbano Bonaerense. On the difference between these two urban informal forms, see María Cristina Cravino, Juan Pablo del Rio, and Juan Ignacio Duarte, "Magnitud y crecimiento de las villas y asentamientos en el Área Metropolitana de Buenos Aires en los últimos 25 años," in *XIV Encuentro de la Red Universitaria Latinoamericana de Cátedras de Vivienda* (Buenos Aires: Facultad de Arquitectura, Urbanismo y Diseño, Universidad de Buenos Aires, 2008).

2. Cravino, Rio, and Duarte, "Magnitud y crecimiento de las villas y asentamientos en el Área Metropolitana de Buenos Aires en los últimos 25 años," 2.

3. Cravino, Rio, and Duarte, "Magnitud y crecimiento de las villas y asentamientos en el Área Metropolitana de Buenos Aires en los últimos 25 años," 13. For diverse descriptions of living conditions in shantytowns, see Javier Auyero, *Poor People's Politics: Peronist Networks and the Legacy of Evita* (Durham, NC: Duke University Press, 2001); and Javier Auyero and Débora Swistun, *Flammable: Environmental Suffering in an Argentine Shantytown* (New York: Oxford University Press, 2009).

4. See Andrea Catenazzi and Juan D. Lombardo, *La cuestión urbana en los noventa en la región metropolitana de Buenos Aires* (Buenos Aires: Universidad Nacional de General Sarmiento Instituto del Conurbano, 2003), 2–10.

5. INDEC, *Incidencia de la pobreza y de la indigencia en el Gran Buenos Aires* (Buenos Aires: INDEC, 2003).

6. Oscar Altimir, Luis Beccaria, and Martín González Rozada, "Income Distribution in Argentina, 1974–2002," CEPAL *Review*, no. 78 (2002): 54.

7. Given the lack of reliable official data, considerable polemics revolve around existing figures.

8. Agustín Salvia, "Consideraciones sobre la transición a la modernidad, la exclusión social y la marginalidad económica: Un campo abierto a la investigación social y al debate politico," in *Sombras de una marginalidad fragmentada: Aproximaciones a*

la metamorfosis de los sectores populares de la Argentina, edited by Agustín Salvia and Eduardo Chávez Molina (Buenos Aires: Miño y Dávila, 2007), 28.

9. Pedro Pirez, "Buenos Aires: Fragmentation and Privatization of the Metropolitan City," *Environment and Urbanization* 14, no. 1 (2001): 3; and Maristella Svampa, *Los que ganaron: La vida en los countries y barrios privados* (Buenos Aires: Biblos, 2001).

10. Mike Davis, *Planet of Slums* (London: Verso, 2006); Eileen Stillwaggon, *Stunted Lives, Stagnant Economies: Poverty, Disease, and Underdevelopment* (New Brunswick, NJ: Rutgers University Press, 1998); United Nations Human Settlements Programme, *The Challenge of Slums: Global Report on Human Settlements 2003* (London: Earthscan, 2003).

11. Defensor del Pueblo de la Nación Argentina, *Informe especial sobre la Cuenca Matanza-Riachuelo* (Buenos Aires: Defensor del Pueblo de la Nación Argentina, 2003).

12. Stillwaggon, *Stunted Lives, Stagnant Economies*, 110.

13. Auyero and Swistun, *Flammable*.

14. Alfred Schutz, *The Problem of Social Reality: Collected Papers I* (The Hague: Martinus Nijhoff, 1964), 280. In one of the many versions of the Greek myth, early in life Tiresias surprises Athena while she is taking a bath. As punishment for having seen his daughter naked, Zeus blinds young Tiresias but comforts him with the gift of seercraft.

15. Pierre Bourdieu, *Pascalian Meditations* (Stanford, CA: Stanford University Press, 2000), 237.

16. For general treatments, see Michael Flaherty, *A Watched Pot: How We Experience Time* (New York: New York University Press, 1999); Anthony Giddens, *The Constitution of Society* (New York: Polity Press, 1986); Edward T. Hall, *The Silent Language* (New York: Anchor Books, 1959); Robert Levine, *A Geography of Time* (New York: Basic Books, 1997); Nancy Munn, "The Cultural Anthropology of Time: A Critical Essay," *Annual Review of Anthropology* 21 (1992); Schutz, *The Problem of Social Reality*; and Pitirim Sorokin and Robert Merton, "Social Time: A Methodological and Functional Analysis," *American Journal of Sociology* 42 (1937). For empirically informed reports, see Michael Flaherty, Betina Freidin, and Ruth Sautu, "Variation in the Perceived Passage of Time: A Cross-National Study," *Social Psychology Quarterly* 68, no. 4 (2005); Clifford Geertz, *The Interpretation of Cultures* (New York: Basic Books, 1973); Leon Mann, "Queue Culture: The Waiting Line as a Social System," *American Journal of Sociology* 75 (1969); Julius Roth, *Timetables: Structuring the Passage of Time in Hospital Treatment and Other Careers* (Indianapolis, IN: Bobbs-Merrill, 1963); Alford Young, *The Minds of Marginalized Black Men* (Princeton, NJ: Princeton University Press, 2004); and Eviatar Zerubavel, *Patterns of Time in Hospital Life* (Chicago: University of Chicago Press, 1979).

17. See Auyero, *Poor People's Politics*; and Pierre Bourdieu, *Outline of the Theory of Practice* (Cambridge: Cambridge University Press, 1977).

18. See Pierre Bourdieu, *Practical Reason* (Stanford, CA: Stanford University

Press, 1998); and Sherry Ortner, *Anthropology and Social Theory* (Durham, NC: Duke University Press, 2006).

19. Roth, *Timetables*.

20. Stanley Cohen and Laurie Taylor, *Psychological Survival: Experience of Long-Term Imprisonment* (Harmondsworth, UK: Penguin, 1972).

21. Paul E. Willis, *Learning to Labor: How Working Class Kids Get Working Class Jobs* (New York: Columbia University Press, 1981).

22. E. P. Thompson, "Time, Work-Discipline, and Industrial Capitalism," *Past and Present* 38, no. 1 (1967).

23. Arlie Russell Hochschild, *The Time Bind: When Work Becomes Home and Home Becomes Work* (New York: Metropolitan Books, 2001); Jerry Jacobs and Kathleen Gerson, *The Time Divide* (Cambridge, MA: Harvard University Press, 2004).

24. Edna O'Brien, "Waiting," in *The Best American Essays*, edited by J. Kincaid and R. Atawan (Boston: Houghton Mifflin, 1995), 177.

25. Barry Schwartz, *Queuing and Waiting: Studies in the Social Organization of Access and Delay* (Chicago: University of Chicago Press, 1975).

26. Schwartz, *Queuing and Waiting*, 856; see also Megan Comfort, *Doing Time Together* (Chicago: University of Chicago Press, 2008).

27. Frances Piven and Richard Cloward, *Regulating the Poor: The Functions of Public Welfare* (New York: Vintage Books, 1971), 160; Cristina Redko, Richard Rapp, and Robert Carlson, "Waiting Time as a Barrier to Treatment Entry: Perceptions of Substance Abusers," *Journal of Drug Issues* 36, no. 4 (2006).

28. Bourdieu, *Pascalian Meditations*, 228; Comfort, *Doing Time Together*, 2008.

29. Schwartz, *Queuing and Waiting*, 856.

30. Bourdieu, *Pascalian Meditations*, 228.

31. Franz Kafka, *The Trial* (New York: Schoken Books, 1998).

32. Kafka, *The Trial*, 187.

33. Defensor del Pueblo de la Nación Argentina, *Informe especial sobre la Cuenca Matanza-Riachuelo*; and Dorado, "Informe sobre Dock Sud."

34. Auyero and Swistun, *Flammable*.

35. Gerald Markowitz and David Rosner, *Deceit and Denial: The Deadly Politics of Industrial Pollution* (Berkeley: University of California Press, 2002), 137.

36. UNEP and UNICEF, *Childhood Lead Poisoning: Information for Advocacy and Action* (New York: UNEP-UNICEF, 1997), 1.

37. UNEP and UNICEF, *Childhood Lead Poisoning*, 5.

38. Between June and September 2009, Divina Swistun, a professional photographer, taught elementary-aged schoolchildren the basics of photography. Their final project was to take twenty-four pictures of the things they like about their neighborhood and the things they dislike. See Auyero and Swistun, *Flammable*, 30–35, for the results of the first photographic exercise with a different group of students from the same elementary school.

39. Auyero and Swistun, *Flammable*, 51.

40. I make a similar argument about the meaning of politics among the main

actors in the food riots of 2001 in Javier Auyero, *Routine Politics and Collective Violence in Argentina: The Gray Zone of State Power* (Cambridge: Cambridge University Press, 2007).

41. Auyero and Swistun, *Flammable*, chapter 3.

42. Auyero and Swistun, *Flammable*, chapter 4.

43. Bourdieu, *Pascalian Meditations*, 229.

44. Bourdieu, *Pascalian Meditations*, 229.

45. The account that follows was reconstructed on the basis of newspaper accounts (from *Clarín* and *Página 12*), reports published by the Fundación Ambiente y Recursos Naturales and the Centro de Información Judicial on their websites, and the Supreme Court sentence (available at http://www.farn.org.ar, accessed June 3, 2012).

46. Corte Suprema de Justicia, "Mendoza Beatriz Silvia and Others v/ the National State and Others Regarding Damages Suffered (Injuries Resulting from the Environmental Contamination of the Matanza-Riachuelo River)," 2008, accessed July 9, 2012, http://www.farn.org.ar/areas/riachuelo/causa-ante-la-corte, 2.

47. Fundación Ambiente e Recursos Naturales, *Annual Environmental Report* (Buenos Aires: Fundación Ambiente e Recursos Naturales, 2009), 88.

48. Corte Suprema de Justicia, "Mendoza Beatriz Silvia and Others v/ the National State and Others Regarding Damages Suffered," 1.

49. Corte Suprema de Justicia, "Mendoza Beatriz Silvia and Others v/ the National State and Others Regarding Damages Suffered," 9.

50. The report was published jointly by the Cuerpo Colegiado para la Participación Ciudadana en la Ejecución de la Sentencia de la Corte suprema de Justicia de la Nación en la Causa Matanza Riachuelo (Task Force for Citizens' Participation in the Supreme Court Sentence on Matanza Riachuelo), the group of NGOs recognized as third parties in the original lawsuit, who are in charge of monitoring the progress in the fulfillment of the objectives mandated by the Supreme Court.

51. Fundación Ambiente e Recursos Naturales, *Annual Environmental Report*, 88.

52. Gabriel García Márquez, *No One Writes to the Colonel* (New York: Harper and Row, 1979), 60, 62.

53. Márquez, *No One Writes to the Colonel*, 26.

54. Márquez, *No One Writes to the Colonel*, 60.

55. Márquez, *No One Writes to the Colonel*, 17, 24.

56. Robert Merton, "Three Fragments from a Sociologist's Notebooks: Establishing the Phenomenon, Specified Ignorance, and Strategic Research Materials," *Annual Review of Sociology* 13 (1987).

BIBLIOGRAPHY

Abramo, Pedro. "A dinámica do mercado de solo informal e a mobilidade residen-cial dos pobres." *Coleção Estudos Cariocas*, no. 20030101 (January 2003). Accessed July 18, 2013. http://portalgeo.rio.rj.gov.br/estudoscariocas/download/2340_Mobilidade%20Residencial%20na%20Cidade.pdf.

Abreu, Maurício de Almeida. *A evolução urbana do Rio de Janeiro*. Rio de Janeiro: Instituto Pereira Passos, 1987.

———. "Reconstruindo uma história esquecida: Origem e expansão inicial das fa-velas do Rio de Janeiro." *Espaço e debates*, no. 37 (1994): 34–46.

Academia Brasileira de Letras, ed. *Aspectos do Distrito Federal*. Rio de Janeiro: Sauer, 1943.

Agache, Alfred Donat. *Cidade de Rio de Janeiro: Extensão, remodelacão, embelleza-mento*. Paris: Foyer Brésilien, 1930.

Agencia Bolivariana de Noticias. "La Alameda: Abre sus puertas una casa cultural en San Agustín." April 15, 2005. Accessed April 14, 2007. http://www.nodo50.org/alameda/espacio_aniv2.php.

Agier, Michel. "Between War and City: Towards an Urban Anthropology of Refu-gee Camps." *Ethnography* 3, no. 3 (2002): 317–41.

Aizen, Mário. *Bairro Peixoto: O oásis de Copacabana*. Rio de Janeiro: Prefeitura da Cidade do Rio de Janeiro, 1992.

Alsayyed, Nezar. "Urban Informality as a 'New' Way of Life." In *Urban Informality: Transnational Perspectives from the Middle East, Latin America, and South Asia*, edited by Ananya Roy and Nezar Alsayyed, 7–30. Lanham, MD: Lexington Books, 2004.

Altimir, Oscar, Luis Beccaria, and Martín González Rozada. "Income Distribution in Argentina, 1974–2002." CEPAL *Review*, no. 78 (December 2002): 53–82.

Andrews, Frank M., and George W. Philips. "The Squatters of Lima: Who They Are and What They Want." *Journal of Developing Areas* 4, no. 2 (1970): 211–24.

Arendt, Hannah. *On Violence*. New York: Harcourt Brace, 1969.

Arndt, H. W. *Economic Development: The History of an Idea.* Chicago: University of Chicago Press, 1987.

Associação dos Geógrafos Brasileiros, Seção Regional do Rio de Janeiro. *Aspectos da geografia carioca.* Rio de Janeiro: Conselho Nacional de Geografia, Instituto Brasileiro de Geografia e Estatística, 1962.

Atkinson, G. A. "Mass Housing in Rapidly Developing Tropical Areas." *Town Planning Review* 31, no. 2 (1960): 85–102.

Auyero, Javier. *Poor People's Politics: Peronist Survival Networks and the Legacy of Evita.* Durham, NC: Duke University Press, 2001.

————. "Researching the Urban Margins: What Can the United States Learn from Latin America and Vice Versa?" *City and Community* 10, no. 4 (2011): 431–36.

————. *Routine Politics and Collective Violence in Argentina: The Gray Zone of State Power.* Cambridge: Cambridge University Press, 2007.

————. "'This Is a Lot Like the Bronx, Isn't It?': Lived Experiences of Marginality in an Argentine Slum." *International Journal of Urban and Regional Research* 23, no. 1 (1999): 45–69.

Auyero, Javier, and Débora Swistun. *Flammable: Environmental Suffering in an Argentine Shantytown.* New York: Oxford University Press, 2009.

Azevedo, Aluísio. *The Slum: A Novel.* Translated by David Rosenthal. Oxford: Oxford University Press, 2000.

Azuela, Antonio. *La ciudad, la propiedad privada y el derecho.* Mexico City: El Colegio de México, 1989.

Azuela, Antonio, and María Soledad Cruz. "La institucionalización de las colonias populares y la política urbana en la ciudad de México (1940–1946)." *Sociologia* 4, no. 9 (1989): 111–33.

Backheuser, Everardo. *Habitações populares: Relatório apresentado ao Exm. Senhor Doutor J. J. Seabra, Ministro de Justiça e Negócios Interiores.* Rio de Janeiro: Imprensa Nacional, 1906.

————. "Onde moram os pobres." *Renascença: Revista Mensal de Letras, Sciências e Artes* 2, nos. 13 and 15 (March and May 1905): 89–94, 185–89.

Baptista, Felix, and Oswaldo Marchionda. "¿Para qué afinques?" BA thesis, Universidad Central de Venezuela, 1992.

Barcellos, Caco. *Abusado: O dono do Morro Dona Marta.* Rio de Janeiro: Record, 2004.

Barreto, Paulo. "Os livres acampamentos da miséria." In *Vida vertiginosa*, 143–52. Rio de Janeiro: Garnier, 1911.

Bazant, Jan. *Periferias urbanas: Expansión urbana incontrolada de bajos ingresos y su impacto en el medio ambiente.* Mexico City: M.A. Porrúa, UAM-A, 2001.

Bazzanella, Waldemiro. "Industrialização e urbanização no Brasil." *América Latina* 6, no. 1 (1963): 3–27.

Benchimol, Jaime L. *Pereira Passos, um Haussmann tropical: A renovação urbana da cidade do Rio de Janeiro no início do século XX.* Rio de Janeiro: Prefeitura da Cidade do Rio de Janeiro, Secretaria Municipal de Cultura, Turismo e Esportes, Departamento Geral de Documentação e Informação Cultural, 1990.

Bengelsdorf, Irving. "Latin America Breeds Misery." *Los Angeles Times*, June 30, 1967.

Benmergui, Leandro. "The Alliance for Progress and Housing Policy in Rio de Janeiro and Buenos Aires in the 1960s." *Urban History* 36, no. 2 (2009): 303–26.

Berner, Erhard. "Informal Developers, Patrons and the State: Institutions and Regulatory Mechanism in Popular Housing." Paper presented at ASF-N Aerus Workshop, Brussels, May 25–26, 2001.

Bezerra, Daniel Uchoa Cavalcanti. *Algados, mocambos e mocambeiros*. Recife, Brazil: Instituto Joaquim Nabuco de Pesquisas Sociais MEC, Imprensa Universitária, 1965.

Bishop, Elizabeth. "The Burglar of Babylon." In *Elizabeth Bishop: The Complete Poems, 1927–1979*, 112–18. New York: Farrar, Straus and Giroux, 1984.

Bomeny, Helena. "Salvar pela escola: Programa especial de educação." *Sociologia: Problemas e Práticas*, no. 55 (September–December 2007): 41–67.

Bourdieu, Pierre. *Outline of the Theory of Practice*. Cambridge: Cambridge University Press, 1977.

———. *Pascalian Meditations*. Stanford, CA: Stanford University Press, 2000.

———. *Practical Reason*. Stanford, CA: Stanford University Press, 1998.

Bracker, Milton. "Beneath the Ferment in Latin America." *New York Times*, February 13, 1949.

Bravo-Heitman, Luis. "Retrospectiva de 50 años de vivienda social." In *Chile: 50 años de vivienda social, 1943–1993*, edited by Luis Bravo-Heitman and Carlos Martínez Corbella, 3–72. Valparaíso: Universidade de Valparaíso, Faculdad de Arquitectura, 1993.

Breese, Gerald William. *Urbanization in Newly Developing Countries*. Englewood Cliffs, NJ: Prentice-Hall, 1966.

Bromley, Rosemary. "Introduction: The Urban Informal Sector; Why Is It Worth Discussing?" *World Development* 6, nos. 9–10 (1978): 1033–39.

Burgos, Marcelo. "Dos parques proletários ao Favela-Bairro: As políticas públicas nas favelas do Rio de Janeiro." In *Um século de favela*, edited by Alba Zaluar and Marcelo Burgos, 25–60. Rio de Janeiro: FGV, 1998.

Burke, T. Robert. "Law and Development: The Chilean Housing Program." *Lawyer of the Americas* 2, nos. 2–3 (1970): 173–99, 333–69.

Caldeira, Teresa Pires do Rio. *City of Walls: Crime, Segregation, and Citizenship in São Paulo*. Berkeley: University of California Press, 2000.

Cámara de Diputados [Chile]. *Boletín de las sesiones ordinarias*. Santiago: Congreso Nacional Cámara de Diputados, June 16, 1965.

Campello, José. "Os aspectos sociaes e económicos do mocambo." *Folha da Manhã*, July 30, 1939.

Canguilhem, Georges. *The Normal and the Pathological*. New York: Zone Books, 1991.

Carvalho, Fernando José de Lacerda Jr., and Celso Funcia Lemme. "O impacto da violência criminal urbana no preço dos imóveis residenciais na região da Tijuca, cidade do Rio de Janeiro: Um estudo exploratório." *Cadernos* EBAPE.BR 3, no. 3 (2005). Accessed July 18, 2013. http://bibliotecadigital.fgv.br/ojs/index.php /cadernosebape/issue/view/570.

Castells, Manuel. *The City and the Grassroots: A Cross-Cultural Theory of Urban Social Movements*. London: E. Arnold; Berkeley: University of California Press, 1983.

———. *La lucha de clases en Chile*. México: Siglo Veintiuno Editores, 1975.

Castro, Cecília Maria Neder, and Miriam D'Ávila Calvacanti. "Notas técnicas 8 e 9: Tijuca / Vila Isabel e Leopoldina." *Coleção Estudos da Cidade, Rio Estudos* no. 98 (April 2003). Accessed July 18, 2013. http://www.armazemdedados.rio.rj.gov.br /arquivos/95_notas%20técnicas%20do%20plano%20estratégico%20n°%208% 20e%209.PDF.

Castro, Josué de. *A cidade do Recife: Ensaio de geografia urbana*. Rio de Janeiro: Livraria-Editôra da Casa do Estudante do Brasil, 1954.

———. *Documentário do nordeste*. Rio de Janeiro: J. Olympio, 1937.

———. *Geografia da fome: A fome no Brasil*. Rio de Janeiro: O Cruzeiro, 1946.

———. *Homens e caranguejos (romance)*. São Paulo: Ed. Brasiliense, 1967.

Catenazzi, Andrea, and Juan D. Lombardo. *La cuestión urban en los noventa en la región metropolitana de Buenos Aires*. Buenos Aires: Universidad Nacional de General Sarmiento Instituto del Conurbano, 2003.

Caulfield, Sueann. *In Defense of Honor: Sexual Morality, Modernity, and Nation in Early-Twentieth-Century Brazil*. Durham, NC: Duke University Press, 2000.

Cavalcanti, Mariana. "Do barraco à casa: Tempo, espaço e valor(es) em uma favela consolidada." *Revista Brasileira de Ciências Sociais* 24, no. 69 (2009): 69–80.

———. "Of Shacks, Houses and Fortresses: An Ethnography of Favela Consolidation in Rio de Janeiro." PhD dissertation, University of Chicago, 2007.

Cavalcanti, Sandra. *Rio, viver ou morrer*. Rio de Janeiro: Editora Expressão e Cultura, 1978.

Centro para el Desarrollo Económico y Social de América Latina. *Aportes para un programa de promoción popular*. Santiago: Centro para el Desarrollo Económico y Social de América Latina, 1966.

Chalhoub, Sidney. *Cidade febril: Cortiços e epidemias na corte imperial*. São Paulo: Companhia das Letras, 1996.

Chavez, Roberto. "Urban Planning in Nicaragua: The First Five Years." *Latin American Perspectives* 14, no. 2 (1987): 226–36.

Cheetham, Rosemond. "El sector privado de la construcción: Patrón de dominación." *Revista Latinoamericana de Estudios Urbanos Regionales (EURE)* 1, no. 3 (1971): 124–48.

Cleaves, Peter. *Bureaucratic Politics and Administration in Chile*. Berkeley: University of California Press, 1974.

———. *Developmental Processes in Chilean Local Government*. Berkeley, CA: Institute of International Studies, 1969.

Clemenceau, Georges. *South America To-day: A Study of Conditions, Social, Political and Commercial in Argentina, Uruguay and Brazil*. New York: G. P. Putnam, 1911.

Cohen, Stanley, and Laurie Taylor. *Psychological Survival: Experience of Long-Term Imprisonment.* Harmondsworth, UK: Penguin, 1972.

Comfort, Megan. *Doing Time Together.* Chicago: University of Chicago Press, 2008.

"Com Getúlio, isto não aconteceu." *O Radical,* May 20, 1949.

Comissão Censitária dos Mucambos do Recife [Pernambuco]. *Observações estatisticas sobre os mucambos do Recife, baseadas no censo efetuado pela Comissão Censitaria dos Mucambos, criada pelo Dec. no. 182, de 17 de setembro de 1938.* Recife, Brazil: Impr. Oficial, 1939.

Conniff, Michael L. *Urban Politics in Brazil: The Rise of Populism, 1925–1945.* Pittsburgh: University of Pittsburgh Press, 1981.

Connolly, Priscilla. *Urban Slum Report: The Case of Mexico City.* Washington, DC: Habitat-UN, 2003.

Cope, R. Douglas. *The Limits of Racial Domination: Plebeian Society in Colonial Mexico City, 1660–1720.* Madison: University of Wisconsin Press, 1994.

Corporación José Domingo Cañas 1367. *Tortura en poblaciones del Gran Santiago (1973–1990): Colectivo de memoria histórica.* Santiago: Corporación José Domingo Cañas, 2005.

Côrtes, Geraldo de Menezes. *Favelas.* Rio de Janeiro: Ministério da Educação e Cultura Serviço de Documentação, 1959.

Cravino, María Cristina, Juan Pablo del Rio, and Juan Ignacio Duarte. "Magnitud y crecimiento de las villas y asentamientos en el Área Metropolitana de Buenos Aires en los últimos 25 años." In *XIV Encuentro de la Red Universitaria Latinoamericana de Cátedras de Vivienda,* 1–25. Buenos Aires: Facultad de Arquitectura, Urbanismo y Diseño, Universidad de Buenos Aires, 2008.

"The Crisis in Our Hemisphere." *Life,* June 2, 1961.

Cunha, Euclides da. *Os sertões: Campanha de Canudos.* São Paulo: Atelie Editorial, 2002.

Curtis, William Eleroy. *The Capitals of Spanish America.* New York: Harper and Bros., 1888.

Davis, Mike. *Planet of Slums.* London: Verso, 2006.

Defensor del Pueblo de la Nación Argentina. *Informe especial sobre la Cuenca Matanza-Riachuelo.* Buenos Aires: Defensor del Pueblo de la Nación Argentina, 2003.

Departamento de Geografia e Estatistica [Federal District, Rio de Janeiro]. *Censo das favelas.* Rio de Janeiro: Departamento de Geografia e Estatistica, 1949.

Departamento de Publicaciones Presidencia de la República [Chile]. *Sexto mensaje del presidente de la República de Chile don Eduardo Frei Montalva al inaugurar el período de sesiones ordinarias del Congreso Nacional.* Santiago: Departamento de Publicaciones Presidencia de la República, 1970.

Departamento de Saúde e Assistência, Inspectoria de Estatistica Propaganda e Educação Sanitaria [Pernambuco]. *Recenseamento do Recife, 1923.* Recife, Brazil: Secção Technica da Repartição de Publicações Officiaes, 1924.

Diário de Notícias. "Os casos dolorosos da cidade: Caso 956." February 2, 1948.

Dias da Cruz, Henrique. *Os morros cariocas no novo regime, notas de reportagem*. Rio de Janeiro: Grafica Olímpica, 1941.

Dietz, Henry. "Urban Squatter Settlements in Peru: A Case History and Analysis." *Journal of Inter-American Studies* 11, no. 3 (1969): 353–70.

Dirección de Estadística y Censos [Chile]. *II censo de vivienda 1960: Resumen país; Levantado el 24 de Abril de año 1952*. Santiago: Instituto Nacional de Estadísticas, 1960.

Dirección General de Planificación y Presupuesto Ministerio de la Vivienda y Urbanismo [Chile]. *Política habitacional del Gobierno Popular: Programa 1972*. Santiago: Editorial Universitaria, 1972.

Dorado, Carlos. "Informe sobre Dock Sud." Unpublished manuscript. Buenos Aires, 2006.

Drake, St. Clair, and Horace R. Cayton. *Black Metropolis: A Study of Negro Life in a Northern City*. New York: Harcourt, 1945.

Duarte, Adriano Luiz. *Cidadania e exclusão: Brasil 1937–1945*. Florianópolis: Editora da UFSC, 1999.

Duhau, Emilio. "Política habitacional para los sectores populares en México: La experiencia de Fonhapo." *Medio Ambiente y Urbanización* 7, no. 24 (1988): 34–45.

———. "La política social y la gestión estatal de la pobreza." In *Dinámica urban y procesos socio-políticos*, edited by René Coulomb and Emilio Duhau, 235–54. Mexico City: OCIM, UAM-A, CENVI A.C., 1993.

———. "La regolarizzazione dell'habitat popolare in México." *Storia Urbana* 23, nos. 88–89 (1999): 65–92.

Duhau, Emilio, and Angela Giglia. "Espacio público y nuevas centralidades: Dimensión local y urbanidad en las colonias populares de la ciudad de México." *Papeles de Población* 10, no. 41 (2004): 167–94.

Durand-Lasserve, Alain, and R. Lauren Royston. *Holding Their Ground: Secure Land Tenure for the Urban Poor in Developing Countries*. London: Earthscan, 2003.

Dyckman, John W. "Some Conditions of Civic Order in an Urbanized World." *Daedalus* 95, no. 3 (1966): 797–812.

ECLA (Economic Commission for Latin America). *Social Development of Latin America in the Post-war Period*. New York: UN Economic and Social Council, 1963.

Edmundo, Luiz. *O Rio de Janeiro do meu tempo*. Rio de Janeiro: Imprensa Nacional, 1938.

Elsey, Brenda. *Citizens and Sportsmen: Fútbol and Politics in Twentieth-Century Chile*. Austin: University of Texas Press, 2011.

Epstein, David G. *Brasília, Plan and Reality: A Study of Planned and Spontaneous Urban Development*. Berkeley: University of California Press, 1973.

Equipo de Estudios Poblacionales, Centro de Investigaciones del Desarrollo Urbano y Regional. "Reivindicación urbana y lucha política: Los campamentos de pobladores en Santiago de Chile." *Revista Latinoamericana de Estudios Urbanos Regionales (EURE)* 2, no. 6 (1972): 55–82.

Escobar, Arturo. *Encountering Development: The Making and Unmaking of the Third World*. Princeton, NJ: Princeton University Press, 1995.

Espinoza, Vicente. *Para una historia de los pobres de la ciudad*. Santiago: Ediciones Sur, 1998.

Falcão, Waldemir. "O ministro do trabalho reafirma o seu apoio à campanha contra o Mocambo." *Folha da Manhã*, September 8, 1939.

Favela-Bairro. *Morro dos Cabritos*. Rio de Janeiro: Instituto Pereira Passos, 2002.

Fernandes, Edésio. "Regularizing Informal Settlements in Brazil: Legalization, Security of Tenure and City Management." Paper presented at ESF-N Aerus Workshop, Brussels, May 23–26, 2001.

Fernandes, Florestan. *A integração do negro na sociedade de classes*. São Paulo: Dominus Editôra, 1965.

Ferreira, Jorge Luiz. *Trabalhadores do Brasil: O imaginário popular, 1930–45*. Rio de Janeiro: Fundação Getulio Vargas Editora, 1997.

Finn, William, and James Converse. "Eight Assumptions Concerning Rural-Urban Migration in Colombia: A Three-Shantytown Test." *Land Economics* 46, no. 4 (1970): 456–66.

Fischer, Brodwyn M. *A Poverty of Rights: Citizenship and Inequality in Twentieth-Century Rio de Janeiro*. Stanford, CA: Stanford University Press, 2008.

Flaherty, Michael. *A Watched Pot: How We Experience Time*. New York: New York University Press, 1999.

Flaherty, Michael, Betina Freidin, and Ruth Sautu. "Variation in the Perceived Passage of Time: A Cross-National Study." *Social Psychology Quarterly* 68, no. 4 (2005): 400–410.

Folha do Povo. "Vivendo na lama e comendo carangueijo: 100,000 párias devastados pela fome a padecer miserias nos 20,000 mocambos do Recife." October 23, 1935.

Fortes, Alexandre. *Na luta por direitos: Estudos recentes em história social do trabalho*. Campinas, Brazil: Editoria da Unicamp, 1999.

———. *Nós do quarto distrito: A classe trabalhadora porto-alegrense e a era Vargas*. Caxias do Sul, RS: Educs; Rio de Janeiro: Garamond, 2004.

Foucault, Michel. *The Birth of the Clinic*. New York: Vintage Books, 1975.

"4 UN Units Help Latin Slum Plan." *New York Times*, December 26, 1961.

Freire, Américo, Bianca Feire Medeiros, and Mariana Cavalcanti. *Lu Petersen: Militância, favela, urbanismo*. Rio de Janeiro: FGV, 2009.

Freitas, Otavio. "Um século de medicina e higiene no Nordeste." In *O livro do nordeste*, edited by Gilberto Freyre, 29–35. Recife, Brazil: Arquivo Público Estadual, 1979.

French, John D. *Drowning in Laws: Labor Law and Brazilian Political Culture*. Chapel Hill: University of North Carolina Press, 2004.

Freyre, Gilberto. *The Mansions and the Shanties: The Making of Modern Brazil*. Berkeley: University of California Press, 1986.

———. *Mucambos do nordeste, algumas notas sobre o typo de casa popular mais primitivo do nordeste do Brasil*. Rio de Janeiro: Ministerio da educação e saude, 1937.

————, ed. *O livro do nordeste*. 2nd ed. Recife, Brazil: Secretaria da Justiça, Arquivo Público Estadual, 1979.

Frieden, Bernard J. "The Search for Housing Policy in Mexico City." *Town Planning Review* 36, no. 2 (1965): 75–94.

Fundación Ambiente e Recursos Naturales. *Annual Environmental Report*. Buenos Aires: Fundación Ambiente e Recursos Naturales, 2009.

Garcés, Mario. *Historia de la comuna de Huechuraba: Memoria y oralidad popular urbana*. Santiago: ECO, Educación y Comunicaciones, 1997.

————. *Tomando su sitio: El movimiento de pobladores de Santiago, 1957–1970*. Santiago: LOM, 2002.

Geertz, Clifford. *The Interpretation of Cultures*. New York: Basic Books, 1973.

Giddens, Anthony. *The Constitution of Society*. New York: Polity Press, 1986.

Gobierno del Distrito Federal, República Bolivariana de Venezuela. *Anuario Estadístico de la Gobernación del Distrito Federal*. Caracas: Gobierno del Distrito Federal, República Bolivariana de Venezuela, 2000.

Godoy-Blanco, Julio César. "El proceso de estructuración urbana de Managua: 1950–1979." PhD dissertation, Universidad de Costa Rica, 1983.

Goldstein, Daniel. *The Spectacular City: Violence and Performance in Urban Bolivia*. Durham, NC: Duke University Press, 2004.

Gomes, Angela Maria de Castro. *A invenção do trabalhismo*. Rio de Janeiro: Instituto Universitário de Pesquisas do Rio de Janeiro; São Paulo: Vértice, 1988.

Gominho, Zélia de Oliveira. *Veneza americana x mucambópolis: O estado novo na cidade do Recife (décadas de 30 e 40)*. Recife, Brazil: Cepe, 1998.

Goshko, John. "Success Shatters a Dream in a Latin Slum." *Washington Post*, April 10, 1966.

Goulart, José Alípio. *Favelas do Distrito Federal*. Rio de Janeiro: Ministério da Agricultura, Servico de Informação Agrícola, 1957.

Grandin, Greg. *The Last Colonial Massacre*. Chicago: University of Chicago Press, 2004.

Greenbaum, Susan. "Backgrounds of Political Participation in Venezuelan Barrios." BA thesis, University of Kansas, 1968.

Gross, Jacqueline. "As the Slum Goes, So Goes the Alliance." *New York Times*, June 23, 1963.

"Guerra assusta Zona Sul." *O Dia*, March 23, 2009.

Guevara, Ernesto. *Venceremos: The Speeches and Writings of Che Guevara*. New York: Simon and Schuster, 1969.

Guimarães, Valéria Lima. *O PCB cai no samba: Os comunistas e a cultura popular, 1945–1950*. Rio de Janeiro: Governo do Rio de Janeiro, Arquivo Público do Estado do Rio de Janeiro, 2009.

Gunther, John. *Inside Latin America*. London: H. Hamilton, 1942.

Hall, Edward T. *The Silent Language*. New York: Anchor Books, 1959.

Handelman, Howard. "The Political Mobilization of Urban Squatter Settlements:

Santiago's Recent Experience and Its Implications for Urban Research." *Latin American Research Review* 10, no. 2 (1975): 35–72.

Hann, C. M. "Introduction: The Embeddedness of Property." In *Property Relations: Renewing an Anthropological Tradition*, edited by C. M. Hann, 1–47. Cambridge: University of Cambridge Press, 1998.

Hansen, Asael T. "The Ecology of a Latin American City." In *Race and Cultural Contacts*, edited by E. B. Reuter, 124–42. New York: McGraw-Hill, 1934.

Harvey, David. *The Condition of Postmodernity: An Enquiry into the Origins of Cultural Change*. Oxford: Blackwell, 1990.

———. *Cosmopolitanism and the Geographies of Freedom*. New York: Columbia University Press, 2009.

———. *The New Imperialism*. Oxford: Oxford University Press, 2003.

———. *Paris: Capital of Modernity*. New York: Routledge, 2003.

Hauser, Philip Morris, ed. *Urbanization in Latin America*. Liège, Belgium: UNESCO, 1961.

Helper, Rose. *Racial Policies and Practices of Real Estate Brokers*. Minneapolis: University of Minnesota Press, 1969.

Hiernaux, Daniel. "Ocupación del suelo y producción del espacio construído en el valle de Chalco, 1978–1991." In *Espacio y vivienda en la ciudad de México*, edited by Martha Schteingart, 179–202. Mexico City: El Colegio de México, 1991.

Hobsbawm, Eric. "Peasants and Rural Migrants in Politics." In *The Politics of Conformity in Latin America*, edited by Claudio Veliz, 43–65. London: Oxford University Press, 1967.

Hochman, Gilberto. *A era do saneamento: As bases da política de saúde pública no Brasil*. São Paulo: Editora Hucitec, ANPOCS, 1998.

Hochman, Gilberto, and Nísia Trinidade Lima. "Condenado pela raça, absolvido pela medicina: O Brasil descoberto pelo movimento sanitarista da Primeira República." In *Raça, ciência e sociedade*, edited by Marcos Chor Maio and Ricardo Ventura Santos, 23–40. Rio de Janeiro: Fiocruz / CCBB, 1996.

Hochschild, Arlie Russell. *The Time Bind: When Work Becomes Home and Home Becomes Work*. New York: Metropolitan Books, 2001.

Hodges, Donald C. *Intellectual Foundations of the Nicaraguan Revolution*. Austin: University of Texas Press, 1986.

Holston, James. *Insurgent Citizenship: Disjunctions of Democracy and Modernity in Brazil*. Princeton, NJ: Princeton University Press, 2008.

———. *The Modernist City: An Anthropological Critique of Brasília*. Chicago: University of Chicago Press, 1989.

Holston, James, and Arjun Appadurai. "Cities and Citizenship." In *Cities and Citizenship*, edited by James Holston, 1–20. Durham, NC: Duke University Press, 1999.

Huntington, Samuel P. *Political Order in Changing Societies*. New Haven, CT: Yale University Press, 1968.

IBGE (Instituto Brasileiro de Geografia e Estatística). *As favelas do Distrito Federal e o Censo Demográfico de 1950*. Rio de Janeiro: IBGE, 1953.

IBGE (Instituto Brasileiro de Geografia e Estatística), Serviço Nacional de Recenseamento. *VI recenseamento geral do Brasil*. Rio de Janeiro: IBGE, Conselho Nacional de Estatística, 1954.

"Imagens de dona Vitória condemam mais um traficante de Copacabana." *O Globo*, October 19, 2006.

INDEC (Instituto Nacional de Estadísticas y Censos) [Argentina]. *Incidencia de la pobreza y de la indigencia en el Gran Buenos Aires*. Buenos Aires: INDEC, 2003.

Iracheta, Alfonso. "Políticas e instrumentos de generación de suelo urbanizado para pobres por medio de la recuperación de plusvalías." In *Los pobres de la ciudad y la tierra*, edited by Alfonso Iracheta and Martim Smolka, 13–40. Toluca, Mexico: El Colegio Mexiquense, 2000.

Jacobs, Jerry, and Kathleen Gerson. *The Time Divide*. Cambridge, MA: Harvard University Press, 2004.

James, Preston. "Rio de Janeiro and São Paulo." *Geographical Review* 23, no. 4 (1933): 271–98.

Jesus, Carolina Maria de. *Child of the Dark: The Diary of Carolina María de Jesus*. New York: Dutton, 1962.

Jornal do Brasil. "Favela política." December 24, 1964.

Kadt, Emanuel de. "Religion, the Church and Social Change in Brazil." In *The Politics of Conformity in Latin America*, edited by Caludio Veliz, 192–220. London: Oxford University Press, 1967.

Kafka, Franz. *The Trial*. New York: Schoken Books, 1998.

Karasch, Mary C. *Slave Life in Rio de Janeiro, 1808–1850*. Princeton, NJ: Princeton University Press, 1987.

Karst, Kenneth J. "Rights to Land and Housing in an Informal Legal System: The Barrios of Caracas." *American Journal of Comparative Law* 19, no. 3 (1971): 550–74.

Kennedy, John F. "Text of Kennedy Message to Congress on Latin Aid." *New York Times*, March 15, 1961.

Knight, David B. "Identity and Territory: Geographical Perspectives on Nationalism and Regionalism." *Annals of the Association of American Geographers* 72 (1982): 514–31.

Kopytoff, Igor. "The Cultural Biography of Things: Commoditization as Process." In *The Social Life of Things: Commodities in Cultural Perspective*, edited by Arjun Appadurai, 64–91. Cambridge: Cambridge University Press, 1986.

Lacerda, Carlos. "O Partido Comunista e a Batalha do Rio de Janeiro." *Correio da Manhã*, May 21, 1948.

Lago, Luciana Correa do. *Desigualdades e segregação na metrópole: O Rio de Janeiro em tempo de crise*. Rio de Janeiro: Revan FASE, 2000.

———. "Favela-loteamento: Re-conceituando os termos da ilegalidade e da segregação urbana." Paper presented at the 10 Encontro Nacional da ANPUR, Belo Horizonte, Brazil, May 2003.

Lancaster, Roger. *Life Is Hard: Machismo, Danger, and the Intimacy of Power in Nicaragua*. Berkeley: University of California Press, 1992.

———. *Thanks to God and the Revolution: Popular Religion and Class Consciousness in the New Nicaragua*. New York: Columbia University Press, 1988.

Latham, Michael. *Modernization as Ideology: American Social Science and "Nation Building" in the Kennedy Era*. Chapel Hill: University of North Carolina Press, 2000.

Leeds, Anthony. "The Anthropology of Cities: Some Methodological Issues." In Anthony Leeds, *Cities, Classes, and the Social Order*, edited by R. Sanjek, 233–46. Ithaca, NY: Cornell University Press, 1994.

———. "O Brasil e o mito da ruralidade urbana: Experiência urbana, trabalho e valores nas 'áreas invadidas' do Rio de Janeiro e de Lima." In *A sociologia do Brasil urbano*, edited by Anthony Leeds and Elizabeth Leeds, 84–143. Rio de Janeiro: Zahar, 1978.

Leeds, Anthony, and Elizabeth Leeds, eds. *A sociologia do Brasil urbano*. Rio de Janeiro: Zahar Editores, 1978.

Leite, Ricardo. "Recife dos morros e corregos." Paper presented at the *Encontro Nacional de História Oral (X)*. Recife, Brazil, April 26–30, 2010.

Levine, Robert. *A Geography of Time*. New York: Basic Books, 1997.

Lewis, Oscar. *The Children of Sánchez: Autobiography of a Mexican Family*. New York: Random House, 1961.

———. "The Culture of Poverty." In Oscar Lewis, *Anthropological Essays*, 67–80. New York: Random House, 1970.

———. *La Vida: A Puerto Rican Family in the Culture of Poverty—San Juan and New York*. New York: Random House, 1966.

———. "Urbanization without Breakdown." *Scientific Monthly* 75, no. 1 (1952): 31–41.

Lima, Nisia Trinidade. *Um sertão chamado Brasil*. Rio de Janeiro: IUPERJ, Editora Revan, 1999.

Lindón, Alicia. *De la trama de la cotidianidad a los modos de vida urbanos: El Valle de Chalco*. Mexico City: El Colegio de México, El Colegio Mexiquense, 1999.

Lira, José Tavares Correia de. "Hidden Meanings: The Mocambo in Recife." *Social Science Information* 38, no. 2 (1999): 297–327.

Logan, John, and Harvey Molotch. *Urban Fortunes: The Political Economy of Place*. Berkeley: University of California Press, 1987.

Lomnitz, Larissa Adler de. *Networks and Marginality: Life in a Mexican Shantytown*. New York: Academic, 1977.

Machado, Maria Helena Pereira Toledo. *O plano e o pânico: Os movimentos sociais na década da abolição*. Rio de Janeiro: Editora UFRJ; São Paulo: Edusp, 1994.

Magalhães, Agamenon. "Ainda o problema dos mocambos." *Folha da Manhã*, September 14, 1939.

———. "O ciclo do carangueijo." *Folha da Manhã*, July 6, 1939.

———. "Concentração urbana." *Folha da Manhã*, July 18, 1939.

———. "O gosto pela habitação." *Folha da Manhã*, July 4, 1939.

———. "O pequeno agricultor." *Folha da Manhã*, July 1, 1939.

———. "Triste pregão." *Folha da Manhã*, July 15, 1939.

Mangin, William. "Latin American Squatter Settlements: A Problem and a Solution." *Latin American Research Review* 2, no. 3 (1967): 65–98.

Mangin, William, and John C. Turner. "The Barriada Movement." *Progressive Architecture*, no. 49 (May 1968): 154–62.

Mann, Leon. "Queue Culture: The Waiting Line as a Social System." *American Journal of Sociology* 75, no. 3 (1969): 340–54.

Mar, J. Matos. "Migration and Urbanization—The Barriadas of Lima: An Example of Integration into Urban Life." In *Urbanization in Latin America*, edited by Philip M. Hauser, 170–90. Liège, Belgium: UNESCO, 1961.

Marín, Luis Muñoz, and Donald Robinson. "The Governor of Puerto Rico Tells How We Can Save Latin America from Castro." *The Sun* (Baltimore, MD), December 16, 1961.

Markowitz, Gerald, and David Rosner. *Deceit and Denial: The Deadly Politics of Industrial Pollution*. Berkeley: University of California Press, 2002.

Márquez, Gabriel García. *No One Writes to the Colonel*. New York: Harper and Row, 1979.

Marrero, Antonio "Pelón." *San Agustín: Un santo pecador o un pueblo creador*. Caracas: Fundarte, 2004.

Marx, Karl. *Capital*. Vol. 4. Moscow: Foreign Languages Publishing House, 1963.

Marx, Karl, and Friedrich Engels. "The German Ideology." In Karl Marx, *Selected Writings*, edited by David McLellan, 159–91. Oxford: Oxford University Press, 1977.

Massey, Douglas, and Nancy Denton. *American Apartheid: Segregation and the Making of the Underclass*. Cambridge, MA: Harvard University Press, 1993.

McCann, Bryan. *Hard Times in the Marvelous City: From Dictatorship to Democracy in the Favelas of Rio de Janeiro*. Durham, NC: Duke University Press, 2014.

———. *Hello, Hello Brazil: Popular Music in the Making of Modern Brazil*. Durham, NC: Duke University Press, 2004.

———. *Throes of Democracy: Brazil since 1989*. London: Zed Books, 2008.

McKee, David L., and William H. Leahy. "Intra-urban Dualism in Developing Economies." *Land Economics* 46, no. 4 (1970): 486–89.

Medeiros, Amaury. *Saúde e Assistência 1923–1926 doutrinas, experiências e realizações*. Recife, Brazil, 1926.

Medina, Carlos Alberto de. *A favela e o demagogo*. São Paulo: Martins, 1964.

Melo, Marcus André B. C. de. "A cidade dos mocambos: Estado, habitação e luta de classes no Recife (1920/1960)." *Espaço e debates*, no. 14 (1985): 45–66.

Melo, Mário Lacerda de. *Pernambuco: Traços de sua geografia humana*. Recife, Brazil: Jornal do Comercio, 1940.

Melo, Mário Lacerda de, Antônio Carolino Gonçalves, Paulo Maciel, and Levy Cruz. *As migrações para o Recife*. 4 vols. Recife, Brazil: Instituto Joaquim Nabuco de Pesquisas Sociais, 1961.

Merton, Robert. "Three Fragments from a Sociologist's Notebooks: Establishing the Phenomenon, Specified Ignorance, and Strategic Research Materials." *Annual Review of Sociology* 13 (August 1987): 1–28.

Miller, Nathan. "Catholic Leaders Warn: Need for Basic Reforms Voiced in Latin America." *The Sun* (Baltimore, MD), August 14, 1963.

Milton, Cynthia E. *The Many Meanings of Poverty: Colonialism, Social Compacts, and Assistance in Eighteenth-Century Ecuador.* Stanford, CA: Stanford University Press, 2007.

Ministério de Agricultura, Indústria e Comércio, Diretoria Geral de Estatística [Brazil]. *Recenseamento do Brasil, 1 de Setembro de 1920.* Rio de Janeiro: Tipografia da Estatística, 1924.

Ministerio de Planificación y Cooperación [Chile]. CASEN, *encuesta de caracterización socioeconómica nacional 2000.* Santiago: Ministerio de Planificación y Cooperación, 2002.

Ministério do Trabalho, Indústria e Commércio, Serviço de Estatística da Previdência e Trabalho [Brazil]. *Estatística predial do Districto Federal, 1933.* Rio de Janeiro: Departamento de Estatística e Publicidade, 1935.

Mintz, Sidney, and Eric Wolf. "An Analysis of Ritual Co-parenthood (Compadrazgo)." *Southwest Journal of Anthropology* 6, no. 4 (1950): 341–68.

MINVAH (Ministerio de la Vivienda y Assentamientos Humanos) [Nicaragua]. *Programa Integral de 2,800 Viviendas para Managua.* Managua: MINVAH, 1980.

Mitchell, Timothy. "The Work of Economics: How a Discipline Makes Its World." *European Journal of Sociology / Archives Européennes de Sociologie* 46, no. 2 (2005): 297–320.

Molina, Jennifer. "El Alameda cuenta la historia de San Agustín." *Parroquia Dentro* 3, no. 17 (2004): 3.

Montalbán, Olafo. "Autogestión comunitaria en la Venezuela Bolivariana." Accessed April 14, 2007. http://www.nodo50.org/alameda/autogestion.php.

Mooney, Jadwiga Pieper. *The Politics of Motherhood: Maternity and Women's Rights in Twentieth-Century Chile.* Pittsburgh, PA: University of Pittsburgh Press, 2009.

Morales, Eduardo, and Sergio Rojas. "Relocalización socio-espacial de la pobreza: Política estatal y presión popular, 1979–1985." In *Espacio y poder: Los pobladores,* edited by Jorge Chateau, 77–120. Santiago: FLACSO, 1987.

Morse, Richard. "La Lima de Joaquín Capelo: Un arquetipo latino-americano." In Richard Morse and Joaquín Capelo, *Lima en 1900,* 11–48. Lima: Instituto de Estudios Peruanos, 1973.

———. "Recent Research on Latin American Urbanization: A Selective Survey with Commentary." *Latin American Research Review* 1, no. 1 (1965): 35–74.

———. "Trends and Issues in Latin American Urban Research, 1965–1970." *Latin American Research Review* 6, no. 1 (1971), 3–52.

Morse, Richard M., and Joaquín Capelo. *Lima en 1900.* Lima: Instituto de Estudios Peruanos, 1973.

Moura, Cristina Patriota de. "As trajetórias da formalização: Condomínios horizontais em Brasília." Paper presented at the 32° Encontro Anual da ANPOCS, São Paulo, 27–31 October, 2008.

Moura, Vitor Tavares de. "Favelas do Distrito Federal." In *Aspectos do Distrito Federal*, edited by Academia Brasileira de Letras, 255–72. Rio de Janeiro: Sauer, 1943.

Munn, Nancy. "The Cultural Anthropology of Time: A Critical Essay." *Annual Review of Anthropology* 21 (1992): 91–123.

Murphy, Edward. "Developing Sustainable Peripheries: The Limits of Citizenship in Guatemala City." *Latin American Perspectives* 31, no. 6 (2004): 48–68.

———. *Historias poblacionales: Hacia una memoria incluyente*. Santiago: CEDECO, 2004.

———. "A Home of One's Own: Finding a Place in the Fractured Landscape of Urban Chile." PhD dissertation, University of Michigan, 2006.

National Commission on Truth and Reconciliation [Chile]. *Report of the Chilean National Commission on Truth and Reconciliation*. Notre Dame, IN: University of Notre Dame Press, 1993.

Nun, José. "The End of Work and the 'Marginal Mass' Thesis." *Latin American Perspectives* 27, no. 1 (2000): 6–32.

Nunes, Guida. *Favela, resistência pelo direito de viver*. Petrópolis, Brazil: Vozes, 1980.

O'Brien, Edna. "Waiting." In *The Best American Essays*, edited by J. Kincaid and R. Atawan, 177–82. Boston: Houghton Mifflin, 1995.

O'Donnell, Guillermo. *Counterpoints: Selected Essays on Authoritarianism and Democratization*. Notre Dame, IN: University of Notre Dame Press, 1999.

Oliveira, Jane Souto de, and Maria Hortense Marcier. "A palavra é: Favela." In *Um século de favela*, edited by Marcos Alvito Alba Zaluar, 61–114. Rio de Janeiro: Fundação Getúlio Vargas, 1998.

Onis, Juan de. "Stevenson Saw Latins' Hardship." *New York Times*, June 25, 1961.

Orlando, Artur. *Porto e cidade do Recife*. Pernambuco, Brazil: Typ. do "Jornal do Recife," 1908.

Ortner, Sherry. *Anthropology and Social Theory*. Durham, NC: Duke University Press, 2006.

Paiva, Cláudio. *O Planeta Diário: O melhor do maior jornal do planeta*. Rio de Janeiro: Desiderata, 2007.

Pandolfi, Dulce Chaves. *Pernambuco de Agamenon Magalhães: Consolidação e crise de uma elite política*. Recife, Brazil: Fundação Joaquim Nabuco, Editora Massangana, 1984.

Parisse, Luciano. *Favelas do Rio de Janeiro: Evolução, sentido*. Rio de Janeiro: Pontifícia Universidade Católica do Rio de Janeiro, Centro Nacional de Pesquisas Habitacionais, 1969.

Park, Robert. "The City: Suggestions for the Investigation of Human Behavior in the City Environment." *American Journal of Sociology* 20, no. 5 (1915): 577–612.

Parks, Gordon. "Shocking Poverty Spurs Reds." *Life*, June 16, 1961.

Pastrana, Ernesto, and Mónica Threlfall. *Pan, techo y poder: El movimiento de pobladores en Chile, 1970–73*. Buenos Aires: Ediciones Siap-Planteos, 1974.

Perlman, Janice E. *The Myth of Marginality: Urban Poverty and Politics in Rio de Janeiro*. Berkeley: University of California Press, 1976.

Petzoldt, Fania, and Jacinta Bevilacqua. *Nosotras también nos jugamos la vida: Testimonios de la mujer venezolana en la lucha clandestina; 1948–1958*. Caracas: Editorial Ateneo de Caracas, 1979.

Pimenta, João Augusto de Mattos. *Para a remodelação do Rio de Janeiro*. Rio de Janeiro: Rotary Club, 1926.

Pires, José Luis. *Minhas verdades: Histórias e pensamento de um negro favelado*. Rio de Janeiro: Reflexus, 2004.

Pirez, Pedro. "Buenos Aires: Fragmentation and Privatization of the Metropolitan City." *Environment and Urbanization* 14, no. 1 (2001): 145–58.

Piven, Frances, and Richard Cloward. *Regulating the Poor: The Functions of Public Welfare*. New York: Vintage Books, 1971.

Poole, Deborah. "Between Threat and Guarantee: Justice and Community in the Margins of the Peruvian State." In *Anthropology in the Margins of the State*, edited by Veena Das and Deborah Poole, 35–66. Santa Fe, NM: School of American Research Press, 2004.

Portes, Alejandro. "Rationality in the Slum." *Comparative Studies in Society and History* 14, no. 3 (1972): 268–86.

———. "Urbanization and Politics in Latin America." *Social Science Quarterly* 52, no. 3 (1971): 697–720.

———. "The Urban Slum in Chile: Types and Correlates." *Land Economics* 47, no. 3 (1971): 235–48.

Portes, Alejandro, Manuel Castells, and Lauren A. Benton. *The Informal Economy: Studies in Advanced and Less Developed Countries*. Baltimore, MD: Johns Hopkins University Press, 1989.

Powelson, John, and Anatole A. Solow. "Urban and Rural Development in Latin America." *Annals of the American Academy of Political and Social Science* 360 (July 1965): 48–62.

Power, Margaret. *Right-Wing Women in Chile: Feminine Power and the Struggle against Allende, 1964–1973*. University Park: Pennsylvania State University Press, 2002.

Pozas, María de los Ángeles. "La burocracia y la acción estatal en Monterrey." *Medio Ambiente y Urbanización* 7, no. 24 (1988): 15–33.

Prebisch, Raúl. *Towards a Dynamic Development Policy for Latin America*. New York: United Nations, 1963.

Quintero, Rafael. "El Grupo Madera." In Rafael Quintero, *Vivir en Marín*. Accessed April 14, 2007. http://www.nodo50.org/alameda/madera.php.

———. "La lucha contra el desalojo del Centro Cultural Simón Bolívar." In Rafael Quintero, *Vivir en Marín*. Accessed April 14, 2007. http://www.nodo50.org/alameda/lalucha.php.

Rabinow, Paul. *French Modern: Norms and Forms of the Social Environment*. Cambridge, MA: MIT Press, 1989.

Ramos, Alejandra, and Jesús Quintero. "Relato de una experiencia: Grupo Madera." In *Seminario Nacional de Investigación Participativa*. Caracas, 1980.

Ramos, Nelly. "Trabajadora cultural a tiempo completo." In *San Agustín: Un santo pecador o un pueblo creador*, edited by Antonio "Pelón" Marrero, 173–82. Caracas: Fundarte, 2004.

Ray, Talton. *The Politics of the Barrios of Venezuela*. Berkeley: University of California Press, 1969.

Recife, Brazil, Eudoro Correa, and Alfredo Vaz de Oliveira Ferraz, eds. *Recenseamento realizado em 12 de outubro de 1913*. Recife, Brazil: Escolas Profissionaes do Collegio Salesiano, 1915.

Redfield, Robert. "The Folk Society." *American Journal of Sociology* 52, no. 4 (1947): 293–308.

Redko, Cristina, Richard Rapp, and Robert Carlson. "Waiting Time as a Barrier to Treatment Entry: Perceptions of Substance Abusers." *Journal of Drug Issues* 36, no. 4 (2006): 831–52.

Rengifo, Felipe "Mandingo." "Embajador de San Agustín en Alemania." In *San Agustín: Un santo pecador o un pueblo creador*, edited by Antonio "Pelón" Marrero, 157–66. Caracas: Fundarte, 2004.

Ribeiro, A. C. Chagas. *Mocambos . . . romance*. Recife, Brazil: Mozart, 1935.

Rios, José Arthur. "Favelas." In *Aspectos da geografia carioca*, edited by Associação de Geógrafos Brasileiros, 213–24. Rio de Janeiro: Conselho Nacional de Geografia, Instituto Brasileiro de Geografia e Estatística, 1962.

————. "Operação Mutirão." *Cuadernos Latinoamericanos de Economia Humana* 6, no. 12 (1961): 250–54.

Roberts, Bryan R. *Cities of Peasants: The Political Economy of Urbanization in the Third World*. Beverly Hills, CA: Sage, 1978.

Rocha, Mercedes González de la. "From the Marginality of the 1960s to the 'New Poverty' of Today." *Latin American Research Review* 39, no. 1 (2004): 183–203.

Rodgers, Dennis. "Each to Their Own: Ethnographic Notes on the Economic Organization of Poor Households in Urban Nicaragua." *Journal of Development Studies* 43, no. 3 (2007): 391–419.

————. "Living in the Shadow of Death: Gangs, Violence, and Social Order in Urban Nicaragua, 1996–2002." *Journal of Latin American Studies* 38, no. 2 (2006): 267–92.

————. "Managua." In *Fractured Cities: Social Exclusion, Urban Violence and Contested Spaces in Latin America*, edited by K. Koonings and D. Kruijt, 71–85. London: Zed Books, 2007.

————. "A Symptom Called Managua." *New Left Review* 49 (January–February 2008): 103–20.

————. "When Vigilantes Turn Bad: Gangs, Violence, and Social Change in Urban Nicaragua." In *Global Vigilantes*, edited by D. Pratten and A. Sen, 349–70. London: Hurst, 2007.

Rodrigues, Liziane. "Um sinal em Copacabana." *Passos* (Rio de Janeiro), September 2009, 24–27.

Rosas, Alexis. *Objectivo Chávez: El periodismo como arma*. Caracas: Editorial Texto, 2005.

Rose, Carol. *Property and Persuasion: Essays on the History, Theory, and Rhetoric of Ownership*. Boulder, CO: Westview Press, 1994.

Rosemblatt, Karin. *Gendered Compromises: Political Cultures and the State in Chile, 1920–1950*. Chapel Hill: University of North Carolina Press, 2000.

———. "Other Americas: Transnationalism, Scholarship, and the Culture of Poverty in Mexico and the United States." *Hispanic American Historical Review* 89, no. 4 (2009): 603–41.

———. "Por un hogar bien constituido: El estado y su política familiar en los Frentes Populares." In *Disciplina y desacato: Construcción de identidad en Chile, siglos XIX y XX*, edited by Lorena Godoy and Corinne Antezana-Pernet, 181–222. Santiago: SUR / CEDEM, 1995.

Rostow, W. W. *The Stages of Economic Growth, a Non-Communist Manifesto*. Cambridge: Cambridge University Press, 1960.

Roth, Julius. *Timetables: Structuring the Passage of Time in Hospital Treatment and Other Careers*. Indianapolis, IN: Bobbs-Merrill, 1963.

Roy, Ananya. "Slumdog Cities: Rethinking Subaltern Urbanism." *International Journal of Urban and Regional Research* 35, no. 2 (2011): 423–38.

———. "Urban Informality: Toward an Epistemology of Planning." *Journal of the American Planning Association* 71, no. 2 (2005): 147–58.

Roy, Ananya, and Nezar Alsayyed. *Urban Informality: Transnational Perspectives from the Middle East, Latin America, and South Asia*. Lanham, MD: Lexington Books, 2004.

SAGMACS (Sociedade de Análises Gráficas e Mecanográficas Aplicadas aos Complexos Sociais). "Aspectos humanos da favela carioca." *Cuadernos Latinoamericanos de Economia Humana* 4, no. 12 (1961): 237–49. Orig. pub. *Estado de São Paulo*, April 13 and 15, 1960.

Saldaña-Portillo, María Josefina. *The Revolutionary Imagination in the Americas and the Age of Development*. Durham, NC: Duke University Press, 2003.

Saltman, Juliet. "Housing Discrimination: Policy Research, Methods and Results." *Annals of the American Academy of Political and Social Science* 441, no. 1 (1979): 186–96.

Salvia, Agustín. "Consideraciones sobre la transición a la modernidad, la exclusión social y la marginalidad económica: Un campo abierto a la investigación social y al debate político." In *Sombras de una marginalidad fragmentada: Aproximaciones a la metamorfosis de los sectores populares de la Argentina*, edited by Agustín Salvia and Eduardo Chávez Molina, 25–65. Buenos Aires: Miño y Dávila, 2007.

Salvia, Agustín, and Eduardo Chávez Molina. *Sombras de una marginalidad fragmentada: Aproximaciones a la metamorfosis de los sectores populares de la Argentina*. Buenos Aires: Miño y Dávila, 2007.

Sampaio, Alde. "A casa tropical." *Boletim de Engenharia* 3, no. 2 (1927): 31–43.

Sampaio, Júlio César Ribeiro. "Bairro Peixoto: A mobilização preservacionista da Associação de Moradores do Bairro Peixoto." BA thesis, Universidade Estadual do Rio de Janeiro, 1988.

Samper, Miguel. *La miseria en Bogotá y otros escritos*. Bogotá: Universidad Nacional, Dirección de Divulgación Cultural, 1969.

Santos, Boaventura de Souza. "The Law of the Oppressed: The Construction and Reproduction of Legality in Pasargada." *Law and Society Review* 12, no. 1 (1977): 5–126.

Santos, Carlos Nelson Ferreira dos. *Três movimentos sociais urbanos no Rio de Janeiro*. Rio de Janeiro: Zahar, 1981.

Santos, Wanderley Guilherme dos. *Cidadania e justiça: A política social na ordem brasileira*. Rio de Janeiro: Editora Campus, 1979.

Sassen, Saskia. "Whose City Is It? Globalization and the Formation of New Claims." In *Globalization and Its Discontents*, edited by Saskia Sassen, xix–xxxvi. New York: New Press, 1998.

Scheper-Hughes, Nancy. *Death without Weeping: The Violence of Everyday Life in Brazil*. Berkeley: University of California Press, 1992.

Schteingart, Martha. *Los productores del espacio habitable: Estado, empresa y sociedad en la Ciudad de México*. Mexico City: El Colegio de México, 1989.

Schulman, Sam. "Family Life in a Colombian Turgurio." *Sociological Analysis* 28, no. 4 (1967): 184–95.

———. "Latin American Shantytown." *New York Times*, January 16, 1966.

Schutz, Alfred. *The Problem of Social Reality: Collected Papers I*. The Hague: Martinus Nijhoff, 1964.

Schwarcz, Lilia Moritz. *O espetáculo das raças: Cientistas, instituições e questão racial no Brasil, 1870–1930*. São Paulo: Companhia das Letras, 1993.

Schwartz, Barry. *Queuing and Waiting: Studies in the Social Organization of Access and Delay*. Chicago: University of Chicago Press, 1975.

Scobie, James R. "Buenos Aires as a Commercial-Bureaucratic City, 1880–1910: Characteristics of a City's Orientation." *American Historical Review* 77, no. 4 (1972): 1035–73.

Secretaría General del Censo Dirección General de Estadística [Chile]. *XII censo general de población y I de vivienda: Levantado el 24 de Abril de 1952*. Santiago: Instituto Nacional de Estadísticas, 1953.

Segre, Roberto. "Formal-Informal Connections in the Favelas of Rio de Janeiro: The Favela-Bairro Programme." In *Rethinking the Informal City: Critical Perspectives from Latin America*, edited by Felipe Hernández, Peter Kellett, and Lea K. Allen, 163–78. Oxford: Berghahn Books, 2010.

Sennett, Richard. *Flesh and Stone: The Body and the City in Western Civilization*. New York: W.W. Norton, 1994.

Sevcenko, Nicolau. *Literatura como missão: Tensões sociais e criação cultural na Primeira República*. São Paulo: Companhia das Letras, 2003.

Shoumatoff, Alex. *The Capital of Hope: Brasília and Its People*. Albuquerque: University of New Mexico Press, 1987.

"Shriver Says Reds Peril Latin America." *New York Times*, November 20, 1963.

Sigmund, Paul. *The United States and Democracy in Chile*. Baltimore, MD: Johns Hopkins University Press, 1993.

Silva, Eduardo da. *As camélias do Leblon e a abolição da escravatura: Uma investigação de história cultural*. São Paulo: Companhia das Letras, 2003.

Silva, Luíz Antônio Machado da. "O significado do botequim." *América Latina* 12, no. 3 (1969): 160–82.

Silva, Maria Lais Pereira da. *Favelas cariocas, 1930–1964*. Rio de Janeiro: Contraponto, 2005.

Silva, Osvaldo Luiz de Souza, and Alice Brasileiro. "Avaliação de imóveis no Rio de Janeirio: A depreciação do valor de imóveis circumvizinhos aos assentamentos habitacionais espontâneos e o tratamento de políticas públicas para essas áreas." Paper presented at the VII Seminário Internacional da Latin American Real Estate Society, São Paulo, September 19–21, 2012.

Simmel, Georg. *The Philosophy of Money*. London: Routledge, 2004.

Skrabut, Kristin. "Recognizing (Dis)order: Topographies of Power and Property in Lima's Periphery." In *The Housing Question: Tensions, Continuities and Contingencies in the Modern City*, edited by Edward Murphy and Najib Hourani. London: Ashgate, 2013.

Skurski, Julie, and Fernando Coronil. "Country and City in a Postcolonial Landscape: Double Discourse and the Geo-politics of Truth in Latin America." In *Views beyond the Border Country: Raymond Williams and Cultural Politics*, edited by Dennis Dworkin and Leslie Roman, 231–59. New York: Routledge, 1992.

Solow, Anatole A. "Housing in Latin America: The Problem of Urban Low Income Families." *Town Planning Review* 38, no. 2 (1967): 83–102.

Sontag, Susan. *Illness as Metaphor: AIDS and Its Metaphors*. New York: Doubleday, 1990.

Sorokin, Pitirim, and Robert Merton. "Social Time: A Methodological and Functional Analysis." *American Journal of Sociology* 42, no. 5 (1937): 615–29.

Soto, Hernando de. "Foreword." In *A Possible Way Out: Formalizing Housing Informality in Egyptian Cities*, edited by Ahmed Soliman and Hernando de Soto. Lanham, MD: University Press of America, 2004.

———. *The Mystery of Capital: Why Capitalism Triumphs in the West and Fails Everywhere Else*. New York: Basic Books, 2000.

———. *The Other Path: The Invisible Revolution in the Third World*. New York: Harper and Row, 1989.

Stillwaggon, Eileen. *Stunted Lives, Stagnant Economies: Poverty, Disease, and Underdevelopment*. New Brunswick, NJ: Rutgers University Press, 1998.

Sturman, Rachel. "Property and Attachments: Defining Autonomy and the Claims of Family in Nineteenth-Century Western India." *Comparative Studies in Society and History* 47, no. 3 (2005): 611–37.

Sulzberger, C. L. "A Tale of Too Many Cities—and Ourselves." *New York Times,* December 4, 1961.

Svampa, Maristella. *Los que ganaron: La vida en los countries y barrios privados.* Buenos Aires: Biblos, 2001.

Tacca, Fernando de. "O Cruzeiro versus Paris Match e Life Magazine." *Libero* 9, no. 17 (2006): 63–71.

Taussig, Michael. "Maleficium: State Fetishism." In *Fetishism as Cultural Discourse,* edited by Emily Apter and William Pietz, 217–47. Ithaca, NY: Cornell University Press, 1993.

———. *The Nervous System.* New York: Routledge, 1992.

Telles, Vera da Silva, and Robert Cabanes. *Nas tramas da cidade.* Paris: IRD; São Paulo: Associação Editorial Humanitas, 2006.

Thompson, E. P. "Time, Work-Discipline, and Industrial Capitalism." *Past and Present* 38, no. 1 (1967): 56–97.

Tinsman, Heidi. *Partners in Conflict: The Politics of Gender, Sexuality, and Labor in the Chilean Agrarian Reform.* Durham, NC: Duke University Press, 2002.

Torre, Lidia de la. *Buenos Aires: Del conventillo a la villa miseria (1869–1989).* Buenos Aires: Educa, Editorial de la Universidad Católica Argentina, 2008.

Turner, John C. "Lima's Barriadas and Corralones: Suburbs versus Slums." *Ekistics* 19, no. 112 (1965): 152–55.

"Uma favela que começa em Botafogo e termina nas Laranjeiras." *O Globo,* May 25, 1949.

UNEP (United Nations Environment Programme) and UNICEF (United Nations Children's Fund). *Childhood Lead Poisoning: Information for Advocacy and Action.* New York: UNEP-UNICEF, 1997.

UN Habitat. *State of the World's Cities 2010/11: Bridging the Urban Divide.* Washington, DC: United Nations, 2011.

United Nations Human Settlements Programme. *The Challenge of Slums: Global Report on Human Settlements 2003.* London: Earthscan, 2003.

Valenzuela, Arturo. *The Breakdown of Democratic Regimes.* Baltimore, MD: Johns Hopkins University Press, 1978.

Valladares, Licia do Prado. *A invenção da favela: Do mito de origem a favela.com.* Rio de Janeiro: Editora FGV, 2005.

———. *Passa-se uma casa: Análise do programa de remoção de favelas do Rio de Janeiro.* Rio de Janeiro: Zahar Editores, 1978.

———. *Repensando a habitação no Brasil.* Rio de Janeiro: Zahar, 1983.

Valladares, Licia do Prado, Lidia Medeiros, and Filippina Chinelli. *Pensando as favelas do Rio de Janeiro, 1906–2000: Uma bibliografia analítica.* Rio de Janeiro: Relume Dumará, URBANDATA, 2003.

Varley, Ann. "¿Clientelismo o tecnocracia? La lógica política de la regularización de la tierra urbana 1970–1988." *Revista Mexicana de Sociologia* 56, no. 4 (1994): 135–64.

Vásquez, Laura. *La Alameda de los sueños.* Documentary. Caracas: Consejo Nacional de la Cultura (CONAC), 2005.

Vaughan, Dianne. "Theorizing Disaster: Analogy, Historical Ethnography, and the Challenger Accident." *Ethnography* 5, no. 3 (2004): 315–47.

Vaz, Liliana Fessler. "Contribuição ao estudo da produção e transformação do espaço da habitação popular: As habitações coletivas no Rio antigo." MA thesis, Universidade Federal do Rio de Janeiro, 1985.

———. *Modernidade e moradia: Habitação coletiva no Rio de Janeiro, séculos XIX e XX*. Rio de Janeiro: 7 Letras, 2002.

Vekemans, Roger, and Ramón Venegas. "Marginalidad y promoción popular." *Mensage*, no. 149 (1966): 218–22.

Velasco, Alejandro. "A Weapon as Powerful as the Vote: Street Protest and Electoral Politics in Caracas, Venezuela before Hugo Chávez." PhD dissertation, Duke University, 2009.

"Venezuelan Town Honors Kennedy." *New York Times*, December 1, 1963.

Verdery, Katherine. *The Vanishing Hectare: Property and Value in Postcolonial Transylvania*. Ithaca, NY: Cornell University Press, 2003.

Vianna, Hermano. *O mistério do samba*. Rio de Janeiro: J. Zahar Editor, Editora UFRJ, 1995.

Wacquant, Loïc. *Urban Outcasts: A Comparative Sociology of Advanced Marginality*. Cambridge, UK: Polity, 2008.

Ward, Barbara. "The Uses of Prosperity." *Saturday Review*, August 29, 1964.

Ward, Peter. "Introduction and Overview: Marginality Then and Now." *Latin American Research Review* 39, no. 1 (2004): 183–87.

Washington Post. "Latins Have 'Rebel' Slums." May 19, 1968.

Williams, Raymond. *The Country and the City*. New York: Oxford University Press, 1973.

Willis, Paul E. *Learning to Labor: How Working Class Kids Get Working Class Jobs*. New York: Columbia University Press, 1981.

Wolf, Eric R. "Types of Latin American Peasantry: A Preliminary Discussion." *American Anthropologist* 57, no. 3 (1955): 452–71.

Young, Alford. *The Minds of Marginalized Black Men*. Princeton, NJ: Princeton University Press, 2004.

Zaluar, Alba. *A máquina e a revolta: As organizações populares e o significado da pobreza*. São Paulo: Brasiliense, 1985.

Zerubavel, Eviatar. *Patterns of Time in Hospital Life*. Chicago: University of Chicago Press, 1979.

Zylberberg, Sonia. *Morro da Providência: Memórias da favela*. Rio de Janeiro: Prefeitura Secretaria Municipal de Cultura Turismo e Esportes, 1992.

CONTRIBUTORS

Javier Auyero is the Joe R. and Teresa Lozano Long Professor of Latin American Sociology at the University of Texas, Austin. He is the author of *Routine Politics and Collective Violence in Argentina: The Gray Zone of State Power* (2007), among other works.

Mariana Cavalcanti is an assistant professor of anthropology at the Centro de Pesquisa e Documentação of the Fundação Getúlio Vargas in Rio de Janeiro.

Ratão Diniz is a photographer for Imagens do Povo and the Observatório das Favelas in Rio de Janeiro.

Emilio Duhau was a professor of sociology at the Universidad Autónoma Metropolitana, Azcapotzalco, Mexico City.

Sujatha Fernandes is an associate professor of sociology at Queens College and the Graduate Center, City University of New York. She is the author of *Cuba Represent! Cuban Arts, State Power, and the Making of New Revolutionary Cultures* (Duke University Press, 2006), *Who Can Stop the Drums? Urban Social Movements in Chávez's Venezuela* (Duke University Press, 2010), and *Close to the Edge: In Search of the Global Hip Hop Generation* (2011).

Brodwyn Fischer is a professor of history at the University of Chicago. She is the author of *A Poverty of Rights: Citizenship and Inequality in Twentieth-Century Rio de Janeiro* (2008).

Bryan McCann is an associate professor of history at Georgetown University. He is the author of *Throes of Democracy: Brazil since 1989* (2008) and *Hard Times in the Marvelous City: From Dictatorship to Democracy in the Favelas of Rio de Janeiro* (Duke University Press, forthcoming, 2014).

Edward Murphy is an assistant professor in the Department of History and the Global Urban Studies Program at Michigan State University. He is an editor of *Anthrohis-*

tory: Unsettling Knowledge, Questioning Discipline and the author of the forthcoming *A Home of One's Own: Property and Propriety in the Margins of Urban Chile, 1965–2010.*

Dennis Rodgers is a professor of urban social and political research at the University of Glasgow, United Kingdom. A social anthropologist by training, he focuses on the interdisciplinary study of urban development, conflict, and violence (youth gangs in particular), and the politics of urban planning in Nicaragua, Argentina, and India. His most recent publication is the co-edited volume *Latin American Urban Development into the 21st Century* (2012).

INDEX

Note: Page numbers in *italics* refer to illustrations.